A Footballer For All Seasons

A Footballer For All Seasons

- the true story of Frank Newton

Nicolas J. de Jong

A Footballer For All Seasons - the true story of Frank Newton

Published by The Conrad Press Ltd. in the United Kingdom 2024

Tel: +44(0)1227 472 874

www.theconradpress.com

info@theconradpress.com

ISBN 978-1-915494-83-2

Typesetting and Cover Design by: Charlotte Mouncey, www.bookstyle.co.uk
Cover design based on a photo of Frank in full cry against FC Austria, December 3, 1934.

The Conrad Press logo was designed by Maria Priestley.

Printed and bound in Great Britain by Clays Ltd, Elcograf S.p.A.

In loving memory of 'Pung' Chaimueang, a great, young soccer enthusiast, sadly taken far too early, 2008-2021, and of my sister, Sidonia, 1940-2023, for her constant interest and support.
May they rest in peace.

Contents

ACKNOWLEDGEMENTS

My concern in returning so long after embarking on this journey is that someone will be overlooked. Many have assisted me since first I undertook this endeavour and I most sincerely thank them for their contributions and support. As it is impossible to thank everyone I have limited these acknowledgements.

Firstly I wish to recognise the late Denis Turner for his early interest and support at the outset, and so too thank Alex White for kindly responding to my later enquiries. Alan Sedunary also provided information around Frank's time at Reading FC. Invaluable help too was forthcoming from James Baxter, a long time friend from McGill University days, and numerous institutions and organisations, including the Stockport Central Library, the South Wales Borderers Museum in Brecon, the British Library, the Marple Local History Society and a number of the football clubs with which Frank Newton, or his brothers had a connection.

Particular thanks must also go to Marcus Heap, among other things historian at Stockport County FC, who not only provided steadfast support, but very importantly introduced me to Keith Newton, Frank's surviving son. Keith's assistance was greatly appreciated as he and his wife Pauline welcomed me into their home where I was permitted access to Frank's collection and Scrapbook. Mention must also be made of David Downs, Reading FC historian, and Robin Nye, long time friend and accredited author, for his valued contribution in bringing this project to fruition.

Thanks are due also to Simon Griffith for his constant encouragement, and also my long suffering sister, Sidonia, for her support and assistance throughout this whole undertaking.

Finally, I wish to thank Mrs Lynda Graham for providing great impetus to the work's progress as she managed to transfer my longhand hieroglyphics to the printed page. Appropriately, Lynda has been a lifelong supporter of Blackpool FC, a side Frank's friend and playing colleague Joe Smith managed in 1953. And to square the circle, the 1953 'Matthews Final' was the very first game that I watched live on TV!

Nicolas de Jong, April 2024

FOREWORD

Shadows lengthened as the sun went down over Doi Suthep, heralding the onset of another Chiang Mai '*l'heure de l'apéritif*'. I had passed a pleasant afternoon on the roof terrace of a good Aussie mate, Simon, during which I had consulted my well travelled copy of *FULHAM: A Complete Record, 1879-1987*. No surprise in that, for I first visited Craven Cottage on December 22, 1956. A less than auspicious occasion as Fulham went down 1-0 to Nottingham Forest.

However, on that now distant day, during the walk from Putney Bridge Station, along the Thames embankment towards Stevenage Road, I recognised that I was experiencing levels of anticipation, intensity and expectation that were new to me. These increased immediately outside the ground as programmes, peanuts and a variety of paraphernalia exchanged hands. Then it was through the turnstile, up to the terrace and the first glimpse of the manicured swathe. For some reason, when recalled, the pitch was always bathed in sunshine. There followed, over a number of seasons, many thrills, much humour, the barracking of both players and officials, a few ecstatic moments and inevitably disappointments. But the atmosphere throughout was always compelling, and I became addicted in short order.

The humour of the terraces, at least to a young novice supporter, was an important element and at times a revelation. With a man down injured, an anguished cry might go up, 'Don't just stand there Fulham, PRACTICE!'.

J. N. Haynes [JNH] was the outstanding member of the side at that time. One who benefited greatly was his Edmonton schoolfriend 'Tosh' Chamberlin. JNH's entertaining and popular left-wing partner, once tipped in the London evening press for a Wales cap was, like JNH, a one-club player. JNH was subsequently joined by Jimmy Langley, George Cohen, Alan Mullery, Tony Macedo, Maurice 'Rockface' Cook, Bill Dodgin, and in the early '60s Bobby Keetch. These were halcyon days for the young Fulham supporter, and on occasion emotions were ratcheted up when members of the first team stopped by the Queen's Elm on the Fulham Road. I can still recall asking JNH if he had received a poem I had sent to him via the 'Cottage'. I was more than thrilled when he responded, upon reflection diplomatically, that he had it 'in doors', and would 'publish it in my memoirs'! Such moments were part of it all, and provided much of the cement that bound me to football and the club for life.

I attended all but one of England's '66 World Cup games, and on each occasion I acquired my ticket outside the ground. Unbelievably, on final day, I parted company with all of a 'fiver' on Wembley Way! Brilliant, but never to be repeated.

Such was my long-standing affection for the club that many years later I briefly worked the turnstiles on alternate Saturdays. This was at the time Louis Saha was performing his magic. On the 'home' gate the response to derogatory references to 'Lightning' etc., were countered with a robust, 'Any more of that and you won't be coming in'. More pressing were the problems posed by the open nature of the kiosks, those allowing access to the terraces, on a windy day. All rather late Victorian, and I certainly remember trying to clutch notes out of the air while calculating the cost for three youngsters, at half price, and two adults. But the 'away' gates were considerably more challenging. I vividly recall one occasion, the arrival of a group of Birmingham City fans, who, after the best part of three hours in the local hostelries, were in no mood to be denied. Arriving approximately ten minutes before the start, control was immediately lost; even the police recognised this was 'mission impossible', as the fans crawled under, or jumped over the turnstile gate. Little in the way of cash exchanged hands!

With my affiliation to Fulham FC, previously a practising archivist of twenty plus years and a published historian, it was not unreasonable that I had noted that one, Sydney Elliott, had enjoyed an extraordinary 1927-28 season with Fulham FC. In what proved to be his only season at the club he played in all 42 games. He led the line on 38 occasions, and in his first 26 outings scored 23 goals. A remarkable success for a player who came to Fulham during the closed season of 1927 from Durham City. However, after scoring a hat trick against Wolverhampton Wanderers on February 4, 1928, he scored in only one of the remaining 16 games, a hat-trick against Bristol City. By the close of the season his figures were less spectacular as he registered 26 goals in his 42 appearances. Nonetheless, these statistics prompted Fulham's Stamford Bridge neighbours to come calling, and John Dean was quick to accept Chelsea's considerable £3,600 transfer offer.

Unfortunately, there was no ready replacement in the Fulham squad, and despite many being tried, or transferred in over the following 3 seasons, none succeeded in claiming the jersey. Finally, Frank Newton, Stockport County's high scoring centre forward, arrived at the Cottage in the summer of 1931. He came via Ashton National FC, a side for which he never actually played, and made Fulham's number 9 slot his own. At least briefly, for after scoring 72 league goals in 74 league games, and 4 goals in 6 FA Cup appearances he was transferred, in September 1933, to Reading FC, for the derisory sum of £650. In itself a quite extraordinary development, and one that deserved further investigation.

As the context of Frank's life was revealed I found his story increasingly compelling. What follows is something around this gifted Romiley lad's sporting and musical talents and his many noteworthy achievements.

CHAPTER I

EARLY YEARS IN A FOOTBALLING FAMILY

In June of 1933 one Frank Newton, at the time a highly successful centre forward with the Fulham Football Club, was described as bringing 'JULES VERNE UP TO DATE'. In the 'Sporting Chatter' column of *The People*, under the heading 'ROUND THE WORLD FOOTBALLER', Frank's career to that point was summarised:

> 'Frank Newton, Fulham's crack centre-forward, is a difficult problem to opposing centre-halves; he keeps on roaming about the field. Have a look at Frank's career: he has been a roamer all his life. At the early age of sixteen he joined the Navy, then he hopped over to India with the British Army. He got his discharge there, then sailed round the world on a cargo boat. Back again to India, this time as a sergeant in the Calcutta Police. Engineering on the East India railway was the next job. Then Frank suddenly discovered he could play football, so he came over to England and signed for Stockport. His goal scoring ability attracted Fulham to secure his transfer. Now Frank is blowing a trumpet in his spare time for the Mortlake brass band'. [1]

It is interesting that Frank's Player Profile on the fulhamweb still includes much of the above almost 90 years later.[2] So who was this colourful character who evidently had packed so much into the first thirty years of his life? What follows is an attempt to update this profile and put it into a coherent context.

There is no question that Frank Newton was one of the most prolific goal scorers to have played in the English Football League. Between March 31, 1928, the date of his first team debut with Stockport County, and December 1, 1934, he had achieved an extraordinary strike rate of 0.92 goals per game in first team league and FA Cup matches. Following his first team debut at Ashington at the end of March 1928, aged 25, he played a further 223 games and scored 206 goals. However, in fairness it must be noted that these figures benefit from the unfortunate and sudden termination of his football career. It was a fateful December day in 1934, when playing against F.K. Austria, at Craven Cottage, Frank broke his right leg. Hence, in his case the years of diminishing returns were avoided.

Frank was born in Romiley, Cheshire on November 12, 1902, to George Edward and Sarah Newton, and was baptised on December 2 of that year.[3] At the time of the 1901 census George, aged 43, was a felt hat finisher and married to Sarah, 41. George died on December 31, 1906 and Sarah on July 10, 1915. Sarah was born in Lane Audenshaw, historically part of Lancashire, and George in Cheadle, Cheshire. They were married on January 12, 1879 in St. Stephen's Church in Audenshaw.

In the 1901 census 9 children are listed. These were: Emma, Sarah Elizabeth, both born in Lane Audenshaw, aged 16 and 11 respectively, Harry and William, twins aged 9, Andrew, 7, Maggie, 6, George, 4, Edith Anne, 2 and Fred, 10 months, all born in Romiley. At the time the family was residing on Hole House Fold at the junction of what is now the Stockport Road. [4]

Unfortunately, the 1901 enumerator at some point became confused, and quite understandably. Firstly, Andrew at the time of his death in 1960 was aged 67, which gives him a birth date of 1893, he had no twin. His age, therefore, in 1901 should read 8, and by way of confirmation it is given as 18 in the 1911 census. The ages of the twins, William and Harry, in 1901 should read 10 as in 1911 they were 20. For his part, William was often confusingly referred to as 'Andy', and his twin 'Harry', christened Herbert, by 1901 answered to Harry. Fred, aged 10 months in 1901, remained, to the best of my knowledge, Fred. In 1911 he was 11 and attending school. The potential for overall confusion was only added to by the arrival of Frank, another F. Newton, on November 12, 1902. [5] By way of their occupations in 1911, the four oldest boys were all employed as labourers at the 'Bleach Works'. [6]

After the Newton wedding in January, 1879 a steady succession of children followed. The first was Albert Edward born in Manchester during October, 1879. There followed twins, Hannah and Juliana, born at 'Openshaw' [Audenshaw] in April, 1881, then John, born 'about 1883', in Denton, Emma, mentioned above, and Annie, born 'about 1886', very probably more twins, both in 'Openshaw' [Audenshaw]. Of these six youngsters only Emma is listed as living with the family 1901. In total there were nine children living at the Hole House Fold address in 1901.[7] Therefore, Frank was the fifteenth surviving child born to the union.

Locally, the family was recognised as one which had 'the

footballing instinct deeply implanted'.[8] And in the local press coverage of Frank's wedding, on October 31, 1928, it stated: 'He [Frank] is a member of a well known local family, and has several brothers who have done well in first class football'.[9] Of the 5 boys enumerated in 1901, at least 3 went on to play professionally.

But it was Frank, born in 1902, who had the largest impact in the game. He debuted for Stockport County in their Reserve side, in a Cheshire County League game at Mossely on December 3, 1927.[10] After which he played with the Stockport A XI until he was called back to the Reserve side for a second round Cheshire Senior Cup tie against Tranmere Rovers. For Frank that proved to be a transformational afternoon, for not only did he score a second half hat-trick, he also 'signed a professional form for the County'. He was considered 'one of the best captures of the season'.[11] Just eleven weeks after his 25th birthday he was a professional footballer. He then had to wait a further 10 weeks before he was selected for the County's first team to play Ashington, at Portland Park, on March 31,1928.[12]

Thereafter he played in the Reserve side until he was called up for his Edgeley Park debut on December 1, 1928, aged 26.[13] Certainly no spring chicken, but what followed was quite remarkable.

The exploits of his brothers are worth a passing mention as their involvement with football raised the family's profile in the local community, and most certainly had an impact on young Frank during his salad years. If nothing else it must have fired Frank's enthusiasm for a 'sporting life' centred around Association football.

In a press interview conducted during the week of March

24, 1929 Frank stated:

> 'I came from a football family, for my two brothers have seen service with first class teams. One was Billy Newton of Manchester City. He could play in either of the two full-back positions. And my brother Andrew played for Manchester City and Port Vale'.[14]

In the years before the outbreak of hostilities in 1914 the surname Newton appeared periodically in football press reports. Prior to 1913 few of these are thought to be associated with Frank's branch of the Newton family. Subsequently however, the Newton name crops up and can be connected with a club for which one or other of the Romiley based brothers played. Inevitably, certain of these connections are speculative, but given the manner in which the boys later flourished in local footballing circles it is worth making an attempt.

The earliest reference appeared in the *Burnley Express* on February 26, 1913, wherein the name Newton appears twice. One was playing for Denton FC, at left back, in a Lancashire Combination Division I match against Nelson FC, which Denton lost 3-0. On the same day another Newton was playing at centre forward, again in a Combination Division I game, between the Hyde and Coln football clubs. Hyde won that game 4-1 and Newton scored twice.[15] Also, approximately six weeks later, Coln, by then in last place in Division 1 of the Lancashire Combination League with 13 points from 30 games, played Denton, 8 points ahead of them, and won 4-1. In this game a Newton was again playing at left back with Denton.[16] Given his preference for playing in that position in later years, my feeling is that this was probably Andrew, then aged 19 or 20, [but then again, it could have been one of the twins William (Andy), or possibly Herbert (Harry)] incorrectly noted as the eldest Newton boy in the 1901 census, but in fact born a year after the twins. Andrew was residing at home at the time. He played for a number of local amateur sides including Romiley St. Chad's, Park Albion, Marple Amateurs, Newton Heath and then Hyde FC, as the Hurst club was then called.

He may also have played for the Hyde club prior to 1917, but there is no mention of him doing so before the club suspended operations at their Ewen Fields ground to grow vegetables to assist in the War effort.[17] This event may have prompted Andrew to play with Burnley FC as a Newton was listed to turn out for them against Stockport at Edgeley Park, on January 20, 1917, in a Lancashire League fixture. On the same day, another Newton, I believe 'Harry', but possibly William ['Andy'], was to play at left half for Manchester City against Rochdale also in a Lancashire League match. As the participants of both teams were named in the Saturday edition of *The Sportsman* it is clear that both Andrew's place in the Burnley side, and that of either 'Harry' or William in Manchester City's were pre-planned.[18]

One Newton, almost certainly 'Harry', is identified as playing at left half for Manchester City in three further Lancashire League matches on January 27, February 10 and 17, 1917 against Bolton Wanderers, Oldham Athletic and Preston North End respectively.[19]

Then over Easter there were numerous Newton entries; the first was in a Lancashire Section Subsidiary Competition game, on Good Friday, April 6, 1917. Either 'Brennon (or Newton)', probably 'Harry' but again possibly William, was to play at centre half for Manchester City at Hyde Road against Stoke. On the following day April 7 a Newton, 'Harry' or William, was selected to play centre half again, in the same competition against Manchester United.[20]

On the Easter Monday one of the Newton boys played for Manchester City in the return fixture at Stoke City's Victoria Ground. In that game either William or 'Harry' played at inside right, alongside the great Billy Meredith on the right wing,[21] in a 5-0 defeat.[22] Later, on April 14 I believe Harry was named at inside left in the City side against Port Vale.[23] The final positive identification located for Harry occurred on May 5, 1917 in what was, I suggest, a charity match between Manchester City and Hurst FC. The game ended in a 2-2 draw in which H. Newton and Lomas scored for City.[24] There were other matches played regularly throughout the period prior to May but while scores were published, game reports and team selections were seldom mentioned in the *Manchester Evening News*.

A further report noted a Newton playing for Stockport County on October 6, 1917, in a return match with Blackpool that the County won 3-1.[25] 'Newton was brought in to partner Goodwin in the defence, this being the latter's first appearance this season'.[26] This statement is incorrect as 'latter' should read 'former' given that Goodwin played the previous week for the County against Blackpool.[27] But, it does indicate that this Newton played for Stockport in the 1917-18 season.

William (Andy) also played the following week for Stockport against Rochdale, but on this occasion at inside left.[28] However, by March 16, 1918, he had moved on to Burnley and was joined there by Herbert, or 'Harry' his preferred handle. It was reported in the *Burnley News* on March 20, 1918 that

Burnley fielded a very weak side which included 'six new men, which completes their tally of 70 players tried this season'.[29] Included were A. (Andrew) Newton who 'last season assisted Manchester City on fourteen occasions, and H. Newton has only previously played minor football'.[30] The boys went straight into the Burnley side at Stoke's Victoria Ground, at right and left back respectively, and with six new faces in the side it was no surprise that Burnley crashed in front of a crowd of some 6,000. 'Suffice to say that for fully 20 minutes Burnley made quite a respectable show.' The score at half time was 3-0 but the 'Potters' went on to score 6 more. It was a baptism of fire and must have been a torrid afternoon for both Newton boys to be on the wrong end of a 9-0 drubbing. The headline in the *Burnley Express* was brutal: 'PULVERISED IN THE POTTERIES'.[31] The correspondent in the *Lancashire Evening Post* was equally as scathing: Stoke were 'infinitely superior in every department'.[32] Unsurprisingly neither Newton was selected to play the following week in the return fixture at Turf Moor, where Burnley again failed to score but only went down 2-0. This second Stoke victory meant that the club won the Lancashire Section of the League.[33]

Afterwards Harry appears to have played in 4 Subsidiary League matches for Manchester City during the 1918-19 season and is credited with scoring one goal.[34] He then joined Hurst FC and between 1919 and 1924 played 174 times for them, scoring on 9 occasions.

However, William ['Andy'] did play for Burnley again on March 23, 1918 in a Lancashire Section Subsidiary Competition match versus Preston North End at Deepdale. Burnley lost 2-1 but W. Newton was credited with scoring

Burnley's goal from long range. 'W. Newton took a shot from the half-way line, and Goddard, who had gone into goal, was unable to keep it out'.[35] Given that two Newtons also played in this match it is safe to conclude that William played at left back as G. Newton turned out at inside left.[36] George was probably roped in as a very late replacement since Burnley were desperately short of players, 'the Turfites having to borrow two players to complete the team.'

Burnley encountered problems in fielding a team over the course of a number of wartime seasons, and one account illustrates the type of bizarre issues that could periodically arise. The description of the pre-match confusion before playing at Blackpool, on Good Friday March 29, 1918 provides a brilliant example. The game started about a half an hour late as a result of a 'chapter of accidents [which] rendered Burnley's chances of making a good show rather hopeless.' Firstly, on account of 'the inadequate railway accommodation half the team could not get on the train, and had to go in taxi-cabs.' Then the kit bag with the 'players' outfits went astray' which meant the club's officials had to rush around for 'boots and costumes' that were eventually provided by the R.A.M.C. [Royal Army Medical Corps] Football Club.[37] Finally, 'Dawson and others could not get to Blackpool', and the home side had to lend Burnley two players.[38] Two of the Newton boys participated in this game, William at left back and Andrew or more probably George at centre forward. The confusion arises as the initial of the second Newton was omitted when the team had been announced in the *Burnley Express* on March 27.[39] On the following day, Easter Saturday, March 30, G. Newton was listed as playing in a Lancashire Section, Subsidiary Competition fixture at Deepdale. William also played at left back in this 2-1 loss to Preston North End.[40]

Reviews of Burnley's seasons of 1916-17, 1917-18 and 1918-19 offer further insights. An item overviewing the 'concluded campaign' of the 1916-17 season appeared in the *Burnley Express* on March 28, 1917. It noted that 'as the season advanced the club experienced great difficulty in placing a full side on the field. This is plainly shown by the fact that on only two or three occasions did the side selected actually take part in the proceedings.' In the League games proper, 42 players were called upon to play in the 31 game schedule. William Newton is noted as having turned out just once, presumably in the game with Stockport County.[41]

Similarly, the summary of Burnley's 1917-18 season did not make for good reading. In fact it was described as one of the darkest, or 'most unlighted in the history of Burnley FC.' A total of 76 players appeared in the Burnley club's colours during the season, and of these as many as 37 appeared on only one occasion in the Lancashire Section of the League proper. It had been necessary for the club to

> 'borrow players from Everton, Port Vale, Oldham, Liverpool and Blackpool and ... to resort to all manner of devices to fill up the team, even to picking up juniors in the streets of the town which they [were] visiting'.

It was all pretty appalling and is well summed up by the fact that of the seven penalties awarded to the side, no less than six were missed![42] It was probably of some relief to the Newtons that none of them were listed as having played in 5 matches or more!

At the beginning of the 1918-19 season it was noted in the *Burnley News* that both W. and A. Newton were available for the upcoming season, at back and half-back respectively.[43] However, neither played in either of the club's pre-season practice games.[44] But on September 7, 1918 Andrew did play at inside right 'in the first match of the season at Turf Moor' against the might of Everton. The home side went down 6-0.[45] It appears that William made his first appearance for Burnley on October 12, at left back against Blackburn Rovers. Andrew participated in this game at left half.[46] Burnley won what was a close encounter at Ewood Park 4-3. Then on November 16, 1918 three Newtons played for Burnley at the Old Recreation Ground, Hanley against Port Vale. The third Newton was F. Newton and he played at inside right. This was most probably Fred as Frank only turned 16 on November 2 and was just 7 months into his Army training. The name F. Newton did not appear again. Port Vale won the game 4-2.[47] Both William and Andrew played their last games for Burnley at Old Trafford in a 4-0 loss to Manchester United on March 1, 1919.[48]

In April 1919, at the close of Burnley's 1918-19 campaign, the *Burnley Express* published a summary of Burnley's season. It stated that Andrew Newton had 'donned the jersey most frequently at half back', in total 21 times over the 30 game season, during which some '80 players have been requisitioned'.[49] He evidently also played outside right against Bury in a 0-0 draw at Gigg Lane and scored Burnley's second goal in a 4-1 romp over Port Vale.[50] Andrew then signed in July 1919 for Port Vale and 'played fairly regularly in the team until February, 1920 when he lost his place. He was released by the club in May, 1921'.[51]

Early in the 1921-22 season he moved to non-league Ashton National FC [formed in 1921 and sometimes referred to as Ashton National Oil and Gas, as the side was financed by a company of that name based in Ashton-under-Lyne. They played, appropriately, in the National Stadium.] and turned out for them at left half against Connah's Quay, in a Cheshire League match in September 1921. Another Newton, F. also played in this game at inside left and was credited with the match winning goal.[52] This was either Frank, perhaps home on Embarkation Leave, or more probably Fred, who played once for Burnley before joining Barrow AFC.[53] Andrew stayed with Ashton National and played at half back for them when required in 1921 and then once in March 1922. However, the last reference located to his varied footballing career was his participation in a Cheshire County League match between Hurst and Chester in October, 1924. Andrew played at left half in a 2-1 home victory.[54] He died on September 27, 1960, aged 67.

William ['Andy'] initially played for Droylsdon FC, a village side that won the Ashton & District League in the 1913-14 season. Andrew would not have played in that side as on February 22, 1913 he played at left back for Denton FC, against Nelson a team in Division I of the Lancashire Combination League. On the same day another Newton, William I imagine, played for Hyde against Colne in a Cheshire League game and scored the third goal in a 4-1 victory.[55] Subsequently William transferred from Hyde FC to Hurst FC in October 1916.[56] He made his debut for them at Atherton Town's Howe Bridge ground on October 14, 1916. However, the *Burnley Express* reported on January 21, 1917, that W.A. Newton of Hurst, it is assumed this was William 'Andy', was one of 2 new faces included in the Burnley side to play Stockport County at Edgeley Park. William played at right back in that game which Burnley lost 1-0.[57] This appears to have been the only Lancashire League game he played for Burnley as he is mentioned in the 1916-17 review of Burnley's season as having made just the one appearance. In fact he may have been 'loaned' by Hurst FC to Burnley for the game. In the season overall Burnley FC had played a total of 30 league games and no fewer than 42 players had been called upon.[58] Additionally, on March 31, 1917, William again played at left back for Burnley. This fixture was against Blackburn Rovers, at Ewood Park, where the side lost 4-0. This was the club's first match of their Subsidiary League campaign, and as such would not have been included in the 30 game league schedule.[59]

However, William was also mentioned in the summary of Burnley's 1918-19 season in which he had 'figured most frequently at back', in total 18 times. He also assisted Manchester City during this season for whom he played in 5 Principle League games in the Lancashire Section, scoring one goal, and 2 Subsidiary League matches in Group C of the Lancashire section.[60] During the following season William made only 2 League appearances and on August 7, 1920 the *Daily Mirror* reported that Newton was one of four players released by City, 'all of whom migrated to Southend to play in the Third Division'.[61] I understand that William then played 29 times for Southend United, scoring one goal before he moved on to Hurst FC in 1921.[62] He did not stop long at Hurst, as he was selected to play in Accrington Stanley's

Reserve side against Rochdale FC on August 27, 1921, and in their senior side, at left back, in their first home match of the season in the return game with Rochdale a week later.[63] The final reference located to William as having played with Accrington was carried in the *Lancashire Daily Post*, 'Special Edition', on September 24 in which he and Richardson were described as 'sound full backs'. That game was played between the Accrington Stanley Reserve side and Leyland Motors on September 17, 1921.[64] Sadly, William died of pneumonia in March, 1931, aged just 34.[65]

Clearly, William Newton's preference for the handle 'Andy', and Andrew for his baptismal name caused confusion in contemporary accounts and make it impossible now to be specific. Given the difficulties often encountered in just running a club, raising a side, and related issues during the War years, means that the records raised by clubs, those that kept them at all, are very often incomplete. The above is no more than an approximation, but it does indicate that both William and Andrew were serious and consistent participants.

Frank's two remaining brothers both played competitive football at a serious level, but did not enjoy similar success. Fred who was 10 months old at the time of the 1901 census, turned out for Burnley FC, Barrow AFC, an unidentified team in the Manchester League, and very probably Ashton National. He played with Burnley in the last two Subsidiary League games, alongside both Andrew and William, against Blackburn Rovers, at the conclusion of the 1917-18 season. It was noted prior to the first outing that a youth who has played in the Manchester League '… was coming with the Newtons.' The youth was Fred Newton. In the first match, at Turf Moor, which Burnley won 3-0, he played on the left wing, and in the last game of the season, at Ewood Park, where Burnley lost 2-1, he was at inside left.[66] He also turned out the following season, against Port Vale, at inside right in a losing cause, on November 16, 1918.[67] In the Spring of 1919 Fred was mentioned once more in the *Burnley Express*:

> 'It is announced in a contemporary that "Barrow A.F.C. have signed on Fred Newton, of Burnley, who can play either full back or half back." He is a brother of W Newton and A Newton and appeared with the claret and blues against the Rovers in the two concluding games last season, at outside left and inside left successively'.[68]

At the start of the 1921-22 season Fred may have signed with Ashton National for a Newton, F., as previously mentioned, played for Ashton against Connah's Quay in early September.[69] By 1924 he appears to have moved on to Atherton FC as he played with them in 2 Lancashire Combination matches, both against Lancaster Town FC. In the first game, played on March 22, correspondent 'LUNESIDER' considered that Atherton had been 'well served' by Newton, at inside left, and were unfortunate to lose by a penalty goal to nil.[70] In the second game, played three weeks later, Lancaster again were fortunate to win by the only goal. The same correspondent wrote: 'Frankly, the better team did not on this occasion emerge victorious, and the Luneside players will be the first to confess their good fortune'. Again Newton, playing on the left wing, was commended for his performance.[71]

Finally, George would also have participated in minor

football before making his only senior appearance located to date. On March 30, 1919, he played in a Subsidiary League game for Burnley, with his brother William, against Preston North End FC. George was playing at inside left in the match which Burnley lost 2-1. However, both he and William were mentioned in the game report in the *Lancashire Daily Post*, Late Edition. William as he had scored a remarkable goal driving 'the ball in from the half-way line, and with Goddard unable to reach it Burnley equalised in unexpected fashion.' Unfortunately, George's contribution was less spectacular. In the final fifteen minutes of the first half, 'Burnley had the greater share of the game, but G. Newton missed a fine opening close in …'.[72] As no further references have been located it is assumed that George returned to local football.

From the above veritable Rubik's cube of names, teams, clubs, dates, grounds and appearances, it is clear that football certainly was deeply ingrained in this generation of the Newton family, and no doubt the boys would have enjoyed a degree of local celebrity. There must have been endless discussions, speculation, conversations and arguments around the beautiful game. Spare a thought too for Mrs Newton and the girls since the washing load on a Monday morning must have been of a different order between August and May. Improvised games involving the constant kicking of balls would undoubtedly have been a feature of the Newton household and must have proved invaluable in the development of the boys co-ordination, particularly their eye to hand and foot skills.

As the youngest son in a large family, Frank would have looked up to his brothers, but of necessity must have developed a degree of independence and an ability to stand up for himself. He would also have come to realise that a level of compliance was required to survive well in a competitive family environment. And, like many sports people, he occasionally exhibited a superstitious side to his nature. Overall it was through this family background that Frank's great sporting abilities developed, and they served him well throughout his time. In later life I understand he enjoyed recounting aspects of his varied life experiences, particularly when amongst his family.[73]

In the 1911 census, 6 boys were living at home, Fred and Frank, aged 11 and 7, were at school. The others, the twins William and Harry, aged 20, Andrew, aged 18 and George 14 were all employed at a 'Bleach Works'. Locally, one was part of the Elder Mill, situated by the Peak Forest Canal, near Hatherlow Mills, in Romiley or Chadkirk. The Elder Mill was a joint stock limited liability company which was completed in the late nineteenth century.[74] Alternatively, they could have been employed at the Chadkirk Printworks, in 1911 part of the Calico Printing Association, a distance of just over a mile from the centre of Romiley. Thus, in 1911 the Bleach Works at Chadkirk could have provided a steady source of employment.[75] However, they were most probably employed at the Joshua Schofield & Sons Ltd, Spring Water Dye Works, located on Dye Lane which ran off Hole House Fold where the family resided. One Hubert Dudley lodging with the Newton family was also employed at a 'Bleach Works'.[76]

Of the Newton boys listed as working in 1911, only George appears to have signed up for a period of military service during the 1914-18 war. This strongly suggests that the others were employed locally in an occupation of national importance, in their cases possibly at the Schofield Dye Works, or in a local colliery.

There is evidence that George Newton had enlisted by October 1915. It reads:

> 'TELEGRAM. OHMS. TREESHEATH CAMP [?] WHITECHURCH SHREWSBURY 2/10/15. Attest Shrewsbury. C438 Please forward documents 12/13792 Pte G. Newton Transferred from 12th Battn [?] very urgent [– C ---dy] 14th Cheshires. Reply – no dup docs rec'd from Oc 12th'.

I believe that this record was part of a 'Service at Home' record series and that George signed up initially until March 18, 1916. At the time he gave his next of kin as Sarah Elizabeth [Newton/Ryan?], then residing at 4, John St., Romiley.

There is also an Identification section, in what is a Record of Discharge, that states in part: 'Inspected this man fit for military service at Home. 15/4/21'. George's apparent age is given as 24, and height 5'10". His complexion was fresh, and his colour of hair and eyes were brown. He was a member of the Church of England, and he now gave William A. Newton, brother, as his next of kin. At the time William resided at 40, Water St., Hyde, Cheshire. It notes that George signed up on April 15, 1921 in Cardiff and was discharged on July 6, 1921. His character was 'good', and he had served 81 days of what was originally a 90 days Emergency Service agreement. This form also notes that George was born on 20/11/1896, was single and a general labourer by trade. Importantly his previous service with the 12th and 14th Cheshire Regiments is referenced, and his Corps/Army/Regimental number was 13792. The document was signed off by a member of the 7th Battalion of the Welch Regiment.[77]

CHAPTER II

FRANK NEWTON JOINS THE MILITARY

It was reported that Frank Newton attended a Navy school in Liverpool.[1] This very probably would have been after his mother, Sarah, 1860-1915, died in July when Frank was aged just 12 years and 10 months. I believe he left school in Romiley prior to Easter 1916 as he was entitled to do since the school leaving age was not extended to 14 until 1918.[2] He then very probably proceeded to a Liverpool Naval school, later referred to as the Navy League School, armed with a glowing letter of reference from his former headmaster dated 13/4/1916. This would partially explain why Frank enlisted in Liverpool on April 8, 1918 with the South Wales Borderers [SWB]. Afterwards he attended Sniggery Camp, a training establishment at the time located near Little Crosby, Lancashire. His Army Registration number was 3903429. He gave his trade as that of musician, and named his sister Mrs E. Ryan of 4, John St., Romiley, Cheshire as his next of kin. However, in a later document, Army Form B 178a, signed on 11/1/1922, he states his employment prior to enlisting was that of Seaman in the Merchant Service.[3] This indicates that Frank served in the Mercantile Marine for a time after leaving the Navy League establishment in Liverpool. This timeline also lends credence to the family's understanding that Frank was aboard a vessel torpedoed in the North Atlantic, possibly in the 'Western Approaches', prior to April 1918. In fact so traumatic may he have found the experience that it very probably determined him to join the Army.

In a press interview conducted in March 1929, Frank responded as follows when asked where he was born:

> 'Romiley to be exact. That was 27 years ago, but I'm taken to be much older. That is down to the fact that I joined the Army when I was 14 years of age. Just reckon it up for yourself. I was in the Army for nine years and have been out just two'.[4]

Had the reporter followed Frank's advice and reckoned it up, he would have calculated that there was a void of over a year. It was during this period that Frank attended the Navy League school and served briefly as a merchant seaman. This appears to be the correct timeline as in a 'STATEMENT BY A SOLDIER CONCERNING HIS OWN CASE', signed by Frank on 11/1/1922, it clearly states that Frank was a seaman in the Merchant Service prior to joining the Army.[5]

However, when interviewed later, in September, 1931, by B.J. Lewis of London's evening paper, *The Star (London)*, Frank states:

> 'As a boy I went to the Navy League school at Liverpool, and then was away at sea. Next I joined the Army, playing soccer at once for the boys of my regiment. While still

a soldier I assisted Pontypridd in the Welsh League, and then sailed to India'.[6]

Again, this statement lacks detail. Many of Frank's sporting endeavours are well documented in the local Brecon press and no mention of his having assisted any Pontypridd side has been located. However, given the proximity of the two locations it could have happened, but I feel only on the rare occasion.

His interest in sporting pursuits was certainly well recognised. These and certain of his other attributes were mentioned in the glowing letter of reference, mentioned above, which was signed on 13/4/1916 by William Warburton his former headmaster at the Romiley Council School. It was a letter that Frank surely would have produced in support of any application he made.

> 'I have known Frank Newton many years. He has spent the whole of his school life with me. I have found him honest & upright. He was regular and punctual, diligent & persevering, willing and obedient. He is a strong healthy boy, and very keen at sports. He has several brothers who have answered their country's call, and I have no hesitation in recommending him for what he now seeks.
> Wm. Warburton
> Headmaster'.[7]

Frank also had a real interest in music and was quite happy to perform in public, something he did throughout his lifetime. His interest would have developed early and was probably self taught although his performing skills would have been enhanced during his formal education, initially at St. Chad's day school and later at Romiley Council School. Frank was noted for his willingness to take on any challenge, and also for both his physique and good health. He would have played football at school and was evidently a member of 'The Romiley Lads'.

He most certainly had confidence in his musical skills since he described himself as a 'musician' when he enlisted at the age of 15 years and 5 months. A signed but undated note from his sister Sarah reflects his interest in music.

> '27 Water St Hyde
> Cheshire
> I give my consent for my brother Frank Newton to join the band of the 1st Batln South Wales Brdrs he is very keen on joining the army and I hope he will make a good boy.
> Signed Sarah Elizabeth Ryan
> Sister of Frank Newton'[8]

Drummer Newton shortly after he enlisted in the South Wales Borderers in April 1918, aged 15 years and 5 months.

During his time in the SWB, prior to his promotion to Lance Corporal, Frank was often referred to as 'Bandsman' or 'Drummer' Newton. Considerably later he played the cornet in the Mortlake Brass Band; during and after his time with Fulham FC and when with Reading FC he performed a trombone duet, 'The Troubadours', at a well attended concert given by 'The Guild Concert Massed Band' in Reading Town Hall.[9] During his time at Reading he also played with the Salvation Army band and 'was good enough to play professionally' at the County Theatre.[10] Later still, in 1943, Frank was Band Sergeant and Deputy Conductor of the 49th, County of Lancaster Home Guard Band.[11]

It seems probable that young Frank, on half pay until he turned 18, stayed first at Sniggery Camp, Hightown, for some while, given his age when he enlisted. Unquestionably, during this period his musical talents would have benefited from further formal instruction and equally as important he would have honed his considerable sporting abilities. In terms of football, given the limited facilities available at the small Sniggery establishment, he may well have practised and played on the Hightown Club ground where Liverpool Ramblers AFC played from September 1919.[12] It is unclear as to exactly when Frank was transferred from Hightown to Chatham, but he was posted from Chatham to the SWB's Regimental Headquarters in Brecon on August 12, 1919.[13]

Once the Armistice had been signed, finally terminating the horrors of the 1914-18 conflict, society slowly started to return to peace time conditions. Sporting activities were inevitably included in this for, despite the shocking influenza pandemic and the sharp economic recession, everybody was desperate to find a new normal. The people of Brecon were no exception and on August 21, 1919, the *Brecon County Times* [*BCT*] published a letter from 'Soccerite' requesting either The Brecon Sports Club, or the Mayor call a meeting 'to get a good football team together' given that another season was fast approaching.[14]

Prior to this, after the hostilities, the *BCT* had reported on just one local football match. That game was played on April 26, 1919 in aid of The Brecon Infirmary, between a team from the SWB Depot and a Brecon Town XI. This charity match was played on the Depot ground and resulted in a 2-1 victory for the military. Unfortunately, the participants were not identified.[15]

Later, in the August 21 edition of the same newspaper, there appeared an announcement for a boxing event to be held in the Brecon Market Hall on September 27, 1919. This was a soirée in which Frank participated.[16]

On August 28, 1919, Mr W.H. Parry de Winton, Mayor of Brecon, had a letter published in the *BCT* acknowledging: 'that a great deal of energy is being put into various efforts to put Association football on its feet again now the war is over.' In support of the cause he was willing to provide the Council Chamber so that a round table conference could be held to further the re-establishment of the Brecon Association Football Club. A similar meeting was held in Llanfaes where it was also decided to run a Llanfaes Brigade side once more.[17]

As the Mid-Wales Association Football League had not yet commenced, another friendly match was played, on September 20, 1919, again between sides from the Brecon Sports Club and the SWB Depot. Unfortunately, the participants were not named, but this may have been just as well for the Depot's players as they were thrashed 11-1. In fairness, it was noted that the soldiers, out of necessity and as the score indicated, had to field a 'scratch' side.[18]

The first specific reference to Frank Newton participating in a Brecon sporting event was in the aforementioned Boxing Tournament held in the Market Hall on the evening of September 17, 1919. When he ducked through the ropes he was still some 6 weeks shy of his 17th birthday. The *BCT* reported that:

> 'Excellent music was played at intervals by the Band of the Depot S.W.B. The tourney opened with a set-to between Drummer Newton and Pte Howells, both S.W.B. lads, but the former was too much for his oponent [sic] who gave up at the end of the first round'. [19]

Frank's first recorded SWB footballing appearance occurred just over a month later on November 1, the eve of Frank's 17th birthday, when he turned out for the Brecon Depot side in a Mid-Wales League fixture against Builth Wells. Private Newton played on the left wing but his performance failed to warrant a mention in the local press report. The Depot lost 3-0, but it was noted that the soldiers had not yet got together a regular team. Nonetheless, they were felt to be 'a very well balanced young side' and recalling their previous outing this result may have been considered something of a success.[20]

A further game, again a friendly, was played on November 25, 1919, on the Depot ground between 'the recently returned cadre of the 1/1st Breckonshire Battalion S.W.B.' and a team representing SWB Headquarters. The latter won a closely contested battle 1-0, but excuses were made for the 'Terriers' as it was felt they 'were not properly shod, and were also feeling the effects of the change of climate.' Yet again the individual participants were not named.[21]

On Saturday, December 6, another Mid-Wales League match was held in Brecon when the Depot took on Llandrindod Wells. At half time the Depot were 4 goals up. Frank playing on the left wing, scored shortly before the interval but disappointingly the side had to settle for a 4-4 draw. The game report noted it 'was not a match to be very critical about, the weather conditions were too bad.' Given that all the goals were scored in the same net there was very probably a near gale blowing the length of the ground, a not unusual occurrence in Brecon![22]

The following two Mid-Wales League fixtures played by the SWB Depot XI were accorded the briefest of mentions in the *BCT*. The first was against the Hay club on December 13 and resulted in a heavy 5-1 defeat. In fact, the game was more competitive than the final score would suggest. The Depot were only trailing 2-1 at half time and there was no further scoring until 20 minutes from the end. However, the soldiers, by then reduced to just 9 men through injury, collapsed and conceded 3 more times. There followed a 2-2 result when the Depot entertained the Brecon Sports Club on December 20. In neither of these games were the players identified.[23]

Frank continued to revel in his sporting life as between the two above mentioned games he once more ducked through the ropes to participate in a boxing tournament on Wednesday, December 17, 1919.

'The large gymnasium at Brecon Barracks was filled ... for a boxing tournament. There was a long – rather too long – and varied programme, and despite the non-appearance of a local "star", the audience had value for their money. In this connection it may be pointed out that the boxing tournaments at the Barracks are only intended to be self-supporting, the underlying nature being to encourage the recruits of the The South Wales Borderers in their training for physical fitness. No question of profit enters into the consideration of the promoters in fixing the prices of admission.

The disappointment of the evening was the non-attendance of the clever Brecon boxer, Tom Hoddinott, who had been matched in a ten-round contest with Ted Collins of Merthyr. The former won the Army welter weight championship in India whilst serving there with Brecknocks and three months ago defeated Young Sharkey of Ystradgynlais, in Brecon Market Hall. The latter brought home the Army welter weight championship of Egypt'.[24]

Drummer Newton's six round contest was the final bout of the evening and the enforced waiting period for Hoddinott's arrival would have done nothing for the nerves of the 17 year old. In the event 'Young McCarthy', also from Ystradgynlais, triumphed 'on points in a fairly level contest'.[25] The detail provided around this tournament and the charging system was probably to ensure that it was differentiated from the professional boxing tournament scheduled for the Brecon Market Hall on Boxing Day evening 1919.[26]

The Depot XI performed well in their Mid-Wales League

fixture against Talgarth, played at home on December 27, and the holiday crowd left delighted. Frank played at inside left, and all on the home side were noted as tryers:

> 'and there was little or any "fiddling" amongst the forwards when near goal. Talgarth had a fair share of the play, but halves and backs were better spoilers than the visitors' defending division. Newton opened the scoring with a good "header" from a well placed free kick, when the first half was nearly over'.

A second was scored by Bates almost immediately afterwards, and at the interval the Depot led 2-0. Both Frank and Bates scored again in the second half and the home side ran out worthy 4-1 winners. The local correspondent concluded that the Depot side had 'improved greatly since the season began, and on Saturday's form they will take a lot of beating'.[27]

The weather early in January turned foul and the return fixture with Llandrindod Wells was postponed.[28] However, despite more 'wretched weather' the match with the Llanfaes Brigade XI did go ahead on January 10, 1920. 'Quite a hurricane blew across the ground, and the heavy rain, if it did not damp the enthusiasm of those present, must have soaked the majority to the skin.' Consequently the game, played on Newton Meadow, was a disappointing spectacle. But Llanfaes Brigade, playing with several reserves, started 'pretty well' and the teams were tied 2-2 at the interval. The soldiers improved in the second half and Frank, now playing on the right wing broke the deadlock with a 'splendid shot'. The Depot continued to dominate for the balance of the match and at the close the local correspondent concluded the side thoroughly deserved their 3-2 victory.[29]

Now on the brink of three straight victories the Depot XI visited the Brecon Sports Club. The ground was reported to be in good condition, the weather was dry, and a strong wind blew down the ground. The Sports Club pressed from the opening and went one up from a penalty. 'This seemed to put life into the "Tommies" and the game took a decided turn.' Nonetheless, the hosts maintained their 1-0 lead until half time. Then it was the turn of the Depot, with the wind now behind them, to press forward and they equalised also from a penalty. This encouraged the 'soldiers to put their whole heart into the game … Newton [again on the right wing], Bates and Watson were the pick of the forwards.' The Depot extended their winning streak with a well deserved, cleanly contested 4-1 victory.[30]

A good sized highly expectant crowd was on hand for the return fixture against the previously defeated Llanfaes Brigade side. It had rained heavily in the morning but a fairly strong wind had dried the ground considerably by kick off. Surprisingly, despite the soldiers' supporters encouraging their heroes with loud shouts of 'Play-up the "Two-and-a-Four"', which seemed to be the regimental war cry, the Depot XI quickly found themselves three goals in arrears. The Llanfaes defence had not been severely tested but for 'one or two runs by Newton and Watson, both of whom sent in good shots …' In fact, with the wind in their backs 'the Llanfaes forwards seemed to do as they liked with the soldiers, who were badly off their usual game.' At half time the home side, having conceded a late own goal, were trailing by 4 goals.

> 'With the wind in their favour it was hoped that the Depot would "show-up" and although Newton sent two or three beautiful shots from the wing early on, the Brigade were never in any serious difficulty. The game which had been strenuously contested from the start now became remarkable for the number of "lay-outs" that occurred'.

Watkins of the Depot was off injured for some time, Llanfaes' Sear seemed to be in great pain and Lewis was accidentally kicked in the head. 'Although the game would not be described as 'rough', at the call of time very few of the players seemed to be without honourable scars.' Ten minutes before the end the Brigade's 'Davies was warned for an infringement, and, after entering into an altercation with the referee, he was sent off.' Nonetheless, the Depot continued to press but failed to trouble the scorer. Thus, in what appears to have been an ill tempered game, Llanfaes ended the Depot's brief Mid-Wales League unbeaten run.[31]

The Depot XI were no more successful in their next League fixture, at home against Talgarth on February 7, when they lost 3-0. Frank was playing on the left wing in this encounter but despite his side's losses in the two league games, the seventeen and a half year old must have been pleased to be selected to play for the 'Rest' against the 1914 League winners, Llanfaes Brigade.[32]

However, the restricted selection basis and the match itself must have made it something of an anti-climax for Frank. First, the players were chosen from just two teams, the Brecon Sports Club and the SWB Depot XI. Secondly, the medal ceremony, which was to be conducted by none other than

Mayor W.F. Parry de Winton, the Old Etonian scholar, had to be postponed as the medals did not arrive. Thirdly, the match almost inevitably lacked any 'edge' although shortly after the start one player was 'crocked' and a second had to leave the field injured. Overall the first half was judged to be very tame - 'players going about their business in a lackadaisical way'. The only goal was scored by Llanfaes from the penalty spot. There was some improvement after the interval and Perry, Waite and Newton were singled out as having performed well for the 'Rest'. However, their efforts were not sufficient to prevent the 1914 League winners from triumphing 3-1.[33]

To this point in the 1919-20 season the inclement weather had taken a toll on fixture lists and by the third week of February a backlog was building. As a result the SWB Depot's game with Llandrindod Wells was played on Wednesday, February 18. Fortunately, the weather was fine and the attendance 'was as good as could have been expected. The soldiers brought their strongest side – but Llandrindod had three or four regular men absent.'

It was reported that the visitors were unfortunate not to take the lead when Newton, playing on the left wing, 'drove in a splendid shot that hit under the bar and came out again.' The scores were tied at the interval but 25 minutes later the hosts went ahead. This caused the 'Breconians' to surge forward once more for they were far from beaten. Having won a corner that:

> 'was beautifully placed ... Newton cleverly headed the equaliser. Brecon made several more attacks, in which Newton had a big share. The Depot outside left looked like getting through again, but was "grassed" by one of

the home defenders'.

Subsequently, it was Bates who scored the winner and it was felt that the Depot deserved their 3-2 victory.

> 'The soldiers possessed many clever tricks, and one great advantage they had over the home eleven was heading the ball. The Depot played clean football and created a good impression among the spectators ... Newton and Bates were the pick of a splendid line of forwards'.[34]

The league leading Rhayader side visited the SWB Depot just three days later for a match which generated a good deal of local interest.

> 'Great things were expected from the visitors but the large crowd on the ground were disappointed at the display they gave. The visitors were over an hour late, owing to a breakdown and the match did not commence until after a quarter to four'.

The ground was in good condition and even at this late hour the weather still fine. Frank again played on the left wing and the Depot pressed forward from the start. But matters did not quite go to plan. In fact, given that the 'Wyesiders' had only been in the soldiers' territory twice, they 'were extremely lucky to be two goals up whilst the soldiers had had by far the best of the game.' But the Depot's persistent pressure eventually paid off as they scored two unanswered goals. After which the game 'became very interesting and was carried from end to end with amazing rapidity ...' Nonetheless, the score remained deadlocked at the interval.

After the break it was Rhayader that went ahead again, but the

> 'Depot once more took up the running and goaded on by leather-lunged N.C.Os. and shrill voiced recruits bombarded the visitor's goal. Newton beat the backs and fell but with an extraordinary twist whilst on the ground screwed the ball from near the touch line into the goal ... With the score again level things got lively. Newton again secured and after beating several opponents was fouled by the Rhayader right-back'.

The Depot scored from the resulting penalty and went on to see out the keenly contested encounter 4-3.

The local view was that the Depot fully deserved their victory but should have scored more goals, particularly during the first half. Newton, Ray, Waite and Watson were considered the outstanding Depot players and all contributed magnificently to overcome the league leaders.[35]

At the beginning of March 1920, the standings in the Mid-Wales League were more a reflection of the games played than the points gained. At that time the Brecon Sports Club had seven games remaining whereas the SWB Depot, Hay and Newbridge each had only three. The last games of the season were to be played on April 24, 1920. Thus the Depot's league schedule was unusually light as the side was due to play only once in March and twice in April.

As the season wound down so also did the column inches

devoted to reporting local football. The Depot's match in March against Newbridge warranted no more than a succinct reference stating it was played on the Depot's ground in continuous rain and resulted in a 1-1 draw. Newbridge scored first and held on until the final minute of the match.[36]

The Depot's penultimate fixture was against Hay, a side locked in a battle royal with Newbridge to avoid the wooden spoon. The match was scheduled for April 3, 1920, but neither an account of the game nor the score appeared in the local press.[37] This was because the Brecon Sports Club won the Kington Cup which locally was of significantly more importance. The Sports Club accomplished this feat after finally defeating Hereford United, at the 4th attempt in the semi-final before winning the final against Ludlow 2-1.[38]

As thoughts turned to summer pursuits, the Depot took on Builth Wells, on April 24, in their final game of the 1919-20 season. This marked the first occasion that Drummer Newton played at centre forward. And while the 'Military put up a good fight and during the first half got away nicely on more than one occasion…', it was Builth Wells that went on to win 3-1 having enjoyed both wind and lady luck after the interval.[39] More coverage perhaps should have been afforded this game, since Builth's victory meant the team clinched the Mid-Wales League title with 23 points, a single point ahead of Llanfaes Brigade. The SWB Depot XI finished fifth with 17 points, having won 7, drawn 3 and lost 6.[40]

For young Frank Newton it was a memorable season. He commenced playing for the Depot XI on the eve of his 17th birthday, against Builth Wells, in what was his team's first post war competitive league match. Given his success and versatility

I believe he very probably played in all sixteen league fixtures. Unfortunately, no reports have been located for three of the Depot's league games, and in a further three the players were not named. However, we know Frank participated in at least ten of his side's 16 matches, scored 9 goals and demonstrated his versatility as he turned out in 5 different positions: centre forward; inside left; centre half and on both the left and right wings. And finally, he was selected, from a limited player base, to play for 'The Rest' against the 1914 league winners, Llanfaes Brigade, as the league was suspended during the war years. It was certainly a most satisfactory start to Bandsman Newton's formal amateur footballing career.

Prior to the outset of the 1920-21 league season changes had arisen in the membership of the Mid-Wales League. Both the Brecon Sports Club and Llanfaes Brigade had decided to compete in the Glamorganshire League, while Llanwrtyd Wells joined the Mid-Wales League. Consequently, in the 1920-21 season each side was scheduled to play 14 matches in the 8 team Mid-Wales League.[41] Both Llanfaes and the Sports Club published their fixture lists for the 1920-21 season. The two teams were playing in the same league although the league was not identified.[42]

Immediately before the Depot XI started their competitive games, Frank would have been well satisfied to have his developing talents recognised when he was again selected to play for the 'Rest', this time at outside right, against Bluith Wells the then reigning champions of the Mid-Wales League. In this instance the 'Rest' side was drawn from all the other sides competing in that league.[43]

In the first game of their new season, on September 25, 1920, the SWB Depot visited Llanwrtyd Wells, the league's new participants. In fine weather the Depot produced a convincing display winning 3-1. Frank playing at centre forward opened his and the Depot's account with 'a beautiful shot shortly before the interval'; however, it was also mentioned that he missed at least one relatively straight forward opportunity. After the interval the soldiers continued to outperform the opposition and came away with what was a well deserved victory. It was reported locally that the Depot XI had made 'a very promising start … and their progress will be followed with keen interest'.[44]

This 'keen interest' was probably sincerely intended but thereafter reports of Mid-Wales League matches appeared only sporadically in the *BCT*, and when they did they were short on detail. In summary, with respect to the SWB Depot XI, no coverage appeared for 2 of their 12 games; succinct reports of 2 further games, in which no names were given, and in the 7-2 romp over Newbridge-on-Wye the scorers of only 3 goals were identified.

The Depot played their second game of the season against Talgarth, at home, and won convincingly 4-1. Frank was selected to play on the left wing, and very probably feeling his first duty was to his team mates, he forfeited his opportunity to play for the 'Rest' XI against Bluith Wells. Nonetheless, on that afternoon he was a young man inspired, scoring a hat-trick before half time!

> 'It is a pity there was not a bigger gate as the match was at times decidedly interesting and well worth watching all through. The Depot mustered a strong team, and the visitors were rather overwhelmed at first, Newton scoring twice within the first quarter of an hour. Nothing

could have been prettier than the way in which he negotiated the second goal, and his unerring judgement and accurate shooting render him an invaluable asset to his side. He scored again for the depot before half time'.

The sides exchanged goals in a more evenly contested second half, but Talgarth were unable to overcome the half time deficit and the Depot were left to enjoy their decisive 4-1 victory.[45]

The following Saturday, October 16, the Depot again turned out at home to take on Llandrindod Wells. In what proved to be a hard fought, workmanlike performance, the Depot secured another 'well earned victory' by 3 goals to 1. The home side led 1-0 at the interval, but Llandrindod levelled early in the second half. Subsequently, 'both teams fought gamely for a decision, the Depot's ultimate triumph being secured by shear [sic] hard work.' The second Brecon Depot goal came from a penalty. But the result was not settled until five minutes from time when 'after a good deal of strenuous play' Frank, again playing on the left wing, finally put the game beyond reach when he netted the third.[46]

The Depot side had started the season impressively having secured three straight victories. The soldiers had improved considerably compared to the inexperienced side that had been crushed 11-1, in a pre-season friendly, by a Brecon Sports Club XI just a year earlier.

The following week, on October 23, 1920, local interest was running high when the soldiers visited the defending league champions, Builth Wells. The home side were forced to give a number of fresh players a run out on account of 'unavoidable absences.' Frank was playing at outside left, and Mr D. Bird, of Llandrindod Wells, was overseeing proceedings on what was a fine afternoon.

Bluith, playing with the sun behind them, were quickly into their stride and a fast game ensued. The home side enjoyed a period of dominance which produced their first goal. A second came from a penalty, so at the interval Bluith were two up. Unfortunately, the second half proved to be somewhat shorter than the first.

> 'The referee awarded Bluith a penalty and when the kick was about to be taken a Depot player crossed the line. The kick, however, was taken and Hughes stopped the shot. The referee, maintaining that he had sounded the whistle before the goalkeeper played the ball, ordered the kick to be taken again, upon which the Depot team left the pitch. The referee also left the field'.

After consulting amongst themselves the Depot side returned and 'expressed their willingness to proceed with the game.' But, too late! Mr Bird had flown and was on his way back to Llandrindod Wells. An 'Unfortunate Occurrence', and an unhappy end to the Depot's brief unbeaten run.[47]

Such unruly conduct was promptly considered at a league committee meeting held at Llandrindod Wells on November 3, 1920. The final decision resulted in the Depot's captain, Corporal Harold John Ray, being suspended until January 1, 1921. This was because his team walked 'off the field as a protest against the referee's ruling in the match between the Depot and Builth Wells'.[48]

The Depot's game that preceded this meeting was played at

Newbridge-on-Wye on October 30. The game was reasonably well attended, and 'the visitors were in good form and played as brilliantly as ever …' The forwards were quick, and well supported by their half backs. Frank headed the first goal and at the interval the solders were 3 goals ahead. In the second half Newbridge performed a little better and scored twice, but they were unable to effectively plug their porous defence and the Depot added 4 more to romp home 7-2. Unfortunately those who scored the six other Depot goals were not identified.[49]

The news of Corporal Ray's suspension, from a purely practical point of view, might well have been welcomed in the Davies household at St. John's Cottage, Pendre, Brecon. This would have been because the good Corporal, 'the well known captain of the Depot football team', was due to marry Florence the youngest daughter in the Davies' family. From Harold's standpoint, with his upcoming honeymoon set for Swansea, he probably had few, if any regrets that he would not be leading the side out again until New Year's Day for the fixture with Hay![50]

Also, in light of the suspension, it was fortunate that the Depot XI played only once between November 6, 1920 and January 1, 1921. On the former date Llanwrtyd Wells visited Brecon and lost by the only goal of the game. With Frank playing on the right wing the soldiers played with their 'usual ability' throughout a game in which the 'pace was fast all through.' The goal came in the second half and was scored by Captain Gottwaltz 'after a brilliant piece of combination work between Cook and Newton'.[51] The Depot were then scheduled to play Talgarth on November 13.[52] This match was postponed however as the first round of the Hando Cup, in which Talgarth was drawn against the Brecon Sports Club, took precedence.

Otherwise the league schedule between November 27 and New Year's Day only specified that the Depot would play Hay on the latter day.[53]

Despite the schedule no reference to the Hay game has been located and it is doubtful that it was actually played. In this context it should be noted that at a meeting of the Mid-Wales League committee, held at the Lamb Hotel in Bluith Wells on January 5, 1921, the Secretary reported 'that owing to numerous cup-ties some League matches had been postponed'.[54] Indeed, the early rounds of various cup competitions came thick and fast in the New Year, and it would appear that the Depot v Hay match was a casualty of crowded fixture lists. In fact a postponement would have suited both sides as the Depot were to play Builth Wells in the 4th round of the Ludlow Cup on January 5, while Hay were scheduled to take on Builth Wells 3 days later in the 1st round of the Llandrindod Wells Cup.

Playing at home the 4th round Ludlow Cup match was one the SWB Depot was expected to win. 'The fact that the visitors triumphed [3-2] was chiefly due to inexcusable lapses on the part of their opponents, does not in any way detract from their success.' Frank played at inside left and since his contribution warranted no mention, it can be assumed that on the day he was not at his sparkling best.[55]

In the John Hando Cup the Depot XI received a bye in the first round.[56] But in the second the team faced a tricky away fixture against the Brecon Sports Club. The game was played on Saturday, January 8, in miserable weather.

> 'It was impossible for either Sports Club or Brecon Depot to do themselves full justice ... the weather conditions

were bad enough to dishearten the best of players. The result was a draw – never a satisfactory outcome but in this instance perhaps the fairest one.

The Depot team had been considerably strengthened, and its performance was very different from that of the preceding Wednesday. Sports Club played with their customary verve, and their tactics were often successful. Not withstanding the inclemency of the weather, large numbers of supporters of both teams turned out and followed the vicissitudes of the game with close attention. In the opening stages of the game the advantage was with the Depot, who developed a skilful attack, the forward line giving at times a very smart exhibition of combination work. Captain Gottwaltz scored first for the Depot after receiving from Newton'.

At half time the score stood at a goal apiece. The second half opened "briskly", despite the inclement conditions, and the visitors attacked again.

'After a corner, Newton dropped the ball in front of goal and Smithers hooked in a goal with his head. After this play shifted further to mid-field, and later the homesters were once more pressing vigorously. The appalling state of the ground made shooting exceedingly difficult, but some notable attempts were made'.

The Sports Club were finally rewarded with an equaliser, but despite 'strenuous efforts' by both sides the score remained 2-2.[57] The replay took place on the following Saturday, January

15, when the Brecon Sports Club rode their luck and won 3-2. Frank actually did not turn out for this encounter, and although no reason was given, it very probably related to his impending move to Aldershot.[58]

The Depot's next outing involved a visit to Talgarth on Wednesday, January 26, a team with which the soldiers were tied at the head of the Mid-Wales League. This battle of the league leaders attracted a reasonable crowd which included Mr Harry Hadley, the former England International, and now manager of Merthyr Town FC, a side enjoying its first season in the new Third Division of the Football League.

The soldiers with the wind in their backs pressed hard from the start. But Talgarth absorbed the early pressure, and by the interval could well have been ahead. For their part, the Depot's chances were few and the best of them arose when Frank, playing at inside left, unleashed a fierce drive which travelled just over the bar. When the sides resumed after the interval 'play was very fast and both teams gave of their best, the ball being taken from end to end in double quick time.' And then almost as quickly, in the space of just two minutes, the Depot conceded twice. Talgarth played well and by the end were clear leaders of the Mid-Wales League having played 10 games. Mr Hadley presumably was also impressed by the performance of the home side as he interviewed 2 of their players after the game.[59]

The soldiers now had a month to reflect upon this loss as the side was not due to play Rhayader until February 26. Talgarth on the other hand, played a further two league matches in the intervening period and won them both which put them 6 points ahead of the Depot XI. A win against Rhayader therefore was critical if the Depot was to retain, at best, an outside chance of winning the league title.

When Rhayader arrived at Brecon on Saturday, February 26 a close encounter was anticipated. However, the soldiers found their best form and administered a thumping, despite Frank's absence, the final score being 5-1.

> "The visitors began in good style, and were successful in registering the first goal, but in the later stages of the game their play deteriorated until they were completely outplayed, much to the chagrin of their supporters. The Depot, on the other hand, showed themselves to be in excellent trim once they really got going, and except for one or two occasions their ascendancy was not seriously challenged. It was thought that the loss of Newton would prove a big handicap to the homesters, but if they can always turn out as strong a team as they had last Saturday they need not fear much in the future."[60]

Prophetic words indeed! The Depot's next game was against the cellar dwelling Hay side which had endured another less than memorable season. After twelve league games the team had amassed just 2 points having won one match. Playing at home the soldiers would have been heavily favoured to win, that is unless things went spectacularly wrong, and of course they did!

However, from Frank's perspective the game was of no immediate significance. Clearly from the above report it was common knowledge, prior to the game, that Frank would not participate. In fact he had only turned out once for the team, against Talgarth, since the drawn game, in the 2nd round of the John Hambro Cup, versus the Brecon Sports Club, played back on January 8, 1921.[61]

Matters military had now impinged on Frank's sporting activities. In October 1919 the 1st Battalion had moved to Aldershot, and were stationed at Blackdown. Then in June 1920, the 1st battalion 'received orders for transfer to Ireland, leaving for Dublin on June 20th.' The Battalion was first quartered at Dollymount, a suburb of Dublin, from where it moved to County Meath, 'not one of the more disturbed parts of Ireland' in September 1920.[62]

At some point during the period between January 27 and February 26, 1921 Frank probably transferred to the Blackdown barracks, Aldershot and may also have done so in 1922 since a brief report in the *Reading Mercury* of September 1933, shortly after Frank's controversial transfer from Fulham FC to Reading FC, stated:

> 'Newton has always liked the town of Reading, and has always had a desire to live in the town. When as a band boy at Aldershot he used frequently to pass through the town and always noticed its cleanliness'.[63]

Frank's return to the Brecon barracks would have occurred in late September or early October, 1921 for he resumed his football endeavours on October 15 when he turned out for Brecon 'A' against Aberpergym.[64]

During Frank's absence from Brecon, a Mid-Wales League meeting was held on May 24, 1921 during which it was determined that all 'uncompleted fixtures' would be played at the beginning of the 1921-22 season. However, the meeting's primary purpose was to discuss the question of establishing a

Central Welsh Section of the National Welsh Football League. It was hoped that it would incorporate every part of Wales. The matter was resolved when it was agreed that all teams within the area would have to join the Central Wales Section, and if any team made an attempt to join any other league they would be advised that there was a league provided for them within their own area.[65]

On August 30 at a meeting of the Builth Wells Football Committee, the Chairman advised that in his view the Central Wales Section, so far as the Mid-Wales teams were concerned, was in a state of chaos. He reported that Talgarth and Hay had chosen to join the Herefordshire League which left only 3 clubs in the senior division, Llandrindod, Rhayader and Builth Wells. The Committee recorded that they considered they had been very let down since they had been advised that teams within the area would be compelled to join their own League.[66] Clearly they were not.

A little over a month later representatives of the Mid-Wales clubs, those left in the Central Wales Section of the Welsh National League, met again in Builth Wells. Briefly, it was decided the 3 remaining sides in the senior division would ask Llanidloes and Newtown to enter the Mid-Wales Division. Also, a second division, to consist of 9 sides, would operate and the reserve sides of the remaining 3 senior teams would compete therein.[67]

Possibly in anticipation of some disagreement and confusion around the upcoming structural changes, Brecon determined to form a new team, Brecon United AFC, which was to compete in the Welsh League (Division II).

'In preparation for the first season of the Brecon United Association Football Club, from which local enthusiasts are naturally expecting great things, a trial match was played on the Depot ground on Saturday last. It was a gruelling hot afternoon, but full time was played and some good form was shown. The 'A' team will play Troedyrhiw on Saturday [away], in the Second Division of the Welsh League, and the 'B' team will go to Ystalyfera the same day with a guarantee to assist in the opening of a new ground'.

Judging from the names of those participating in these games it appears that Brecon United drew on players who formally played for the SWB Depot and Brecon Sports Club sides. Frank being still at Blackdown did not participate in these games.[68]

Despite the change the Depot still put out a side and played two games against a Brecon Albion XI. The first was played on September 28, and the second on October 5, 1921. The soldiers won both easily, 5-1 and 5-0. Unfortunately again, the names of the participants were not given.[69]

Finally, on October 15 Frank played locally again, on the left wing, for Brecon 'A' against Aberpergwm.

'Aberpergwm visited Brecon and soundly defeated the local team. The visitors brought with them the reputation of not having won a match in the last eight, but from their play on Saturday they were easily the best team that has visited Brecon this season. The opening passages were fairly even till the visitors got the measure of their opponents, and seemingly encamped for good on the territory of the home team ... Spasmodically the Brecon left wing showed there were possibilities left in them, but the opposing defence was too good. All the weaknesses of the home team were intensified by the smartness of the visitors, who took advantage of them all'.

Clearly there were few positives the locals could take from the game, but given the side only lost 1-0, the defence must have performed reasonably well.[70]

The following Saturday, October 22, Brecon 'A' faced Rhayader in a preliminary round of the Wales Amateur Cup. Unfortunately, the names of the players again were not published, but their involvement was brief as Rhayader won 4-0.[71]

The following week the 'A' side participated in a Welsh League Division II match at Abergaveny which ended 1-1. The initial impact that the side had made was succinctly summed up: 'Brecon showed that they are not quite the negligible factor in Div II of the Welsh League that the league table might indicate.' Faint praise, particularly as Abergaveny missed two penalties. Frank may have played in this game as he did not participate in the 'B' side's 2-1 home loss to Talgarth, in the first round of the Herefordshire Challenge Cup.[72]

However, on page 8 of this edition of the BCT there appeared an announcement, not a report, that Brecon had beaten Henged 5-2 in a South Wales Cup tie. It noted: 'Good performances by Thomas, Newton, Davies and A. Blake.' Other than stating the score was 1-1 at half time, it offered nothing further. The very short lead time, the format and brevity of the announcement, and its positioning on page 8, suggest that the game was played on November 2.[73]

It was now the turn of the Aberdare Reserve side to visit Brecon, and on November 5 they provided a stern test which the 'A' side failed miserably.

> 'The Aberdare Reserves arrived on Saturday with a reputation of being second to none in Division II of the Welsh League, and perhaps partly because of this Brecon were beaten from the kick-off. Immediately the whistle sounded, the Aberdare forwards invaded the territory of the home team; the Brecon attack fell back to help the defence, and stayed there for the greater part of the first half. Aberdare played their first team goalkeeper, but he was not able to put in much practice during the game. Leslie Rowlands, their centre forward, is a native of Brecon and well-known in the district. He has already eighteen goals to his credit this season and added three more on Saturday'.

As the half progressed the 'debacle continued, the home attack becoming more and more demoralized.' The game was as good as over by half time as the visitors led 4-0.

With the wind in their backs during the second half Brecon were more successful in holding the visitors. But there remained an outstanding defect in this Brecon side which had 'always been the lack of a good centre forward. And against such a team as Aberdare the deficiency was considerably emphasised.'

Frank playing on the left wing was briefly mentioned as a rallying force, 'but had no assistance from the inside' and his attacking efforts were quickly nullified. The final result, 6-0, was conclusive and well deserved as Aberdare 'played splendid football and their combination was perfect. They had Brecon beaten individually and collectively.' The only possible relief for the home supporters among the large crowd was provided by the musical selection, played by the Buff's Band, before the game and during the interval.[74]

After such a dispiriting mismatch, Frank was probably delighted to return to the Depot XI and turn out for a first round match, at Builth Wells, in the Hay Challenge Cup. The draw was made on 19/10/1921 at a meeting of the Hay Challenge Cup Association, at the Wye Temperance Hotel, Hay. The game was noted as being between Builth Wells & the Brecon Depot.[75] The Depot went off at a rapid clip and Frank, playing at centre forward, scored the opening goal with 'a fine first time shot.' The soldiers controlled the opening period and led 3-1 at the break. Builth, with the wind behind them, improved considerably in the second half, and 'pressed vigorously and dominated the play almost continuously. The visitors satisfied with their lead fell back on the defence' and suffered the almost inevitable consequences. Builth pulled a goal back, and having previously missed a penalty, were awarded another just before full time, and equalised.[76]

The drawn game was replayed on the Depot's ground the following Wednesday, November 16, 1921, and on this occasion the Depot XI were considerably more focused. 'In the first half the soldiers were all over their opponents and piled up a comfortable lead of six goals to nil.'

The second half was slightly more entertaining, but the Depot did not release their grip on this game, although they failed to increase their lead, 'despite the earnest attempts of

Newton, who banged the ball home at every opportunity.' The final score was 6-2, but the individuals who scored were not named.[77] It appears that Frank was injured during the proceedings as a note signed by the Depot team captain, J.H. Ray, states that Drummer Frank Newton 'was kicked in the groin whilst playing against Builth Wells' and had to leave the field for a short time.[78]

Nevertheless, Frank's sporting day was not yet done as he was on the Depot's Boxing Tournament card to fight in the last of that evening's four round contests. After an increasingly nervous wait and before a large, baying crowd, Drummer Newton once more ducked through the ropes, adrenaline pumping, to fight one Private Lewes. The contest

> 'created much interest, Newton being well-known as a football player in Brecon. The first round opened rapidly. Newton setting the pace and putting his man down twice. Lewes rallied in the second round, but could not hold his opponent. He fought gamely, but Newton got home some terrific body punches that decided the bout in his favour early in the second round'.[79]

Frank's sporting endeavours continued just three days later when he lined up for the Brecon 'B' side in a Herefordshire League match against a weak Bromyard team.

> 'The Brecon 'B' team were in splendid form on Saturday when they were at home to Bromyard ... The visitors arrived with a rather shaky record, having drawn two and lost three of the five matches they have played. The

home team quickly demonstrated their superiority and played well together'.

Despite missing an open goal early in the game, Frank partially made amends when he scored from a penalty, putting 'a terrific shot passed Saunders'. By half time the Depot were three goals up although they were reduced to ten men after I. Brookes 'was knocked out'.

Brecon maintained the pressure in the second half and continued to dominate. For his part, Frank was firing on all cylinders. He tested Saunders again and, in the space of a few minutes, he twice headed over the bar.

'Then calamity fell on Bromyard and their defence utterly went to pieces. It was not so much a question of getting goals that the home team had to decide, but who was to be given the honour'.

Newton began the 'deluge' to put Brecon four up and then added the sixth. Now rampant, the home side surged forward and despite Frank again heading over, Brecon added four further goals.

'The chief factor of the play was the splendid performance of Newton at centre. He is not yet a very clever player, but his shooting is always dangerous. His long passing was perfect, and he understands his position, and is the best pivot that the 'B' team has had. He simply rained shots at Saunders who was lucky to be generally in their way'.

This was 'decidedly the best game' the 'B' side had played at home, and as the final score, 10-0, indicated was little more than a walk in the park.[80]

There followed a rearranged 'A' team fixture at Aberpergwm, originally scheduled for October 22, but postponed because of the Welsh Amateur Cup game with Rhayader.[81] The journey up would have been more enjoyable than the return leg during which the side no doubt reflected on their 5-0 drubbing. The correspondent for the *BCT* was left to wonder if extra terrestrial forces might have had a bearing. 'Not yet have the Brecon 'A' team emerged from the haze of mysterious bad luck that envelops them. In fact it seems to deepen.'

More probably Brecon on the day were simply in over their heads, a situation which did not improve after Frank failed to convert a first half penalty. By the interval Brecon had shipped 3 goals and the home defence were in no mood to let the visitors back into the game. The combination of Aberpergwm's strong defence and Brecon's 'weak and futile' finishing ensured yet another Welsh League Division II defeat.[82]

It remains uncertain, but Frank very probably played a part in a rare Brecon 'A' victory at Trecynon the following week on December 10. What is certain is that his name did not appear on the 'B' side's team sheet for the game against Leominster, played on the same day. The 'A' team took a young side to Trecynon and won convincingly 2-0. The very brief game report merely noted that the Brecon defence had 'stood firm', but neither the goal scorers, nor the team members were named.[83]

The following Saturday, December 17, a Hereford Thistle XI duly arrived in Brecon to play the 'B' side in a Hereford

League encounter. A good number of spectators turned out to watch the proceedings despite rain and a strong wind blowing down the ground. A close, hard fought encounter raged which in turn was dominated by the respective defences, although on the slippery surface progress was at times erratic.

Unexpectedly, Hereford Thistle, although playing into the wind, pressed strongly from the outset.

> 'The visitors' play was much the better at this period, Brecon were never allowed to get out of hand and it seemed that the home team's chance of victory would be slender when the visitors got the advantage of the wind'.

What limited response Brecon were able to muster came through the efforts of Frank at centre forward. He had a couple of good efforts early on, and from one, Baird put the rebound over the bar.

> 'Newton was unfortunate, some fine first time shots being interrupted unintentionally before reaching their objective. The Hereford backs played a splendid game and smothered the home attacks with aggravating persistence. Both teams were fully extended, but the visitors played with a kind of quiet confidence that enabled them ... to anticipate events. The combination of the home team was haphazard and their attacks were spasmodic and not pushed home. The ball was seldom fully under control and there was an obvious tendency to kick and chase it'.

In fact the half finished scoreless and Hereford, now with the wind in their backs, were favoured.

However, the Brecon 'B' team previously had demonstrated an ability to scrape through in other matches, often defying the odds stacked against them. Judging from the action in the first half, the home side must have appeared 'easy pickings'.

> 'But on the resumption of play they [Brecon] ... carried the game to their opponents ... Again the home team pressed and Newton got in a terrific shot that the visitors' goalkeeper was lucky to reach. He fisted clear and from the subsequent mix up in the goalmouth Watson got home and Brecon were one up'.

Thereafter Brecon continued with renewed vigour, and although there was little finesse about their attack, it displayed 'a certain happy-go-lucky quality that contrasted unfavourably with the nice combination and footwork of the visitors.' The home side continued to press but, against the run of play, the Thistle equalised from a corner. This set up a barn storming finish, but a deciding goal was not forthcoming and the match ended in an acceptable draw.[84]

There followed, on Tuesday, December 22, a 'friendly' against Merthyr United which was also played at Brecon. As a spectacle this game, the insertion of which in a crowded schedule went unexplained, was spoilt by the very high wind that prevailed throughout. Brecon's only goal came in the first half and was scored by Frank from 'a splendid screw shot'. However, this game too ended in a draw after Merthyr scored from a penalty.[85]

The return match with Trecynon was played on Boxing

Day. Having suffered a home defeat to the Brecon 'A' side in their previous Welsh League Division II encounter, the visitors were intent on revenge. In what became another vigorously contested match, Frank, playing on the right wing, opened the scoring with 'a fine angle shot'. After which the Brecon defence fell apart for no apparant reason and by the interval Trecynon had established a 4-1 lead. Matters failed to improve after the interval as the visitors added a fifth, and Frank yet again missed a penalty. However, Brecon did score a second following a period of intense pressure. But this arose only when all semblance of seasonal goodwill had evaporated after the visitors' goalkeeper was ejected for whacking an opponent![86]

For Frank there followed what appears to have been a fallow period as he is not mentioned in any football reports until his selection to play for Brecon 'A' against Pengam on February 4, 1922. In this context it is worth noting, as a possible explanation, that a number of issues had arisen at the Brecon club, one of which was team selection.

A 'Brecon Clear-up Meeting' was held on January 9, to address certain 'Grievances amongst some players and supporters' which had prompted W.R. Price, the Club's Secretary, to tender his resignation. As a result of a 'full, free and frank' discussion, a motion in favour of the General and Selection Committees remaining in office was carried by a majority of more than two to one'.[87]

There is no evidence that Frank had any involvement in the meeting, but there was an issue around team selection and this may have resulted in Frank limiting his availability. Alternatively, he may have been due a spot of leave and travelled back to visit the family in Romiley. Be that as it may, he was back playing at centre forward against Pengam on February 4. There was but a very brief report of that game which is unfortunate for Frank was at his imperial best as Brecon led by four goals, all scored by Frank, inside the first 30 minutes.[88]

Frank's next recorded appearance for Brecon was on March 11, in another Welsh League Division II match, against New Tredegar. Again he played for the 'A' side, was judged an influential force in a hard fought contest, and came close in the first half when a 'brilliant shot' was well saved. Nevertheless, the visitors went one up, but Brecon equalised shortly before the interval.

'The second half opened quietly. Like well mannered opponents the teams watched warily for an opening ... In this period the best football of the match was played. Individual and tip-and-run methods were discarded. The players kept their positions better and there was a lining up of forces before an attack got going that gave it more vitality than mere momentum'.

New Tredegar scored a second following a spell of tenacious pressure, but Brecon once more equalised, a goal recounted in extraordinarily convoluted detail.

'Ray wrapped himself round a visitor and it was some time before they could be unravelled. Baird got possession, and Newton being in close attendance, the pair reconnoitred the position. It looked good. Baird drew the defence, and placed the ball in position for Newton. The latter was not quite satisfied with it and returned it again. Baird juggled with the ball long enough to confuse the defence and then stood aside while Newton with a demonstration shot equalised the score'.[89]

This was possibly an attempt at a more creative style of reportage, but thankfully one not encountered elsewhere.

Despite 8 fixtures remaining on the Brecon 'A' side's Division II schedule, this was the last match of the 1921-22 season in which Frank is reported to have participated. It was in this season that Frank, still only 19, was more regularly selected to fill the centre forward slot. This reflected an improvement not only in his understanding of the game, and therefore his ability to lead the line, but also in his finishing and distribution skills. At 11 stone, he assumed a quick and increasingly robust presence on the football field, qualities which mirrored his periodic appearances in the boxing ring. During the season he certainly played 6 games for Brecon 'A' and twice for the 'B'" side. In one other match the team was not specified, and he also turned out in the 'friendly' with Merthyr United. In League and Cup matches he unquestionably scored 6 times for the 'A' side, and 3 for the 'B'. And besides scoring against Merthyr he was very probably amongst the scorers in the South Wales Amateur Cup game with Henged. Frank also played for the Brecon Depot side on at least 3 occasions; the first two at the beginning of the season were straight forward victories over Brecon United, and the third was in the Hay Challenge Cup match.

When Frank played his first game for Brecon in the 1922-23 season on September 30, he was probably well aware that he would shortly be shipping out to join the Regiment's 2nd Battalion in India. As a result he played only 4 times for Brecon early in the season, the last on October 21, 1922. The first was a Division II game against Trecynon, on their 'Gas Works' field. At the time the hosts were unbeaten and in fourth place in the Welsh Division.

Frank was selected to play at inside left, and for the first time 'the attack was as good as the defence.' Overall it was judged Brecon's best performance of the season, and it can be assumed that Frank was one of the three referred to:

> 'the speed of the forwards and their first time combination provided many interesting and exciting moments. Brecon turned out a very strong team that included three of the most successful of last year's forwards not yet seen out this season'.

Conditions underfoot were difficult as it rained heavily from the start. Play was evenly balanced throughout the first half and no goals were forthcoming. The best opportunity fell to Frank.

> 'From the throw in Webb passed out to Crimmings, who beat his man and gave the ball to Newton. Surrounded by opponents though he was, Newton tested Mundy with a fast angle shot that was unlucky to find the goalkeeper waiting to receive it. It was one of the most spectacular shots of the game and thoroughly deserved the applause it evoked'.

Brecon surged forward after the interval and put the Trecynon defence under sustained pressure. Both Brookes and Crimmings played well and but for a solid defence Newton or

Webb would have opened the scoring. 'The agility of Crimming [sic] was remarkable, and Newton's effective shooting kept the defenders well in the goal area, for his shots gave little to spare.' Brecon almost snatched victory at the death when Crimmings put the ball through to Frank, but he was well challenged by Philips, and could do no better than hit the outside of the upright. The game ended in a scoreless draw.

Troedyrhiw visited Brecon the following Saturday, and a fiercely contested Welsh League battle ensued and resulted in a narrow 1-0 Brecon victory, the side's first Division II win of the season.

> 'Newton scored almost sensationally from the kick-off for the home team. The game developed into a Homeric struggle on the part of the homesters to preserve their lead and vigorous offensive tactics on the part of the visitors to rest [sic] it from them. Seldom has such a fast and exciting game been seen on the local ground, but the football, except at intervals, was not of a very high quality. The homesters' tactics, however, were successful if not spectacular'.

Brecon attempted to press home their early advantage. Twice Frank, at inside right, came close with 'terrific drives', and Webb, at centre forward, was prominent. For their part Troedyrhiw came more into the game and dominated after the interval, but the Brecon defence, although stretched, covered effectively. Finally, after both goals had narrow escapes, Brecon were awarded a penalty and believed they had scored. However, the referee ordered it to be retaken and then, almost inevitably, it was missed. Both sides rode their luck in equal measure, but it was felt the visitors were overly dependent upon their offside trap which held up, but only just. For Brecon it was a hard earned win that, on balance, the side narrowly deserved.[90]

Frank's final league game for Brecon 'A' was played the following week against Dowlais. Frank played on the left wing in what was for Brecon a rare occurrence in Division II, back to back victories. The published report was extremely brief and noted merely that the home support was, not surprisingly, delighted with the 2-1 victory. The game itself was succinctly dismissed as very fast in which 'all the players acquitted themselves well'.[91]

In what proved to be Frank's last game in the colours of the Brecon Club was played on October 21, 1922. Appropriately, he was selected to lead the line in a 1st round Welsh Amateur Cup match against Builth Wells.

The day broke fine, but it was bitterly cold and a strong wind prevailed throughout. Upon winning the toss Brecon chose to play down wind and immediately went on the attack. Despite Frank having to temporarily leave the field through injury, Brecon were 3 goals up at half time. Builth recovered briefly after the interval and scored twice in short order. However, once the Brecon defenders had adjusted to the conditions they provided their forwards with some excellent opportunities from which 2 goals resulted. Appropriately, the last of these was scored by Frank, his second of the game, and was judged to be 'the best of the match'.[92]

In another report of this game "THE KEEPER" offered a somewhat different perspective.

'When a big wind blows from goal to goal as it did in this match at Brecon, ... it is not much use to the forwards playing with it or to the defence who have to face it. In short it completely spoiled what, one believes, would have been a far more interesting game otherwise. Add to this militating factor a light, dry ball, which was blown about like a balloon, and cut innumerable capers on a turf which is not yet of the best on the new ground, accurate and good football could not well have been expected. Not withstanding, we had a vigorous and not alltogether [sic] an uninteresting game, especially, ... when the home side who were undisputedly the stronger if not the better together, had to play against the hurricane. The greatest defect in the Breconian's team, who did not play as well together as one has seen them, was the forward line. The selection appeared to be at fault. Why play such a brilliant outside left as Newton at centre, when Ivor Brookes was available for that position? Had he been in the middle with Lewis inside left and Newton outside, the line would have been the stronger and combination better. Brecon thus enters the next round, but they will have to play very much better together than they did in this game if they want to get any 'forrader' in the competition'.[93]

If the team did so, it was without Frank who almost certainly had departed for home to enjoy his three week leave entitlement, prior to his approximately 5 year deployment to India. At the time British soldiers were allowed three weeks Embarkation Leave, and a similar length of Disembarkation Leave upon their return. Ordinary Ranks and NCOs were not entitled to home leave during their deployment. However, they were permitted local, or recreational leave while in India.[94]

CHAPTER III

INDIA, 1922-1927

At some point in November 1922 Frank left the Brecon Depot and sailed, probably from Liverpool, to join the Regiment in India. Previously the 2nd Battalion of the SWB had landed in what was then Bombay on November 18, 1919, and then deployed to Jhansi, Uttar Pradesh. It remained there until November 1922 when it was ordered to Barrackpore and Dum Dum, West Bengal, where it was stationed until December, 1925. Available evidence suggests Frank arrived in Barrackpore on December 6, 1922, as one of a draft of 'one sergeant and 55 other ranks'.[1] It is clear from the Ministry of Defence file that Frank Newton, Army Number 3903429, served in India after 4/11/1922, which it is assumed approximates the date he left the Brecon Depot.[2]

Frank remained with the SWB until April 20, 1927 when he transferred from the 2nd Battalion to the Army Reserve, Identity Number, N13. The 'Cause of transfer to the Army Reserve' was the 'expiration of Colony Service K.R. para 362 (1)', dated 20/4/1927. This notice of transfer advises that he was moving to the Calcutta Civil Police, and could be contacted, C/O Calcutta Police, Lal Bazaar, Calcutta.[3]

Part 1 of this form provides additional detail. Frank's complexion was given as 'fair', both his hair and eyes were 'brown', he had a tattoo on each forearm, a mole on his left shoulder and a scar in the centre of his forehead. He held a third class education certificate, his Military Character was 'Very Good', and the serial number to the Character Certificate is noted as: 2/SWBdrs/303. Frank's 'Character in Testimonial form as recorded on Character Certificate' reads: 'Has been in the Regimental Band and is a fair cornet & trombone player. A smart hardworking [sic] & sober man. Very keen on games & a good all round performer at athletics and games.' His 'Proficiency Pay Classification' was '1st Class'. He was a 'Marksman (Rifle, Table "R" 1926-27)', and was entitled to a period of furlough between April 6 and 20, 1927. Other details included his vital statistics, boot, cap, steel helmet sizes and the length of rifle butt best suited for him. This transfer to the Army Reserve was signed off in Agra at the end of April, 1927. Meanwhile, Frank was issued with a 'Protection Certificate' that allowed him to proceed 'to Calcutta on the 6 April 1927 on furlough until the 20 April 1927, pending transfer to the Army Reserve.' Both L/Cpl. Newton and Major G.H. Burkett, Commanding 2nd Battalion The South Wales Borderers, signed.[4]

Sporting activities were one of the mainstays of military life overseas, and such pursuits were certainly at the top of Frank's agenda. Being highly competitive, possessing a robust physique, speed and good eye-hand-foot coordination, he was well suited to avail himself of most sporting opportunities, and this he did whenever they arose. It is fair to say that he exhibited far more interest in his sporting activities than advancing through the ranks.

Sporting seasons appear to have overlapped in India. Athletic track and field competitions were held in January and February. Hockey followed and dominated the sporting calendar between February and April. Football was played primarily between May and July and was followed by Rugby in September. Boxing events were held throughout the year, and cricket matches tended to be held in November and December. Frank participated in all these activities and also played tennis and badminton. Clearly there were ample sporting opportunities throughout the year that provided a period in Frank's life that he thoroughly enjoyed.

FOOTBALL

Frank was assigned to HQ Company, and it was this Company that won the Inter Company Football Challenge Cup on December 15, 1922. There is no evidence that he participated in this particular event. However, Frank's sporting life in India took off very shortly thereafter. Having participated successfully in Athletic, Hockey, and I believe Boxing events, he subsequently travelled with his footballing colleagues to Calcutta to represent the Battalion in the Calcutta Football League in May 1923. At this time the League was comprised of 8 teams which played each other twice. In addition a 'Charity International', between England and Scotland, was held at the mid-point of the 14 game schedule.

On May 8, 1923 Bandsman Newton led the Borderers' line against Calcutta FC, in their first Calcutta Football League match which the solders lost 2-0. Nonetheless it was reported in *The Statesman* that 'Fenner was a tower of strength to the Borderers' defence, while Newton was prominent in their forward line'.[5]

Then just two days later the team drew 3-3 with the Cameron Highlanders. Again Frank played at centre forward and scored the goal which briefly gave his side the lead. 'A hard drive by Newton, of the Borderers, which had immense possibilities, went wide; but a minute or two later the same player gave his team the lead by a short, stinging shot,' that was past the Highlanders' goalkeeper in a flash.[6]

The Rangers XI were the next up, on May 12, and were crushed 5-1. Bandsman Newton led the charge in what was considered a 'singularly uninteresting League fixture'. The game was played on the Mohun Bagan ground.

> 'The soldiers' win did not, however, indicate any great prowess, for with such poor opposition with which to cope, they should have done very much better ... until Newton got the first point. The Borderers then went hard at it, Newton being prominent all the time, although ably backed-up and fed by his four colleagues. He just missed a "sitter", but made amends by scoring a second and third goal in rapid succession'.[7]

In all Frank netted four.

However, on May 15 the Borderers ran up against an unyielding Aryans XI defence, a game in which both sides failed to register a goal.

Eight days later the SWB were defeated 2-1 by Dalhousie. Frank again played at centre forward, but no match report has been located. The Borderers bounced back on May 25 and hammered an unfortunate Calcutta Customs side 5-0. Frank scored once in a game dominated, despite the scoreline, by the weather.

> 'The storm, combined with the weak display of the Customs, came very near to rendering the Customs – S.W. Borderers match on the Customs' ground on Thursday evening an unqualified farce. At the finish the score stood 5-0 in favour of the Borderers, but it is doubtful if 50 per cent of the spectators and even some of the players themselves were quite sure how many goals were scored and who were responsible for them. For fully half an hour, during the closing stages of the first half, and the greater part of the second, it was literally impossible to see what was going on half way across the field owing to the dense clouds of dust and, later on, driving rain. It may be a matter of opinion as to whether the Customs' defence, especially in the first half, was not sounder than that of the soldiers, but this certainly could not be said of the half backs. Hardinge has seldom been so useless, and Templeton has obviously a lot to learn'.[8]

Frank led the SWB line, once more in miserable weather, on May 30 when the side defeated the East Bengal Railwaymen by a single goal.

> 'The conditions were, of course not favourable to good football - a strong, erratic breeze bothered the players and the ground was very rugged. Newton at centre forward, might have been more effective had he not been so unselfish. On occasions when he might have

got through on his own the ball was swung out to the wings, and this policy on a hard and uneven ground with a strong wind was certainly not a profitable one'.[9]

The Borderers final game in the first half of the schedule, took place at the beginning of June against Mohun Bagan. The soldiers won 1-0, and it was Frank who slotted the goal.[10]

At the mid point of the season the SWB had played 8, won 4, drawn 2 and lost 2. However, the side was enjoying a run of good form having won their last three matches.

There then followed one of the highlights of both Calcutta's social and football seasons, the keenly contested 'Charity International'. This annual fixture between teams representing 'England' and 'Scotland' was drawn from the teams participating in the league. Frank was one of three members selected from the ranks of the Borderers XI, to play for England in what proved to be a keenly contested struggle that England finally won 3-2.

'Probably the most enjoyable, as it was the best football contest seen in Calcutta for many years, was the annual charity "international" match between the teams representing England and Scotland respectively witnessed by nearly 10,000 people on the Calcutta ground last evening. Bunting fluttered over the enclosure, and pleasing music was supplied by the pipe bands of the Cameron Highlanders and the Cassipore Artillery respectively, their plaids and kilts and green-coloured bag-pipes adding a picturesquely Celtic touch to the scene'.[11]

The SWB opened their second half schedule against Calcutta

FC in what was described as a close fought encounter.

> 'Newton, Jenkins and Simpson, ... combined effectively, on several occasions, their short passing often being a treat. The trio also tried a good few shots, and their hustling tactics worried the opposing halves'.

However, despite putting their opponents under pressure, the Borderers failed to score, and eventually went down 1-0.[12]

The team should then have played the return fixture with the Cameron Highlanders. But this match never took place as the Camerons withdrew from the League. The Associated Press article of June 8 read in part:

> 'Some controversy is taking place in the sporting circles in Calcutta over the action of the Indian Football Association in suspending for two years two members of the Cameron Highlanders football team which has resulted in that team's withdrawal from the League. The trouble occurred during the game against the Aryans, an Indian team, last week. Prior to that match the Camerons were second in the League, being one point only behind Calcutta; but in that match they met with [an] unexpected reverse, being two goals down a few minutes before time. It is alleged that some members of the side then indulged in rough play and that one man struck the Aryan's goalkeeper; following a melee in front of the Aryan's goal. This was the signal for the crowd to break on to the ground and order had to be restored by the police, the game being abandoned.

The Officer Commanding the Camerons suspended three of his men and in a meeting on Monday the Football Association awarded the game to the Aryans and decided to suspend two of the Camerons regular players for two years. In view of this step the Camerons have withdrawn from the League, not as a protest but because, owing to injuries added to these suspensions, they are unable to raise a side without depleting the strength of their "B" team, which is at present at the head of the second division of the League. The removal of the Camerons from the first division deprives the League of much of its interest'.[13]

There followed a 1-0 victory over the Rangers XI, played on June 6. But it was considered a poor match, as it was played on a hard surface and in a high wind. The lone goal was scored, seven minutes into the second half, by Simpson from 'an excellent opening made by Newton'.[14]

The Aryans provided the opposition for the SWB's next outing in which:

'Despite the fact that the soldiers' centre forward [Newton] blundered frequently, particularly in the second half, their forward line played a steady and well planned game, grasping opportunities with readiness and success. Newton too did much to maintain his high reputation by testing Das with a magnificent drive in the second half'.

Nonetheless what, from the above, must have been a poor

performance on his part, Frank would still have enjoyed the routine 4-0 victory. The side continued to build their winning streak with a 2-0 victory over Dalhousie on June 18, avenging their loss in the first half of the schedule. The game report, in *The Englishman*, contained little of interest about another straight forward win.[15]

The Customs XI was next up, on June 25 and as previously, the side offered only token resistance. This game, in which Frank scored three times, was reported in *The Englishman*, as being:

> 'one sided but there was not an unpleasant incident in the whole match, the play of the Borderers in particular being of a model character. The soldiers gave a good exhibition of forward play, and that too despite poor support from their halves. Newton delighted the crowd by shooting three clever goals and the visiting team's centre-forward apart from his shooting was always in close touch with his wings ... Within eight minutes of the start as a result of fine combination the Boarderers [sic]were attacking and from Jenkins' centre Newton scored. Only three minutes elapsed before Newton scored again '.[16]

The Borderers heavy scoring continued, and towards the end of June the side took on the East Bengal Railway [EBR] club and won 7-2.

> 'The telling character of their [SWB's] play was due to the marked superiority of their forwards who individually

> as well as collectively showed all the art which this sport contains. Scarcely ever has one seen this season a stout defence out-manoeuvred so gloriously and easily too'.

From the outset the Borderers' forwards swarmed around the EBR's defence and within three minutes Newton opened the scoring with a fine drive. However, his afternoon did not pass unblemished for yet again he failed from the penalty spot.[17]

SWB played their final game in the league at the beginning of July and unexpectedly lost to Mohun Bagan 1-0. "Rex" in his report in *The Englishman* stated that Frank while being very much in the 'mix', did not appear to have his shooting boots on as he 'was none too lucky with his one-timers'.[18]

There then followed a special charity match in aid of the Entally Orphanage, on July 7, between the Europeans and the Indians. The teams were selected from the Calcutta, Dalhousie and SWB sides on the one hand, and a team chosen from two Indian sides, Mohun Bagan and the Aryans. It proved to be a somewhat one sided affair which the Europeans won comfortably 3-0.[19]

The Indian Football Association Challenge Shield [IFACS] got underway the following week and in a first round match the SWB took on the India Jute Mill XI.[20] The game, played on the Calcutta Club's ground, as they all were, was won 3-1 by the soldiers.[21] In the second round the SWB beat the Caledonians in a tight match 1-0.[22] The soldiers then went on to win their third round encounter, on July 19 against Dalhousie, by a similar score.[23] However, the SWB were eliminated in the semi-final, losing 2-0 to the Calcutta Club. 'Owing to the rain the ground was heavy and slippery, but the winners were the better team on the day's play'.[24]

Overall, the SWB side enjoyed a good 1923 season, winning 9 of their Calcutta Football League matches, drawing 1 and losing 4; the side scored a total of 34 goals and conceded 12. The team also did well in reaching the semi-finals of the IFACS. Unfortunately, published accounts of games in this tournament were brief, and individuals were not identified.

Frank also enjoyed a successful season. He was noted as having led the line in all the SWB's Calcutta League matches, and had scored at least 10 of his side's goals. In the process he established a high reputation for his footballing abilities, his fierce shot, an unselfish approach to his colleagues, his line leadership and his high level of cohesion with his wings. In addition, he was selected at centre forward for the annual 'England v Scotland', charity match. However, one or two shortcomings were noted. Frank was not perhaps the surest of penalty takers; he was judged to not always adjust his game to best advantage, and of course he missed his share of the standard 'sitters'. However, at twenty years of age he was still relatively inexperienced, but unquestionably his footballing talents were progressing.

Frank's participation in sporting activities was curtailed early in 1924, for an unspecified misdeed, but not before he competed in the Regimental Athletic Sports event, The Moffat Cup, in which he again placed 3rd in the Shot Put. This was followed on February 23 by the first round of the Murree Football Cup. Bandsman Newton played at centre forward, but, despite his best efforts, the team lost by the only goal of the game, a penalty, to the 2nd Durham Light Infantry. This game marked the end of Frank's competitive sporting activities until the 5th round of the Calcutta Football League played at the end of May 1924.

The specific details of his misdemeanour rest somewhere in the mists of time, but on April 4, 1924 a meeting of the General Sports Committee of the SWB was held in Barrackpore. There were no fewer than 10 members present when the Committee sat down to 'discuss and investigate' the case of Bandsman Newton, and any such matters arising therefrom.

> 'Minute 1. The President explained the facts of the case to the committee. [Bandsman Newton called and retires.] Minute 2. After hearing the case the committee discussed amongst themselves the most suitable action to be taken. It was proposed by Bt. Lieut.-Colonel T.C. Greenway, D.S.O., and seconded by Lieut. W.L. Hughes, M.C., that Bdm. Newton should not be suspended but simply dropped from all forms of sport and receive a severe lecture. The motion was carried'.[25]

No details of the case were mentioned, but Frank's sporting prowess would have been common knowledge, and the committee would have been mindful of Frank's contribution to the Regiment's standing on the sporting fields of India. As a result Frank was not suspended and at the end of May 1924, no doubt having absorbed the 'severe lecture', he travelled to Calcutta to lead the Borderers' line in the fifth round of the 1924 Calcutta Football League.

Frank made an immediate impact when, reinstated at centre forward, he scored both goals in the Regiment's 2-0 victory against the Aryans XI. There followed a hard fought match with the strong Calcutta FC which the Borderers won by the only goal of the game. Almost inevitably, Frank played a part, as noted in the Battalion's Sports Diary of 1924: 'we scored in the second half from a centre by Morgan which was going out when Newton ran in and headed it to Simpson who scored'.[26]

The two matches immediately prior to the mid season break were both tough, but inconclusive encounters. That played on June 3, against the 51st Company of the Royal Garrison Artillery, resulted in a 1-1 draw. Bandsman Newton, again at centre forward, left it late but scored the equaliser some five minutes from the end. The last game was played just 2 days later against Mohun Bagan, and resulted in a 0-0 draw. Whoever wrote the relevant entry in the SWB's Regimental Sports Diary perhaps felt that Frank could have done better. He confided, that 'Newton at centre forward looked very like scoring several times'.[27]

The mid-season 'Charity International' followed, but this year Frank, quite understandably given the number of games he had missed, was not selected. In the first match after the break the SWB took on Dalhousie. Frank again spearheaded the line and scored late in the first half. However, he disappointed later after being brought down heavily in the penalty area. Surprisingly Frank took the resulting penalty which he missed, and then immediately left the field injured. Nonetheless, the SWB went on to register a 2-0 victory.[28]

Frank was '*hors de combat*' for the next three games, but this proved no handicap as the team hit top gear and rolled off three straight victories without conceding a goal. The games against the Rangers FC and the Cameron Highlanders were won 1-0, and the Customs XI were seen off 3-0. Frank returned for the game against Calcutta FC, on June 21, which resulted in a goalless draw. This run of success, 4 wins and a draw, placed the Borderers in second place in the League after 13 games. The side trailed Dalhousie by a point, but were 2 ahead of the Cameron Highlanders, who had a game in hand, and 3 up on the Calcutta club.[29]

There followed another 0-0 draw against the Aryans side. On this occasion Frank played at inside left in what proved to be a lacklustre game. *The Statesman* carried a report which called out the performance of the Borderers' forwards.

> 'In the first half when the Borderers had the advantage of a slight breeze they monopolised the game, but the forwards manoeuvred aimlessly in front of their opponents' goal, many transfers being misdirected or easily intercepted. Accurate shooting was also not a feature of their game and Newton and Davies had some fine chances to repair their early errors from Cook's centres, but both shot yards wide'.[30]

The stout performance of the Borderers' defence continued, and in their next match the Royal Garrison Artillery side was shut out. The difference in this encounter was that the recently underperforming forwards managed to score a brace. Frank, at inside left again, scored the first: 'Kelly then put forward a fine pass to Newton, who after rounding an opponent sent in a low shot which Skinner failed to hold …' Frank then set up Davies for the second.[31]

The last round of these Calcutta League games was scheduled to be played on July 5, 1924. The league standings were finely poised with Dalhousie, the 1st Battalion of the Cameron Highlanders and the 2nd Battalion of the SWB, all having an opportunity to take the honours. The SWB must have fancied their chances as they were due to play Mohun Bagan who were fully 10 points behind them in the league standings, having just 12 points from 15 games. However, the win eluded them, and despite the defence remaining intact, for the sixth consecutive game, the forwards failed yet again. The reports in *The Englishman* and *The Statesman* both called out Frank and Davies for missing the proverbial 'sitters'. As a result of what was a disappointing draw, the SWB finished second on goal average.[32]

The final placings at the top of the Calcutta Football League in 1924 were as follows:

Team	Plyd	W	D	L	GOALS		PTS
					F	A	
1st Btn. Q.O. Cameron Highlanders	16	9	5	2	28	7	23
2nd Btn. SWB	16	8	7	1	19	7	23
Dalhousie	16	9	5	2	19	10	23
Calcutta FC	16	6	8	2	23	7	20[33]

Again the conclusion of the Calcutta League did not mark the end of the football season as the IFACS started two weeks later on Saturday, July 19. The SWB played the Dacca based Wari Athletic Club in the first round. The match was played in conditions that were considered to favour the Athletic club. However, the soldiers acquitted themselves well enough to earn a 1-1 draw, and it was Frank who scored with a 'capital rising shot'.[34]

The teams replayed on the Monday following, when the SWB recorded a relatively straight forward 3-0 victory in which Frank scored from a set piece. In the match report it was considered that the Wari side were handicapped by the conditions under foot, and that their defeat was 'chiefly due to the wet ground, which was like a fen … Undoubtedly the wet ground spoilt the Indians' game, and even the booted team slipped all over the field'.[35]

Frank again led the SWB line in the second round against the Aryans XI, a match the soldiers narrowly won by the only goal of the game. In the semi-final the victors came up against the familiar Calcutta FC XI and lost 1-0. This was the final appearance of the SWB side in 1924.[36]

After 1924 it becomes more difficult to follow Frank's footballing exploits as the SWB's Sports Diary was maintained more casually and all the relevant newspapers are not immediately available. The Battalion did not enter a side in the Army Football Championship of 1925 to be played in March, nor did a side travel to Calcutta to take part in the Calcutta Football League. The fact that the Battalion was due to deploy to Agra probably had some bearing on the latter decision, and there is no reference to the tournament in the Battalion's Sports Diary. Nonetheless, a team was entered in the 1925 IFACS. It was noted too, on May 25, 1925, that Frank, now Lance Corporal Newton, was 'one of those selected to referee games in the 1st and 2nd Division of the Inter Platoon Association Football League.' Increased responsibilities in the sporting arena, it would appear, were commensurate with promotion.[37]

Frank once more led the SWB line in the IFACS. In the first round, played in July, as in the previous year, the Battalion was drawn against Kumartuli, a local Calcutta team that played in the Second Division of the Calcutta League. An unidentified press reporter considered the outcome of the game a formality, and so it proved. 'The inevitable goal was soon forthcoming, Newton in a quick break-away scoring with a shot that gave Ganguli no chance.' This was the first of two goals scored by Frank in the side's 3-0 victory.

The East Bengal Engineering College, also based in Calcutta, provided the opposition in the second round and were dismissed 6-0. Frank again scored twice, the first after just six minutes and the second, finally, from a penalty! However, in the semi-final matters did not go so well as the Royal Scottish Fusiliers provided sterner opposition and defeated the Borderers 2-0. Nonetheless, this was a closer result than that recorded in the final in which the Fusiliers swamped the Cheshire Regiment 5-1.[38]

In December 1925 the Battalion finally moved to Agra, Uttar Pradesh, and on January 24, 1926, played the Royal Warwickshire Regiment in the first round of the Murree Association Football Cup. The match ended in a draw and was replayed the following day when the SWB won another close encounter 3-2. In the next round they disposed of the Delhi Independent Brigade to advance to the semi-finals against the Northumberland Fusiliers. I believe this match was played on February 17; Frank played on left wing and the SWB XI lost 2-0. Regrettably, to date no detailed accounts of the matches have been located.[39]

The next documented football event in which the Battalion XI participated was the IFACS held in Calcutta in July 1926. The Battalion played an East Indian Railway XI in the first round. Frank, now captain, led the team out and playing inside left scored the first goal. Unfortunately, that was as good as it got, as the Railwaymen came back to win 2-1 and advanced to the second round.[40]

In 1927 there is but one brief reference to the 2nd Battalion's football team, and no doubt there would have been others had the Sports Diary been regularly maintained. This single reference recorded the appearance of the 2nd Battalion's XI in the final of the Delhi Independent Brigade, Agra Football Competition. A game the Borderers won easily, beating the Royal Warwickshire Regiment 6-2. L/Cpl Newton played at centre forward in what was considered 'a very hard game', despite the score line.[41] Unfortunately, nothing further has been located relating to the SWB's footballing journey in India prior to the Battalion's departure for Aden in 1927.

However, Frank was not a spent footballing force by 1927, as became apparent after Frank transferred to the Army Reserve, on April 10, 1927, some nine years after he enlisted. He moved to Calcutta and joined the Calcutta Police, which allowed him to continue his footballing exploits. On May 18 Frank turned out for the Police XI, in a Division II match, against the North Staffordshires' 'B' side.

> 'There was a good attendance on the Police ground when the home side met the North Staffords "B" and won by 3-0. It was a game worth seeing, the visitors having the better of the first half but the home side pressing home the attack in the second.
> For the Police, Newton was undoubtedly the outstanding player at centre half'.

The score was tied 0-0 at the interval, but the Police upped their game in the second half and Frank headed their first from a corner. Two further goals followed which put the game out of reach for the soldiers.[42]

A second report of this game, which Frank not surprisingly placed in his Scrap Book, was headed "BRILLIANT NEWTON". Much of the content is a tribute to Frank's versatility and opportunism, but it also makes reference to the change in his military status.

> 'Newton, late of the South Wales Borderers, and at present one of the outstanding men of the Police team, had a big share in the victory gained on Wednesday by that team against the North Staffords Reserves. The margin was three goals to nil, and it was well deserved.
>
> In a game that could by no stretch of the imagination be said to have produced even average football, Newton's display impressed itself. In the first period he played centre half, displacing Greenhorn, who joined the attack. Newton lost no time in showing that he can be a brilliant centre half. The attacks of the soldiers nearly all ended with him, for he showed uncanny ability to head the ball away at the right time.
>
> After the interval Newton went up into the forward line and it was not long before he showed himself a rare opportunist by heading in the first Police goal from a corner. Thenceforward he returned to the defence, not only repulsed the Staffords raids, but also gave material assistance to his own forwards. Towards the end, when the Staffords woke up, Newton was a full back, and here

too he pulled his side out of many a tight corner. Truly a versatile and useful footballer. It is no exaggeration to say that he was the most conspicuous man on the field, for it was his efforts - and his alone - that helped to raise the game from being deadly dull'.[43]

There then followed, on June 9, a match 'between the Dalhousie 'B' and the Calcutta Police, the champions of the Second Division League, on the former's ground,' for the Hardinge Shield. It was a game, played before a large crowd, that the Police should have won, but the side folded in the second half. The Police led 1-0 at the break, and within 5 minutes of the restart went 2 up, 'Newton netting off a free-kick from just outside the penalty area.' However, 'The Dals forwards then made a great rally' and scored the winning goal 'a few minutes before the close'.[44]

Frank must certainly have been playing regularly for the Calcutta Police, despite their being a Division II side, as he was selected to play for England in the annual charity game against Scotland on June 11, 1927. "Rex" described that year's colourful, social Calcutta highlight in some detail:

'The seventeenth international meeting between England and Scotland on the C.F.C. ground on Saturday ended in a draw of three goals all. This being the case, the custody of the medals depended upon the toss of a coin, and Scotland won. These were presented by Mrs F.E. James with both teams lined up and meeting with due appreciation for the fine exhibition given on either side. The Hon. Mr Justice Buckland, President of the

I.F.A., presided. In addition to his share of the medals presented by the I.F.A., Davidson, the Scottish skipper, was the recipient of a smokers' cabinet, which incidentally included a bottle of White Horse whisky, presented by Messrs. Samuel Fitze and Co. The cabinet, by the way, is made of oak taken from the scene of the Battle of Bannockburn and therefore one to value.

The 'Charity International, England XI', 1927. Played on the Calcutta Sports Ground against their Scottish counterparts, June 11, 1927. The game ended 3-3. Frank front row, 2nd from right

Clearly, "Rex" and the Samuel Fitze Company recognised the commercial value of donating a bottle of whisky for the occasion. An astute move by the management of the business, incorporated in 1898 and still, in 2023, welcoming its customer base at their highly rated Chinese restaurant in Kolkata. However, the composition of the cabinet may require more of a stretch since the Battle was fought in 1314. One wonders how many items must have been so described in the intervening years?

"Rex" continued:

> 'With the flag-bedecked enclosure, the scene was a gay one, and this helped not a little to raise the enthusiasm of a large gathering, amongst whom it was good to see a large number of Indian enthusiasts who can have had no other object than to see a good game. As usual the Pipes of the Cossipore Artillery were very much in evidence and their playing, walking up and down the field in their picturesque attire, was quite one of the tit-bits of the afternoon both before the match started and in the interval. Whereas they played the Scottish team on to the field, the Band of the North Staffords heralded the English side, and they too helped very materially to pass away the spare time pleasantly. They gave a distinct invitation to the onlookers to take part in "community" singing but, apart from a few somewhat timorous attempts from the Press Box, this was not taken up'.

Overall, "Rex" considered that Scotland were somewhat fortunate to draw, although there was considerable discussion around whether the third English goal was off-side, and 'had the referee not been well up with the play their first goal might not have been awarded'. He emphasised the neutrality of the proceedings, the referee, Mr C.R. Clayton, 'being an Irishman, was in every way an ideal referee', and even 'the ball was neutral, being green. It was one of the latest laceless [sic] balls, but one doubts whether the colour, deceptive in flight, will find favour.' He described the conditions at game time, and gave his considered opinion around the players' performances. In particular

Steele at centre forward, who scored a hat-trick, and Frank

> 'were the pick of the forwards. The former was dangerous whenever he had the ball near goal and showed plenty of dash, and the latter gave him many a promising "through" pass which might have led to a score at any time, kept Luby well fed and took a big share of the defence'.

It was noted that Frank did not play in the 1926 game, but he was clearly very much at home in this company.[45] And this was confirmed by his selection to play, at inside right, in the upcoming Europeans vs Indians International on July 2.[46] The game was played on the Calcutta FC ground which, as the Associated Press reported, was:

> 'thronged by thousands to witness the annual International soccer match between Europeans and Indians. His Excellency the Governor and Lady Jackson were present, this being the first football match they have witnessed here. Lady Jackson gave away the medals after the game ... The crowd was the largest seen this season and every possible point of vantage was taken. People fought for admission, the tickets having been sold out hours before the game commenced and thousands had to remain content with seeing what they could through periscope or be satisfied with a bird's-eye view of the game from the approach to the ramparts of Fort William'.

The weather was fine and this was considered to help the bare-footed Indian side, and it was they, despite the Europeans being favoured, who ran out winners by the only goal of the game. In particular the Indian defence stood out and 'was brilliant and undoubtedly assisted enormously towards the victory.' On the other hand, the Europeans were lacklustre, exhibited poor cohesion and were unable to press home their attacks. In particular Steele at centre forward was effectively marked out of the game. The run of play ebbed and flowed, and it was the Indian XI that scored after hitting the woodwork to deservedly lead 1-0 at the break. The Europeans improved somewhat in the second half and Newton, Steele and Banks all went close. In fact the 'Europeans were very unfortunate not to net during this period', but Talukdar in the Indians' goal pulled off a couple of wonderful saves to ensure victory. 'The end heralded the fourth consecutive victory for the Indians, who undoubtedly played brilliant football'.[47]

Another but similar report of the game appeared in *The Englishman* on July 7, 1927. Again the European forwards came in for faint praise, 'Bell too played below form as did also Newton and Knight who remained starved for the most part.' Steele too 'seemed to have been overpowered by Gossain who shadowed him throughout'. The Indian team were judged to be fully deserving of their victory, and perhaps 'what served as an extra impetus to the players and spectators alike was that the match was honoured by the presence of his Excellency the Governor of Bengal and Lady Jackson.' As mentioned, Lady Jackson presented the medals, and Sir Stanley addressed the gathering stating that 'he had seen many big matches in England but he could not remember one that had been productive of as clean a game as the one he had witnessed'. He commented also on the high standard of play, and 'spoke highly of the CFC ground, which he, at the very first sight of it, thought was a cricket ground, since it appeared too good for a football match and was as good as many of the first class county grounds'.[48] Sir Stanley would have been well informed on this as he played cricket for Yorkshire between 1890 and 1907, played in 20 Test matches for England between 1893 and 1905, and led the side to their celebrated Ashes victory in 1905.[49]

At some point between early July and August 27, Frank moved, or transferred from the Calcutta Police to the East Indian Railway Company [EIRC], where, true to form, he quickly became involved with their football side. On August 21 the EIRC entered the Durand Football Tournament, held annually in Simla, at the time the summer capital of British India, and it was anticipated that they would 'bring a formidable side'. The following week the EIRC XI left Calcutta for Simla, and *en route* played a friendly match at Allehabad.

The Tournament proper got underway in Simla on Saturday, September 10. The first report covering the East Indian Railway side was a second round match, played on September 17, against the Royal Scots Fusiliers. The game was attended by many of the local glitterati, including His Excellency the Viceroy, E.F. Lindley Wood, known as The Lord Irwin, the Hon. Miss Wood, Sir Clement Hindley, Chief Commissioner of Railways for India, and Sir B.N. Mitra, a member of the Viceroy's Executive Council and later Indian High Commissioner in the United Kingdom.

The Royal Scots Fusiliers, from Ferozepore, were favoured but it was a match in which 'the railway team shone beyond expectation.'

'From the outset the Railway side, after stemming an initial attack by the Fusiliers, settled down to serious football. Chakrabati made an effort to draw first blood, when Whelan made a great save by tipping over ... Chakrabati and Samad again got going on the right when the latter was charged in the area and the Railway were awarded a penalty, from which Newton scored'.

Later in the half Chakrabati combined with Frank, his centre forward, who scored a 'fine goal, the ball striking the inside of the upright'. At the break the EIRC XI led 2-0, and added a third shortly after the resumption. After conceding a fourth the Fusiliers frustration got the better of them and, when Frank broke through again, he was 'tripped and injured, necessitating his removal from the field. Later Samad was similarly fouled and the referee sent Collins off the field.' However, the Fusiliers did score a late consolation goal when the referee perhaps felt he should even the penalty count.[50]

In the third round, played on September 24, the Railwaymen defeated the holders of the Lahore Trades Cup, the King's Own Yorkshire Light Infantry [KOYLI], 2-1. It was a hard fought, intense encounter, played out before a large crowd of spectators and even more of the glitterati, including His Highness the Maharaja of Faridkot.

'The game was played in a clean, sportsmanlike spirit and though the honours of the day go to the East Indian Railway by the odd goal in three, the KOYLI were by no stretch of the imagination an inferior team'.

Both defences were subjected to periods of intense pressure, but the soldier's short passing game ultimately proved ineffective. The battle raged on and towards the end of the first half:

> 'the Railway side redoubled their efforts and they were the one team in the picture for some time. Newton broke through but his shot was smothered ... Then Bose sent in from the left, Ford bringing off a fine save, but Bose ran down the line again and centering accurately, Samad headed into the corner of the net. Again did the Railway attack, when McMullen made Ford save a fine shot and a minute later Chakrabati ran through the KOYLI defence and snapped in a second goal for the Railway side. Two goals in the lead, the Railway continued to attack, Bose sent in another centre which Newton just put over. Then the KOYLI, steadying themselves, set about reducing the deficit, but they would persist in the short passing game, which failed more often than not'.

The soldiers attacked more vigorously after the break, and despite Frank doing his best to 'set his forward line going', the soldiers were the more persistent attacking force, and it was not long before the margin was reduced. 'Great enthusiasm now prevailed and the KOYLI made a great bid to draw level. The Railway defence, however, went all out to stem onslaught after onslaught'. In this the side was successful, and the EIRC side advanced to the semi-final to take on the 1st Battalion of the Royal Fusiliers.[51]

Saturday, September 28 proved to be 'an ideal day for football; the sky was overcast and the cool air was exhilarating.

The Railway won the toss and elected to play downhill. The Fusiliers immediately launched a menacing offensive', the first of several throughout the first half. Ryan in goal for the Railway XI performed heroically, and his and the defenders' efforts were rewarded late in the half when Bose got down the line and centred for

> 'Samad to score easily ... The Fusiliers who had done the bulk of the attacking, appeared to slacken momentarily, for the Railway forwards, ably led by Newton, had the Fusiliers defence in difficulty'

but they failed to capitalise further before the break.

In the second half the civilians came more into the game. Frank shot over the bar and was judged unlucky not to score on two further occasions after he had split the defence. Likewise, Samad tested Clements in the soldiers' goal after 'a brilliant solo run', and Clements pulled 'off a great save from almost off Samad's too [sic: toe] and before he was able to recover himself Newton tried a hard shot', but 'amidst thunderous applause', Samad was ruled off-side. The Fusiliers stormed back but Ryan again stood firm. By the close neither side had been able to 'score again and a great game ended in a win for the Railway'.

This, the second semi-final game was played out before a 'huge' crowd, which now included Sir Cyril Deverell, Quartermaster-General of India, and Sir Umar Hayat Khan, member of the Governor-General of India's Imperial Council, in an atmosphere of 'tense excitement'. There was a high level of interest attached to what the East Indian Railway team had achieved as they were:

> 'the first civilian team to enter the final of the tournament since 1897, when with a meagre entry list of only five, the 2nd [Simla] PVRC lost to the then redoubtable Black Watch, who followed up their success by annexing the trophy outright'.[52]

The final, a social highlight, was played on Saturday October 1, between the York and Lancaster Regiment and the EIRC XI, in what was a carnival atmosphere. Prior to the match Messrs Syed A. and M. Wazir Ali, the local Army Contractors, judiciously were 'At Home' to a large group of guests which included His Excellency the Governor of the Punjab, Sir William Hailey, and others in the Viceroy's party.

> 'Seldom, if ever, has Simla witnessed so great a Durand match as this afternoon, when all previous gate records were broken and with gorgeous weather prevailing, many made it a whole-day affair by picnicing down at Annandale in Epsom Day style. Not only were the stands overflowing, but every coign of vantage on the hill-side was requisitioned and what added lustre to the proceedings was the full band of pipers of the Seaforth Highlanders, who marched down the field before the match and at the interval'.

The Railway side were strong favourites to sweep all before them and when they 'emerged from their dressing tent the crowd exhibited the wildest enthusiasm'.

The game was dominated by two strong defensive units, but both sides had good chances in the first half. Frank and

McMullen went close and the soldiers missed a penalty. But five minutes before the interval the Railwaymen conceded. The second half was very much a repetition of the first; again Frank and McMullen threatened, and while the Yorks and Lancs played the more aggressive football, their poor finishing let them down. And, inexcusably, a second penalty was missed. Nonetheless, seven minutes from time the outcome was finally settled when the soldiers scored from a direct free kick. The two goalkeepers were singled out for their outstanding performances: Ryan for the East Indian Railway, and Lees in the soldiers' net who remarkably had not been beaten once throughout the tournament.

Following the game Sir John Thompson, President of the Tournament Committee, requested Lord Irwin to award the various cups and prizes, and he also expressed the view 'that this year's Tournament would live in the memory of those who watched it as one of the best Tournaments since the War.' Thanks were expressed to the Quartermaster-General, the referees, the sponsors of the special cups and prizes, the Army Contractors (who had taken the place of the Army Canteen Board which had gone into liquidation, possibly to the relief of many), and not least the Simla public for the warm welcome extended. The event wrapped up after Lord Irwin 'presented the cups and medals, amidst scenes of enthusiasm'.[53]

Finally, an article that appears to have been filed on October 4, by *The Englishman*'s 'Own Correspondent' in Simla, reported on a banquet given the previous evening by Mr A.M. Hayman, Finance Director of the Railway Board and Mr D.H. Framjee, in honour of the Durand Cup Finalists. The soiree was very well attended, with many distinguished guests among the 500 present. Mr Hayman made the obligatory speech during which he mentioned:

> 'he could not disguise the fact that the railway officials were disappointed at the E.I.Ry. Team not having won the tournament and thereby making history by annexing the most coveted trophy in the field of sport in India, yet the great display of clean and clever football that the side had given had produced very good results in that two of the Agents of the big railways in India had promised to send teams to next year's tournament'.

He went on to assure his audience that it was Mr G. Colvin, the sporting Agent for the EIRC, who had agreed to send the side, and had also 'found the funds to keep them up at Simla for such a long time.' He congratulated the Yorks and Lancasters on their deserving win and expressed the hope that an EIRC side would emulate them 'in a year or two.'

For his part, Mr Colvin said he was pleased with what the team had achieved, and 'even more proud that his team was the only one composed of different communities, and he held it out as an example of what could be accomplished if the different communities would work together as a team in any game of life.' Then Lady Hindley presented the awards:

> 'a cup to the E.I.Ry. Team, a cup to Newton, a cup to Corpl. Stones, captain of the Yorks and Lancs., a cup to A. Bhattacharya, captain of the E.I.Ry. Team, a medal to Glover, who had to stand down, and the Colvin medal to Mr Tawse, the trainer of the E.I.Ry. Team'.

There followed further speeches from distinguished members of both the Railway Board and the Railway Department, before the proceedings wound up with dancing. It was noted that certain of their Ladyships 'and several other ladies set the example by dancing with the players' of both teams. Unfortunately, no reason was given for the awarding of the silver cup to Frank. Possibly it was for services rendered on the football field as the final marked his footballing swansong on the playing fields of India.[54]

ATHLETICS

Having arrived in India at the end of 1922, it was not long before Frank got into the sporting mix and quickly impressed his abilities upon his colleagues. The competition for the 'Moffat Cup', awarded to the Company that won the Regimental Athletic Sports Competition, was held in Barrackpore over 2 days, on January 22 and 23, 1923. The results record that Private Newton, of HQ Company, came second in the Shot Put. This event marked the launch of Frank's remarkably full sporting life in India. It was one in which he engaged fully whenever possible, and contributed greatly to his enjoyment during his time in India, as he said, 'I had a great time out East'.[55] This result also provides the first formal evidence of his having arrived in India.[56]

In the same event in 1924 he came third, a result he repeated the following year. [57] In 1925 he also won the long jump with a leap of 19' 2". A year later the 'Moffat Cup' competition was held on February 3, in Agra, and Frank, now L/Cpl Newton, continued to perform well in his chosen field events. He came first in the Shot Put, with a throw of 35'5", and third in the long jump.[58] The latter result would have been something of a disappointment to him as the winning distance was 6" shorter than his winning effort in1925.

Later, on October 10, 1926 he travelled to Darjeeling, undoubtedly with the Battalion's Athletic Team, to compete in the Darjeeling Athletics Meet, held at St Joseph's College. Once more Frank excelled for he not only won the Shot Put, but also, although at best a marginal field event, won the 'Throwing the Cricket Ball' competition![59]

The following year the 'Moffat Cup', Frank's last, was held on February 7 and 8, 1927 again in Agra. Once more Frank was competitive winning the Shot Put, with a throw of 34' 1", well below his personal best, and qualified for the Long Jump final, but failed to finish in the top three.[60]

HOCKEY

In the first week of February, 1923 the Regiment played off against the Cameron Highlanders for the lone vacancy to participate in the First Division of the Calcutta Hockey League. On the day, February 6, the SWB encountered little opposition and swamped the 'Camerons' 6-1.[61] Frank almost certainly did not participate in that game. However, because it was necessary to make 'several alterations to the team, owing to the indisposition of some of the regular players', he did travel with the side to Calcutta for the round robin tournament. In their opening game the Borderers were up against the powerful, domestic league leading Calcutta Rangers, with a less than settled line up.

'Newton was pressed into service and tried on the left wing ... These translations and alterations, instead of weakening the Borderers, as a side, seemed to work excellently and they gave their best exhibition of the season and with a little luck they may have beaten the League leaders'.

The game ended in a surprising 1-1 draw and it was none other than Frank who equalised ten minutes into the second half.[62]

In the four following games, played in quick succession, Frank retained his place on the left wing. The first two of these matches were drawn; 0-0 against the Greer Club, and 2-2 with the Apprentices XI. The third versus the Medicals XI was won 1-0, but the SWB were well beaten 4-1 in the last game by St. Xaviers. However, the Borderers solo goal was netted when Newton went down on his own and beat Lee-Emery.[63] Of the five goals the SWB scored in the competition Frank accounted for at least two.

Bandsman Newton apparently did not participate during the 1924 hockey season, perhaps because he chose to play in the Murray [Murree] Football Cup competition which the Borderers XI exited when defeated 1-0 by the 2nd Durham Light Infantry on February 23, 1924. Frank played at centre forward in the game. However, his failure to appear subsequently was almost certainly related to Bandsman Newton's sporting misdemeanour mentioned previously.[64]

Even so, he was back on the hockey field in March 1925 as he participated in the Inter Unit Hockey Tournament. In the first round, played on March 26, the Borderers defeated a team from the Cheshire Regiment 3-1. Just two days later, in the final held at Barrackpore, the Regiment, with Frank at left back, once more easily disposed of the Cameron Highlanders 6-0.[65]

South Wales Borderers hockey XI that competed for the Beighton Cup in April 1925, on the Calcutta Sports Ground. Frank, back row right.

The Borderers also competed in the Beighton Cup and in the first round, played on April 14,1925, once more defeated the hapless Cameron Highlanders, but only 3-0. The defensive qualities of the side were mentioned: 'The backs too are dependable as both of them, especially Newton, the Soccer centre forward, showed clever interception'.[66]

In the second round the soldiers faced off against the Customs XI, a match that ended 1-1. Again L/Cpl Newton performed well at full back, as mentioned in *The Englishman*: 'Newton at back is worthy of every praise – he showed clever anticipation, was energy personified and hit cleanly.' No faint praise, but the defence failed in the replay, and the 4-1 defeat sent the Borderers back to barracks.[67]

The final entry in the Regimental Sports Diary relating to the Battalion's hockey exploits in India is brief. It notes only that in the elimination competition for the Army Hockey Championship, the Battalion played the Devonshire Regiment XI, on February 13, 1926, in Agra. L/Cpl Newton again played at full back, but the team went down 1-0 and accordingly were eliminated.[68]

However, Frank again represented the Regimental Hockey XI, on October 14, 1926, when he was reported to have been injured. There is a statement signed by L/Cpl C. Binnie, witnessed by L/Cpl G.C. Simpson, reporting that Pte. Richards of A Company, in attempting 'to clear the ball, hit L/Cpl Newton on the knee (with the ball)'. As a result Frank had to be carried from the field with what was thought to be a damaged patella.[69] This match was part of the Darjeeling Athletics Meet, held at St. Joseph's College.

BOXING

Boxing was high on Frank's sporting agenda from the outset of his army career, but regrettably the SWB Sports Diary contains no detailed accounts of the numerous boxing competitions held between 1923 and 1927. However, it can be taken as given that Frank's reputation as a boxer of ability, earned back in Brecon, was common knowledge to those involved in organising the District Team Boxing Tournament, held at the end of January, 1923. The event ran over three days and it is a racing certainty that Frank participated. The tournament was won by the Cameron Highlanders; the SWB finished second and the 'Lincolns' third. In addition, the SWB Inter-company boxing competition was held between April 6-10, 1923, but no detailed results have been located.[70]

Then 6 months later, on October 12, 1923, an "Interesting 10 rounds contest" was held in Calcutta's Empire Theatre. The featured fight on the card was a catchweight contest between George Thorogood, weighing in at 8 st. 2 lbs., and Manila's "Kid" Castro, 7 st. 4 lbs.. Featured on the under card, in one of four, four round fights, was Bandsman Newton of the SWB versus the pride of Katihar, Syd Parrott. Frank weighed in at 11 st. and Parrott 10 st. 12 lbs.. The fight ended when Frank knocked the unfortunate Parrott off his perch in the second round.[71]

There is also irrefutable evidence of Frank's boxing prowess in his trophy cabinet in the form of a fine silver trophy, hallmark: Birmingham, 1922, and inscribed:

CALCUTTA EXHIBITION
1923
MILITARY BOXING
6 ROUND COMPETITION
WINNER

I believe that this was the trophy that Frank won when he knocked Syd Parrott out, in the second round, at Calcutta's Empire Theatre in October 1923, and any confusion regarding the number of rounds is of little importance.

Frank the pugilist. Most probably taken after he won the Military Boxing, 6 Round Competition at the 1923 Calcutta Exhibition.

In 1924 the Inter-Company Boxing competition was held in March, but no reference to a District Tournament has been located. However, one was held in Calcutta on Wednesday and Thursday, February 18-19, 1925, in which the SWB placed second. And then in May a further District Tournament was held between the 'Cheshires', the Royal Artillery, the Queen's Own Cameron Highlanders and the SWB. The results were particularly impressive as the Borderers won 18 and drew 1 of their 24 bouts.[72]

The following year, 1926, the Battalion held their Inter-company Boxing Tournament, now called the Gurkha Shield, in Agra during April. The Regimental Tournament of 1926 was held during August at Bandikui, Dansa. Once more the Battalion made a strong impression, winning 8 of the 12 bouts held.[73]

Although none of the participants are named in any of the above events, there is little doubt that Frank continued to duck regularly through the ropes to represent the Regiment. If he had not, there would have been no reason to include the name of L/Cpl. Newton on a list of 33 non-commissioned officers and men who were ineligible to enter Novice Boxing Competitions. A note was made on September 2, 1926 that the rules governing Novice Boxing Competitions, at para 5, prohibited those classed 'A' to enter such competitions.[74]

The Regiment's final Inter-company Boxing Tournament, before departing for Aden was held in Agra on February 23, 1927 and was won by C company.[75]

RUGBY

In 1924 the inaugural India and South East Asia Rugby Championship was played on Indian soil. The game of Rugby Union was certainly very well established and keenly followed throughout the ranks of the SWB. In 1925 the 1st Battalion, then based in Devonport, England embarked on a remarkable run when the XV won the Army Cup, an achievement the 1st Battalion repeated in 1926, 1927 and 1928.[76] It would have come as no surprise therefore that the 2nd Battalion entered the inaugural All India & South East Asia Rugby Tournament in 1924.[77]

Unfortunately, the rugby records relating to the Battalion are fragmented, and were not consistently maintained and remain far from complete. However, it is clear that the 2nd Battalion ran two sides in 1925, and the 1st XV again entered the South East Asia Rugby Tournament. Frank participated in the first 4 matches played by the 1st XV. In the opening game he played at centre three-quarter against the Bengal Nagpur Railway XV, a match the soldiers won 6-0. His preference for this position probably reflected his knowledge of Rugby League rather than Union. He certainly played in the following 3 games in which it is assumed he continued at centre three-quarter. There followed a 0-0 draw with the Calcutta Club XV, and a 6-5 defeat inflicted by the Calcutta Scottish. Frank's final outing in this tournament resulted in a resounding victory, 27-0, against La Martinière Old Boys.[78]

This tournament was followed by the All India Rugby Cup in which the Battalion XV also participated, but there is no record indicating Frank was involved.

Over the course of the 1925 season the SWB fielded two sides, both of which compiled good records.

	P	W	D	L	Points For	Points Against
1st XV	13	9	2	2	177	20
2nd XV	6	5	0	1	77	27[79]

The 1926 side was less successful. At the end of July the Battalion XV played the 2nd Battalion of the Gloucester Regiment, in Jhansi, and won 6-0. However, they lost the return encounter, held in Agra, 9-6.[80]

In September the SWB XV competed in the Calcutta Rugby Cup and in the first round knocked out the Jubbalpore Signals XV in a close contest, 3-0. Their second round game, held on September 25, against the Welch Regiment XV was also fiercely contested, but on this occasion the SWB were knocked out, going down 5-3.[81]

The Borderers' XV commenced their last rugby season in India with a tour of Uttar Pradesh. They set off at the end of July 1927, visited the cities of Jhansi, Jubbalpore and Allahabad, and played two games in early August. The Regimental Sports Diary contains nothing further. However, at the end of August the side competed in the Cawnpore West Cup, and in the first round, recorded a relatively straight forward 13-0 victory over what may have been the Gymkhana 2nd XV. On September 2 the Borderers swept all before them in the semi final when they hammered the Lincolnshire Regiment 32-0, and a couple of days later the side beat their hosts, Cawnpore, to win the trophy.[82]

The XV's final appearance on Indian soil, in what may well have been an exhibition match, was less successful as they lost to the Bombay Gymkana 'A' XV 19-0. But no matter, for on that day the West Rugby Cup was presented to the Battalion by A. West Esq. himself, '… as a parting gift and as a memento of the excellent games which they played in the recent Rugger Final in September last.'

The presentation took place on October 25, 1927 a week before the Battalion departed for Aden.[83]

Given Frank's inclusion in the side in 1925, it is reasonable to suggest that he would have turned out for the first or second XV in 1926. Weight is added to this suggestion in the interview, cited below, conducted by B.J. Evans in September 1931. Frank states that one choice he could have made was taking up Rugby League professionally. In my view, Frank's statement strongly suggests that he would have played rugby regularly prior to his transfer to the Army Reserve.

CRICKET

As previously mentioned, Frank won a 'Throwing the Cricket Ball' event at the Darjeeling Sports meet in October 1925. It would seem probable that his interest in such a marginal event was prompted by his only recorded involvement in the Regimental cricket team, a sport in which his batting endeavours were less than spectacular. The side performed well in the 1924-25 season, winning 8 matches, drawing one and losing 3. Few details are available, but Frank certainly played in at least 5 of these matches and very probably more given the side's good win record. As a lower order batsmen Frank would have been called upon to bat on fewer occasions. Clearly Frank struggled with the bat as his season's record at the crease indicates:

Also Batted	Innings	Runs	Not Out	Highest score	Average
L/Cpl. Newton	5	30	0	15	6[84]

It comes as no surprise that he finished bottom of the batting averages. There is no mention of any bowling performances, which may have been just as well.

RETURN FROM INDIA TO ENGLAND

An advance party of the Battalion departed Agra on October 27, 1927, for Bombay, and there embarked on the S.S. Razmak which sailed for Aden before the end of the month. Then, on the last day of October, a Baggage Train and party was followed by two trains comprising the remaining Battalion personnel. They arrived in Bombay in the morning of November 3, embarked, 'in spite of the Embarkation Staff', and sailed for Aden at about 4.00 p.m.. The Battalion arrived there on November 10, and other than those detailed for the UK, of which Frank was one, disembarked. [85]

It was fortunate for Frank, in terms not only of his sporting interests, that he sailed directly on to the UK since Aden was considered to resemble '"Hell with the lid off"... [and] was not a very attractive station.' Or, as mentioned in the Digest of Service in November: Aden:

> 'Has not got a prepossessing appearance, rock, dust and a complete lack of organization. Crater is about 5 miles from Steamer Point and possesses practically no facilities for entertainment'.[86]

Indeed, such was the nature of the place that an entry in the Digest on November 19 reads: 'The Commanding Officer decided that, owing to the lack of suitable ground and the enormous expense necessary, that the Regimental Sports would not be held'.[87] However, by this time Frank, possibly regretting the November weather in the East Atlantic, was somewhere in the Bay of Biscay, and no doubt eagerly anticipating his return to Romiley and his family.

When interviewed by B.J. Evans of London's evening *Star* newspaper on September 26, 1931, Frank succinctly summarised his time in India, and the prospects awaiting him upon his return to England.

'I had a great time out East, playing for the Army in 27 representative games at Soccer, Rugger and hockey. I was also a boxer, and was the uncrowned light heavyweight champion of India. On leaving the Army and coming home, I was torn between three sports! Should I become a professional at Soccer, Rugby or boxing? I could have taken my place in a Rugby League team at centre three-quarter; while Johnny Basham thought I should have made good as a boxer. But I am sure I chose the right game!'[88]

On the threshold of his professional football career, after some 9 years with the SWB, Frank Newton, aged 25, was a confident, loyal and respectful team player. He held a strong belief in both his sporting and musical talents, and after almost five years away in India he wished now to be close to his family and was content to return to his Romiley base.

CHAPTER IV

STOCKPORT COUNTY FC, DECEMBER 1927- MAY 1931

The Newton family, as previously recounted, was well known in Romiley as something of a footballing family, and it was to his Cheshire home that Frank returned. It was not in his nature to 'hang about', and clearly he fancied his chances of establishing a sporting career. No doubt he would have discussed with his brothers, all of whom had excellent local football contacts, as to where he might have the best chance of success.

I have read that Frank went along to a Stockport County practice and that he was invited to join in after he returned the ball from the sidelines with some considerable force.[1] However, the arrangement was more structured, as Frank acknowledged during an interview conducted by B.J. Evans in 1931. 'Norman Rogers [sic: Rodgers], the Blackburn Rovers centre forward, befriended me; taught me a good deal and sent me to Stockport County for a trial'.[2] Rodgers played 156 times, between 1911 and 1919 for Stockport, scoring 72 goals, and Blackburn Rovers between 1919 and 1923, scoring 21 times.[3] The timeline supports this view as Frank arrived home on November 18,[4] and on December 2, 1927 the football correspondent for the *Cheshire Daily Echo* was able to announce that Frank Newton was to make his debut in the Stockport County Reserve side on Saturday December 3, 1927, aged 25.

> 'What the team requires ... is a good centre forward, built on the heavy side ... perhaps the Club has the needed player in Newton the ex-soldier, who took the position at Mossley this afternoon. I hope he fulfils the expectations which his form in training have raised ... and [he] has a good reputation as an all-round athlete'.[5]

Indeed, Frank was to prove himself a fast, robust, forceful type of centre forward, ever willing to use his physical attributes to advantage, as a number of goalkeepers in later years could attest. He could also shoot powerfully with either foot, and exhibited an extraordinary ability to score goals.

The game report of his Stockport County Reserve team debut, against Mossley, noted:

> 'The forward line had more life and vigour, and the changes made an appreciable difference. Newton, the new centre forward, who has recently left the Army with a splendid record for goal scoring – his total is 475 goals in six seasons – made no spectacular debut, but he undoubtedly knows the game well, ... [and] he should make his presence felt in the forward line'.[6]

Frank's recall of his County debut was a little different: 'I played my first match in the County's colours in a Reserve match against Mossley in the Cheshire League. I can well remember it, for I was nearly frozen stiff'.[7]

Nonetheless, Frank certainly made his presence felt as he scored 27 goals for the Reserve side over the remaining 22 games of the Cheshire Senior League season. He signed as a professional with Stockport County on December 11, 1927, just 8 days after his amateur debut. That was also a memorable day as he scored a hat-trick, at Prenton Park, to knock Tranmere Rovers out of the Cheshire Senior Cup.[8]

> 'The County played F. Newton, the ex-Army player, at centre forward. He made his first appearance with the Reserve team at Mossley on December 3. In this match, after an indifferent start, he proved an able forward, quick to take opportunities, and an accurate marksman. In the second half he performed the "hat trick," and each of his three goals was a good effort. The best of the three was the first. Receiving the ball in the goalmouth, he successfully got it past three of the Tranmere defenders, and placed it neatly into goal between the right upright and the goalkeeper, with only a few inches to spare on either side'.[9]

Despite his goal scoring abilities, he was limited to just one first team appearance in the 1927-28 season, a 4-1 defeat to Ashington played on March 31, 1928. That day Frank lined up at inside left.

> 'Ashington achieved their proudest success of the season at Portland Park on Saturday when they beat Stockport

County by 4-1. The County were second in the running for League promotion, but if their chances of overtaking Bradford were vague then they are almost negligible now. Ashington have a peculiar habit of upsetting Second League aspirants and the County were only another addition to a rising list of victims that has steadily accumulated in the past. No one was more surprised than the Stockport team that the play which had succeeded against teams of better repute than Ashington should have failed to find the compensation which had brought them to be regarded as rivals to Bradford'.[10]

His opportunities to lead the line in the 1st XI were limited initially as Joe Smith, formerly of Bolton Wanderers and England, had successfully filled that role in the County's senior side since March 1927.[11]

Joe Smith, Bolton Wanderers, England and Stockport County. Frank's early mentor at County, later team mate, friend and willing participant in Frank's sudden move to Reading where Joe was manager in September 1933.

Now at the end of the 1927-28 season, around the time of Frank's only 1st team appearance, the *Derbyshire Football Express* reported:

> 'Stockport County turned a deaf ear to all overtures made for their players last week, because the officials believe that if they keep their present team together for the next season they will win promotion. There may be a shortage of money at Edgeley Park, but the best way of getting money is to have a winning side, not to sell players and then lose money weekly through diminishing gates'.[12]

True to their beliefs, the County management retained the nucleus of the successful 1927-28 side, and Frank Newton was one of those named on the retained list. Clearly, Frank had impressed the management from the outset. Not only had he been offered professional terms 8 days after his amateur debut at Mossley, but he had demonstrated his goal scoring abilities over the balance of the Reserve side's season. Despite a number of clubs deciding, as was customary, to cut down summer wages to the lowest possible minimum, former L/Cpl Newton was on the cusp of becoming a lower league, scoring celebrity.[13]

1928-29 Season

At the start of the 1928-29 season Frank continued to hone his skills in Stockport's Reserve side. But as the season progressed, the Club's management, recognising Joe Smith was approaching the end of his illustrious career, commenced the search for his successor. On November 10, 1928, the *Derbyshire Football Express* reported that Stockport was:

> 'the scene of the latest football sensation, for when the Hatters turned out a week ago it was found that popular Joe Smith the ex-Boltonian had been left out of the side. The decision was not made until a few minutes before the match, and no explanation has been proffered. It has this week been a big topic in football circles, but the mystery may be solved as being merely a desire to try an experiment with a younger player'.[1]

Joseph Everest was the player concerned, but on the day 'his all round display was barely satisfactory'.[2]

A week later the same newspaper advised that:

> 'The dropping of Joe Smith, ... a fortnight ago, has only been a nine day sensation, for he was back in the leadership when the side visited Southport a week ago. Exactly what was behind his being dropped remains a mystery, for the official explanation that the team selectors wished to see if they had a good understudy is hardly one that holds water'.[3]

Lyme Grove, Romiley where Frank resided at the time of his marriage to Florence Edwards on October 28,1928

Against this background of pending change, Frank surrendered his bachelorhood when he married, on October 31, 1928, a local lass, Florence Edwards, the youngest daughter of Mrs H. Edwards of Romiley. The bride was given away by her brother-in-law, Mr R. Ratcliffe, and Miss Nellie Wilde was her bridesmaid. The service was conducted by Rev. W.E. Parry, Rector of St. Chad's, Romiley. Mr Arthur Sumner was the best man, and Fred Newton, Frank's youngest brother, was the groom's man. The reception was held at the bride's home, and the Stockport club released Frank for a short honeymoon which the happy couple spent at New Brighton.[4] In addition, the club gave Frank a clock, 'Presented to Frank Newton by the Players and Staff of the Stockport County FC Ltd on the occasion of his wedding, October 31, 1928'.

Frank and Stockport County colleagues gathered around an HMV gramophone believed to have been an additional wedding present to the happy couple, in recognition of Frank's musical talents.
From front, l to r: Jack Jobson, Walter Cook, Fred Westgarth (trainer), Alf Townsend (behind Frank Newton), Frank Newton, Ben Boardman, Harry Burgess, Billy Tompkinson, Ernie Helliwell, Billy Bocking and Billy Newton.

Meanwhile the club's selectors maintained their interest in finding a replacement for Joe Smith, and Frank continued to learn his trade in the Reserve side, awaiting his opportunity. By the end of November, 1928 he had scored 9 goals in Cheshire Central League matches, and as "Observer" pointed out in the *Cheshire Daily Echo*, the Central League provided an excellent opportunity for the 'up and coming' player.

'The Central League is certainly the finest training ground the players could have for fitting them for the first team, and I am convinced that the standard of football in that League is quite equal to anything in the

Northern Section. In the Central League the majority of the teams are composed of players with 1st League experience and so if there is not the rush and bustle of Northern Section football, there is a good standard of play and the players we meet do try to play class football'.[5]

At the end of November reports of a rift between Stockport County's directors and the Supporters' Club appeared in the local media. The details are not important here, but warranted comment from "Busy Bee" as the directors withdrew the use of all facilities on the ground from the Supporters Club, and 'forbade that organisation using the name of Stockport County.' As he noted the details were fully reported in the *Cheshire Daily Echo* of November 30, he continued:

> 'Those who wish for the success of the club are defeating their own object if they adopt a hostile attitude to the Directors, for that is the surest way of damping down public enthusiasm. The County needs all the help it can get during the next few months. At the present moment the club looks like turning the corner. Our chances are bright both in the League and the FA Cup, and there never was a time when the club had such an excellent band of reserves at their disposal. The first team is better than it has been for several seasons'.[6]

Inevitably, Frank's big break, perhaps delayed by the honeymoon, finally arrived on December 1, 1928. With Joe Smith unavailable through injury, Frank was summoned to make his first team home debut almost exactly a month after his 26th birthday. It was a total success. South Shields, the 'Seasiders',[7] or 'Plate Enders', were crushed 7-1, and two of the goals, the third and seventh, were scored by the debutant. The County's forwards were in deadly form and scored 4 times in the space of 12 minutes to lead 4-1 at half time.

The reporter in South Shields' *Football Gazette* did not consider Stockport to be 'worth a margin of six goals.' However, he did acknowledge that:

> 'the Stockport forwards were at the top of their form and snapped up practically all the scoring chances that came their way. The County have an exceptionally strong side, and it so happened that South Shields met them when they were on their best behaviour'.[8]

On match day, because of print deadlines, it was standard practice for the *Football Gazette* to cover only the first half of the game in question, and on this occasion Frank featured.

> 'The Stockport forwards were playing dashing football and from another strong attack Newham [sic] headed in from short range and Shevlin just managed to save. FIELDING rushed up and scored the County's fourth goal. Newton was going through when he was fouled, and the deferee [sic] awarded a free kick just outside the penalty area. The kick was taken by Newton, who sent in a delightful shot which Shevlin tipped over the bar very smartly. F. Newton made several attempts to break through the Shields defence, and the visiting backs found him difficult to hold'.

Nonetheless, Frank's strong showing was qualified somewhat as Davies, the 'Seasiders' centre half, was described as 'a great plodder'.[9]

The correspondent in the *Stockport Express* was succinct when he commented upon Frank's display:

> 'The play of Newton [F.] was most commendable. He is a finely built youth, who never spares himself, and he has a good idea of the duties of centre-forward, whilst his shooting was generally on the mark'.[10]

However, 'Busy Bee', columnist for the *Cheshire Daily Echo*, was considerably more forthcoming and elaborated on Frank's performance.

> 'Newton in his first appearance as a centre-forward for the first team, fully justified the confidence reposed in him. When I commented on his play against Derby County I pointed out that all he needed to become a really brilliant centre-forward was better positional play. He showed in the second half against South Shields that he needed little tuition on that score. Given the ball and only one man to beat, Newton is a masterful player, and his final shots are terrific. If he has not the craft of Joe Smith he has the extra yard in speed which Smith has lost, and the question as to whether he shall retain his place in the side will have to be seriously considered, although it cannot be denied that Smith has been a factor in the team's success in the past. With two inside forwards to play to him like Burgess and Boardman and wingmen

> who can put across such good centres as Tompkinson and Fielding do, Newton had a chance of showing what he can do, and he made full use of it'.[11]

'Busy Bee's' comments above relating to Frank's performance against Derby County in a Reserve team match played at the Baseball Ground on November 27, were well intended. In comparing the two opposing centre forwards he commented:

> 'Ruddy lacked the forcefulness of Newton, but he did not attempt as much and there lay his effectiveness. The Stockport pivot played a fine game in many respects, but if he attempted less and let the opposing centre half run after him he would find his task much easier. Newton made several attempts to score which would have beaten a less skilful goalkeeper. He is a player with many fine points and this little friendly advice is offered so that he will be able to do himself justice. His only fault is over-anxiety for the success of his side, but if he will wait for the ball coming his way and try to have only one man to beat he will come up to the high expectations which many of us have of him'.[12]

The Saturday following Frank's home debut, December 8, Smith was again unavailable, and Frank retained his place. On this occasion, a third round FA Cup encounter against Southport, the County had little difficulty in winning 3-0. Frank duly delivered a brace. "Busy Bee" described his first goal and commented further upon Frank's improvement.

'It was not until a minute from the interval that F. Newton set our fears at rest by scoring a magnificent goal. He received a pass from Tompkinson and beating Martin swerved to the right to avoid Worrall. The back, however, managed to upset him in the penalty area, but also fell to the ground. Newton was the first up and putting his foot to the ball without hesitation he found the left hand corner of the net well out of reach of Halsall, who was unsighted. It was as fine a goal as one could wish to see. F. Newton again justified his selection. A pleasing feature of his display was the way he is cultivating the art of putting the ball out to the wings. His positional play is improving, and he certainly played no small part in the County's victory'.[13]

The view in the *Stockport Express* was also supportive.

'The County again demonstrated their all-round ability, and considering the insecure foothold some of their work was exceedingly creditable. ... Frank Newton again showed ability as leader of the attack. He may be lacking in the finer points of the game, and hardly welds the line as a more experienced player would do, but there is no denying his value as a marksman, and the manner in which he scored the opening goal was a tribute to his opportunism'.[14]

Frank's recall of the game was a little different. In a newspaper article that appeared under his name after he had joined Fulham, he wrote:

> 'There are twenty-two players who will say that the last time Stockport met Southport in the Cup was their worst game. They had every excuse. The weather conditions were awful. The ground was covered in snow and was harder than concrete. It was my first experience of a cup-tie. I don't know how I would have faced the ordeal under ordinary conditions. As it was, the frost-bound ground was of great help to me! I scored two goals and, in each case, I doubt if I would have scored in the ordinary way. My second goal, for instance, was scored when the goalkeeper, two backs and the centre-half opposing me were all on the ground'.[15]

The County took on Doncaster Rovers on December 15, and before a crowd of some 8,000 inside Edgeley Park, beat them decisively 4-1. The game was reported in glowing terms in the *Stockport Advertiser*, and the victory was considered well deserved.[16] The following day, in his *Cheshire Daily Echo* review of the week, "Busy Bee" waxed almost lyrical about Frank:

> 'Frank Newton again appeared with success at centre forward. He is one of the finest discoveries the County have made for several seasons, and it is remarkable what a great improvement has been shown in his form since he came on the first team. Of course, I put some of it down to the co-operation of his colleagues. In the first team he has not got to do so much foraging for the ball. He can wait until he gets his opening, and then we find out what he can do. His goals in the last three matches - and he obtained two each week - have been amongst the finest

> efforts I have seen on a football field. Today [December 22, 1928]we will have a chance of seeing how he fares on foreign soil with the first team. He will be well backed up, and if he gets his customary two goals I think we [Stockport] will win'.[17]

The correspondent for the *Stockport Express* agreed that Frank benefited from good support.

> 'Frank Newton maintained the promise of his previous appearances and his consistency as a marksman looks like assuring his place in the team. He was always ready for a run through and his shooting was generally well directed. His colleagues in the line rendered admirable support, the Fielding-Burgess wing again showing to advantage'.[18]

The game at Barrow on December 22, 1928 marked the beginning of the heavy Christmas programme when 3 games were played in the space of just 5 days. The County won the encounter 4-2, and Frank scored a goal in each half, the second resulting from an 'excellent shot'.[19] On Christmas Day the County entertained Rotherham United. The weather was fine, and it was considered worthy of note that, given the time of year, 'the ground [was] in excellent condition.' Nonetheless, Stockport failed to reproduce their sparkling form of previous weeks. The result was a hard earned County triumph, the winning goal being scored half way through the second half. Frank's contribution was limited to forcing Best, in the Rotherham goal, to make 'a wonderful save ... from close range', but in taking the shot Frank twisted his knee and was off the field for some five minutes.[20]

The return encounter on Boxing Day resulted in a 3-3 draw, a game "Busy Bee" thought the County should have won.

> 'These holiday games are always a big strain on the players and seldom produce the highest class of football. This game however, was much more interesting than the one at Edgeley Park on Christmas Day and produced a thrilling struggle for mastery'.

The first goal was scored by Frank, yet again from an 'excellent shot', after 25 minutes, and the County went on to lead 2-0 at the interval. However, just before half time Frank was the recipient of an errant boot. He was felled and had to be assisted off the field. Nonetheless, he resumed at the start of the second half and continued to lead the line. But the County's performance fell away over the next 25 minutes and three goals were conceded. It became increasingly clear that Frank was struggling, so after Stockport surrendered the third goal, he was moved to outside right. Burgess then led the reshaped forward line, and fortunately for Stockport he scored the equaliser ten minutes before time.[21] "Busy Bee" considered 'the injury to Frank Newton proved a big handicap to the County, and it was unfortunate' that he was not moved to the wing earlier. The injury itself, a 'badly swollen left foot', was reasonably serious as Frank did not return to first team duties until January 12, 1929, against Bradford City in a second round FA Cup match. On that day Stockport lost 2-0 at Valley Parade before a crowd of approximately 30,000. 'It was a fierce struggle for mastery' in which Bradford's superiority in the mid field proved decisive. But the Cup battle, between the two top teams in the Northern Division, was a good day out, and enjoyed by many.

> 'Exciting scenes were seen at Bradford station just before the departure of the return trains to Stockport, where several thousand County supporters assembled, cheered the County players, sang lustily, and behaved as if the County had won, not lost. One thing they brought back with them was the Bradford war song, "Hello, Hello!"'.[22]

League duties resumed the following Saturday, January 19, when the County took on Halifax Town at home. Conditions under foot were atrocious, and were described, before the game finished, as '... like a section of No Man's Land after shell fire.' It was felt that to 'play for ninety minutes on such a ground was a great feat of physical endurance in itself, and it was indeed marvellous how, [sic] both teams kept pegging away resolutely to the very end.'

For his part, Frank added another brace in the first half, in what was a comfortable 3-0 victory.[23] As a result Stockport retained their one point lead, over Bradford City, at the head of the Northern Division. After 25 games Stockport had 35 points, Bradford City 34 and Wrexham 32.[24]

There followed on Tuesday, January 22 a surprising and most disappointing 4-1 loss to Nelson. The *Nelson Leader* proclaimed that the home side:

> 'thoroughly deserved the victory – the best of the season – and there has not been more enthusiasm since the

season opened. It was a pity that there were not crowds to see the performance. The gate was a poor one, fog and frost keeping many away. The ground was as hard as iron and the ball did curious twists and turns, when it fell. Stockport did not master the conditions as Nelson did, for the home team played splendidly, and with an abandon bordering on dangerous'.[25]

The Stockport press coverage was damning.

'The performance was so unsatisfactory from a promotion point of view that one would prefer to talk about anything but the actual game, and in this case it happens that both going to the match and coming back to Stockport afterwards there was much by which to remember the visit. However, "the play's the thing," and football, or the lack of it, must come first. It was a match which the County ought to have won easily. Nelson had four or five reserve players, and one of these practically a novice, was responsible for two of their goals'.

The County led 1-0 at the break, but it all went downhill thereafter. 'The County backs had one of their worst days of the season', and on a 'frost-bound ground', the surface of which 'was like a sheet of ice', Stockport conceded four goals.[26]

Unfortunately, Frank was injured again during this encounter and did not play again until February 29, 1929, when the County visited Carlisle.[27] However, in the intervening period, with Frank '*hors de combat*', the County secured an important 2-1 win over Bradford City at Edgeley Park. Such was the intense interest in this game that for the first time in the Stockport club's history '... the notice "Ground Full"... had to be posted'. It was estimated that over six thousand people travelled from Bradford and swelled the attendance at the game to 25,000.[28] Afterwards Stockport enjoyed a 5 point margin over Bradford, still their closest rivals in the Division. It was very probably the comfort of this advantage and Frank's unavailability that prompted the management to again experiment with Everest at centre forward.

> 'Stockport County are confounding their supporters by strange experiments in their centre-forward birth [sic], for recently they rang the changes between Joe Smith and Frank Newton, and a week ago they added to the mystery by playing John [sic] Everest in the leadership at Accrington ... He is hardly ripe enough for this company'.[29]

Once fit again, Frank accompanied the team North to Carlisle. At the time Carlisle United enjoyed an exceptional home record for the team had not lost on their own ground, Brunton Park, in three seasons. But on February 23, 1929 the County side rolled in and reduced the local fortress to rubble. "Busy Bee" reported gleefully:

> 'Stockport County showed remarkable form in their match at Brunton Park with Carlisle United and their 5-0 victory ranks amongst the finest performances in the history of the club. This was Carlisle's first defeat on their own ground for three seasons ... According to

some of the United's leading supporters the County had given one of the finest exhibitions of football ever seen at Carlisle'.

Frank scored yet another brace which prompted the following comment:

> 'F. Newton scored a capital goal after a characteristic solo effort, screwing the ball in from the left at a difficult angle well out of reach of Prout ... Frank Newton, who returned to the attack, owing to the injury to Joe Smith, after five week's absence, gave one of his best displays. His positional play was better than it has been, and he was always a menace to the Carlisle defence'.[30]

The report in the *Cumberland Evening News* was generous in its assessment. Headed 'Sparkling Stockport: Leaders' Polish too much for Carlisle', their local correspondent considered that any team capable of playing such champagne football was worthy of promotion.[31]

In turn, the account in the *Stockport Express* almost went overboard in recounting the afternoon's events.

> 'This will rank as one of the finest achievements ever attained in the annals of the club. On arrival at the ground a telegram awaited the County captain from Councillor E. Barlow, Chairman of Directors, wishing all the "boys" good luck. It must have acted as a tonic. They played as a team inspired, and during a very long association with the club the writer cannot recall a finer

display than that served up in the opening "45". The machine-like precision underlying the repeated advances on the Carlisle stronghold was little short of perfection, and evoked the repeated appreciation of the crowd, who were most impartial in their favours. What a pity the Edgeley Park devotees were denied the pleasure of witnessing such a display, which puts into the shade anything given at home this season. The general opinion after the match was that the winners were booked for the Second Division, and on Saturday's form it seems a pretty safe assumption ... Burgess was always noticeable for crafty footwork, his return to his best form being a welcome feature. Boardman also showed clever initiative, with such capable henchmen Newton was given every opportunity to make ground, and the Romiley youth responded with a most virile display, his speedy dashes up the middle repeatedly harassing the defence. The wingmen also rendered good service'.[32]

The reaction of the promotion-chasing Bradford City fans to Stockport's demolition job was commented upon in the *Derbyshire Football Express.*

'More than fifty per cent of the Valley Parade crowd stayed on the ground a week ago after the game was over. They were waiting for the result of Carlisle – Stockport game, and when the news came through that the County had won by 5 goals to nil it hardly describes the scene when it is said that the crowd was amazed. It was, indeed, thunderstruck. City had expected that the Carlisle hurdle would have proved too difficult for the County to have overcome'.[33]

A more nuanced view was provided in the *Athletic News*:

> 'Stockport County have possibly never played more brilliant football than they did at Carlisle. They reached a remarkably high standard, and the 11,000 spectators who saw them administer to Carlisle United a crushing home defeat could not fail to recognise that here was a team certainly worthy of higher League status. It was their great form and not Carlisle's poorness which gave them their triumph'.[34]

By early March 1929, Frank had scored 11 goals in the 8 first team games in which he had played. A very creditable performance, but the County were in a tough promotion battle along with Bradford City and Wrexham. Given that only the Northern Section Champions would be promoted to the Second Division, the Stockport management, despite indicating otherwise, were anxious for yet more goals.

> 'Stockport County officials pretend to be undismayed by the heavy scoring which Bradford City indulged in last week, and declare themselves as pinning their faith to the motto, "Steady does it." Nonetheless, it is a well known fact that the Hatters have rung the changes with Smith, Frank Newton and Everest at centre forward, and that these changes were made because goals were not scored frequently enough. This week it was whispered that the Hatters are angling for a new leader'.[35]

As March came in, Stockport were top of the Northern Section with 43 points from 30 games, second were Bradford City, 39 points after 29 games, and third were Wrexham also with 39 points, but from 30 games. In some ways the concerns of the Stockport management are understandable, but goals scored would not appear to have been a major concern. The respective for and against goal figures for the three clubs at that time were: Stockport: 88 – 43; Bradford: 81 – 39 and Wrexham: 70 – 48. Clearly, Wrexham had more reason for concern.[36]

After their truly impressive performance at Carlisle, the County faced a difficult encounter on the Racecourse Ground, home of their promotion rivals Wrexham. Locally, games between promotion chasing rivals were not only stern tests, but often significant social events.

> 'The visit of the leaders aroused unusual interest in the town and the district, so much so that all junior football was "held up" in order that the big match on the racecourse enclosure could be witnessed. The result was an attendance of 16,800 --- a record for the ground, exceeding the gate at the recent international by a few hundreds. The County's great triumph at Carlisle, coupled with ideal weather conditions, induced a large following, and there were animated scenes at Tiviot Dale Station, from whence two closely packed excursion trains were dispatched shortly after noon. The band which usually discourses at Edgeley Park also made the journey, and enlivened the waiting period on the ground with a selection of popular airs, in which the Welsh and English

> national anthems were given lusty vocal support. There had been snow at Wrexham earlier in the week, which had been cleared from the playing area, but the effects of the sun made the "going" very treacherous, and accounted for numerous slips during the game. Most of the big-wigs in the Principality were present, including genial "Ted" Robbins, secretary of the Welsh F. A., without whom no football function in Wales would be complete. Fred Jones, of Oswestry, who assisted the County at centre-forward a few seasons ago, also turned up to renew acquaintance with former colleagues'.[37]

Despite the build up it was not to be the County's day and they went down 2-1, and Frank, who it was felt under performed, failed to score.[38]

"Busy Bee" commented that the pitch was in poor shape as the surface had thawed, but 'underneath the ice was still in the turf, and this made it difficult for the players to keep a foothold. Under these circumstances the County' should not be blamed for failing to reproduce their display at Carlisle. He also observed that Wrexham's pivot, Bellis, 'successfully held F. Newton, who did not play as well as usual'.[39]

The account in the *Liverpool Echo* summarised matters:

> 'For three-quarters of the game at the Racecourse, Wrexham were on top of their rival promotionalists [sic], Stockport, but when the Welsh team began to play as though they were six up and only a few minutes to go they asked for trouble – and got it! The spice of a game which attracted a record crowd for a league match was in

the last quarter of an hour, when after being two goals down, Stockport were given the opportunity of making a fight of it'.[40]

However, it was all to no avail, but despite this loss, Stockport remained at the top of the table with 43 points from 31 games. The club was now two points ahead of Wrexham, and three of Bradford City, although the latter still had a game in hand.[41]

A further development arising from this defeat was Frank's relegation, almost certainly much to his surprise and annoyance, to the County's Reserve side for a game on the following Monday, March 4, against Birmingham City's counterparts. However, having been out injured for five weeks, the management very probably felt that Frank lacked match practice and peak fitness. Unfortunately, from Frank's point of view, he failed to sparkle against Birmingham; in fact he was considered to be 'off form'.[42] Consequently he was excluded from the first team to play New Brighton, at Edgeley Park, the following week. Instead he travelled to Goodison Park where the County Reserves lost 2-1 to Everton's Reserve side. Possibly Frank's only consolation on that day was the goal he scored a minute from full time.[43]

Frank was less than impressed with his demotion and he took decisive, possibly impulsive, action. As a result, a minor sensation was reported in the local press on March 16 advising that F. Newton, at his own request, had been placed on the transfer list.

'I am writing these notes on Friday, and I am therefore not in a position to say much in regard to the question of Frank Newton being placed on the transfer list at his

> own request. In the first place I did not make use of the information that Newton was on the transfer list because these matters are private and confidential. The intimation from one club to another that they are willing to part with a certain player is sent on a form, printed in red ink, which is marked private and confidential. Whoever gave the information to the Press was guilty of a betrayal of confidence. It often happens that a player is put on the transfer list and then the matter is amicably settled and the transfer does not take place. We shall all be sorry if Frank Newton goes, because he has made himself a general favourite with the County's supporters'.[44]

Having come to professional football comparatively late in life, Frank understandably was a man in a hurry, and eager for success. He had confidence in his abilities, a depth of sporting experience, a strong sense of loyalty, a high expectation of how he should be treated, and possibly at times an impulsive nature which he later amply demonstrated. Fortunately the County's management did not progress the matter, but they took the message on board. Frank was promptly reinstated and led the line the following week against Rochdale. Nonetheless, the management did not want to give the impression that they had capitulated too easily, and final team selection was left 'until just before the match, when it was decided to play Frank Newton at centre forward in place of Joe Smith'.[45]

The County beat Rochdale 3-0, and the team's performance was one of the best of the season, '… if not quite equal to that at Carlisle, it is certainly worthy of being ranked alongside the victory at Lincoln.' Frank marked his return by scoring twice.

The first was memorable as it resulted from 'a remarkable shot from 30 yards range, the ball striking the back of the net and rebounding into play. It was a magnificent shot …'[46]

"A. W." in the *Stockport Express* reported that the 'introduction of Newton speeded up the County front-line, and his goals were well taken, both shots being of the unstoppable order'.[47] Or, as the *Staffordshire Sentinal* described it, the game at Rochdale's ground was played 'in ideal weather, before 12,000 spectators. Play was fast and very keen from the start and after 15 minutes F. Newton scored for the visitors from 30 yards'.[48]

Frank had now scored 13 goals in the 10 games he had played in the County's first team. Following his recall against Rochdale, Frank was selected for every remaining league match, 9 in total, but disappointingly for him he only scored three further goals.[49] Something of a late season dip in form.

Shortly after the game at Rochdale "Busy Bee" provided an interesting assessment of the contrasting playing styles of Joe Smith and Frank.

> 'Frank Newton and Smith present a good contrast in styles of play. I have heard it said that the other forwards do not play to Newton as well as they play to Smith. The reason for this is due to the different styles of play of the two players. Joe Smith goes foraging for the ball himself and the result is he appears to combine better with the other forwards than does Newton, who plays the game he has been told to play, namely, to harass the opposing backs. A centre forward cannot shine in midfield play and at the same time be close to the backs. The modern

game is for the centre forward to be well up, waiting for a chance to dash through. It is a game which Newton is specially qualified to play, both by physique and speed. It is a method for which Joe Smith is not suited. His abilities lie in other directions. Joe by temperament and training is still an inside left, a glutton for work and always eager to be on the ball. Whether they "give it to Joe" or not, he could not help himself but be in the thick of the "hurly-burly." Personally, I can admire both styles of play. As I said once before, if we could combine the abilities of Joe Smith and Frank Newton we should have a centre forward good enough to take Dixie Dean's place on the England side. There is no truth in any suggestion that the other players do not do as much for Newton as they would for any other player. Playing well on the backs Newton cannot have the ball as often as Joe Smith, for the latter goes hunting for it if it does not come his way, whereas Newton has had it impressed upon him that he must play as close to the backs as he can without being given offside, and that he must harass the opposing defence as much as possible. One way he can do this is by taking up position especially when one of his inside forwards has the ball. If, for instance, the inside left has the ball, Newton, by veering to the right causes the opposing defence to follow him and thus gives the man with the ball more room in which to work. Without actually touching a ball it can be realised that by positional play a centre forward can play havoc by the mere fact that the other side is worried lest he get the ball. A good axiom for a centre forward is "Make the other side run after you."'[50]

By March 22 the promotion battle was developing into a desperate affair between Stockport County, Bradford City and Wrexham. The County were still top with 47 points, Bradford were one point behind and Wrexham two. All had played 33 games.[51] However, results went against Wrexham on March 23, after which the side slipped out of contention being 4 points behind Stockport. In addition Bradford City now had the better goal average. Stockport were 96 for and 48 against, whereas Bradford comparatively were 110 and 40.[52]

The County did enough to maintain their position when they narrowly beat Southport at home, 2-1. Frank did not score in the game but was interviewed shortly afterwards. The report read in part:

> '"A hard fight on Saturday against Southport, Frank?" "Yes, it was a good fight, and we deserved to win," replied Frank Newton, Stockport County's centre-forward. "You didn't find the net, eh?" "No, but where is the man who can score every week?" He laughed. "It was the great goalkeeping of Jones in the Southport goal that prevented me getting more goals. He played a really splendid game and deserves great credit."'

Frank went on to say:

> 'it is a great joy for me to know that I can get a game in the first team, when there is such a great player as Joe Smith for the position. I may add that if a fellow cannot succeed with such expert guidance as I get from Trainer

Westguard, Joe Smith, Hudspeth, and Curry then he must be a dud'.

He was then asked for his view of the tense promotion battle between Stockport and Bradford City.

'"And what of Stockport's chances of promotion, Frank?" "Great; we've a good chance, and a good point in hand. Bradford City did themselves a good turn on Saturday by beating Wrexham, whose chances as challengers have diminished somewhat. All I can say is that it's going to be a ding-dong struggle, with no quarter given. Still, I fancy we will pull through in the end."'

The unidentified interviewer then provided reassurance around Frank's recent transfer request.

'Newton with ordinary luck should make a name for himself. He did not cost Stockport County anything, and his recent request that he should be placed on the transfer list has been withdrawn. Frank Newton is perfectly happy at Edgeley Park, and he has high ambitions of playing in Second Division football next season. He turns the scales at 12st. 7lb. and is 5ft. 9 1/2 in'.[53]

With the crowded Easter schedule upcoming, certain of the cognoscenti maintained a degree of scepticism:

'Stockport County keep bagging the points, even if the manner of their doing so is not nearly so convincing as that of their new sole rivals, Bradford City. The Edgeley Park management has spent more money on new men this season than it can reasonably afford, and if the club misses the prize one wonders what will happen. There will have to be sales of some sort. The Hatters are up against a big struggle, and on paper look as though they may be pipped at the post'.[54]

At the beginning of April, Wrexham were effectively out of contention as the side was then 5 points behind Stockport. Both teams had played 37 games, but Bradford City headed the Division on goal average, with 48 points, and had a game in hand over the County. At the onset of the Easter programme the teams remained locked in a fierce promotion battle. The *Stockport Express* reported:

> 'with Bradford City piling up goals in phenomenal style it behoves the County to get a move on in the same direction if they are to seriously contest the issue with the "Tykes." On Saturday [March 23] after making due allowances for the brilliance of Jones in the visitors' goal, many opportunities were neglected of improving the goal average, and much of the sparkle associated with the front-line in earlier engagements has been lacking recently'.[55]

In addition, the scheduling of matches was unfortunate as Stockport had to play 3 games, of which two were away from Edgeley Park, in just 4 days. On the other hand, Bradford City played just twice, on March 30 and April 2.

The County hosted Crewe Alexandra on Good Friday, a side they had lost 2-0 to at Gresty Road in early September. Surprisingly, this return fixture was played in June like weather, '... more suitable for cricket', and although the low sun made it difficult at times for the players, it had 'a beneficial effect on the coffers of the club, the "gate" reaching to about 14,000, including a large contingent from the railway centre'.[56]

The result, a 2-2 draw, from the County's standpoint was a disaster. It was a game the home side should have won and the point dropped cost them dearly. After 12 minutes Frank was fouled inside the penalty area. Hudspeth, Stockport's left back stepped up, placed the ball and shot, unfortunately, directly at Davies in the Crewe goal. His colleagues congratulated Davies heartedly for his prowess, but so enthusiastic were they that the goalkeeper suffered a slight injury, '... necessitating attention so he could resume.' Despite this Stockport persisted and Burgess, County's inside right, opened their account. But '... hardly had the cheers died away before the Railwaymen equalised.' Nonetheless, the County went ahead a second time, shortly before the interval, when Frank set up Burgess for his second goal.

The second half was noteworthy as Crewe scored again after 20 minutes, but then Davies unaccountably pulled the County's right winger, Tompkinson, down in the goalmouth. A stone cold penalty. This time Burgess was entrusted with the spot kick, probably to allow him to complete his hat-trick. But much to the dismay of the faithful, he shot well wide.[57] The local press did not have to spell it out; missing two penalties was inexcusable, and the dropping of a crucial point at home, particularly in a tight promotion battle, was for many unforgivable.

Consequently the upcoming game at Darlington now became a 'must win' encounter, again played in seasonably unusual weather. 'Considering the extremely hot weather the match ... was fought at a great pace [with] the fresh green turf on the adjoining cricket ground affording a striking contrast to the more sombre aspect of the football pitch'.[58] Although the County dominated at the outset they fell behind when Hudspeth conceded a penalty after just 11 minutes. However, Stockport levelled when Burgess buried a cross from Tomkinson on the half hour. But the "Quakers" were not to be denied and went ahead again shortly before half time, although 'hardly a correct reflex of the play'.[59]

Stockport continued to press after the interval, but had to wait some 20 minutes before Frank equalised with

> 'a remarkable shot, arresting the ball almost on the goal-line and screwing it just inside the near post ... incidently this marked the County's century of goals, which was duly acknowledge by the "quid-nuncs"'.[60]

The County were now under immense pressure to take both points and after 70 minutes it was Burgess who slotted the much needed winner. Darlington failed to respond as it became increasingly apparent that the extraordinary heat had taken a toll on all the participants, 'the homesters especially'.[61]

The *Stockport Advertiser* reported that additional interest was provided to this encounter:

> 'by reason of the fact that the game was controlled by a

Mr A. Josephs, of South Shields, who has been appointed referee for the FA Cup Final at Wembley. Mr Josephs after the match confessed that he did not expect the Cup Final would be any harder to control than the game at Darlington had been. As a matter of fact he had during the game two lapses which are perhaps unusual in his experience. The first came after eleven minutes when Hudspeth deliberately handled the ball in the penalty area.

Darlington made a strong and persistent claim for a penalty, which Mr Josephs did not allow until after he had consulted the linesman. In this case the offence occurred while he was unsighted. The incident which led to Darlington's second goal could not be excused for Eden was clearly offside when he got away with the ball. Here again the referee was in a bad position to judge and it is evident the linesman did not give him the right cue'.[62]

The *Athletic News* considered both teams were over anxious, and from Stockport's standpoint this significantly detracted from their performance.

'Desperately in need of points, one side to win promotion and the other to avoid relegation, Darlington and Stockport County gave Mr Arnold Jacobs, the Cup Final referee, a rather worrying time at Feathams. They allowed their anxiety to override their discretion, particularly Stockport, and the result was that several players were spoken to in the first half, and after an incident in the second half some Stockport names were taken. If the County had shown their customary steadiness they would have won by a bigger margin'.[63]

Stockport had temporarily maintained their promotion challenge, as had Bradford City by winning 3-0 at home against New Brighton. The County's game at Wigan on Easter Monday was therefore of critical importance since Bradford were not scheduled to play Hartlepools United until the following afternoon.

Unfortunately for Stockport the weather broke most foul and by game time, particularly for those inside Springfield Park, it was appalling. "A. W." writing in the *Stockport Express* commented:

'A regular hurricane prevailed and made accurate football impossible, but the homesters profiting by an early goal against the breeze, never relaxed their hold, and using the elements to the best advantage had the distinction of inflicting on the County their heaviest reverse of the season [4-0], a feat that was keenly relished by a holiday crowd of some 15,000'.[64]

The *Stockport Advertiser* reported on this distressing result.

'Stockport County's chances of gaining promotion were considerably diminished on Easter Monday ... The strong wind which blew down the ground was all against good football, and the game was completely spoiled. The conditions may be judged from the fact that in the first half Crowther did not have a goal kick, and in the second half

Preedy, the Wigan goalkeeper, did not have one. The County had the wind in the first half, but did not make the use of this advantage that they ought to have done. Wigan scored a lucky goal after five minutes. Crowther fumbling with the ball and letting it slip through his hands into the goal ... With this lead Wigan were content to play on the defensive for the rest of the first half. They conceded corners galore, and placed into touch on every possible occasion. In the second half, ... the County could not afford to play a purely defensive game. The players fought like Trojans in the teeth of the gale to get the ball down, but they never managed to get it beyond the Wigan penalty line'.[65]

On the following afternoon, April 2, Bradford City did not falter and thumped Hartlepools United 4-1. By that evening therefore, both Bradford and Stockport had 52 points, but Bradford had a game in hand and a superior goal average having scored 115 and conceded 41. Stockport's totals were 101 and 58. However, there remained plenty to play for as Bradford drew their next match with Rochdale while the County beat Nelson 3-0 to return to the top of the table.

The headline in the *Stockport Advertiser* on April 12 read:

'COUNTY'S PROMOTION HOPES REVIVED.'

'Although Nelson put up a stern fight at Edgeley Park they were no match for the County and were beaten by three goals to nil. The fall in popular enthusiasm following the defeat at Wigan, was reflected in the attendance

> which was between seven and eight thousand, but the discouraging sign had no effect on the players, who gave a sparkling display and thoroughly deserved their victory ... The result ... places the County at the head of the League table again, and they have a good chance of promotion if they win their remaining four matches for Bradford City are by no means certain of getting full points from their visits to Southport, Nelson and Rochdale'.

Tompkinson scored early for the County and Frank added a second 10 minutes after the interval, before proceeding to net the third. His first was set up by Boardman and the second followed 'a clever elusive run by Burgess'.[66]

A vital visit to Horsley Hill followed on April 13, 1929 where the County achieved their fifth double of the season, winning a close contest 1-0. The South Shields club, recently relegated from Division II, was experiencing difficult times, and like many clubs in the Northern Section were:

> 'suffering from [a] lack of support from the sporting public. The attendance at this match did not exceed 6,000, and this is a much larger "gate" than they have been receiving in recent matches despite the fact that they had previously only lost two matches at home'.

The County directors and management must have been much relieved with the result as so '... precious were the points to Stockport that the players have been undergoing a course of special training at Roker Park during the week.' In itself, unquestionably a significant investment.

In fact, the 'Seasiders' might well have considered themselves unfortunate to have conceded the only goal of the game after 18 minutes, although it was recognised that the County 'played with excellent understanding and their teamwork was very effective'.[67]

> 'The winning goal was the reward of F. Newton's opportunism. W. Newton had dropped the ball in and his namesake attempted to head it, but it went to Dunn, who kicked it against Newton's back. The centre forward turned rapidly round and shot the ball into the net, well out of the reach of Shevlin'.[68]

A similarly close result was recorded against Ashington, on their Portland Park ground, the following Saturday. This was a rearranged fixture previously scheduled for December 8, but postponed owing to the FA Cup fixture with Southport. The significance of this result was well recognised.

> 'The County, who had had a day's rest at Whitley Bay, in view of the importance of the game, motored over, to Ashington just after noon, and had a pleasant journey through rural Northumberland with its mining villages dotted here and there. Ashington is a place with a population of 35,000 who depend almost entirely on the mining industry. A large proportion of the residents have suffered acutely during the past three years owing to the slump in the coal trade, and as a result the support accorded to the football club has dwindled down and down, until now an attendance of one

thousand is considered a large gate. On Saturday the "gate" numbered 1,350, which is remarkably small in view of the importance of the match. The "Colliers" are now in the position of having to apply for re-admission to the Northern Section, and in view of their poor financial backing, and the keen competition which is promised from new applicants to the League, their chances of re-election are not very bright'.[69]

Despite this bleak prospect, and as a result of losing the game Ashington was bottom of the Northern Section, behind Hartlepools United. Nonetheless, Ashington:

'on anything but their best form, proved a proposition that was almost too much for Stockport County. Hard, rugged miners who spend the best part of the week underground ... whose [the Ashington club's] weekly wages bill does not exceed sixty pounds. The County is a team of professionals and their wages account is a little short of two hundred pounds a week, and yet they were by no means the goal superior'.[70]

The promotion battle raged on, and in their penultimate fixture against Doncaster Rovers the County secured a vital 2-0 victory, placing the club once more at the head of the Section.

'With one match to play and enjoying the narrow lead of a single point against Bradford City's two games yet to play Stockport County are bang in the Third Northern limelight. On Saturday, at Doncaster, they proved themselves the better side. They played like promotion candidates, and even if the game as a spectacle did not reach expectations there was sufficiently good aggressive football shown – at least by the visitors – to keep the crowd of over 9,000 on tip-toe throughout the 90 minutes'.[71]

Sadly from the County's standpoint, despite beating Barrow 3-0 in their final game, it was not enough. Bradford won their remaining matches and thus took the Division title by a single point. It was a close run matter, and the County certainly gave it their best shot, winning their four remaining games without conceding a goal.

"Busy Bee" summed up the season in his column of May10, 1929. Tribute was paid to Bradford City on gaining promotion.

'It has been a great struggle between the County and Bradford City, the latter having had one of the most remarkable runs of successes in the history of the League. ... The Valley Paraders sustained their last defeat on February 2nd, when they were beaten 2-1 by the County at Edgeley Park. Since then they have managed to escape defeat, ... and in the end they have gained promotion by a lead of one point on the County and a record goal average'.[72]

Stockport's retained list of players was referred to in the same piece and confirmed that Frank, despite having had 'one of the most unfortunate games of his career', in the 3-2 home win against Barrow, had superseded Joe Smith as the club's centre forward for the season upcoming; the latter was not retained.[73]

"Busy Bee" also paid tribute to the manager, Lincoln Hyde, the trainers and players:

> 'This season they are second, with the finest record any County team has ever had. The players have been a steady, loyal, and enthusiastic body, keenly devoted to the interests of the club and a good deal of the spirit of fellowship which exists amongst them is largely due to Mr Hyde's way of handling the team. He has a kindly but firm way of dealing with the players and they all admire and respect him. The trainers, Mr Fred Westgarth, for the first team, and Mr Harry Catterick, for the second team, have both given loyal and devoted service, and have made a substantial contribution to the playing successes of the teams'.[74]

For his part, "A. W.", in his review of the 1928-29 season, concluded by expressing his appreciation for the uniform courtesy extended to him

> 'on all occasions, but especially on the outward engagements, when the fine spirit of comradeship among the "boys" [plus the lively wit of the comedians "B. & B."] tended in no small measure to the good results on the field'.[75]

Later, in September, 1931, Frank was interviewed by B.J. Evans who at the time is thought to have been with *The Star (London)* newspaper. The article was published on September 29, and in it Frank paid a generous tribute, typical of him, to Joe Smith and his influence on Frank's early professional career:

> 'I have to thank Joe Smith, who is now the manager of Reading, for teaching me how to be a centre forward. He spent hours teaching me in ball-control, heading and shooting; and was the finest tutor a man could have. Absolutely true blue is Joe; a man I admire immensely'.[76]

The 1928-29 season was transformational for Frank, as not only did he make his first team debut at Edgeley Park, but he established himself as the County's first team centre forward in place of Joe Smith, in itself a fine achievement. Initially Frank enjoyed almost unbelievable success, netting 7 times in his first 5 games, 11 times in his first 8, and finished with 16 in his 19 league appearances. However, it is noteworthy that he lost some of his aggressive spirit and suffered a late season dip in form, scoring just three times in his last nine games.

Frank was considered a robust, finely built man who was unsparing in his efforts as a team player. He was a consistent marksman with a terrific shot, and while he was lacking in some of the finer points of the game he improved over the course of the season. At the time of his Edgeley Park debut on December 1, 1928, his 26th birthday was behind him. He was therefore under some pressure since he had married at the end of October 1928, and was well aware that to succeed he needed regular first team football. Importantly, he believed in his own abilities and, after the best part of ten years in the military, was not intimidated by authority, nor overawed by a chain of command. This was amply demonstrated when it emerged that he had submitted a transfer request after he was 'dropped' following the humbling defeat at Wrexham on March 2, 1929. Frank was not prepared to 'carry the can' for the team's failure, and after two games in the reserve side he submitted his transfer request. Fortunately, the management recognised his frustration and he played in all ten remaining fixtures. Unsurprisingly he was included on the club's retained list.

For Frank the 1928-29 season was memorable as he succeeded in establishing himself as a first team professional footballer and had replaced Joe Smith in Stockport's starting line up. Perhaps the only surprise in Frank's steady progress at the club arose when he was passed over to take Joe Smith's spot against Rochdale on November 3, 1928. In March 1929 a further hiccup arose and on this occasion Frank was quick to take the management to task when, after two outings in the County Reserve side, when he requested a transfer. Fortunately the management clearly were unwilling to let him go, and once recalled he retained his place for the balance of the season. Overall, Frank had earned the right to view his 1928-29 season as one of significant achievement.

1929-30 Season

Stockport commenced their 1929-30 season with a practice game at Edgeley Park on Saturday, August 17. "Observer" in the *Stockport Advertiser* was well satisfied with what he saw. It was

> 'an interesting afternoon's football. The players were all in good trim and gave a spirited display. The attendance was not large – about 1500 – but many people were away

> ... and others were kept away by the bad weather'.[1]

The forward line of the previous season, the Whites, were pitted against the squad's defensive unit, the Blues, and despite the forwards having the better of the exchanges only two goals were scored. Both came deep into the second half and were slotted by Frank, 'who showed a return of the old aggressive spirit'. This suggests it was noted as somewhat lacking at the close of the previous season.[2]

The result of the second practice match may have caused manager Lincoln Hyde some concern. The game played on August 24, provided something of an upset as the 'reserve players [the Whites] surprised the spectators, the opposing team, and probably themselves, by defeating the team which ... were last season's first team'.[3]

The match report attempted to downplay any significance that might have been attached to the scoreline. But a few questions must surely have arisen in Mr Hyde's mind. Almost inevitably it was Frank who scored the first goal, in the 22nd minute, to put the Blues ahead. But that was it. Shockingly there followed a succession of goals which resulted in the reserves whipping the Blues 5-1.

> 'The two chief factors of the White's success was the splendid form of Everest, the centre forward, and the excellent goalkeeping of Richardson, the ex-Bury player. Everest if he reproduces this form, will quickly reach the first team. He positively shone on Saturday'.[4]

The 1929-30 season proper started auspiciously for the

County as they drew their opening game 1-1 at Wrexham, and then at Edgeley Park thumped Barrow AFC 5-0,[5] before a crowd of 6,845.[6] For Frank the season started slowly for, despite his setting up two of the goals, the closest he came to scoring was to hit one of the Barrow uprights. Indeed, 'many easy chances were missed, and in this respect the centre forward was the worst offender, failing to score once or twice when it seemed almost impossible to miss'.[7]

Stockport County, 1929-30 pictured at Edgeley Park.
Back row, l to r. Westgarth (trainer), Billy Newton, Bocking, Richardson, Wilson, Helliwell, Vincent. Front row, l to r. Tompkinson, Boardman, Frank Newton, Lincoln, Fielding.

However, the *Lancashire Evening Post* viewed things a little differently: 'Stockport had advantage of height and weight, and the whole team worked well together … Of the forwards F. Newton was outstanding'.[8]

It was not until the fourth game of the new season that

Frank finally opened his goal scoring account. In so doing he revealed the superstitious side of his nature when he reverted to using his 'old boots'. This change was judged to be worthy of comment in the local press.

> 'Like King James of old, he [Frank] believes there are such friends as old shoes. It is rather remarkable that he did not start scoring this season until he went back to his old boots. He wore new ones in the matches against Wrexham, Barrow (at home) and Wigan Borough and scored not at all'.[9]

Having made the change, Frank certainly struck a better run of form and scored twice in the return game with Barrow, a 4-0 romp. It was hoped that this marked a return to business as usual, and his 'old scoring vein'.[10]

There followed a potentially difficult game at Carlisle where the County had won so decisively the previous season. On this occasion the home support was less than generous as their heroes, once again, could only offer token resistance to the County's onslaught.

> 'The Carlisle spectators took the beating badly, and the match was marred by an ugly demonstration on their part against the referee, Mr J. Rennie, of Oldham ... The crowd began to get really bad tempered after Stockport's third goal, McLeod had been warned once for fouling when he deliberately tripped and pushed Jobson the referee without a moment's hesitation ordered him off the field. Mr Rennie was booed and hissed by the

spectators and some of them went to the length of throwing stones. One of these caught him in the back whilst the teams were taking up their positions for a corner kick conceded to the County, and it was some little time before he would permit the game to proceed. The uproar increased in intensity, and at the close the local police marshalled their forces and gave the referee an escort of some twelve constables as he left the field. One of the spectators aimed a blow at him, but he reached the dressing-room in safety'.[11]

The coverage in the *Athletic News* provided a little more context:

> 'In light of the fact that Carlisle United were without four of their leading players ... their home defeat by Stockport County was not unanticipated, but Carlisle's ill-luck did not end with them having to call on five reserves and reshuffle their team. In the second half, when Carlisle were three goals down, the referee, whose decisions in the game had met with much disfavour, ordered McLeod, ... off the field for what appeared to be a most trivial offence. This led to a hostile demonstration by the crowd for this is the first time in the history of the club, extending over 25 years, that one of their players has been given marching orders'.[12]

Stockport again scored five goals at Brunton Park, and despite the crowd's animosity Frank scored two to bring his season's tally to 4 in 5 games.

There were more to come for Frank the following week, in a remarkable home match against an unfortunate Nelson side. The visitors possibly made a mistake in the 28th minute when they took the lead, as this invigorated the County. After Shelvin in the Nelson goal,

> 'had dealt with shots by Newton and Lincoln he was ultimately beaten by the centre-forward who gave him little chance from close range. This occurred after 37 minutes, and the cheers had scarcely subsided ere the lead was obtained, Newton again being the executant. The Nelson defence was now under almost constant pressure, and five minutes from the interval a penalty awarded for a foul on Tompkinson resulted in a third goal. Newton converting the spot-kick and thus accomplishing the "hat-trick" ... Shelvin performed heroically and saved numerous well-directed shots before capitulating again to Newton, who received from Boardman, after his first effort had re-bounded from the bar, and forced both ball and keeper in the net. The little "goalie" was slightly injured in the melee but quickly resumed and was roundly cheered for his pluck. Although now holding a substantial lead the County did not relax their efforts, and just on the half-hour Newton ran up to a perfect centre from Fielding to head a fifth goal – the best of the match. This was followed by another fierce drive from the home centre, who took the ball on the half-turn and rattled the bar with Shelvin beaten'.[13]

A week after the Nelson game "Observer" in the *Cheshire*

Daily Echo acknowledge Frank's achievement.

> 'As it was, it was the poorest crowd, numerically, which has attended a first team match this season, that saw County in its happiest scoring vein against Nelson. For the first 20 minutes the Lancashire side held its own, but the goal which gave them first blood was not altogether deserved ... After this Stockport got into their stride and were soon easily on top. Those who failed to see the match failed to see Frank Newton, the Stockport centre forward, at his best. His five consecutive goals in this match were a record in League football for the day, and it has only once been equalled on the Edgeley ground in recent years. That was two seasons ago, when the feat was achieved by Joe Smith. Newton is a worthy member of a family which has the footballing instinct deeply implanted. During his two seasons with the County he has rendered excellent service to the club, and, young as he is, I feel convinced that we shall see him do still greater things in the future'.[14]

The County then undertook a trip to Southport's Haig Avenue ground where Stockport had never previously won. The home team were in confident mood as they were coming off a good victory over York City and a memorable draw with a Manchester City side in a Lancashire Cup match. The game against the County was described as a '... neck and neck struggle all through, and Stockport only gained the winning goal when the end was near.' It was scored with just 6 minutes remaining and judged the best of the three scored in the game. It resulted from a

> 'clever exhibition of resourceful play by F. Newton. He snapped up the ball, ran forward, was pushed over ... by a defender, recovered himself and the ball in a trice, and scored with a quick, left-footed shot past the advancing 'keeper. After shooting Jones caught the Stockport centre's elbow, and he [Newton] spun round and fell on his left ankle the one he injured at Rotherham last season – and for a time he was hors de combat. The hurt, fortunately, was not serious, ... and he was passed fit for the evening match at Lincoln the following Monday evening'.[15]

The match report carried in the *Lancashire Evening Post* stated:

> 'Southport had every reason to be satisfied with their display against Stockport County. Though beaten they had the satisfaction of knowing they had been worthy of a share of the spoils. It was a game in which the result was always in doubt, and in the end Stockport got the goal which might just as easily have been Southport's. There were differences between the sides, of course, and the most pronounced, perhaps, was the effectiveness of the opposing forward lines. That of the County always impressed, for it had the daringly enterprising Newton and the weighty and dashing Lincoln ... Wynes had the hardest task, though, in having to watch such a fast and clever centre as Newton, the limiting of whose scoring to a single goal, reflected some credit upon the young Southport player'.[16]

The regular League schedule was then briefly interrupted as Stockport had won through to a place in the final of the Cheshire Medal Competition against Tranmere Rovers. The game was played on Tranmere's Prenton Park ground on October 3. Despite fielding five of their Reserve side, the County had no difficulty defeating their hosts and it was a memorable day for Frank. After conceding an early goal Stockport raised their game and went on to record a 5-2 victory, with Frank scoring no fewer than 4 of the County's 5 goals. 'Mr Harry Chase, the Chairman of the Cheshire FA presented the gold medals to the County players'.[17] However, the home support was not particularly appreciative.

> 'They even went to the length of booing one of the Stockport men when Mr Harry Chase ... was presenting the medals ... a very unsportsmanlike action. Mr Chase paid the Stockport players a merited compliment when he stated that they were worthy of the Second Division. Their form in the match left no doubt on this point. For all that they were playing with five reserves, they displayed a brilliance in tactics, ball control, and combination which made the Tranmere football look very poor in comparison. Frank Newton added to his store of goals by scoring four of the County's five. Like King James of old, he believes there are no such friends as old friends. It is rather remarkable that he did not start scoring this season till he went back to his old shoes. He wore new ones in the matches against Wrexham, Barrow [at home] and Wigan Borough and scored not at all. He returned to his old ones for the match at Barrow and scored twice!

Since then he scored one against Crewe Alexandra, two at Carlisle, five against Nelson, one at Southport, and four at Prenton Park'.[18]

Stockport County's 'Clubable' Frank Newton, 1930

By the end of September, Frank had scored 10 goals in the County's 7 league games, all of which were recorded in the last four matches in the month. He was running at full throttle and must have been greatly enjoying his prolific scoring vein.

After the first week in October, it was clear that Port Vale, relegated from Division Two the previous season, were serious challengers for the Division title. At the time they had accumulated 16 points from 9 games, and were followed by the County and Accrington Stanley with 12 from 7 and 8 games respectively. An encouraging start, but disappointingly from their standpoint, Stockport could only muster a further 2 points from a possible 6 in the first 3 weeks of October 1929. On October 5 the County lost their proud, undefeated home record when they went down 3-2 to Crewe Alexandra. Not since April 2, 1927 had the County lost at Edgeley Park, when Bradford Park Avenue turned them over 2-1. Since then

Stockport had played 51 home games without defeat. But the

> 'record went by the board on Saturday, when Crewe Alexandra triumphed after a severe struggle by the odd goal. When it is recalled that the Railwaymen checked the County's promotion aspirations last Good Friday by drawing 2-2 at Edgeley in a game during which two "penalties" were missed by the homesters, and on Saturday they again failed at a "spot-kick," there would appear to be ample ground for the contention that Crewe are regarded as a "bogey" team by the Edgeley players, some of whom apparently had the "wind-up" on Saturday'.

Crewe were 2 goals ahead through "Jimmy" Scullion, formerly of Fulham FC and Stockport, before the County reduced the deficit, when Frank 'lobbed the keeper' five minutes prior to the interval. However, Crewe responded within two minutes of the restart, once more through Scullion, who, enjoying his best season, completed his hat-trick. The County then netted again, and a rare struggle ensued. The 'bulk of the attack work fell to Newton and Boardman. The centre-forward was always on the 'qui vive', and after 15 minutes he recorded his second goal', driving home Fielding's cross from the left wing in fine style. Unfortunately, a clinical finish was missing fifteen minutes from the end when Frank was 'brought down, in full cry', inside the penalty area. The referee immediately pointed to the spot, and walked over to Davies in the Crewe goal, apparently to remind him 'of the new rule regarding a 'goalie's' conduct when the 'spot-kick' is taken.' His behaviour was impeccable, as he turned Frank's drive around the post and in that moment the undefeated home record was lost.[19]

There followed on October 12 a hard fought game, at York City, which the County won 2-1, with Frank scoring the winner late in the second half.[20] But Stockport disappointed in their next match being defeated 2-0, surprisingly, by Tranmere Rovers at Prenton Park. 'Observer' reported on the encounter for the *Stockport Advertiser*, and rated Tranmere good value for their victory. 'Whilst the home team displayed excellent form', the County were well below their best, lacked punch and were unable to penetrate Tranmere's strong defensive unit.[21]

Although the season was still young, Port Vale maintained their winning ways and on October 25, 1929 the *Stockport Advertiser* published the Division 3 (Northern Section) table. Port Vale were 6 points clear of Darlington, who in turn were one point ahead of the chasing pack: Stockport County, Accrington Stanley, Tranmere Rovers and Rochdale. However, Port Vale had played 12 games, Darlington, Tranmere and Accrington 11, and both Stockport and Rochdale 10. Clearly, despite the games in hand, the pressure was already mounting to remain within touching distance of the Hanley club.[22]

Thankfully from Stockport's and their leading scorer's standpoints, the team returned to top form the following week when, on October 26, Halifax Town were seen off 6-0 at Edgeley Park. 'The three goals that Newton scored enhanced his already big reputation as a marksman and consolidated his position as the top scorer in the Northern Section. Again his old boots stood him in good stead'.[23]

On the day the Stockport side was depleted through injury and called up four from the Reserve side, two of whom played in the forward line. Nonetheless, the team combined well and at half time enjoyed a deserved 2-0 lead. The fireworks came in the second half when Stockport added 4 goals inside 18 minutes. Three of them went to Frank, the first from a scramble in the Halifax goalmouth, the next, just two minutes later, headed in from Lincoln's centre, and the third, an 'excellent goal', headed home from a corner.[24]

The result demonstrated that the County enjoyed strength in depth, and it was felt that if the team could maintain their form there was every chance of Port Vale being reeled in. The contribution of the replacements was summarised at some length:

> 'today's team included no less than four reserves, Gee, the young Reddish centre-half, was given his first chance on the Northern Section team, through the unfortunate breakdown of Jack Jobson at Prenton Park, and Cawley, another promising half-back, was at right-back in place of Billy Newton, who pulled a muscle during practice ... The forward line also had two changes, ... Seabrook, the ex-Crewe forward, was on the right wing, and Cooper, who came to Stockport from Lancaster Town last season, appeared on the left ... there had been no cause to grumble about the displays made by the four reserve men ... They were all giving a good account of themselves. Gee was defending strongly and also feeding the forwards well. Cooper was showing plenty of spirit ... and a feature of the game was the excellent understanding which existed between Cawley and Seabrook'.[25]

By the end of October Frank was enjoying great success,

and his importance as the team's talisman was indisputable as he had accounted for 16 of the County's 34 goals. Next came Lincoln with 6, Boardman 4, Tomkinson 3 and Fielding the outside left with 2.[26]

The club next drew 2-2 at Rotherham on November 2, after which Rochdale were entertained at Edgeley Park a week later. The local press reports of that game were ecstatic and proclaimed that the County had performed like 'CHAMPIONS'. This local 'Derby' drew the largest crowd to that point in the season, 12,903, and they were considered fortunate to have witnessed a thrilling encounter which the County won 4-2. Stockport displayed 'real championship form', particularly in the first half. Frank scored the County's third goal just before half time, and when Lincoln scored the fourth 6 minutes into the second half, the game was over. Although Rochdale rallied with two late goals, the result was never in doubt.[27]

A keen tussle at Horsely Hill followed, and in an enthralling game the County managed to beat South Shields 3-2, after falling behind twice. The score was tied 1-1 at the interval, but within 5 minutes Stockport gave away a penalty and the 'Plate Enders' were 2-1 up. Nevertheless, the County continued to play with 'grit and perseverance', and after 10 minutes Lincoln levelled the score. Stockport's winner came 5 minutes later when Frank broke in on goal, drew the 'keeper, and passed to Fielding to unerringly deliver the *coup de grâce,'* into the empty net.[28]

The view of the *Athletic News*' correspondent was that the County thoroughly deserved the win, although there were times when the team had to scrap for every inch of ground to achieve their objective.

'If the visitors had won with twice as many goals it would not have been surprising, because they were so far the dominant note in the game, particularly during the first half. It was a team triumph, with the forward line the outstanding feature. Fielding and Lincoln were a capable left wing, and there was a sparkle in the artistry and speed of the former which stamped him as an individualist of singular capabilities. Both wing pairs dovetailed together nicely and passes were rarely wasted. The leadership of F. Newton had much to do with their success'.[29]

The report in the *Football Gazette* was also unequivocal.

'While it is dire misfortune to concede both points by an odd goal, South Shields were certainly the inferior side on the day's form. Stockport's forwards were a set of big, hustling fellows, who gave no quarter when it came to tackling, while Shields' vanguard on the contrary were anything but aggressive in the Stockport goal area. Newton and Maycock were in distinct contrast, and the comparison was against the Shields leader'.[30]

Port Vale continued to make the running in the Northern Division, and the league positions to November 23 had the Hanley team first with 29 points from 17 games, the County second with 23 from 15, followed by Darlington and Accrington Stanley with 21 and 20 points respectively, both from 16 games.[31]

Off the pitch, Stockport's financial footing remained an ongoing concern, and the County's officials took their supporters to task for failing to give their winning team better support.

The club's games 'in hand' were also a concern as they mounted while Port Vale continued winning. Uncertainty was growing around the County's promotion prospects. It was rumoured that players might have to be sold in an effort to balance the books. Consequently, when Accrington Stanley visited Edgeley Park towards the end of November 1929 'a big array of club managers and paid scouts [attended] this game. Matters are working in the direction of transfers from Stockport'.[32]

The game itself, with Stockport placed second and Accrington fourth, was a 'four pointer'. It was a close, hard fought tussle played out on a very heavy pitch, which resembled a 'sea of mud'. The County carried the game to Accrington throughout the first half, but could not break down a resolute defence and the half ended scoreless. Further rain fell during the interval, and the game continued 'to be strenuously contested, with the County holding the balance, and their visitors defending with skill and judgement'. The struggle was finally settled, some 15 minutes from time, when Frank squared to Tomkinson who slotted the winner from close range.[33]

Thoughts in the lower leagues now focused on the first round proper of the FA Cup in which the County were drawn to face Wellington Town FC (Shropshire). The match was played before a crowd of 7,719, on November 30. Stockport encountered little resistance from their hosts and, as expected, won convincingly, 4-1.

> 'Less than 200 supporters travelled by rail from Stockport ... the early start, coupled with bad weather doubtless being responsible. However, there was plenty of excitement in the old town, excursions from the

surrounding districts being well patronised, the visit of a Third Division team being looked upon somewhat in the nature of a football luxury.

The opening stages of the second-half were strenuously contested, but the visitors gradually got a firm grip on the game, and after F. Newton had obtained the lead following a corner on the left, further goals were registered by Fielding and Tompkinson, the County thus winning somewhat easily'.[34]

By the beginning of the second week in December, after the home fixture with Hartlepools was postponed because of the shocking state of the Edgeley Park pitch, alarm bells were again ringing around the County's promotion prospects.

> 'Stockport are getting behind in their fixture list ... Everything seems to point to the Hanley club being in an almost unassailable position ... At Stockport there is no lack of spirit, but the odds against them are now well realised'.[35]

At the time Port Vale remained at the top of the Northern Section with 31 points from 18 games, and the County were second with 23 points from 15.[36]

Two weeks after winning their Cup match against Wellington Town, the County entertained Barrow in the second round of the FA Cup. "Observer" considered that Stockport's appearance in the third round was as certain as anything can be in football, and so it proved as the County won 4-0. The home side bossed the game virtually from the outset, and Stockport's '... clever play on a holding surface was ... a triumph over the conditions, and amply repaid the onlookers for their loyalty in braving the elements.' Stockport were two up at the interval, Frank scoring the second after 40 minutes when he 'made no mistake with a low cross-drive.' There was little change after half time, despite the persistent rain, on a pitch that had become 'a veritable quagmire.' The County continued to dominate, and the Barrow defence was subjected to 'almost continuous pressure.' The result, as "Observer" predicted was never in doubt.[37]

Between November 23 and February 1, 1930 Stockport were to play 7 of their scheduled 10 games at Edgeley Park, and it was this fact that must have prompted Mr E. Barlow, Chairman of Stockport County, somewhat unwisely, to go on the record in the Manchester press complaining of the unsportsmanlike behaviour of the County's fan base as manifested in the poor turnouts at home games. "Observer" reported on December 7, 1929:

> 'Interest in the controversy regarding the sportsmanship of Stockport people, raised by a Press interview given by the Chairman of the club a fortnight ago does not seem to flag. Below I give two more letters on the subject'.

In the first of these the correspondent, Sam Riley, wrote:

> 'I was not surprised, on reading your notes in last Saturday's issue, to find that you had received several letters of protest respecting the charge of being unsportsmanlike, made against Stockport people by Mr E. Barlow, ... and whilst not being associated in any way with your correspondents "Bob a week" and "Sportsman", I should

> like to point out to Mr Barlow that these charges of non sportsmanship and threats of what will happen if gates do not increase, are causing great annoyance to many staunch supporters of the County. It is easy to understand that the Board are perturbed at the decrease in gates at home matches, seeing that the teams are doing so well. Good luck to them, but surely it must be patent to the directors ... that the fall in receipts is principally due to the great number of men and youths unemployed in the town and district, amongst whom are many of the supporters of the County, who find it impossible to spare the shilling required to enable them to have the opportunity of seeing their club play at home ... Although the situation is disquieting from a management point of view, I do not think the circumstances justify a charge of being unsportsmanlike brought against the people of Stockport'.

On the other hand, "Happy Harry" offered a different viewpoint.

> 'I can well understand Councillor Barlow's exasperation at the attendance at Stockport County's matches. To be able to run a successful team of 1st or 2nd League standard requires an average gate of twelve thousand for the first team and six to eight thousand for the Central League matches. The gates are falling a good deal short of this. But I doubt the wisdom of criticising the public because it does not do a penny worth of good, in fact, it does a great deal of harm ... Public support is part of the County's

stock in trade ... People who run places of entertainment know full well that success breeds success. If the news gets about that a show is drawing big houses it causes other people to want to go. My advice is: "Drop the lack of support" stunt. Put in its place the slogan: "Stockport County has the best team, the best management, and the best lot of supporters in the country'.

"Observer" closed out the discussion as follows:

'Mr Riley raises an interesting point. There are at present some 5,000 people unemployed in Stockport, and it is, of course, likely that some of them are people who, if they had the means, would attend the matches at Edgeley Park. Stockport County are not the only club suffering from economic stress at the present time. Burnley, Halifax Town, South Shields, and Swansea Town are also deploring lack of support, and it would be interesting to know to what extent unemployment is responsible. As I have said previously in these columns, the County, for all that they are well supplied in comparison with other Third Division clubs, need bigger gates than they are getting at present if they are to bring a better class of football into the town. Personally, I should be loath to dub any man unsportsmanlike if the criterion of sportsmanship is to be attendance at a football match, but at the same time, in view of the club's excellent record, ... it seems strange that a town and district boasting a population of 130,000 cannot produce a bigger crowd at Edgeley Park than 8,000'.[38]

The County now faced a difficult and congested Christmas programme which required them to play 6 matches, between December 21, 1929 and January 4, 1930, in just 15 days. Fortunately four of these games were at home, viewed as an advantage despite the extremely heavy going underfoot at Edgeley Park, certainly a very physically demanding surface. Naturally, of the games in prospect, by far the most critical was the 'double header' against Port Vale, to be played over Christmas.

The visit of Chesterfield, a side in confident mood having just knocked Port Vale out of the FA Cup, got the crowded schedule underway at Edgeley Park, on December 21. The visitors produced a 'clever and resourceful' performance, but could not break down the well marshalled Stockport defence. For their part, the County failed to adjust adequately to the heavy conditions and persisted with their short passing game. However, in the second half they came more into their own offensively, yet it was not until 8 minutes from time that Frank latched on to a long clearance and beat Dolman in the Chesterfield net from 15 yards.[39] This was an important result as it moved Stockport back into second place in the Northern Division, and perfectly set up the back to back games with league leaders Port Vale.[40]

The County were fortunate in the first game, played on Christmas Day at 'The Old Recreation Ground', as Port Vale's left wing, Baxter, was injured early in the first half, and thereafter 'was little more than a passenger.' Then, with some ten minutes remaining, Vale's inside right, Rawlings, had to be carried off. However, the match was not reported as being played in an overly robust manner, and these injuries, at least as reported in the local Stockport press, were attributed to 'bad luck'. Predictably, the game was keenly contested and there was little to choose between the two sides throughout most of the first half. But after 45 minutes Stockport were judged to be the more aggressive and would have turned around one up if Frank had not 'ballooned over' from five yards out. A 'golden opportunity' missed. After the break the County continued to improve and scored their first goal, 17 minutes in, when Frank converted a pass from Fielding. Port Vale responded and were credited with a 'hotly disputed' goal with 15 minutes remaining. This temporarily invigorated the home side, but Stockport were in no mood to be denied, and 5 minutes from time Tomkinson fired home from 15 yards. This 2-1 victory was a 'great achievement' for the County, despite Port Vale's injuries, and was of course vital in terms of their promotion prospects.[41]

On Boxing Day the teams were at it again at Edgeley Park before a crowd of some 22,000, the best of the season. Port Vale produced a 'good resourceful' performance in which the strength of their defence stood out. 'There was little to choose between the teams in the first half, and it was not until the later stages of the second half that Stockport definitely gained the upper hand'.[42]

In fact it was Port Vale that opened the scoring just 11 minutes into the game. There followed a spirited response from the County as they strove for an equaliser. This finally materialised, some 20 minutes later, when Stockport's right half, Billy Newton, drove home a 'terrific' shot which 'completely beat Davies from some 20 yards'. At the interval honours were even.

Frank again 'missed a golden opportunity' when, shortly

after the interval, with 'a clear run for goal' he shot straight at Davies. Then less than 10 minutes later it appeared that the County might live to rue Frank's profligate ways when Port Vale again went in front. However, the Edgeley Park faithful were rocking shortly thereafter when Fielding pushed the ball into the goalmouth and Frank:

> 'made no mistake with a terrific drive from short range. After this excitement remained intense as the home players strove might and main to take the lead, and the Vale goal had several very narrow escapes. By this time Stockport were by far the more aggressive side and pressure on the Port Vale goal became intense'.[43]

So it really came as no surprise when, after 78 minutes, Lincoln, at inside left, scored his first of the afternoon to put Stockport ahead. Immediately thereafter Stockport continued to press and Davies was again 'severely tested' by both Frank and Lincoln. Nonetheless, the result was not sealed until, with 10 minutes remaining, Lincoln scored his second.[44]

The *Evening Sentinal* described the games as Port Vale's 'Black Christmas'. The Christmas Day defeat was attributed to the serious injuries to their two men, Baxter and Rawlings, although the report concluded that Stockport's defence and positional play were superior to those of the Hanley club.[45] With reference to the Boxing Day loss, it was felt that it could 'best be described as a material outcome of their mishaps of the previous day'.[46]

These back to back victories exceeded the expectations of all but the most ardent County supporters, and of course enhanced the team's chances of promotion. Nevertheless, Stockport still remained 4 points behind the Vale, but now with 3 games in hand.

Two days later Wrexham visited Edgeley Park and provided

> 'a striking illustration of the vagaries of football. Before the match no one doubted for a moment that its result would add another two points to the six already gained by the County during the proceeding seven days'.[47]

But the County were complacent and, after raising their game against Port Vale, were unable to reproduce the critical levels of intensity required, a pattern often observed in sporting encounters. Consequently, the club lost points and provided Wrexham with their first away win of the season.

"Observer" considered that:

> 'the County were beaten not so much by Wrexham as by their own inability to adapt their play to the conditions ... and remembering that the Edgeley Park has ... been in a bad condition since the heavy rains began in November their failure is rather remarkable ... they were all at sea ... figuratively and almost literally ... in the ankle deep mud and water'.[48]

Unfortunately, Stockport persisted in trying to move the ball on the ground, but the

> 'short passing game is worse than useless in such conditions ... and ... availed the County nothing. Wrexham on

the other hand, did not attempt an uneven struggle with the mud, but kept the ball in the air and kept it moving with strong, lusty passes, despite its weight'.[49]

Wrexham scored their goal in the third minute and subsequently defended resolutely. They effectively dealt with everything in the Stockport forwards' armoury. Unquestionably, they were assisted by the appalling state of the pitch, one half of which was almost completely under water before the end. "Observer" was of the opinion that 'it would have occasioned no surprise' if the referee had abandoned proceedings. He did not, and the County dropped 2 invaluable points from a game they would certainly have expected to win.[50]

Matters improved little on New Year's Day 1930 when Lincoln City took a point away from Edgeley Park. Another very disappointing result, the cause again being the inability of the County players, primarily the forwards, to adapt to the conditions, particularly in the second half, on the 'morass-like ground'. In fact the state of the playing surface at Edgeley Park was becoming something of a handicap to the County, and no doubt many must have been surprised by the side's apparent inability to adjust to the prevailing conditions. However, Stockport pressed from the start and were a goal up inside 15 minutes. After which the home side continued to dominate, and shots from Frank, Tompkinson and Boardman were 'miraculously intercepted.' Then on the half hour, and very much against the run of play, Lincoln equalised. The County forwards were then kept in check throughout a hard fought second half, during which 'they were facing the Shaw Heath end and were attacking over the worse half of the ground'. In particular, the side was let down by the inside forwards who 'were at a loss in the mud and failed to take their opportunities'.[51]

It was to prove a critical point in the County's season. Both these events and the playing conditions were commented upon at length, and probably overstated, by "Observer".

> 'It is often the unexpected that happens in football, but the County's failure to gain more than one point from their last two matches, both played at home, surprised the whole football world. After winning both the Port Vale matches the Stockport club seemed to be in [a] fair way of achieving a record from their holiday matches. Certainly the Wrexham and the Lincoln engagements were considered the easiest of the five which they had to meet during the Christmas period. And yet they produced only one point. It was very disappointing for the club to lose ground in such a fashion after improving their promotion prospects so handsomely by their victories over the League leaders. It has been an unequal struggle with a mud bound ground as far as Stockport are concerned. The ground on Saturday was hardly fit for the match to be played at all, and although most of the water had been drained away on Wednesday, it was still very muddy. And in both matches the County forwards had the muddy half of the playing pitch to attack over in the second half, when it was vital that they should get goals. In both matches Stockport were unfortunate. They were unfortunate on Saturday in not being awarded a goal when Dickie knocked the ball through his own goal after the goalkeeper had been charged by

F. Newton – a perfectly good shoulder charge as far as one could see, but the referee thought otherwise. Had Stockport equalised at this period it would have made a world of difference to their chances. Again Stockport were unlucky on Wednesday or rather Lincoln City were phenomenally lucky. Half a dozen or more shots at their goal deserved success, but in some remarkable way they were intercepted, more by good luck than good management. County's luck was dead out. But having said all this, the fact remains that the County should not have lost three points from these matches. Had they played the same kind of game as Wrexham ... and booted the ball hard instead of trying fancy football in the mud they would not have suffered the ignominy of a home defeat; had their forwards shown any ability to control the ball and take their chances – which were numerous – on Wednesday, they would not have had to concede a point to Lincoln City. The heavy ground routed the team completely. They had the will to win, and no one can say they did not work hard enough. But though they were the chief aggressors in both matches they were unable to apply their industry and energy to the right tactics'.[52]

There followed an interview with Mr George McIndoe, a former Stockport County director, conducted immediately before the upcoming Cup tie with Blackpool, in which he stated: 'In my opinion the state of the ground at Edgeley Park is the cause of the recent loss of points there, which is not due to any faults of the players, who are clever enough but have fallen to kick and rush teams'.[53]

After "Observer" had highlighted the poor state of the Edgeley Park pitch, "Busy Bee" revisited the issue, a year later, in the *Stockport Advertiser* on February 13, 1931. The fact was the drainage of the ground was inadequate and thus the pitch was very often not conducive to the style of football that came most naturally to the team. "Busy Bee" stated:

> 'The Shaw Heath end of the County ground is in a terrible state just now, due to an unfortunate experiment in re-laying two or three seasons ago, for which the present ground staff are not responsible. To play classic football on such a ground is impossible for either attackers or defenders'.[54]

The evidence was clear, vital points were being dropped at home because the County failed to adequately adjust to the conditions underfoot which at times were appalling.

In January 1930 an interesting piece appeared in the *Cheshire Daily Echo* relating to junior footballers. The issue under consideration, by a Commission of the Cheshire FA, was the stress suffered by young, working lads, who were often under nourished, when they were required to play in unreasonable conditions. The matter arose because many youngsters were physically incapable of lasting 90 minutes. Interestingly, Frank was mentioned in this context: 'When a strong player like Frank Newton drops down with exhaustion, who can expect a young lad who may ordinary [sic] perhaps be employed in a hot spinning room during the week to stick it out?' Unfortunately, no reference is made to the match in which Frank's mishap occurred, but it is reasonable to suggest that it would have been in late November, or early December 1929.[55] It should be noted that:

> 'Up to September 1929 had been a very dry year for England and Wales with just 63% of the expected January-September rainfall. October saw a turnaround and the last three months and especially November and December were complete washouts. They were so wet that the last three months of the year contributed 56% of the rainfall total for 1929, compare that to the first three months of 1929 which contributed only 10%. November 1929 is the 4th wettest November on record for England and Wales'.[56]

Edgeley Park unfortunately did not escape the deluge.

At the beginning of January 1930, despite these two disappointing results against Wrexham and Lincoln City, the County remained in touch with Port Vale. The League leaders had 35 points from 22 games played, Stockport were second with 30 points from 20 games, and Darlington followed with 27 points after 23 games. Effectively, it had developed into a two club race.[57]

Newton's goal scoring exploits had continued, and by New Year's Day 1930 he had scored 20 league goals in just 20 games. However, following the match against Lincoln City he was dropped for the next 7 league matches. "Observer" noted that against Lincoln he was 'below his usual form and missed a number of excellent chances'. In fact Frank was experiencing a poor run. Despite the County winning 6 and drawing 2 of their previous 9 games, Frank had scored only 4 goals. For him this was a drought, and Lincoln Hyde decided a change was required, something with which the Chairman, given his concerns, would almost certainly have fully agreed. Frank's only first team appearance, before his recall on February 22 against Tranmere Rovers, was in the County's 2-1 loss to Blackpool, at Bloomfield Road, in the third round of the FA Cup. He was probably preferred then given the strength and experience of the Blackpool defence.[58]

That game on January 11, proved a hard fought one in which Blackpool, then in Division II, rode their luck. "Observer" commented that the 'much vaunted' Blackpool side were a fair match for Stockport and the visitors acquitted themselves admirably. The County engineered some early opportunities but failed to capitalise, and it was Blackpool who went ahead after 25 minutes. However, the County hit back and:

> 'had the hardest of hard lines in not equalising, a terrific shot by Frank Newton striking the crossbar when, had the ball been an inch or two lower, Wolf would have been helpless. This was the finest shot of the game'.

The game in the first half was not a typical Cup tie with end to end thrills, but was rather closely contested with neither team able to dominate. After the interval Stockport took the game to Blackpool, but again it was the home side that scored, and this goal was felt to be no less fortunate than the first. Both were scored by Browell, Blackpool's inside right, the first off his shin, and the second from a rebound off one of the uprights. Nonetheless, Stockport remained unbowed and scored 2 minutes later through Boardman. From that point the County attacked vigorously:

> 'the Blackpool goal had several narrow escapes. Even the heavy hailstorm which swept over the ground did nothing to abate the vigour of the visitors' attacks, and when the final whistle blew Blackpool were a chastened side, extremely thankful that they had managed to keep their lead. The County's display certainly deserved a replay at least. The team had no weak spots. In attack and defence the players gave an excellent exhibition and proved themselves the equals of their highly placed Second League opponents'.[59]

Regardless, Frank was not reinstated to Stockport's first XI, and the *Daily Mirror,* somewhat belatedly, on January18, reported that the County had surprised the football community by dropping Frank for their upcoming home game with Carlisle United.[60] Everest was again selected to replace him, and Frank was nominated to turn out for the Reserve side which somewhat ironically involved an immediate return to Bloomfield Road. Once again the County lost 2-1, but on this occasion Frank scored Stockport's goal, and 'with strange colleagues, could hardly be expected to show his very best form, but with a little luck he would have done the hat trick'.[61] However, the result from Edgeley Park, from Frank's standpoint, was none too encouraging and did nothing to enhance his prospects of a quick return to first team football. Not only did Carlisle crash 7-0, but Everest, Frank's replacement, scored 4 of them!

'Everest's display amply justified his selection for a second trial at centre forward. He played a splendid bustling game, he was quick on the ball, and controlled it well, and his marksmanship was excellent'.[62]

Frank must have been concerned at Everest's electric display in what he must have considered was his rightful first team slot. However, he was certainly prepared to fight for his place, and on January 25 he played again in the Reserve side, at Edgeley Park, against Blackburn Rovers. It was reported that Frank 'was a tireless leader' in that game, and played a large part in Stockport's 4-2 triumph, scoring the second and fourth goals.[63]

On February 3, 1930 Frank was then selected for a Cheshire Senior League, third round Cup match. Sandbach Ramblers provided the opposition and on their own ground proved more than a handful. As expected Stockport played the better football, dominating the midfield, but unexpectedly lost 3-2. The Ramblers adopted 'kick and rush' tactics and these combined with the County's poor finishing put the Ramblers through to the fourth round.[64]

However Sandbach was not the most hospitable of venues, and the County players may have had concerns regarding their safety.

'The spectators who lined the touchline showed great hostility to the County players because the home team was being outplayed, and several times the Ramblers' supporters broke on to the field of play. When Kyle, in checking a Sandbach forward and dispossessing him of the ball, made a quite legitimate tackle, the excited crowd,

> who were irritated by the rock-like defence of the County back, burst through the railings behind the County goal and seized him. The situation had ugly possibilities, and the referee had to stop the game to admonish the crowd, while the village policeman, who was at the other end of the ground, came to the spot to maintain order'.[65]

For Frank it may have all been just a little too much and he was taken ill during the game, but while he played on, he 'was obviously off colour.' The ailment was not specified, but it most probably explains why he was not selected to play against Oldham Athletic reserves the following Saturday. Certainly he had ample time to reflect upon the ignominies of life outside the first team. But he may have drawn some solace from the County's performance at Edgeley Park, in a 2-2 draw with Southport, which was considered to have been 'vastly disappointing'.[66]

Nonetheless, worse was to follow, from Frank's perspective, as Stockport visited the transfer market and acquired a new centre forward. The *Cheshire Daily Echo* reported on February 15 that the club had signed Marshall, a junior Scottish International, from Liverpool. This move was interpreted as a statement of intent on behalf of the County's directors to further ensure that the club would clinch promotion.[67]

The centre forward position remained a concern to management, and it was noted that 'the necessity for some improvement has been obvious.' Everest, Frank's replacement in the drawn game against Southport, 'disappointed at centre-forward. He was slow on the ball and in Dixon, the visitors' centre half, and Little and Lowe, the two backs, he found opponents able to counter his every move'.[68] Later, on February 15, "Observer" reported Everest was 'lacking in the finer points of the game', and a significant further issue was his tendency to play the man rather than the ball. In addition, "Observer" also responded to certain 'Supporters Suggestions', one of which came from Mr J. Noel Sutton of 139, Chapel Street, Edgeley. With particular reference to Frank, Sutton thought the side would have functioned better in the 1-1 draw with Crewe Alexandra, played at Gresty Road on February 2, 1930, if he were to play at inside right with Boardman outside him.

> 'With regard to Newton playing at inside right, I feel confident that he would have a lot more space to work in for shooting, than he had in the centre position, for although centre forwards score more goals than inside men, the 'policing' of Newton was enough to knock any man off his game. Then, by having more room for shooting, he would prove a real danger for opposing defences'.

He concluded by stating that it was far more onerous for defenders to 'look after' Frank than it was Everest.

"Observer" responded:

> 'To take Mr Sutton's suggestion first, it is fairly obvious it is the forward line that has required strengthening, but I do not agree that Boardman would be better on the right wing, or that Frank Newton would do better at inside right. Boardman came to the club as a wingman, but he was never a great success in that position. He is

not a player who wants a great deal of room in which to work. The tighter the corner he is in the more he seems to be able to do with the ball. He has been out of form lately, and that fact, I believe, has had a great deal to do with the lack of efficiency in the forward line as a whole. Frank Newton was tried at inside left this afternoon in the Reserve team, and it will be seen how he fared in that position. Personally I don't think he is cut out for an inside position. He is an opportunist, rather than a constructive forward. That is, when he is in form he is more able to turn to account the chances which are offered to him than to open out the game for the rest of the line'.[69]

In reviewing these developments Frank, now aged 27, would no doubt have questioned whether his future lay with Stockport County. However, there is no evidence to suggest he repeated his audacious transfer request of the previous season. He must have considered the strength of the competition and decided to bide his time.

As for Marshall, he was parachuted straight into the first team against York City, before 9,400 or so of the County faithful. Although he scored on his debut, Stockport went down 3-2 in what was considered a most unsatisfactory defeat. In his second outing the team won a close encounter 2-1 at Darlington, but in the opinion of "Observer":

'Marshall, the new centre forward, did not impress me. His form on Saturday in his first match showed some promise, but in the second match it was not fulfilled, though this time he had many more chances given him than on the former occasion'.[70]

It was time to call for Frank, and "Observer" commented upon this prior to the game with Tranmere Rovers. 'Frank Newton's return for the match today was more or less inevitable. I think he is the best of the three centre forwards available'.[71] For the unfortunate Marshall it had been a baptism of fire as he barely had time to meet his new colleagues, let alone adjust to their style of play. Instant success was required if the promotion challenge was to be maintained. The directors had hit the panic button, and the expectations placed upon Marshall, straight out of the Liverpool reserves, were, to put it kindly, unreasonable.

Against Tranmere, on February 22, Frank set out to re-establish himself in what he surely felt was his rightful position. The result was a 3-1 victory, and both his and the team's performances were lauded locally. The *Cheshire Daily Echo* screamed 'THE OLD COUNTY AGAIN, Brilliant Form Against Tranmere.' Frank played his part to the full, when after almost 15 minutes of constant pressure, County scored their first. 'Frank Newton was showing considerable enterprise and working very hard whenever he got the chance…' The goal resulted from his charging Burrows, Tranmere's goalkeeper, who lost possession, and the ball ricocheted up allowing Lincoln to head home. The second came 10 minutes later.

'Frank Newton splendidly vindicated his return to the team by scoring a truly characteristic goal ... The movement was initiated by Gee ... he pushed it forward to

Newton who was standing near the edge of the penalty area. The centre made a bee-line for goal, forced his way between the two backs and beat Burrows cleverly with a low shot to the left corner'.

The County dominated throughout the first 45 minutes but were only two up at the break thanks to Tranmere's stout defence. The visitors raised their game in the second half and honours were even, each side scoring once.

"Observer" summarised the encounter:

'It was the old County, with all their dash and cleverness, whom 10,000 spectators saw at Edgeley Park against Tranmere. Their splendid liveliness in the forward line, well led by Frank Newton, and the County well deserved their two goals lead at the interval. The Rovers were seldom seen in the home half, and the Stockport defence was well able to cope with all the efforts made by the visitors. Stockport did not have things so much their own way in the second half, Tranmere making a splendid rallying effort and causing the County defenders no little trouble ... a third goal ... made the issue safe for Stockport'.[72]

Victory in this match was vital as it meant the County just maintained contact with Port Vale at the head of the Northern Division. In fact it was now barely a two horse race as the Hanley side had 48 points from 29 games against Stockport's 42 from 28. Darlington were now a distant third having 34 points from 31 matches.[73]

It must have been something of a relief to Frank that he played well and scored on his return to first team duties. That goal was the first of 8 he scored in the first four league games following his recall, and by the middle of March he had netted no fewer than 28 times in his 25 first team appearances.

A week later, on March 1, 1930, the County played at Halifax Town's Shay Stadium, where they recorded a fine 3-0 victory, and in doing so 'completely outclassed' their hosts. Despite being a man short for 25 minutes, Boardman was off with concussion, Stockport were 2 goals up at the interval and cruising. Both goals were scored by Frank, the first coming after 23 minutes. It resulted from a three way passing movement between Fielding, Lincoln and Frank who 'very coolly' beat Matthews from 12 yards out. His second was typically opportunistic, and more spectacular as it resulted from a 'clever hook shot over his head.' Stockport went 3 up almost immediately after half time and subsequently never allowed Halifax back into the game. Nonetheless, it was noted that Stockport wasted a number of good chances.[74]

"Observer" commented upon Frank's performance which he considered confirmed his view that Frank was the best of the three centre forwards at the club. Frank 'led a set of forwards who were easily masters of the opposing defence. Had their finishing been a little better their display would have been without fault'.[75]

The match report in the *Leeds Mercury* could find no redeeming features in the Halifax performance.

'Halifax lacked leadership in the front line and showed very little method in anything they tried to execute. The style of the victors was very different. There was never a move that was not backed by other members of the team, and there was hardly a kick too far or too short'.[76]

The County next entertained Hartlepools United on March 8, a re-scheduled match for that postponed on December 7, 1929. A good result was crucial to Stockport's promotion drive as a win would place them just 3 points behind the recently poorly performing Port Vale XI. Both sides had played 30 games.[77]

A reasonable crowd of almost 4,700 attended that Monday afternoon, at Edgeley Park, and were treated to a rampant exhibition of raw County power. The home side pressed throughout a thrilling first half and were leading 4-1 at the interval. Stockport opened the scoring after 9 minutes and never looked back. Frank headed a fourth before Hartlepools scored, from a breakaway, just before half time. Nonetheless, by then the game was effectively over, and somewhat predictably the County eased up after the interval allowing Hartlepools to recover some of their poise. But it was Stockport that scored the only goal in the half, thus ensuring a comfortable 5-1 victory. It was a welcome result, and an 'invigorating display' that would enhance the side's confidence as the promotion battle intensified.[78]

Rotherham United arrived at Edgeley Park just 5 days later and were dispatched in a similar manner. The game was played in fine weather and would have proved highly entertaining for the majority of the 9,500 fans. Rotherham applied early pressure, but once the County hit their stride the visitors were doomed. Frank opened the scoring after 14 minutes and at half time the County led 3-0. Also late in the half Rotherham's chances further diminished when their left back, after a nasty collision with Frank, had to be taken to the infirmary.

Stockport continued to press immediately upon the resumption, and after just 3 minutes Frank rose to head a fourth goal. Then barely 7 minutes later he headed the County's fifth, and although Rotherham then notched their consolation goal, the final act fell to Frank, who, with just minutes remaining, completed an accomplished second half 'hat-trick'. It was a resounding 6-1 triumph which maintained the 3 point differential with the recently reinvigorated Port Vale side.[79]

After 5 consecutive victories, things went wrong the following week, on March 20 at Rochdale, where Stockport went down 3-1. The game was fiercely contested and there was no scoring before the break. However, the visitors were particularly unfortunate as the Rochdale woodwork was struck twice, a County goal was disallowed, and worst of all Lincoln, at inside left, had to withdraw as a result of ligament damage. Rochdale capitalised midway through the second half scoring 2 quick goals, but with 11 minutes remaining Stockport pulled 1 back. There followed strenuous efforts for the equaliser, but shortly before the end Rochdale hit the visitors on the break to add their third.[80]

The match report in the *Athletic News* described the County's first half misfortunes in some detail.

> 'Stockport in the early stages deserved to score when F. Newton screwed the ball over the head of the goalkeeper into the vacant goal, but it came down slowly, and rebounded from the foot of the post. Butt later hit the top of the goal, and when the ball came down it appeared

> to be over the line, but the referee would not listen to Stockport's claim, and then when F. Newton headed past Lynch the official apparently ruled that the ball had crossed the line before it was centred. It was not Stockport's day by any means'.[81]

This unfortunate loss resulted in some dispirited local reportage.

> 'Stockport County's hopes of promotion this season were finally shattered at Rochdale a week ago, for now only a remarkable collapse on the part of Port Vale can give them the prize. Had this defeat come earlier there might have been some transfer business done at Stockport, but coming on the last day of the transfer rush [March 15, 1930] time was too short, even though the Hatters did telegraph their willingness to sell players to one or two interested clubs'.[82]

The mood did not improve the following Thursday when the County could only draw 1-1 with Doncaster Rovers on their Belle View ground. Despite going behind after just 10 minutes, Stockport fought hard and Frank levelled the score some 17 minutes later. In the second half, with the wind in their backs now, the County were expected to dominate proceedings. This they did, but the Rovers' defence excelled and withstood everything the visitors threw at them. The prospects of promotion were slipping away.[83] Before a small crowd of around 2,000, and with half a gale blowing the County were again considered unfortunate not to have taken both points. [84]

'Since their admission to the Third Division Doncaster Rovers had never gained a point from Stockport until yesterday, and then they were fortunate to do so, for Stockport were attacking for the greater part of the second half, after honours had become even at the interval. At times it was little short of miraculous that the Rovers' goal escaped. On one occasion Tate fell in attempting to save from Bott [Butt] and Newton (F) the Stockport centre-forward, had an open goal presented to him, but Scott got in the way of the ball in the nick of time. It was a poor game, good football being well nigh impossible owing to a blustering wind'.[85]

After this result Stockport were 4 points behind Port Vale and had played one more game. But it was not over for there was yet a further twist in this promotion battle. Consecutive Stockport victories over South Shields, 2-0, and Accrington Stanley, 1-0, raised temperatures once more around Edgeley Park, particularly as Port Vale, almost unbelievably, failed to take points from their matches with Darlington and Hartlepools. Thus by March 31, 1930 the promotion odds were once more finely balanced. Both teams had 53 points and identical goal differentials of plus 52; however, the County still had played one more game.

In their next fixture, against South Shields on March 22, the County started strongly in clear 'but cold weather'. The 'ground was on the soft side after last week's snow', but the County encountered little difficulty in registering a home victory. Frank scored a 'clever' goal in the 36th minute, 'this being followed almost immediately afterwards by a second from LINCOLN. The first goal was the result of a centre by Fielding from which Newton headed through. As soon as the game re-started Tompkinson passed to Newton who headed back to Lincoln for the latter to score from 15 yards range, Carr having no chance to save either of the shots'.[86]

'Thereafter the game went chiefly in Stockport's favour, and for considerable periods in the second half it degenerated into a bombardment of the visitors' goal; but the home forwards, excellent as their constructive methods were, showed [a] lack of efficiency in front of goal, and chance after chance went begging. Frank Newton worked hard throughout, though his marksmanship in the second half was not always above reproach'.[87]

The game against Accrington Stanley was played the following week, and the 'high and boisterous' wind made for a scrappy encounter. The teams were equally matched throughout the first half, but the County shaped better in the second, playing up the slope and with the wind behind them. The respective defences tended to dominate proceedings, but 22 minutes into the second half, Fielding was put through and scored while the Stanley defence looked on appealing for offside. However, to "Observer", not surprisingly, he appeared 'well onside'.[88]

After these games it was reported that:

'Things are getting so tense at Stockport that the big danger is that their players will not be able to do themselves justice in the very critical games that still have to be played ... The Hatters have thrust transfer business right out of their horizon now. They will consider no offers until they know their promotion fate'.[89]

The tension continued, particularly as Darlington, the conquerors of Port Vale two weeks previously, rolled into Edgeley Park on April 5. A crowd of over 10,500 looked on and most would have been highly delighted to witness a decisive 4-0 County victory.

> 'A little bad luck and a continuance of the poor finishing which has been a noticeable feature of the Stockport forward work recently kept their score down to one goal in the first half'.
> However, Stockport improved after the interval, dominated the midfield, and scored a further three.
> 'County's strength lay chiefly in defence, and the excellent constructive work of the halves had a lot to do with the teams' success. In the forward line Brown's individual work was outstanding ... and both the wingmen... played well. Neither F. Newton nor Lincoln was at his true form'.[90]

There now followed a memorable 1-0 victory, on April 12, at West Hartlepool that moved the County to the top of the Northern Division, one point ahead of Port Vale; however, they had played one game more. It was nail-biting stuff, and the County were now slightly favoured to win it all. Despite there being only the one goal in the Hartlepools match, Stockport were unquestionably the better side and evidently, with a little luck, could well have scored six. The County dominated throughout the ninety minutes, yet the encounter was one of hardest of the season. The half backs controlled the midfield and provided the platform for Stockport's 'splendid performance.'

> 'The only goal came within a minute of the interval, shortly after Jobson had struck the upright and F. Newton the crossbar. Brown received the ball from the centre forward and netted after skilfully working a shooting position. In the second half the County's superior attacking methods showed up well ... and the Hartlepools goal was often in danger. Rivers, the goalkeeper, made a brilliant save from a header by the County centre, and the latter had hard lines with a shot that was deflected over the bar by the foot of a defender. The forwards and halves had an excellent understanding and there was some clever combined play. The wingmen, Tompkinson and Fielding, were again in excellent form and Brown did well at inside right. Neither F. Newton nor Lincoln was at his best, though both had hard lines on a number of occasions'.[91]

The Easter programme followed, and on Good Friday the County got off to a disastrous start. The team travelled to New Brighton and went down 3-2, very much to the surprise and horror of the travelling support. New Brighton started brightly, and despite being a man short from the seventh minute, were 3-1 up at half time. Afterwards the 'Rakers', not surprisingly, played everyone behind the ball and invited the County to come on to them. This they did, but New Brighton marshalled a sound defence and Stockport were only able to score once, an excellent effort by Frank some 20 minutes into the half.[92]

The game was summed up in the *Liverpool Echo*:

> 'Yesterday at Rake-lane, before a record crowd for the season, they stopped Stockport County's progress, winning by 3 goals to 2. It was one of the hardest-fought games ever seen on the ground, and New Brighton won, despite an injury to Pither. It was not a fluke win, because in the first half New Brighton took their chances to get three goals to Stockport's one. Stockport easily took the honours of the second half, but were not able to beat a team which played a man short practically the whole of the game'.[93]

Now with just 3 games remaining and trailing Port Vale by 2 points, the visit of Doncaster Rovers was absolutely a 'must win' encounter if the County were to maintain even a remote chance of promotion. Stockport attacked from the outset and, despite the steady rain, after 17 minutes were rewarded when Frank buried a rebound off the crossbar. Increasingly, the County stretched the Doncaster defence, and the second goal resulted from a well worked move between the two wing-men. Fielding played the ball across the pitch to his opposite number, Tompkinson, whose centre found Frank, and 'with a well placed header' he beat Tate in the Doncaster goal. This, Frank's second goal, marked the County's 100th of the 1929-30 season.

Trailing 2-0, Doncaster went on the offensive at the start of the second half, but their revival was short lived when Frank, after 13 minutes, 'completed his hat trick with a brilliant goal.' It 'came from a centre by Fielding and was the result of a remarkably fine first-time drive' which he hit with 'terrific force.' The County maintained their dominance and at the final whistle were considered full value for their victory.[94]

Nevertheless, Port Vale offered the County no respite as the Hanley side maintained its winning ways and remained in pole position.

The County's next assignment was at Sincil Bank, on April 23, for their rearranged fixture against Lincoln City. And it was on this day that the County's promotion prospects were effectively torpedoed as they went down 1-0. The Division title was now Port Vale's to lose, since they led by 2 points, enjoyed a better goal average and held a game in hand over the County.

The tussle at Sincil Bank was an even contest, played in drizzling rain before about 5,000 spectators.[95] Both sides created good chances, and Lincoln City scored what proved to be the decisive goal 32 minutes into the game. It was considered that:

> 'Lincoln just about deserved the points. Stockport had opportunities in the second half to draw level, but their marksmanship was poor, and the side, taken man for man, could certainly claim no superiority over their hosts, whose football at times reached a high standard'.[96]

There followed a potentially difficult encounter at Chesterfield just three days later. To this point in the season, Chesterfield had dropped only 3 points at home and were 4th in the Northern Division. However, the County were into their stride quickly, played splendidly throughout and were full value for their 3-1 victory. The visitors were generally quicker on the ball, and the forwards were sharper and more penetrative than in their previous two games. Stockport's first goal was well contrived and came via Frank's head after only 7 minutes. The second quickly followed when Lincoln latched on to Frank's through ball and beat the goalkeeper from distance. On balance, the County had the better of the exchanges throughout the first half. Chesterfield rallied immediately after the break and pulled a goal back. But Stockport were not fazed, and 17 minutes later the matter was settled when Tomkinson scored the third.

> 'The County played a splendid open game and there was not a weak spot in the side. Frank Newton worked very hard at centre-forward and led the line splendidly. Both he and Lincoln had found their formality again, and were in thrustful [sic] mood'.[97]

As had been predicted, Stockport, despite losing to them on Good Friday, had no difficulty seeing off New Brighton in the last match of the season. Unfortunately, as was evident from the attendance of only 4,100, no promotion issue depended on the outcome. "Observer" commented that such a disappointingly small turn out was:

> 'a poor compliment to a team which has put up such a great fight for League honours. Despite an oppressive atmosphere and for the greater part of the afternoon, heavy rain, there was no end-of-the-season staleness about the game. It was fought at a fair pace though the

County's marked superiority, especially in the second half, robbed the contest of some interest. Stockport were the better side in every department'.[98]

After 18 minutes it was Frank who opened the scoring when he netted his 36th goal on only his 33rd appearance. The second was scored by Lincoln shortly afterwards. "Observer" concluded that the team had given an evenly sound display, and he nominated Frank and Fielding as the pick of the forwards.[99]

From the County's standpoint it was a most disappointing conclusion to a fine season. In the end it was Port Vale, the team that Stockport had twice defeated over the Christmas period, that gained promotion with a total of 67 points, having won 30 games and drawn 7. The Hanley side had scored 103 goals and conceded only 37. Comparatively, the County accumulated 63 points, from 28 wins and 7 draws, had scored 106 goals, at the time a record for Stockport, but had conceded 44. Frank was the team's leading scorer with a total of 36 league and 2 FA Cup goals. Lincoln followed with 25 and 2, while Tompkinson was next with 12 and 1. Nobody else registered in double figures.

There is no question that the management would have been desperately downhearted at the team's failure to gain promotion for the second year in succession, but a steadfast belief remained that:

> 'it is only a case of hope deferred. That the club intend to go on trying is evident from the retained list. Though there is a greater clearing out this time than there has been for several years past, only one member of the first

> team, Tompkinson, is not retained. Even allowing for any developments which may take place in the near future, there will be more than a nucleus of the senior eleven for the next season's campaign'.[100]

Not surprisingly Newton F. was again included on the retained list.[101] However, there were those who considered the Club's officials had contributed to the County's failure to once more gain promotion.

> 'Stockport County are becoming the Plymouth Argyle of the Northern Section in that they keep on filling the runners-up berth. The management cannot place its finger on the weakness though they may have contributed to their own undoing by ringing the changes with their forward talent so often. The selectors have never been afraid of dropping a player, but not every time have they found the right substitute'.[102]

Given Frank's great goal scoring abilities, it is surprising that he was dropped from the first team between January 4 and February 22, as over the 20 games played to that point he averaged a goal a game. However, the criticism for ringing the changes in the forward line, at least in Frank's case, seems a little harsh as the club gained a total of 10 points, from the 14 on offer, over the four away and three home fixtures in which he was not selected.

As mentioned previously, an important factor, and one which undoubtedly impeded the County's promotion efforts, was the state of the Edgeley Park pitch after rain. There were numerous references to its poor condition: 'a veritable quagmire'; 'been in a bad condition since the heavy rains began in November'; a 'morass-like-ground' and 'ankle deep mud and water'. In addition it was felt that the County often adopted the wrong tactics, or failed to adjust to the conditions underfoot. The team exhibited a preference to play a short passing game, and on numerous occasions were criticised for not adopting the kick and rush tactics often employed by their opponents. Certainly the inability to improvise adequately was a contributing factor in the club's promotion failure. "Busy Bee" made reference to this in August 1930 at the outset of the 1930-31 season. He noted that the Edgeley pitch was now in 'excellent condition, and the trouble caused by defective drainage' had been sorted out.[103] Or had it? As noted previously, in February 1931 he reported:

> 'The Shaw Heath end of the County ground is in a terrible state just now due to an unfortunate experiment in re-laying two or three seasons ago, for which the present ground staff are not responsible. To play classic football on such a ground is impossible for either attackers or defenders. These conditions favour big strongly-built players, and are a handicap to men of the type of Boardman, Brown [N], and Webster'.[104]

Frank Newton was undoubtedly one of these physical, 'strongly-built players', and perhaps he benefited from the heavy going, although not necessarily from the management's preference for a short passing style of play. He got off to a slow start at the beginning of the 1929-30 season and failed to score in the first three games. However, there then followed a truly purple patch during which he hit the back of the net sixteen times in eight games. Inevitably, he could not sustain this extraordinary rate, and as the rains increased from early November he scored only four times in the following nine matches, six of which were at home. Frank experienced a loss of form, and was possibly feeling the effects of playing on atrocious surfaces which would partially explain the reference to him dropping 'down with exhaustion'.

The fourth wettest November on record did not enhance attendances which in turn contributed to the financial pressures the club was facing. The tight promotion battle continued unabated and Frank unfortunately suffered a loss of form which prompted the management to drop him after the home defeat to Lincoln on January 1, 1930. Frank proceeded to play in the Reserve side, other than in the Cup tie at Blackpool, until he was recalled to first team duties on February 22, 1930. Initially his place was taken by Everest and then by the new signing from Liverpool, Marshall. Once recalled, Frank's spark returned and he scored sixteen times over the season's last fifteen games. He finished with 36 goals in the 35 league appearances, and 2 in 3 FA Cup matches.

Overall, Frank enjoyed another remarkably successful season. However, he did experience a loss of form which I believe resulted to a considerable extent from physical exhaustion. While Frank was often described as being forceful and physically robust, which he certainly was, I believe the often appalling playing surfaces exacted a toll on his stamina, in particular, playing on a sometimes almost subterranean Edgeley Park pitch. While Frank recovered his goal scoring touch after a spell in the less intense atmosphere of the Reserve side, a pattern of decline towards the end of stamina sapping seasons, can be observed in his goal scoring statistics of later years.

1930-31 Season

The disappointment of again failing to win promotion in the Spring of 1930 had dissipated by August, and a general air of optimism prevailed around Edgeley Park particularly as seven of the successful 1929-30 side remained under contract. However, "Busy Bee" was not one to get carried away. Stockport's

> 'unfortunate experience in the last three seasons, when they have narrowly missed gaining promotion, makes one reluctant to prophicay [sic] that they will gain promotion in the coming season. I fully believe the County will again be in the running'.[1]

The attendance was excellent at the first practice match despite many local residents being away enjoying their Wakes Week holidays. "Busy Bee" noted that 'general satisfaction was expressed at the form displayed.' He reviewed the players, both new and returning, and the positions they might take with either the first or reserve sides.

He mentioned also the pleasant day out Mr Lincoln Hyde, still the County's secretary-manager, the trainers, players and ground staff had spent in Blackpool. On the day they all piled into a 'motor saloon' kindly provided by Councillor George Worsley, one of the club's directors. But, from what followed, the County's season almost ended before it began!

'Whilst the County players were on a machine called the "Big Dipper" the driving chain broke and the machine suddenly stopped and began to run back. The players quickly jumped clear and so escaped any possibility of injury'.

Otherwise the day passed off without incident, thankfully, and all were safely back in Stockport around 10.30 p.m.[2]

"Busy Bee" was also on hand to report on the second practice game, watched by between 3,000 and 4,000 fans, which resulted in a 6-3 win for the 'Probables'.

'As a team the eleven worked very well together, and the new men gave an excellent display, particularly Simmons and Keating on the wings, and [R. W.] Mathews [sic] the centre half. Garner, the ex-Leicester City left back, partnered Bocking and shaped promisingly. In fact, though practice matches may not be taken as an accurate guide in form, the club seems to have solved its team-building problems exceedingly well'.[3]

Singing in the bath. Photo taken early in the 1930-31 season, almost certainly after one of the inter-squad games in August 1930.
From l to r: Garner, Jobson, Frank Newton, Billy Newton, D Matthews, Gowland and Bocking.

The assembled faithful would also have been encouraged to see Frank in 'sparkling form.' 'Five of the six goals registered by the 'Probables' were scored by him, and he was in his happiest vein, quick on the ball and showing his old qualities as an opportunist'.[4]

The 1930-31 season proper got underway on August 30 with a home fixture against the recently relegated Hull City. Neither Mr F. Wightman, trainer, nor his assistant, Harry Catterick, were reported as anticipating any problems in preparing their charges for the season's opener. In this they were not disappointed for the County tore into the previous year's FA Cup Semi-Finalists and were 3 goals up inside 20 minutes.

Frank opened his season strongly, resplendent in the club's new colours, white shirts and black shorts; he virtually stepped from the pages of 'Vogue' to score the second goal and set up the third for his inside left, Andy Lincoln. Hull rallied after the interval, but fell short losing 3-2.[5]

Two days later Stockport hosted New Brighton, before a crowd of almost 8,000, but despite winning 2-0, they were considered fortunate to take two 'hard earned points'.[6] Many felt that the 'Rakers' were hard done by when they had a goal disallowed in the first half. However, their fate was sealed, some 25 minutes after the interval, when Frank collected a through ball from Boardman. He swerved to his left and unleashed a Newton 'special' that had 'the custodian beaten to the world'.[7]

There followed away games at Lincoln and Carlisle which quickly destroyed any momentum that the team may have felt was building. These two games also demonstrated that Stockport had vulnerabilities that could be readily exploited. First, the County crashed 6-1 at Lincoln, the team's worst defeat in the 5 years since their return to the Northern Section.

> 'It was a severe and salutary experience, and coming at the beginning of the season should not be without its lessons. The game was not as one-sided as the score indicates. In the first half the County were the more aggressive side, and did not deserve to be two goals behind. There seemed every possibility that they would wipe out the arrears caused by the two lucky goals of the Imps ... but although the opportunities came the County forwards did not avail themselves of them'.

As a contest the game was over 17 minutes into the second half when Lincoln City scored their third. Frank reduced the arrears a minute later, but there was to be no fight back, and the Imps added 3 more as a 'result of the County's feeble display in the last twenty minutes.' Frank 'although not the worst of the County players, has played better on many occasions'.[8] Elsewhere it was mentioned that Newton 'missed a great opportunity at point-blank range. He sacrificed direction for pace when a goal for his side would have halved the deficit'.[9]

There was a view that the score line flattered the 'Imps', although it was their dominance of the midfield that ultimately made the difference.

> 'Lincoln City were not so superior in their match with Stockport County as the 6-1 score indicates, but they did make better use of their opportunities. Early on the bustling tactics of the home forwards upset the visitors, who never seemed to recover an effective combination.

> Lincoln owed much of their success to their half backs ... In the second half they dominated the game'.[10]

Little improvement was evident 5 days later, on Thursday, September 11, when Stockport delighted the Carlisle crowd by conceding five times at Brunton Park. The report in the *Stockport Advertiser* understandably passed quickly over the proceedings proper, and was comprised of little more than a listing of the Carlisle goal scorers.[11]

But there were also dismissive reports:

> 'Stockport County ... had a rude shock at Carlisle last night, being beaten 5-1. Carlisle were superior throughout, and fully deserved the win'.[12]
>
> 'Stockport County are not the formidable side that many people might suppose. They are hefty, but much below the form displayed by the players who represented this ambitious club last season. Their attack is less than methodical'.[13]

The relief at returning to Edgeley Park for a match with Hartlepools United, on September 13, must almost have been palpable. And predictably, following two heavy defeats Lincoln Hyde made numerous changes to the County's line up:

> 'the inclusion of Brown [N.] and Webster on the left wing, made for improvement. Eddie Vincent, in place of Mathews [sic] at centre-half, was not so successful, and never touched his real form. Cyril Mathews [sic], the ex-Notts County player, made his first home appearance,

and in the opening stages shaped particularly well, though he fell away later'.

The recent defeats combined with the inclement weather resulted in just over 6,000 spectators passing through the turnstiles. Such a poor turnout was considered unfortunate as certain of the associated glitterati, namely the Chief Magistrate, Alderman G.E. Hope JP, Mayor of West Hartlepool, and the Mayor of Stockport, Mr Joshua Preston JP attended. Fittingly, 'prior to the kick-off the players lined-up on the field and were duly "presented" in the Wembley fashion, this little ceremony being heartily acclaimed by the onlookers'.[14]

It was Alderman Hope who was responsible for the gathering as he had advised Mayor Preston that he would be accompanying the Hartlepools side to Edgeley Park. Such was his largesse, and perhaps sensing it to be an opportune time to inflict a further defeat on the 'Hatters', he invited Mayor Preston to join him for a luncheon at the White Lion Hotel. And then, after what he probably anticipated would be a jolly repast, to accompany him to the game.[15]

After the introductions, the action 'fluctuated from end to end' throughout a first half played in steady rain, and at the interval Stockport led 2-0. Unfortunately, the downpour intensified during the break, and

> 'a rush was made by spectators on the popular side to get under cover. The "men in blue" did their best to stem the invasion, but were clearly outnumbered, and to the general amusement some hundreds succeeded in reaching "port" on the stand'.

The second half remained scoreless until the visitors converted a hotly disputed penalty, 2 minutes from full time, which of course produced much 'music' from the home crowd. However, their 'indignation was mollified' a minute later when Frank was on hand to head a 'brilliant' third goal, and preserve the spoils.[16]

"Busy Bee" summarised the proceedings.

> 'The County showed a great improvement in their team spirit. The players pulled together, showed delightful combination at times, and were full value for their victory. Their superiority was even more pronounced than the score would indicate, and in view of the defeats at Lincoln and Carlisle and the drastic changes in the team, it would be unfair to apply a very critical standard to this match. The team was not as good as it will be when the promoted players settle down to the conditions of Northern Section football'.

In addition "Busy Bee" nominated Frank as one of the outstanding Stockport players. In his view Frank had worked hard, 'and if he had been better supported would have got a bag of goals.'

At this early stage in the season, the Northern Section standings showed 7 teams grouped at the top, Lincoln City with 10 points and Stockport in seventh with 8.[17]

Two days later Stockport entertained Carlisle United, in the early evening of the Monday just 2 days after Carlisle had defeated them at Brunton Park. Despite it being the County's third game in 5 days, the team displayed their best form of the season, and won 3-0 before a crowd of over 5,000. The first half was played at a hectic pace and, despite missing a penalty, the County scored twice within 5 minutes, through Matthews and Frank, to lead 2-0 at the break. Then shortly after the restart Frank struck again for Stockport's third. Overall it was considered a 'keenly contested' match in which the changes

> 'in the home side worked to advantage. F. Newton was a forceful leader, and with a little luck would have registered a "hat-trick", several shots late in the game missing the mark by inches'.

There was perhaps some justice in the fact he did not as Kelly, the Carlisle goalkeeper, had to retire 10 minutes from time as the result of a "violent collision" with none other than Frank![18]

"Busy Bee" reported that the game was:

> 'full of thrills. The County from the start gave one quite a different impression than they did in the Hartlepools match, when there were several obvious weaknesses, and the team, although showing neat combination at times did not appear strong enough to gain promotion. Monday's team had all the stamp of a promotion side, in spite of one or two minor failings ... I am satisfied that the County have now got the team that will do justice to the club, and there will not be any need for further drastic changes'.[19]

On the Saturday following, September 20, the County travelled to Springfield Park for their fixture with Wigan

Borough. Unfortunately the team were unable to repeat the form displayed in the return fixture with Carlisle, and went down 2-1. 'To Wigan Borough's credit they fairly and squarely beat Stockport County, and thus checked the latter's promotion struggle'.[20]

There was only a marginal improvement when the "Hatters" returned to Edgeley Park to take on the lowly ranked Nelson side. "A. W." reported on that game in the *Stockport Express*.

> 'Although the afternoon turned out fine there was only a moderate attendance ... and the fare served up did not prove particularly exhilarating ... With the benefit of the wind in the first-half the homesters had the balance of midfield play, but their attempts at scoring were not very convincing, and the Nelson defence was rarely extended. Many corners were conceded, ... but there was a noticeable lack of punch near goal, and with the exception of one or two drives by F. Newton, Shelvin was not unduly troubled. With the exception of the occasional back-pass, ... we do not recall the home goal-keeper having anything to do in this half, ... The standard of play never rose above mediocrity, and it was a fitting conclusion to a scrappy first-half when the interval arrived with a blank score-sheet'.

With some 15 minutes remaining when 'all hopes of a score were beginning to vanish', Frank travelling at speed, ran on to a perfect cross from Webster and provided 'about the only redeeming feature of the match.' However, during the last minute of play:

'in a desperate attempt to add to the score, Frank Newton came into violent contact with Shelvin, being "laid out". The "goalie" was able to resume after attention, but Newton was taken over the touch-line and eventually carried from the field by colleagues and ambulance men. It was an unfortunate finish to one of the poorest displays seen at Edgeley Park for a long time. Nelson are not a good side, but on Saturday the County were very little better, and it was the generally expressed opinion that the eleven as at present constituted will not cut much ice'.[21]

There followed a game at Darlington's Feethams enclosure from which Stockport, ably assisted by a fit again Frank, gained their first away points of the season. Darlington were expected to win, but the County's defence were deserving of credit, although '… (a good left back would still be welcomed) …' Stockport took the lead after 20 minutes when Frank fired home a rebound that Holdcroft in the Darlington net failed to hold. Darlington equalised early in the second half, after which 'the concluding stages were warmly contested, and only some seven minutes remained when Frank Newton came along with a second goal from a pass from Lincoln.' In the final minutes Darlington pressed forward desperately and were awarded a penalty. But after the shot whistled wide of the Stockport goal a relieved County escaped with both points.[22] Frank's contribution was mentioned in the *Athletic News*:

'Frank Newton was the driving force in the Stockport attack, and he was always a great danger in the vicinity of goal. He combined well with his wing men, and got an excellent response'.[23]

Halifax Town were next up at Edgeley Park and succumbed 3-0, or as the local press described it: 'AN EASY VICTORY'. "A. W." reported on events in the *Stockport Express.*

> 'Despite fine weather conditions [for the opening at any rate] there was a very moderate attendance to welcome Halifax Town ... and one wonders whether the industrial condition is wholly responsible for the decline in "gates" so apparent this season. Complaint is made that obvious weaknesses in the side have not been remedied and certainly the eleven compares unfavourably with the one which made such a gallant bid for promotion last season. Prior to the kick-off there was a most impressive little ceremony in memory of the unfortunate victims of the R 101. The club's flag was flown at half-mast, and before the players appeared the band rendered the well-known hymn-tune "Rimington." After the captains had tossed for choice of ends the players took up positions on the field, accompanied by His Worship the Mayor [Joshua Preston, Esq. JP], The County Directors [the football club's directors], and officials of the Halifax club. With the club upstanding and heads uncovered, two verses of "Abide with me" were played. Then followed two minutes' silence, at the expiration of which a verse of the National Anthem concluded a scene the like of which has never before been witnessed at Edgeley Park, and one which will have a lasting impression on all who witnessed it'.

The R 101 was the airship that crashed in Beauvais, France on October 5, 1930, with the loss of 48 lives.

In the game itself Stockport pressed from the outset and led 2-0 at the break. Frank was fortunate to score the second goal for when he was tackled he could only push the ball forward 'at no great speed. Many were under the impression' that it was going wide. This apparently included Bilcliffe, in the Halifax goal, who made no attempt to stop the ball as it swerved slowly into the net. A third goal was added by Andy Lincoln early in the second half, and Stockport went on to what was a routine 3-0 win.[24]

Although the County were not playing particularly well, they travelled on October 18 to York City's Fulfordgate ground, having won 3 games on the bounce. It was reported that the team performed excellently in handing York their first home defeat of the season. Frank struck early when he converted Webster's accurate cross from the left wing. This aroused the "Citizens" and by the interval the scores were level. By all accounts the second half was fiercely contested as both sides strove manfully, in difficult conditions, for a winner. The excitement mounted, and 15 minutes from time Boardman netted to give Stockport the narrowest of victories.[25]

A balanced account of the match appeared in the *Yorkshire Post & Leeds Intelligencer*.

> 'Falling away considerably in the second half of the match at York, the City were deservedly beaten by Stockport County, the visitors securing the odd goal of three before 6,000 spectators. York more than held their own to begin with and were unfortunate when, after seven minutes, a defensive error enabled F. Newton to give the visitors

> the lead. Subsequently the game was played at an exceptionally fast pace the City doing most of the attacking, and they reaped [their] reward just on the interval, ... On resuming, however, Stockport were well on top, and they well deserved the winning goal scored by Boardman midway through the period. Considering the high wind which prevailed, the players on both sides gave a good exhibition of football'.[26]

The visit of Tranmere Rovers was now eagerly anticipated as the Rovers had been in 'exceptionally fine form' and included 'several "lights of other days" – Meston (Southampton and Everton), Kennedy and Livingstone (Everton) and Shears (Liverpool) ...' Consequently, a large crowd was anticipated.[27] The match, played on October 25, attracted just over 8,400, one of the better attended games to that point in the season. The sides were evenly matched and play fluctuated rapidly from end to end. The County went ahead through Frank after 21 minutes, a lead they held until 'extra time' when J. Kennedy, Rovers' inside left, tied it up. "A. W." was less than happy with the County's performance.

> 'Although perhaps fortunate to equalise so near the end, and against a disabled goalkeeper, there can be no denying that the play of the visitors was well worth the point obtained. As a combination the Rovers were ahead of the homesters, whose front-line continues to present a most lopsided appearance. Webster was clever and forceful, and Newton with limited opportunities did as well as could be expected, but the other positions were far from

satisfactory, and until there is improvement here we are afraid promotion hopes cannot be entertained'.[28]

After this result Stockport remained 5th in the Division with 18 points. Ahead of them were Lincoln City with 21, Tranmere on 20, followed by Wrexham and Chesterfield with 19. All teams had played 13 games.[29]

Frank Newton, by the beginning of November had netted 12 times in 12 matches. Then came a game at Chesterfield played in appalling weather, poor light accompanied by heavy rain, and neither side was able to score in the first half. The players turned around without a half time break as the referee did not want to lose the light, and within 5 minutes Stockport took the lead when Frank converted a penalty. The award arose when Chesterfield's left back, Schofield, punched a shot from Frank over the bar.

Shortly thereafter Frank fell heavily and broke his collar bone. He was compelled to retire for a time through injury, and after he resumed Matthews, Stockport's right wing, was off for a brief period. Then for the second time in two weeks the County conceded a late goal, and the game finished 1-1. The vast majority of the 7,512 in attendance was jubilant as Chesterfield had retained their unbeaten home record.[30] Despite his injury, Frank and his namesake William, were named as 'star performers'.[31] Not so good for the County was Frank's broken collar bone, as it kept him *hors de combat* for three weeks, until the home game against Accrington Stanley on November 22.[32]

On that day the ground was sodden, the weather stormy and a disappointingly small crowd which, 'at a generous estimate', did not exceed 4,000. The Accrington goalkeeper Langdale, formerly with Millwall, made his goalkeeping debut and excelled throughout the first half as Stockport applied almost unrelenting pressure. He pulled off a series of good saves and aroused the crowd by saving a header from Frank 'in wonderful style.' A good indication of the County's dominance was the number of corners awarded, 16 in total, of which 13 went to Stockport. Accrington, despite taking the lead very much against the run of play, were justifiably 2-1 behind at the break. Frank scored the first from the penalty spot and Jobson, at centre half, rose to a corner to put the County ahead. The second half was something of a repetition as the County scored twice more. Of these the first arrived after 15 minutes when Frank netted his second. Then, with just 3 minutes remaining Webster knocked in the rebound after Lansdale failed to deal with a 'red hot special' from Frank.[33]

The first round of the FA Cup now followed and the County were drawn against Hartlepools at Victoria Park. The game was played on November 29 and resulted in a 3-2 win for Stockport after what was described as a 'severe struggle'.

> 'The game aroused tremendous enthusiasm at the shipping port, and at one point, when the home team were exercising strong pressure a portion of the supporting rails gave way and precipitated a number of spectators on to the playing surface'.

Despite this distraction and with 'a gusty wind in their favour', the County set the pace and goals by Frank and Lincoln gave them a serviceable 2-0 lead at half time. Hartlepools improved thereafter and outscored Stockport 2-1. With the score at 3-2, 'excitement reached fever heat' as the hosts made a 'gallant attempt' to equalise. But the County defence remained unyielding and the club progressed to the second round, a tricky away encounter with Bristol Rovers to be played on December 13.[34]

Conditions for the visit of Crewe Alexandra, on December 6, were similar to those encountered at Chesterfield, namely poor light, and fog hanging over the ground. This was unfortunate as only some 8,000 were on hand to witness a game that, under normal conditions, should have attracted one of the largest gates of the season. Nevertheless, Stockport started brightly, and within 10 minutes were a goal up when Webster met a cross from Frank and drove 'the ball home in great style.'

The County, however, despite dominating throughout the balance of the half, failed to increase the margin.

> 'The visiting defence was very effective, if over-vigorous at times. Frank Newton and Lincoln "both being in the wars," the centre forward particularly coming in for some rough treatment, which materially affected his game. Mr Ryecroft [the referee] warned more than one offender, but this had little effect, and many felt that sterner measures should have been adopted'.

Because of the failing light Ryecroft turned the teams straight around at half time, and after 22 minutes Webster created an opening and put Frank through to score a 'characteristic goal.' The game continued in a robust vein, but there was no further scoring. The match, a 2-0 triumph, was completed in semi darkness with the County, very much the superior side, still on the attack.[35]

These represented two vital points for Stockport which kept them in close touch with the leaders of the Northern Division. The side retained its position in second place only 2 points behind Lincoln City, with all the top 7 teams having played 17 games.[36]

The week following was spent in preparation for the upcoming Cup tie with Bristol Rovers on their Eastville ground, located next to the local gas works. For this reason the club was nick-named 'The Gas'; however, others preferred 'The Pirates'. On match day, December 13, the pitch was greasy and the going heavy after morning rain. But the locals were not to be denied by the weather, and over 16,000 spectators witnessed 'the most well contested cup-tie seen in Bristol for some seasons.'

A "Bristol Correspondent" reported in the *Stockport Express* that had the County taken their chances they would have at least forced a re-play.

> 'The best of the County was seen in the early stages of each half. At the start of the game they opened up play with long swinging passes and for a quarter of an hour were definitely the better side. Frank Newton, during these stages, failed by inches with a flashing shot and had fortune favoured that effort the game might have pursued a very different course. For a time during the second half, the County similarly dominated play, but the superiority they established during these periods was not maintained'.

Having absorbed the initial pressure, Bristol went ahead

after 20 minutes. Stockport then scored a cleverly worked goal through Lincoln, but the Rovers struck back within 2 minutes. Thereafter excitement levels increased, and the game 'became fast and furious when Frank broke clear with a characteristic burst and again equalised with a gloriously placed long shot, this being the best goal of the match.' Wretchedly for the County, Bristol's celebrated inside left Ronald Dix notched his third of the game just before the interval. Nonetheless, at half time the game hung in the balance. Upon resuming, the County came out 'with such dash and vim that an equaliser looked certain.' Matthews thought he had done just that when 'the ball looked to have definitely crossed the home goal-line', but the referee was not convinced. Then, after Frank unfortunately had 'miskicked in the mud' with the goal literally 'yawning', Stockport conceded once more and the game was effectively over.[37]

"Busy Bee" provided a somewhat different perspective in the *Stockport Advertiser*. While it was generally agreed that the County played one of the better, if not the best, games to be seen at Eastville to that point in the season, he thought that 'Bristol's second goal was the only one they really deserved'. The first should not have been allowed because 'Attwood handled the ball, and the County players stopped playing under the impression that the referee had awarded a free kick,' The third resulted from a defensive 'mix up', and the fourth from a corner 'which never ought to have been given …'. Nonetheless, Stockport's hopes of a lucrative run in the Cup were over, but in no way had they been outplayed.[38]

The Cup match meant that the league game, originally scheduled for December 13 against Wrexham, had to be rearranged and was played the following Wednesday. This encounter was effectively a 'four pointer' as Wrexham were just 2 points behind the County after 17 matches. The contestants met on Wrexham's Racecourse ground and were watched by a crowd of some 4,000, a reasonable turn out on a Wednesday afternoon.

In the first half the game was conducted at an electric pace, during which Wrexham defended resolutely while remaining dangerous on the break. Overall the County had 'slightly the better of the exchanges', and their half backs dominated the midfield until Vincent at left back was injured. He was dispatched, limping badly, to the left wing where he was judged to be of 'no use to his side.' Nevertheless, five minutes before the interval Stockport got their noses in front when Frank fired home from close range.

The County's lead, however, was short lived as just three minutes after the restart Wrexham levelled. The ensuing action remained intense as Stockport continued to press despite being effectively a man short. Their reward came on the hour when 'a brilliant movement … ended in Frank Newton passing to Webster, who found the net with a delightful shot'. Unfortunately, Wrexham then proceeded to score two more goals, and the County, failing to respond, finished losing 4-2.

The report in the *Sheffield Daily Independent* merely recounted that the longer the game went on the better Wrexham played. After twice levelling the score, 'the visiting defenders … could not withstand the pace and cleverness of the opposing forwards.' There was no mention of the County being short handed.[39] Whereas "Busy Bee" considered that Stockport had 'fought a plucky game' and lost primarily because the side had been reduced to 10 men.

After 18 games the County were 5th in the Northern Section, only three points behind the leaders Lincoln City; sandwiched between them were Tranmere, Chesterfield and Wrexham.[40]

The home game against Rotherham, on December 20, marked the beginning of a crowded Christmas programme over which the County were scheduled to play 5 games in just 11 days. The weather in Stockport for the first was poor, mist combined with a drizzling rain. The playing surface was heavy and not conducive to fast, open football. The County pressed from the start, but against the run of play Rotherham went ahead after 10 minutes. Stockport responded 8 minutes later when Matthews crossed, and Frank took the ball 'with his back to goal, swung round, and with a lightning drive fairly shook the rigging, the ball striking the back of the net and rebounding in the field of play.' Matthews then put the County ahead, on the half hour, and the score remained 2-1 at the break.

The second half was evenly contested, and within 10 minutes Rotherham equalised. However, the County and Matthews were not to be denied and he scored his second of the afternoon shortly thereafter. Then play

> 'swung from end to end until the closing quarter, when the County gradually assumed the mastery, and after 40 minutes Boardman was working through ... when he was palpably fouled in the "area" ... A penalty was at once signalled, and Frank Newton made no mistake with the "spot-kick" ... the homesters continued on the attack, and three minutes from the end Lincoln completed the

"nap" hand following a corner'.[41]

The crowded Christmas schedule was off to a fine start. The home game on Christmas Day 1930, against Gateshead, kicked off at 11.00 a.m. before a crowd of almost 10,700. The playing surface was again heavy 'and cut up badly during the game'. Proceedings opened in a 'spirited style', but after 25 minutes Stockport yet again surrendered the opening goal.

> 'This reverse gingered-up the home side, and six minutes later Frank Newton literally threw himself at a centre from Webster, the ball striking him in the face and flashing in the net to the evident astonishment of Crowther and the huge delight of the crowd, who were immensely tickled at the scorer's facial adornment'.

The teams turned around with the score tied which was judged to be a fair reflection to that point. Early in the second half the County were briefly reduced to 10 men when Helliwell, centre half, had to retire for repairs. Although he returned he was no more than a 'passenger' for the balance of the game.

> 'Despite their handicap the County were on top for the major portion of this half, and at the end of a quarter-of-an-hour Frank Newton headed through from a pass by Lincoln, and gave his side the lead. Matthews entertained the onlookers with some tricky wing play, and Boardman lent him valuable assistance, whilst Newton was ever on the look-out for a dash through, and just over the

half-hour he cleverly took a pass from Boardman and left the goalie powerless with a fierce cross-shot, the accomplishment of the "hat-trick" being loudly acclaimed'.

But Frank was not finished with Crowther, and towards the end of the game he spectacularly fired in one of his acclaimed 'specials' which Crowther 'caught, threw away, and then fell like a log, the force of the shot completely knocking him out for a time'.[42]

The County team then spent most of what remained of Christmas Day travelling to Newcastle where the team stayed overnight for the return fixture with Gateshead. The following morning, no doubt much to relief of all, not just Crowther, a pitch inspection was required as 6" of snow had fallen on Newcastle during the early morning. Not surprisingly, it resulted in the Redhough Park ground being declared unfit. The referee, Mr I. Caswell of Blackburn, phoned the news through to the visitors at 11.30 a.m. Whereupon the County team bus was turned around and set out for Hull.[43]

This situation prompted a well judged complaint. It was pointed out that a weary Stockport side had arrived in Newcastle in the early hours of Boxing Day morning to play their second match in two days, only then to have to travel to Hull to take on 'The Tigers' on December 27! It was also mentioned, most justifiably, that to play 'three games in three days, on heavy grounds, is a big strain'.[44] Nonetheless, because of the extensive road trip, the County players must have been mightily relieved to have the one game postponed.

At this the mid point of the season, Stockport remained undefeated at home, and were in fourth spot, on goal average, in the Northern Division with 29 points. Ahead of them were Lincoln City on 33 points, Tranmere Rovers 32, and Chesterfield 29. Both Lincoln and Stockport had played 21 games, one less than Tranmere and Chesterfield.[45]For his part, Frank maintained his deadly goal scoring touch, and had made an enormous contribution to the side having scored 22 of the team's 47 goals in the 18 games in which he had participated. In addition, he had notched a further 3 in the two FA Cup matches.[46]

The second half of the County's season opened at Anlaby Road, Hull on December 27, 1930. Hull were in fine form as they had just thrashed Halifax Town 10-0 at home, on Boxing Day after drawing 1-1 at The Shay the previous afternoon. The conditions underfoot at Anlaby Road were atrocious; the ground:

> 'was a sea of thick, slimy mud, which had all the adhesive qualities of strong glue. It was early evident that the team possessed of the greater stamina would be the winners. Stockport proved to be that team and would, I think, have won with ease had they finished the game with eleven men'.

This match was Hull's third outing in three days and by then the well travelled County's second, so perhaps it was predictable that, despite being a robust game, it ended 1-1 on an energy sapping surface. It was also an ill tempered encounter that did not improve when Stockport's right half, Albert Lambourne, was ejected for allegedly having struck Walsh, the former Stockport player but now the Hull City captain. But as the reporter for the *Stockport Express* diplomatically pointed out, since 'the matter is now sub-judice, the less said the better, but to my mind the punishment was too harsh.' However, the match was overseen by the capable and highly regarded Mr J.O. Rickwood of Sheffield, which was probably just as well as otherwise there could well have been 'serious trouble and many injuries.' The Hull City goal was not commented upon, but the County's was detailed.

> 'The forwards played with commendable skill on the treacherous ground, and Matthews' goal was the result of a cleverly conceived movement. The ball was put across from the left, and Frank Newton, who was marked, let it pass through his legs to Matthews. The outside-right quickly seized his opportunity, and gave Gibson no chance with a fine oblique drive from the fringe of the penalty area'.

Frank's significant contribution to the team over the season was also mentioned and perhaps hinted of things to come.

> 'Frank Newton, who has scored 22 goals in 19 league games [including this game], failed to find the net in this match, thus recording his first miss for 14 weeks. He has done wonderfully well and with a little luck should realise him [sic] ambition of 50 goals this season. I know that a number of First Division clubs are anxious to secure his services, but if the County get adequate "gates" they are not likely to part with the Romiley player'.[47]

The abysmal condition of the playing surface and the resulting effects on the players' performances were well described in the *Athletic News*.

> 'On a surface of thick slush and water Hull and Stockport had an unenviable experience, and for their heroism alone it was right that each should take a League point. Stockport were far better endowed physically for such a trying ordeal, and it was due to this that they were able to force a draw eight minutes from time when Hull's stamina had completely given out. Anything approaching accuracy was always at a discount, and positions were won and lost through sheer luck alone throughout the game. So helpless were the respective forward lines that neither Gowland nor Gibson was given a single serious shot to handle, and occasionally Frank Newton and Raleigh cleared all opposition without being able to propel the ball with sufficient power for it to reach goal, where usually the goalkeeper stood engulfed in mud. Each side's single success was due to chance pure and simple and to the inability of the defenders to remain upright'.[48]

The reporter in the *Yorkshire Post* was far more succinct in his assessment of what the crowd of 10,000 did, or did not see. 'Of real football none whatever was witnessed.' Nonetheless, the gate receipts of £575 would have been most welcome.[49]

The County opened their 1931 schedule on New Year's Day with a 2-0 victory at Rake Lane. There was some discussion in the local press as to whether Stockport rode their luck, but the correspondent in the *Stockport Express* was adamant, '... the County were infinitely the superior team, and the score by no means misrepresented their superiority.' The County pressed from the start and were deservedly 2 goals up at half time. And by the end of the game, 'with Stockport playing down the slope, 'The Rakers' were a well beaten side'.[50]

The view in the *Yorkshire Post* concurred with the assessment that the County 'gained a deserving victory.' It was also mentioned that this was the second consecutive game in which Frank had failed to score. Perhaps a concern, particularly as the faithful were beginning to believe that Stockport could win the Northern Division, if the side could 'maintain their away form'.[51]

An important test followed just 2 days later as Stockport entertained the Division leading Lincoln City. Clearly, the outcome was critical.

> 'A fine afternoon, a record crowd for the season, and a victory of 4 goals to 2 over the leaders of the competition should prove a stimulus to the Edgeley Park players and officials in their gallant race in the promotion stakes. With their splendid record, and also remembering the 6-1 defeat inflicted on the County at Sincil Bank in September last, the visit of the "Imps" had been keenly awaited, and we think it will be generally agreed that a more pulsating struggle has not been witnessed at Edgeley this season'.

Immediately from the kick off the County went on the attack, and with the forwards combining admirably they were a goal to the good after only 4 minutes.

> 'Frank Newton sent the crowd wild with delight by scoring one of the finest goals ever seen at Edgeley. Taking up a pass from his namesake he was immediately challenged by a defender who forces him over to the right, but retaining possession the County centre ran on and from a most acute angle the leather was flashed in the roof of the net like an arrow from a bow'.

This early success unsettled the 'Imps', but they recovered their composure until they conceded a penalty, on the half hour, which Frank converted to put the County two up. The situation improved further, from the host's point of view, as Frank then set up Webster for Stockport's third. The County were bossing the game, and 2 minutes after the interval Frank completed his hat-trick. He again muscled 'his way through, and though harassed by three opponents he managed to steer the ball just inside the post.'

The crowd were now in full cry and baying for more. But it was Lincoln City that rallied and with 30 minutes remaining were awarded a penalty. The decision was hotly disputed but Mr Bristow of Stafford was not to be swayed and Lincoln opened their account. This roused the visitors and within 10 minutes they had added a second. The League leaders now gave sound 'evidence of their prowess by capital mid-field work, and with a real sharp-shooter in their ranks would have caused trouble.' The Stockport defence then doubled down and there was no further scoring. After an enthralling game, and such an excellent result, the home support was in generous mood and appropriately, 'both sides were loudly cheered for their capital display.'

"A. W." viewed it 'a game well worthy of rivals for championship honours.' He felt that Lincoln:

> 'proved themselves a fine well balanced side, their chief failing being the poor finishing of their forwards. And what of the County? They are fortunate in possessing a clever opportunist in Frank Newton. He may have his limitations as a constructive player, but regarding his value as a deadly shot there can be little question. His opening goal in the game will go down in the annals of the club of [sic] the finest ever, and its effects on the team went a long way to the winning of the match. It was a memorable game, in which that first-four-minutes' goal of Frank Newton's will be talked about for many a day'.[52]

Most importantly the win moved Stockport into 3rd place in the League, just 2 points behind Lincoln City with a game in hand over Chesterfield. For Frank, his 3 goals had increased his tally to 25 in just 21 games.[53]

After this exhilarating win it was almost inevitable that the trip to Rochdale on January 10 would prove anti climatic. And so it was; the County had left their 'A' game at Edgeley Park and came out 'flat', lacking both vitality and determination, and proceeded to lose 1-0.

Unfortunately, the weather was miserable and this severely reduced the attendance to a meagre 2,000 for what was anticipated as being one of Rochdale's most attractive home fixtures. In the most trying conditions the sides made a valiant effort, but it was 'a wonder that the game was played.'

> 'Stockport were unfortunate to drop two points at Spotland. They had quite as much of the play as Rochdale. Though the light was fairly good half an hour before the start, fog enshrouded the ground when the players turned out. The teams were not allowed the customary interval, and the light had become bad again long before the end. Three minutes before the end the visitors lost the match in remarkable fashion. Rochdale forced a corner, and Tippett sent the ball in from the kick. In the gloom it appeared as though Gowland deflected the ball into his own goal'.[54]

However, results improved over the next 2 weeks as Stockport first beat Hartlepools United 2-1, on their Victoria Park ground, and the following week, at Edegely, disposed of Wigan Borough more easily 4-1.

The correspondent for the *Stockport Express* wrote:

> 'Hartlepools United have only once beaten Stockport County – that was in 1927. Last Saturday they came very near to achieving their second success over the Cestrians. They were really unfortunate not to do so, and yet the County were the superior side and were worthy of their victory. That statement may seem something of an Irishism, and yet it is only a statement of fact! In the first half the County were facing a boisterous and bitterly cold North-East wind, and in consequence Hartlepools enjoyed the better of the exchanges'.

Initially, Gowland in the County goal was in exceptionally good form, and it was thanks to him and his full backs, Bocking and Beedles, that the County were able to get to the interval on level terms. At the start of the second half Hartlepools found that 'they had indeed been but "dressed in a little brief authority", [and] their defence had an extremely uncomfortable ten minutes.'

Unfortunately for Stockport, Gowland had been kicked in the head prior to the interval, and although he remained in goal he was 'subject to fits of diziness [sic], and at times was unable to see.' Unquestionably a serious handicap, and on this occasion when Hartlepools swung a free kick into the Stockport goalmouth:

> 'Gowland ran out and completely missed the ball, in fact he was no where near it, and Thayne had a simple task to head into the empty net. The custodian told me after the game that he had no idea where the ball was, and only ran out in the futile hope that it might come to him'.

The Stockport goal had a further narrow escape when Beedles, the left back, had to clear off the line after the by now myopic Gowland completely missed a shot. Fortunately the County were well on top 'or there is no telling what may have happened.'

Frank was not 'in deadly shooting form but he opened the game out with … excellent passes.' The 2 goals came from Webster and Lincoln, but on reflection the County must have considered themselves extremely fortunate to have escaped with the win, particularly as their goalkeeper was clearly concussed for over half the game![55]

There followed a more straight forward 4-1 victory, at home, against Wigan Borough, on January 24. Playing yet again on heavy ground, but with the wind in their backs, Stockport went a goal up after 5 minutes when Andy Lincoln netted. As the game progressed certain of the Borough men were:

> 'not over-scrupulous in their methods, free-kicks being rather frequent and it was such a concession that paved the way for the County's second goal. From a few yards inside the Wigan half, the ball was placed straight for home, and just as Mittel was preparing to fist away Newton's head bobbed up and the leather was in the net – fine anticipation on the part of the home centre-forward'.

A third goal was scored just 5 minutes before the interval when Matthews struck a 'remarkable' shot from an acute angle. It was also mentioned that Frank was brought down inside the penalty area, but the resulting appeals were waved away by referee Millward; however, Frank remained pole-axed and required attention before resuming.

In the second half Wigan heads went down, play deteriorated and the visitors seldom challenged 'the issue seriously.' The score did not change until 15 minutes from time when

> 'little Webster, who was too fast for the opposition, got clear on the wing and put across in perfect style for Frank Newton to head just inside the far post, a joint-success which was duly appreciated by their colleagues'.

Although Wigan scored a late consolation goal, they were effectively a well beaten side prior to the interval.[56] Frank's goals, numbers 26 and 27, had been struck in his 24th league appearance. These were truly exceptional figures.

There followed an unsatisfactory 1-1 draw at Nelson in which Frank did not participate because of the injury sustained against Wigan. For Frank this must have been a disappointment as it denied him the opportunity of increasing his goal tally at the expense of a poor Nelson side, lodged in the Division basement, with just 13 points from 26 games. However, travelling conditions were truly appalling and his regrets may well have been tempered. The County set off in a snow storm, and the drifts 'beyond Bury were fairly deep.' A sympathetic note was struck by "Busy Bee" as he considered the whole experience to be very trying for the players who 'suffered acutely from the extreme cold, and it was a marvel to me that they were able to stick it to the end.' Despite the conditions the game went ahead and by the final whistle it was estimated that no less than 4 inches of snow had accumulated on the pitch.[57]

At the beginning of February the County were lying 3rd in the Division, 4 points behind Lincoln City and 1 back of Chesterfield over whom Stockport still had a game in hand.[58]

Although Frank missed the Nelson game, he was declared fit to turn out for the County's Reserve team on the following Monday, February 2, against a Blackburn Rovers Reserve XI. No fewer than five of those who played at Nelson, plus Frank, were selected for the game. This was a strong side, put out in the hope that a win would advance the club's cause and avoid the 'humiliating experience of having to apply for re-election for the second successive season'.

The scheme worked out well as Blackburn were defeated 4-2, and in the process Frank bagged a brace.[59] Consequently, the County Reserves remained third from bottom in the Central League with 19 points, 3 ahead of Liverpool and 6 above Manchester United.[60]

If the first team's 1-1 result with Nelson was poor there was much worse to come. February can be a cruel month, and for the County, February 1931 was memorable for all the wrong reasons. Stockport, one of the League's form sides, unbelievably collapsed completely. To that point in the season Stockport County had scored 60 goals in 27 league matches and were chasing promotion. What followed was truly disastrous as the team inexplicably failed to score a single goal in the 4 matches played during February. In all, just a solitary point was gained in the month, a 0-0 home draw against York City.

This bleak spell started with a 1-0 home loss to Darlington, on February 7, before a crowd in excess of 7,600.[61]

A week later on February 14 the team travelled to Halifax, then second from bottom in the Northern Division, and were comprehensively beaten 3-0.

This result came as a considerable shock. "Busy Bee" thought the match was the most 'unsatisfactory display the County have given this season.' He commented upon the conditions and the County's failure to adapt to them. He felt that the short passing game was fine as far as it went, but certainly was not best suited on a snow-covered pitch.[62]

The correspondent from the *Stockport Express* was of a similar opinion.

'The County at Halifax were like the curate's egg – "good in parts" but unfortunately the good parts came too infrequently to be of any material value. True enough, Stockport played good football, they progressed through the medium of intricate short passes which were undoubtedly pretty to watch, but they were not half so effective as the long swinging passes employed by Halifax. I think that so far as actual football skill was concerned Stockport were the superior side, but the object in football is to get goals, and the County are not achieving that object. Personally, I like the County's style of play, but it would be foolish to let that liking prejudice me against any other method of playing the game. It has been blatantly obvious during the last few weeks that the tactics adopted by Stockport are not the most advantageous on heavy grounds. The close passing has been overdone, and the wing men have been practically starved, with the result that the attack has lost most of its sting, and the County have degenerated into a very mediocre side. I may be wrong, but to me it seems that now more than ever the wing men must be the chief raiders, and to bring this about the short passing must be dropped, and steps taken to open the game out. To say the least, Stockport have been very disappointing of late, and in spite of their fine record at home they are not a very formidable visiting side'.[63]

After this shocking decline in the team's form, 3 losses and a draw in the 6 games played since January 10, it was time to circle the wagons. "Busy Bee" in his *Cheshire Daily Echo* column of February 21 attempted to rally local support.

> '"These are times to try men's souls," and it is a phrase which I think can be applied to the affairs of Stockport County. These are the times to try the loyalty of the supporters. There has been an unexpected lapse in the form of the team, and a series of set backs which have ruined for the time being the County's chances of promotion. But the race is not yet over ... I see no reason to give up hope at this stage ... I am not going to lose faith in the County players, even though they have disappointed us all greatly in recent matches. What they have done before they can do again, and I ask all County followers to suspend judgement until after the matches with Tranmere Rovers and Chesterfield'.[64]

To ram the message home he also included a brief analysis of the financial positions of certain other clubs in the Northern Division. Particular reference was made to Halifax, Nelson, Accrington Stanley and Rochdale. He provided a summary outlining what the supporters of each were doing to assist their respective clubs. He then drew the County into the argument noting:

> 'Unless things mend very soon with Stockport County a similar position will arise here. Since the beginning of the season the gates have been substantially lower than they have been since the County joined the Northern Section'.[65]

The observation was perhaps poorly timed because the County was most assuredly trying to mend things, as elsewhere in the same edition was an article headed: 'County Recruiting.' It detailed that no fewer than four players had been signed by Lincoln Hyde. These included James L. Bilton, an inside forward, obtained from the British Legion FC, Howden-on-Tyne. He was 20 years of age and arrived with a 'big reputation as a goal-scorer in the Tyneside League.' Joining him was John T. Fantham, a 21 year old inside forward, who had been with Wolverhampton Wanderers for 2 seasons. This Sheffield native went straight into the County first team against York City, on February 21, as a replacement for the injured Boardman. In addition, two well regarded amateurs, the brothers Charles R. and Peter R. Hardman, centre forward and inside right, were signed from Manchester United and the Northern Nomads respectively. The Directors were still holding to the line that County could yet gain promotion, but it was also a very clear statement as to where they considered the County were under achieving. If the side's promotion bid failed, changes were coming.[66]

On February 21 Stockport entertained York City and produced what many considered the most feeble performance witnessed at Edgeley Park for many months. Although the County did manage a goalless draw, few in the crowd of some 5,000 were impressed. Because of injuries four changes were made. These were the recently signed Feetham at inside left, Vincent at right half, Horsfall in goal, and Lloyd at left back. These did nothing to improve the side's cohesion. More particularly, all but Vincent were making their first team debuts, and almost unbelievably Horsfall and Lloyd had not previously even played in League football! It was the lack of cohesion that

"Busy Bee" believed was the underlying cause for the recent run of poor results. In fact the new recruits acquitted themselves well, in particular young Horsfall, who 'certainly saved a point for the County'.[67]

"Busy Bee" remained optimistic:

> 'Individually the players are good enough, but they lack understanding. This was never so apparent as in the match with York. The visitors as a team were far ahead of the County. Their passes invariably found the man for which they were intended. The County have struck a really bad patch, but there is no reason at this present stage to give up hope. The return of the injured players and one or two changes will probably effect a transformation'.[68]

Although this undoubtedly was a most disappointing result Stockport still hung on to fourth place in the Division, only 2 points behind Tranmere Rovers and Chesterfield, but now 6 adrift of Lincoln City. Tranmere had scored the massive total of 88 goals, Lincoln 72 and Chesterfield 71. The County lagged well behind with just 60.[69] Of these Frank had accounted for 27 and Webster 10; otherwise nobody had achieved double figures.[70]

The next game, on February 28 against Tranmere at Prenton Park, was one of the benchmarks that "Busy Bee" had highlighted for the side. He believed that if the County could win this fixture then promotion remained a distant possibility, or at least the season could be resurrected. But it was not to be as Tranmere scored 3 unanswered goals and climbed to second place in the Division, just 2 points behind Lincoln City.

Stockport performed reasonably well in the game itself, but Tranmere took their chances whereas the County did not. In midfield Stockport were the better side, and the forwards had more chances to score 'than the home team, but unaccountably failed.'

> 'Frank Newton missed a wonderful chance in the first minute, when Lincoln charged Conner off the ball and left the County centre-forward with only the goalkeeper to beat. Newton took steady aim and tried to put the ball into the far corner of the net, but his shot went just wide – a sheer piece of bad luck, for Newton is not in the habit of missing such chances'.

Webster then did the same moments later, and so it continued throughout the remainder of the game. Stockport 'fought desperately hard, and frequently outplayed the home team', but simply could not convert a single opportunity.[71]

In his weekly review following the game, "Busy Bee" announced that he had discovered the 'Secret of the Recent Lapse.' If any revelations were anticipated the reader would have been disappointed since he offered the stunningly straightforward observation that the County 'ought to have won but did not take their chances.' But he also considered that the team depended too heavily on Frank.

> 'Up to six weeks ago Frank Newton was the leading goal scorer in the Northern Section, but since then he has failed to find the net once, and as he has dropped off no

one-else has made good. During the month of February the County have not scored a single goal – a record for which I cannot find a parallel. The trouble is the County all through the season have relied too much on Frank Newton to win the matches, and his failure has meant the failure of the team. He is not the only forward who has not come up to expectations in recent matches'.[72]

Finally this disastrous run did end with a very 'welcome' 2-1 victory at Edgeley Park, on March 7, against Chesterfield.

'Under more favourable conditions [from a weather as well as a playing point of view] the return engagement with Chesterfield on Saturday would probably have drawn one of the best "gates" of the season. Actually, the attendance was one of the poorest – between three and four thousand. Admitted the extreme cold would account to some extent for this, we are afraid the main reason must be assigned to the recent falling away in the play of the Edgeley side, and their consequent "lag" in the promotion race. This is much to be regretted, for if half the rumours going about are true the club is experiencing a rough time financially, and can do with all the support available'.[73]

Chesterfield opened in determined fashion and rocked the home support when they scored in the first minute. However, County heads did not go down, Stockport retained their poise and Bocking put them back on level terms just before the interval. On resuming the County had the wind at their backs, yet there was no perceptible change in the flow of the game until the visitors focused on protecting the draw. Stockport improved as Chesterfield 'concentrated on defence. Goal-kicks were taken in the most leisurely fashion …, and the half-backs likewise were never in haste when a throw-in was awarded.' Such tactics did not sit well with the home crowd and the visitors were subjected to much caustic abuse. However, such time wasting was to no avail as with just 4 minutes remaining Frank settled matters.[74]

After the County's recent disastrous run this was indeed a welcome victory, but "A. W." believed that 'the general play of the side was far from satisfactory.' He thought that the defence and half backs had performed adequately. But 'the forwards were the disappointing section, and it is here that the chief trouble lies. All their pep and snap seems to have departed'.[75]

The team's form did not improve greatly thereafter, and on March 14 the side travelled to Barrow and went down 1-0, before a crowd of almost 8,000. A truly shocking result, which dismissed any lingering thoughts around Edgeley Park regarding the sunny uplands of Second Division football. Such thoughts were sadly placed on hold for yet another season.

> 'Barrow's dashing display in the first half of their game with Stockport County augured well for their success in the second, and they recorded a well deserved victory ... Frank Newton and Webster were frequently dangerous, ... but they could not penetrate the home defence. Frank Newton was well covered, and not allowed time in shooting'.[76]

The level of local disappointment was reflected in the poor attendance for the County's next home match against Southport.

> 'Stockport County's fall from grace was strikingly exemplified in the meagre attendance at Edgeley Park on Saturday, when with a fine afternoon, and attractive visitors in Southport, not more than some 5,000 passed the turnstiles. Had the County still been challenging the leaders it is almost certain the "gate" would have been nearer three times the number'.

The teams were level at the interval, but 2 minutes after the restart the County went a goal up, scored by Matthews. Stockport subsequently squandered a number of good openings, but were greatly assisted in defence by the brilliant play of Bocking at right back, who 'many times pulled up the line single-handed, and was cheered again and again for his clever work.' Finally, some 10 minutes before the end,

> 'Frank Newton [who had anything but a good day] took up a cross from the right and turned the leather in the net, the Southport defenders easing up under the impression that the scorer was in an off-side position – an opinion shared by many of the spectators'.

However, the referee, Mr G.T. Davies of Bury, did not share their opinion which meant the County reversed the score recorded at Haig Avenue in November.[77]

After this game the County still held on to a respectable

fourth place in the Division, but were now 6 points behind Lincoln City and had played a game more.[78] This situation did not improve when the County could do no better than draw against Accrington Stanley the following Saturday, March 28. It was now apparent to both the club's directors and management that promotion was but a memory. It was time to initiate a rebuilding programme, and to this end the club started to experiment with new combinations in the forward line.

The game at Accrington's Peel Park, ended in a 2-2 draw. Lambourne, at inside left, scored the County's first goal. But this was a day when a blustery, bitterly cold wind swept across the field from end to end and

> 'was responsible for the mediocre display. The ball was almost impossible to control so it can readily be imagined that constructive football was out of the question. Unfortunately, this state of affairs was harmful to only one team, the County. By that I mean the Cestrians were prevented from playing in their normal style simply because their usual methods require skill and judgement, commodities which the wind made impossible to introduce. Accrington on the other hand, have no particular style, in fact they are one of the most haphazard sides I have seen this season'.

Despite their shortcomings, Accrington were 2 goals up at the interval. But this 'Our Own Correspondent' in the *Stockport Express* attributed to the prevailing climatic conditions.

> 'The game can be summed up in [a] very short space, for the first half, with the wind and slope in their favour, Accrington attacked with dash and enthusiasm and gained a two goals lead. In the second half, attacking did not come into their scheme of things at all, but they certainly defended in a resolute and praiseworthy manner'.

He believed also the County would have won but for the experimental state of the forward line. In his view, a purpose was nonetheless served as Lambourne was clearly a much better half back than he was a forward. However, he gave over more column inches to describing Frank's astounding equaliser.

> 'Frank Newton, who has had a very lean time during the last two months, was in something like his real form, and staggered the Accrington crowd with a remarkably spectacular goal. It was so unexpected that I confess I am myself somewhat hazy as to how it happened. I know that the ball was bobbing about in front of the Accrington goal, then Frank Newton, striking a pose that a classical dancer might have envied, hooked the ball over his shoulder into the net. He went flat on his back as soon as he had done it, and so somewhat spoiled the experimental Russian Ballet part of the programme, but as the ball was over head high when he hit it, his collapse was pardoned. As I have intimated, the Accrington people were amazed at this goal, and I suppose it really was a wonderful effort. I say suppose as I have become so accustomed to the Romiley player scoring from impossible positions that I have, I am afraid, become somewhat blasé'.[79]

The correspondent from the *Lancashire Evening Post* viewed events somewhat differently as he reported:

> 'Stockport County against the run of the game, obtained a point at Peel Park. Frank Newton is not more likely to score a luckier goal than from the chance kick that directed the ball into a corner of the net. Stanley were always the more dangerous'.[80]

There now followed the Easter programme during which the County were scheduled to play Doncaster Rovers twice and Rochdale. Stockport travelled to Doncaster for the Good Friday encounter which 'Our Own Correspondent', again in the *Stockport Express*, headlined 'Roughest Game Ever Seen'.[81] The match was described also as a 'peculiar game', one in which the County were 'immeasurably the better team', but lost because they squandered chances with 'heart breaking frequency.' The Doncaster crowd also came in for some criticism:

> 'I was left with a bad impression of the Doncaster crowd for they subjected the County players to a flow of abuse throughout the game. It all started when Vickers rushed at Bocking, came off second-best, and sustained an injury to his knee. From that point onwards the game was one of the roughest I have ever seen, and I am still wondering how it was that more players were not injured'.[82]

This was Doncaster's first victory against the County since the 1926-27 season, and it was well deserved. After a scoreless opening half, Doncaster took control and pressed the

Stockport defence which 'fell away considerably'. Doncaster scored their goals in this half, both resulting from excellent passing movements.[83]

The home fixture with Rochdale came next, and it proved an altogether more docile affair. To the point that 'Our Own Correspondent' described it as 'one of the most spiritless games' played at Edgeley Park for a long time. The pre-match view was that Rochdale would take nothing from the game and the fact that they were able to force a draw was put down to Stockport's defensive blunders, and yet again the poor finishing of the forwards. The latter reflected further experimentation, on this occasion with a new right wing pairing, Butt at inside right and Rathbone outside him. Rathbone was credited with having good ball control and Butt as being clever, but as a pairing they were generally considered ineffective.

> 'And yet poor as the finishing was, I thought that Lincoln and Frank Newton showed greatly improved form. The Romiley player led the line with more zest than has been the case for weeks, and only absolutely cruel luck prevented him from notching at least two goals'.[84]

"Busy Bee" noted that:

> 'The football did not reach a high standard. The ball was kept too much in the air, and the passing very often left very much to be desired. Still the County forwards were much more lively than they have been for some time. If Frank Newton had been about a foot lower with four or five shots he would have at least done the "hat trick." In

his approach work and positional play Newton touched his best form, even though he did not always get the passes he ought to have had. But no one can forgive him above all men for missing such easy chances'.[85]

Perhaps the column inches describing one of Bocking's first time clearances was a reflection of the game's lacklustre nature. In one instance he

'did not add to his popularity, [when] he slammed one ball into the adjoining reservoirs to the obvious indignation of a large flight of seagulls, which were resting there. They wheeled and dipped above the ground protesting vehemently against such ruthless treatment'.[86]

The result of the return game with Doncaster, played at Edgeley Park on Easter Monday, provided a further shock as 'the Yorkshire men achieved something they had never done before, they took a point away from Edgeley Park'.[87]

Mr G. Hewitt again refereed the match and came in for some flack from 'Our Own Correspondent'. He considered that while Hewitt was correct in awarding a hotly disputed penalty resulting in Doncaster's equalising goal, he lacked consistency.

'Had he shown such exact powers of discrimination throughout the game all would have been well, but unfortunately he didn't, and in consequence a number of players got away with very nasty fouls, it was perfectly obvious to me, after the game at Doncaster ... that the return engagement would be contested in anything but a holiday spirit, and as events turned out I was not far wrong'.[88]

Lambourne returned at inside left in this game and the County attack, again like the curate's egg, was good 'in parts'. Frank was responsible for both the County's goals, and he:

'gave a decidedly improved display but he is still a long way from being the goalkeeper's "bogey" that he was in the earlier part of the season. I still think he has the hardest shot with both feet in the country, but of late we have not seen much of his shooting capabilities. He is having a bad time – nobody knows that better than he does – but he is bound to come again. At present he is, I think, lacking in confidence, but that cannot be helped, it is a place through which every footballer must pass at some time in his career'.[89]

Despite Stockport's dismal run of results, just 2 wins in 12 games, "Busy Bee" named Frank, in his brief report, as one of four County players who were outstanding at Crewe Alexandra's Gresty Road ground on April 11. The 'Railwaymen' 'claimed the verdict by the only goal of the match', but the lack of goals was perhaps not surprising. As "Busy Bee" explained, both 'sides were troubled by the ball, which possessed peculiar qualities and did not respond to the efforts of the players, twisting and twirling in an unexpected manner …' He noted too that the pitch 'was in better condition than usual on Saturday owing to the dry spell. But it badly needed a roller'.[90]

The fixture at Gateshead, postponed because of the snow on

Boxing Day morning, came next and was played on April 15. The *Stockport Express* correspondent set the scene.

> 'When South Shields played at Horsley Hill, the North East coast enclosure was always something of a happy hunting ground for Stockport County. However, South Shields commenced a new era in their life as a club when they changed their name to Gateshead and moved bag and baggage to Redheugh Park, which is on the outskirts of Newcastle. Thus the County were breaking new ground last week, and quite evidently the spell they had hitherto cast over the Northumberland side was not as potent on pastures new as it had been on the old ground at Shields, or "Plate-ends" as the "Geordies" descriptively describe the railway terminus. In the good old days [i.e. last season and years previous] the County had more than their share of luck when opposed to South Shields. Unfortunately for the Cestrians, like everything else luck runs in cycles, and last week the pendulum had swung the other way with a vengeance, Gateshead winning by the odd goal of three, after having all the luck that was going'.[91]

For his part "Busy Bee" reported that Stockport 'played better football than they have done for weeks ... and did not deserve to be beaten'. He considered the County would have won but for 'the uneven nature of the ground.' But he was prepared to excuse Frank who 'played with great dash, but was unfortunate near goal, missing two "sitters"'.[92]

'Our Own Correspondent' thought the forwards played well,

'but were lamentably lacking in finish', and he provided the unfortunate detail around the defeat.

> 'Then came the piece of luck which resulted in Stockport being defeated. Sinclair punted the ball downfield, and Bocking came out to clear but the uneven playing surface went all against him, for the ball broke three yards and this enabled McNaughton to run in and beat Richardson at his leisure'.[93]

The long return journey would have afforded the players ample time to reflect upon the drastic decline in the side's fortunes after January, at which time the club was very much in the shake up for the Northern Division title. Inevitably too, with the end of the season fast approaching, there would have been much speculation as to who might be released, retained or placed on the transfer list. The forwards in particular, given their ongoing failings and the emphasis the County's management had recently placed on signing replacements, would have felt particularly vulnerable. Change hung heavy in the air over Edgeley Park, for not only had another promotion challenge been derailed, but a new manager was required as Lincoln Hyde was off to manage Preston North End FC.

There followed the return game with Wrexham at Edgeley Park, on April 18, which provided further evidence, not that any was needed, of the declining interest in the happenings of the County. The attendance numbered no more than 3,000, approximately half the total that turned out to watch the County's Reserve side the week before. Although the weather was bitterly cold, it was argued that the primary reason for the sharp decline was the team's miserable form. And as previously, it was the forwards that were held to be at fault.

The County went on the attack from the outset, but the visitors drew first blood. This spurred Stockport to greater heights and on the heavy ground a 'ding-dong' battle ensued, but try as they might the County could not pierce a stout Wrexham defence. The visitors went in a goal up at the interval and little changed when play resumed. The Wrexham goal remained under an almost continuous but fruitless bombardment. Then with 15 minutes remaining the County were awarded a penalty. As "A. W." reported, the decision was disputed and words were exchanged

> 'before the kick could be taken. When Newton shot from the "spot" Finigan fisted away, but the referee ordered the kick to be re-taken, presumably on the ground that the goalkeeper had infringed, and this time Vincent was entrusted with the kick, and he made no mistake'.

Frank redeemed himself 5 minutes later when he scored to put the County in front. But the lead was short lived as Wrexham equalised just before full time, to earn a 'meritorious draw'. This was the final home game of Stockport County's 1930-31 season, and, although unknown to the County faithful at the time, it also marked Frank's final appearance at Edgeley Park.[94]

The last game of the season was played on Rotherham United's Millmoor ground, and 'Our Own Correspondent' commented:

'Personally, I don't think they have put up a better show away from home this season, and although the Rotherham people were naturally disappointed, they freely admitted that so far as football was concerned the County were by far the superior side. The County were a much more methodical side, and gave one the impression that they could score just when they wanted to. They played delightful football with an air of detachment that might almost be termed nonchalance'.

The scoring in the game was hectic as Rotherham took the lead in the first minute, but 6 minutes later the County's Andy Lincoln tied it up. Immediately following the kick off, Fantham, at one time on the Rotherham staff, playing at inside right, sent Matthews in to score and the County led 2-1 at the break. However, Rotherham responded and equalised shortly after the resumption. The 'Millers' then lost their goalkeeper, Emery, but they were not deterred and with 15 minutes remaining the County conceded a third to trail 3-2. Fantham was then moved to outside right and set up Frank 'with an opportunity which the County leader was quick to seize.' And finally, with just seconds remaining, Webster 'the County's diminutive wing man' completed the County's third 'double' of the season with a fast oblique shot.

"Thus, Stockport finished the season in excellent style", or so 'Our Own Correspondent' in the *Stockport Express* concluded.[95]

It also provided some welcome relief, despite it being only the third victory in the County's last 16 starts. A disastrous run, the ramifications of which were shortly to follow.[96]

By the close of the season, Frank had once more dominated

the club's individual scoring statistics having netted 34 League and 3 FA Cup goals, in 39 league and 2 FA Cup games. In addition, he scored 3 times for the Reserve side in the Central League. Second to Frank was Lincoln who recorded 12 and 2, then came Webster with 12, and 1, and behind him was Matthews with 10 league goals. Nobody else contributed more than 3.[97]

After yet another season in which promotion had eluded the County's grasp, it was time for radical change, or more precisely 'a clear out'. Lincoln Hyde had already announced his departure, and it was common knowledge that the club's captain, Billy Bocking, was off to Everton after seven years at Stockport. Many of the others must have read the writing so clearly on the wall, in particular the under-achieving forwards. Bocking's departure was big news in the local football community and overshadowed the announcement that Frank was not going to be retained.

"Busy Bee" put out in his column of May 2 that Frank was not included on the list of retained players, but was open to transfer. Disturbingly, this was misinformation, or at best created much confusion.

> 'Stockport County's list of players retained, open to transfer, and free transfers will cause quite a stir, for amongst those who have not been re-engaged are five regular members of the first team, including two half-backs and the three inside forwards, amongst whom is the County star goal scorer, Frank Newton'.[98]

It would appear safe to assume that Frank would not have

anticipated that the club would fail to re-engage him, hence placing him on the open to transfer list. This meant that the club had not offered him the minimum wage of £208 per annum as stipulated in the FA's regulations.

Having concluded from the newspaper report that he was on the free transfer list Frank signed with non-league Ashton National on May 5. His doing so reflected his shock and anger at the management's decision and his need for a steady income. In addition this arose at a difficult time for the family as Frank's brother William had died in March from pneumonia.

The headline on the Sports page of the *Stockport Express* on May 7, 1931 screamed:

'NEWTON FOR ASHTON NATIONAL'

> 'It was announced on Tuesday [May 5] that Frank Newton had been secured by Ashton National, a Cheshire County League club, who last season included two former County players on their staff in Billy Wilson and Evan Hooker. The status of the Cheshire League has been considerably enhanced in recent years due to the acquisition of prominent ex-English League players by many of the clubs in membership, and Ashton are evidently determined to keep well in the van'.[99]

Immediately above this announcement was notification of the 'County's Retained List', which clearly stated that Frank had been placed on the Transfer List, not the Free Transfer one![100] "Busy Bee" updated his readership on May 9 when he wrote:

'Last week I announced the list of retained players, but this has since been revised and all those who were given as open to transfer are now on the retained list. As a result none of the players are able to sign for other clubs'.[101]

For Frank this came too late and his move to Ashton was quite understandable as two of his brothers had played for the club and remained associated with it. No doubt he would also have contacted William Hooker and Evan Wilson, the two former County players then with Ashton.[102]

An interesting aside is that 'local knowledge' would have afforded him an insight around wages, and related matters, at the non-league club. A year later the celebrated Alex Jackson did not bring his talents to the Ashton National Stadium for any other reason than the money on offer to him. Or as Jackson expressed it:

'I tell you frankly that with the prospect of £8 as a maximum wage in the League, and unlimited possibilities when playing outside the league – well, what would you do?'

Jackson signed for Ashton during the off-season in1932, initially on £15 a week. However, six weeks later this was changed to a percentage arrangement, based on gate receipts, after the Ashton directors informed Jackson 'his salary was driving the club to bankruptcy'.[103]

In reacting precipitously Frank had created something of a problem as Stockport County held his registration without which he would be unable to play in League football. However, the County were also faced with a dilemma; should the club retain Frank's registration and lose any transfer fees to which the club would be entitled, and certainly needed? Rather than a stand off, a compromise was reached, and on May 19, 1931, the *Daily Mirror* reported that Frank Newton had been transferred to Fulham FC.[104]

To recap the convoluted nature of Frank's transfer to Fulham. First Frank reacted precipitously to the announcement, on May 2, that he had been placed on the 'open to Transfer list'. It was then announced on May 5 that he had signed for Ashton National. Frank could do this, but Stockport held his registration with the Football Association. This meant that he could not play for a side in the Football League, but he could play with non-league Ashton. Matters came to a head when Fulham's management came in with an offer. A compromise was reached, after some involvement from the Football Association, and the transfer fee was divided between the County and Ashton National.

The fee was not disclosed at the time but was subsequently reported as being £575. The funds were split, Ashton National receiving £200 and the County £375. Apparently a further £100 was to be paid should Fulham be promoted at the conclusion of the upcoming season.[105]

The saga was reported upon in the *Athletic News* in May, under the heading: 'A Lesson For Stockport':

> 'League clubs generally would do well to take note of the Football Association's decision not to accept the registration of Frank Newton, the Stockport centre-forward,

who was recently transferred to Fulham. Newton had previously signed for Ashton National, a Cheshire League side, who asked the Football Association to inquire into the matter, the contention being that, as Stockport County had not offered Newton the minimum wage of £208 per year required by FA rules, they had no claim upon him. In this they were right, and they have been upheld. Newton is their player, and as they are not a League club they will not be required to pay a transfer fee for him'.[106]

Two weeks later the *Athletic News* informed its readership:

'Frank Newton the Stockport County centre-forward, who has transferred to Fulham after he had signed for Ashton National, has now been registered by the FA as a player of the latter club. For signing for both clubs Newton has been fined £5. The Ashton National club have been informed that the Emergency Committee of the FA had decided that the notice given by Stockport County to the player as to time and wages offered was not in compliance with Rule 31. Should Fulham still desire the services of Newton I believe Ashton National would not be averse to releasing him, though they would probably require some recompense for his loss'.[107]

The following week it was confirmed, in the same publication, that Frank had moved to Fulham, and that Ashton had 'been true to their word. Though they were entitled to retain him, they had no desire to stand in his way …' and presumably were quite content to trouser their percentage of the negotiated transfer fee. [108]

To summarise Frank's final season with the County (1930-31) got off to a sparkling start for Frank when in the second inter-squad practice game he scored five of the 'Probables' six goals. In the season's early going proper the County did well enough winning 8 and drawing 2 of their first 13 starts, during which time Frank averaged a goal a game. Unfortunately in the 13th game against Chesterfield he broke a collar bone and was sidelined for three weeks. He returned against Accrington Stanley on November 22 and promptly resumed where he had left off, scoring a further 12 goals over the next 8 games. Thus after defeating Lincoln City on January 3, 1931 he had scored 25 times in 23 games, and Stockport County were third in the Northern Section of the Third Division, just 2 points behind the leaders Lincoln City. During this spell he scored hat-tricks against Gateshead on Christmas Day and in the Lincoln City match on January 3, 1931.

However, the club was approaching its high water mark of the season. After the home victory over Lincoln, Stockport lost to Rochdale, followed by 2 further wins and the disappointing draw at Nelson. The side then suffered a devastating collapse, when over the next 14 games just 2 wins were recorded, and 13 goals scored.

After 27 games the County had averaged over 2.22 goals per game and Frank was scoring at the rate of 1.25 in the 24 games in which he had played. Over the balance of the season these numbers collapsed, with the County down to 1.25 goals per game and Frank to a miserable .466, and but for the goals scored at Millmoor in the final game of the season these figures would have been even worse.

There does not appear to be any one reason to which this shocking run can be attributed. Inevitably numerous factors came into play. In February the side was hit by a spate of injuries which necessitated the introduction of inexperienced replacements up front and resulted in a lack of cohesion. The forwards were consistently criticised for poor finishing, and there was a view that the club often still failed to adjust their preference for a short passing game to the prevailing weather conditions.

Frank too came in for his share of criticism, and there is no doubt that his exceptional goal scoring abilities deserted him after January. Nonetheless, he did account for 7 of the side's 17 goals scored during this particularly lean spell.

Finally, he still possessed a devastating shot capable of pole-axing any goalkeeper, his opportunistic instincts as well as the ability to score spectacular goals, certain of which were destined for the annals of the club and recognised as amongst 'the finest ever scored'. These qualities were shortly to be welcomed by the Fulham faithful. For Stockport County their season ended once more in tears, and the inevitable winds of change now howled around Edgeley Park.

CHAPTER V

THE FULHAM YEARS, 1931-1933

1931-32

At the start of the 1929-30 season John Dean, chairman and owner of Fulham Football Club, was becoming increasingly agitated about the club's failure to acquire a first rate centre forward. In November 1929 his thoughts possibly drifted towards the Arsenal, but were more a reflection of Dean's wishful thinking, 'outside the box', rather than based on reality.

> 'Fulham's search for a big, robust centre forward led them to the Arsenal, where they greatly fancied John Lambert, who in six First Division games this season scored seven goals. However, Arsenal are holding on to this player in case of emergency, but, in any case, Fulham could not afford anything like the figure that the Highbury people would want'.[1]

Certainly the view that Dean had overreached himself in hoping to attract a player of Lambert's stature to a Third Division club held sway. But it did not detract from the Fulham owner's great desire to oversee the club's return to the Second Division from which it was relegated at the end of their abysmal 1927-28 campaign.

In December 1930 the *Derbyshire Football Express* reported further that Fulham had

> 'tried a dozen different players at centre forward and the latest of them is experienced enough to make a success of the job. He is Ernest Watkins, a Londoner, and has been with Birmingham, Southend, Brentford and Millwall'.[2]

But the much travelled Watkins, more journeyman than specialist, was not the answer and was moved on to Gillingham in August, 1931.[3] So there remained unfinished business at the Cottage, and evidence suggests some supporters were becoming increasingly frustrated with the situation. There had been rumblings of discontent among supporters early in the 1930-31 season around boycotting certain Fulham home games, and both the *Daily Mirror* and *Daily Express* carried reports of these threats.

> 'A letter has been received by Mr J. Dean, chairman of the Fulham Football Club, threatening a boycott unless a first-class centre forward is secured immediately for the League team. A Fulham official yesterday said that the demand was stated to be a copy of a resolution passed by a body of supporters. "It is impossible," said the official, "for me to imagine that I should not have heard a murmur about the matter if there was really anything in it. We are taking no notice whatever of the letter. In

my opinion the club's supporters are the most loyal in London."'[4]

According to another report, over 5,000 signatures were appended to another petition sent to the directors by a

> 'Fulham FC boycotting organisation asking them to obtain a first-class centre to fit in with Hammond and Price, whom the organisation consider two of the best inside forwards in the country'.[5]

This was certainly quite some action for the supporters to take, and the official, identified as the club secretary, responded 'that I, who have been so long connected with Fulham, and have hundreds of friends among our supporters, should not have heard a murmur' was considered sufficient to dismiss any concerns of a boycott.[6] The two matches identified for such action were against Southend United, on October 25, 1930 and Bristol Rovers on November 8.[7]

It is very probably safe to conclude that Frank had no immediate knowledge of, or interest in any potential boycott, nor indeed the internal workings of Fulham FC. At best he may have been vaguely aware of Fulham's ongoing struggle to fill their number 9 berth for which by the close of the 1930-31 season no fewer than eight players had failed to make their own.[8] The search continued.

The voluble James McIntyre was appointed manager of Fulham FC on April 5, 1931, and guided the side over the last month of the season to a ninth place finish in the Third Division South. His appointment proved to be inspired, and a transformational moment in the fortunes of the Fulham Football Club.

> 'Before arriving at the Cottage he [McIntyre] had steered Southampton to the Third Division South title and then had three seasons in charge of Coventry. From the outset, he tried to raise his and the club's public profile, openly modelling himself on Herbert Chapman. Like his role model, McIntyre had only been a journeyman player but had an aptitude for management learnt from his time in industry and a flair for publicity, for himself and his employers'.[9]

James McIntyre, a successful Fulham manager between 1931-34. Oversaw Frank's somewhat convoluted transfer to the Cottage in 1931. But incurred the wrath of the Club's directors when he took the "unprecedented action" of agreeing to Frank's transfer to Reading "entirely on his own initiative ... for the impossible price of £650"

McIntyre's first task was to improve the squad and he lost no 'time in reconstructing the team in the hope that next season will bring them promotion and [a] return to the Second Division'.[10] With cheque book in hand he set about the exercise enthusiastically and signed 6 players during the closed season of 1931. One of these was Bill Richards, a right winger who McIntyre had managed previously at Coventry and now signed for £100. Another was Eddie Perry, 'a go-getting, dashing centre-forward' from Thames FC; William Hickie, a left back from Newport County, who made just 9 Fulham first team appearances before being moved on to Aldershot; Joe Birch, a defender from Bournemouth who went on to make 187 League appearances for the Cottagers; Albert Wood, an inside right from Sunderland;[11] and finally Frank Newton whose transfer was reported in the *Daily Mirror* of May 19, 1931.[12]

It was felt that McIntyre had begun well by signing Frank, but there was understandably some surprise that Frank agreed to go from Stockport County to another Third Division side. But he may have been convinced by McIntyre's considerable powers of persuasion, or he may have preferred a club at a lower level, within his comfort zone, where he would make a bigger impact if successful.

McIntyre, similar to Herbert Chapman at Arsenal, was an authoritarian who impressed his views upon his charges. By way of example, in the economically difficult days of the early thirties it was not unusual for players, particularly in the lower divisions, to supplement their incomes by holding down a job during the week. But McIntyre was having none of it, and his position was mentioned in 'Tales of the Cottagers', by "The Baker's Man" in one of his regular features in the Fulham FC programme.

'Mr McIntyre's first bombshell was rather a drastic one, for he announced at the beginning of the season that every player would have to devote his whole time to the game. This affected two or three prominent members of the League team, but the mandate was accepted with loyalty, and the results have been eminently satisfactory'.[13]

The suggestion that Fulham's good start to the season could be attributed to this approach was mentioned by the football correspondent Captain Carefree in his 'Exclusive News' column in *Reynold's Illustrated News* on September 6, 1931:

'Is Fulham's very bright start a case of cause and effect? There was very nearly a row when new Manager McIntyre said that no member of the staff should have a job during the week. But he got his own way, and the first steps have been taken to climb to the level of their neighbours at Stamford Bridge. We Chelsea!'[14]

If this was the "first bombshell", the second was possibly McIntyre's absolute insistence that he would not engage with the recently established Fulham Supporters' Club. McIntyre held certain autocratic views and these definitely extended to such clubs. His and apparently the Club's directors' views were spelt out at the Shareholders' Annual Meeting on the evening of October 19, 1931.

'The Fulham FC directors' objection to the newly-formed Supporters' Club was given by the chairman ... When the question of other business was reached, several members spoke in favour of the Supporters' Club, and Mr Mollet asked for an explanation of the directors' "biassed [sic] views" on the matter. Mr Dean, in reply, said the position was that as soon as any member of the Supporters' Club put his foot into the office at Craven Cottage, the threatened resignation of their new manager, Mr McIntyre, would be put into effect'.

Dean continued by stating that during his thirty year association with Fulham FC there had been no talk of a supporters club when financial assistance was required to purchase the ground; nor had anybody, other than the directors invested 'to tide the club over its dark days.' He added that having 'saved your ground from the official receiver' the board and 'my manager, … are strongly against any supporters club.'

Dean did admit, however, that he had been accurately quoted in a press interview conducted a year earlier as saying that it was 'unfortunate that there was no supporters club' at Fulham. But he added quickly that circumstances had now changed as McIntyre 'had come to Fulham on the understanding that there was to be no supporters club; if there was, he intended to leave immediately.' And '"If we have a supporters club here," Mr Dean said, "I shall be missing, my friends will be missing, and you will have to find a new board."'[15]

With such backing McIntyre must have felt his position to be almost unassailable, and he remained adamant that no supporters club would be part of the Club's landscape while he was in post. He held firmly to this view and in the Fulham v Stoke City programme, printed for the game played on November 26, 1932 McIntyre wrote:

'I should like to bring once again to the notice of our loyal patrons that there is no such thing as a Supporters Club attached to the Fulham Football Club, Ltd. Whoever these people are who are trying to foist on the ardent supporter a 1/- entrance fee, etc., they have no connection with this club whatever. What they have done in one season's work we know nothing about and furthermore we don't want to. If Fulham Football Club cannot carry on without donations then it is about time the ground was sold for a wharf or a potato patch. Supporters clubs may serve their purpose with some organisations, but not with Fulham, and I can assure all our supporters that whilst I am in charge of the affairs at Fulham and have the support of my Chairman, Mr J. Dean, and his colleagues there will be no so-called Supporters Club here. The only supporter I try to please is the man or woman who pays at the turnstile. There will be no parrot cries here of "to help and not hinder". If we could advise this so-called Supporters Club what to do with their surplus wealth it would be to pay a visit to the Fulham Welfare Centre who require funds to supply some of the poor of Fulham with Xmas Dinners and a few hundredweight of Coal to keep them warm over a very trying time. This would be a more befitting cause than offering it to a Football Club that does not require it and would not accept it under any circumstances.

Yours sincerely,

J.A. McINTYRE

Sec-Manager Fulham FC'[16]

There was a view in the press that McIntyre's arrival might herald a welcome period of stability at the Fulham club. At least that was the view of an unidentified correspondent when he stated:

> 'I have often wondered if Fulham's failure to regain their lost status has been due to the repeated changes in the management. It will be recalled that in the past few seasons Andy Ducat, Joe Bradshaw, and Ned Liddell have been in charge of the club's fortunes. And now yet another manager has been appointed – Mr J.A. McIntyre. There can be no doubt that these constant changes must have had an unsettling effect on the players. I trust that Mr McIntyre has come to the Cottage for good, and I wish him the best of luck in his new job. I must say that I like the look of the new players Mr McIntyre has secured. In particular, the signing on of Frank Newton, the Stockport County centre-forward, was a fine stroke of business. I have never seen Newton in action, but his record with Stockport is good enough for me. A player who can score well over a century of goals in three seasons must have exceptional ability. I feel sure that the former Stockport man will solve one of Fulham's chief problems. The Cottagers have not had a really strong centre-forward for some time'.[17]

Another opinion of Fulham's prospects for the upcoming 1931-32 season was given by Charles Buchan in the *Daily News* on August 18. He mentioned that Fulham's financial position was 'in none too flourishing a condition', and that 'the desired success may be denied them in the immediate future'; however, he thought Frank would make a positive contribution.

> 'Centre-forwards have come and gone from Fulham without giving entire satisfaction, but the management hope that they have secured the right man for the position in Newton, who has scored 150 [sic] goals for Stockport County during three seasons in the Northern Section. Bolton Wanderers and West Ham United were keenly desirous of obtaining the signature of Newton, who with Hammond, the Sussex cricketer and Wood on either side, should add to his big total of goals'.[18]

Unquestionably, Frank's goal scoring prowess was remarkable, but the figure mentioned by Charles Buchan is incorrect. Altogether Frank made 94 first team League appearances for Stockport, and played in 7 FA Cup games. In 1st team league games he scored 86 goals, 6 or 7 in Cup ties and a further 77 for the Reserve side. In addition, Frank scored freely when playing in both 'A' team and Cheshire Cup matches. His goal tally when playing for the senior sides was 169 or 170. When playing for the Reserve side, Frank scored 53 times in 1927-28, 21 the following season, at least 3 in 1929-30 and 2 in his final season with the County.[19] I do not believe there is an accurate count of the goals he scored when playing for the County's A side.

'The Baker's Man' gave Frank a rousing welcome prior to the opening game of the season with Coventry City. He noted that Frank arrived with an established reputation as a sound leader of the attack, a 'menace to goalkeepers' and a 'passion for scoring'.

> 'The most important change in the personnel of the team is at centre forward, and a man who can score 150 [sic] goals for Stockport County in three seasons of rugged Third Division football should be ideal. There was some difficulty before the transfer of Frank Newton was obtained, but he was eventually signed'.[20]

Frank made an immediate impact at his new club when, in the first pre-season practice game played at Craven Cottage on August 15, he scored 3 goals and 'led the probable first eleven attack in fine style. His excellent leadership was a feature of the match'.[21] Frank did not play in the second practice game, possibly because he had already ensured his selection for the opening fixture at home against Coventry City; a game Fulham won handily 5-3 and Frank reinforced the appraisal of 'The Baker's Man'. The following day's headlines spoke volumes.

'FULHAM FIND A CENTRE,
NEWTON THE MAN THEY WAITED FOR'.[22]

Both Frank and Jim Hammond scored a brace. And the local press report was enthusiastic, 'Newton, whose leading of the forward line was one of the brightest spots of the game', then added:

> 'Hammond in his usual brainy style initiating a movement which Richards took up, dribbling the ball through for Newton to equalise. The effect of this goal was electrical, and the Cottagers proceeded to gave [sic] an exhibition in their most brilliant style'.

In conclusion, the report maintained the win was well deserved and that the forward line had 'received a decided fillip from Newton, who lived up to his reputation as a goal-scoring genius'.[23]

The team then travelled to Exeter for a midweek fixture on the following Wednesday. Fulham won the encounter 3-0 with all the goals being accounted for by the 'goal-scoring genius'! It was a 'capital performance' on Fulham's part, 'and throughout they proved much stronger in attack'.[24]

James Parker, the *Exeter & Plymouth Gazette's* man on the spot, reported on the game, Exeter City's first at St. James's Park that season, and played before a crowd of some 7,000. Although the 'Grecians' enjoyed 'a fair share of the play' they were unable to break down the 'rock-like' Fulham defence. After Frank had scored his second, Parker observed there 'was a better understanding among the visiting forwards, whose attacks were delivered with speed and precision.' And when Frank scored his third 'by crashing home a centre from Penn after whirlwind football that left the Exeter defence standing,' he concluded:

> 'Fulham are a smart team, fast and confident, able to stand up to the hurly-burly, lacking nothing in physique in those positions where physique is needed. They will not be a long way from the top at the end of the season, if my judgement is correct'.[25]

An away game at Gillingham followed on September 5 where Fulham went down 2-1. Played on a rough surface, 'and in a high wind the team gave a below par performance.' Not surprisingly, even at this early stage of the season, Frank's explosive scoring had been noted and he was effectively marked out of the game by their 'giant of a centre half, Collins'.[26]

Prior to Monday evening's home game on September 7 against Torquay United, 'The Baker's Man' was quick to point out that prospects were bright.

> 'Fulham's early efforts have captivated the critics good and proper. They have come to the conclusion that we are in for a great season and many pleasant things have been said regarding our prospects for the season'.

And he could hardly have been more supportive of Frank's contributions over the first three games.

> 'There have been one or two features about the games so far which auger well for the future. First of all we have a dandy goal scoring centre in Frank Newton, who seems determined to keep up his Stockport County record of 150 [sic] goals in three seasons. It looks like a rare tussle for supremacy between him and Simpson, the Crystal Palace leader. Apart from his valuable goals, however, Newton has dropped into the Fulham scheme of attack as no other centre has done for years. His understanding with Hammond and Price, his inside wing players, was perfect, and it is already evident that the many clever movements which have hitherto gone astray will be turned to useful account'.

He felt compelled in the same article to acknowledge Frank's earlier performance in the 3-0 win at Exeter on September 2:

> 'Afterwards our team developed brilliantly, and the thrilling attacks they made were something to be proud of. Frank Newton completed the triumph by scoring all three goals, and Manager McIntyre emphatically declares that he has never seen three better ones put into a net. He also got a fourth, which the referee disallowed for hands. As a matter [of] fact he did not handle the ball; it struck him on the chest'.[27]

Following the disappointment at Gillingham, the Cottagers bounced back with a vengeance on the Monday evening against what was generally regarded as a weak Torquay side. During the first half Frank netted twice, and the other forwards once each putting Fulham 6-0 up at the break. Hammond then went on to score a second half hat-trick, and Price added a tenth; unquestionably, a great, early season boost to the goal average. Despite winning 10-2, a word of caution surprisingly crept into the local match report. 'The fact that two goals were scored against them makes the results of their next month's fixtures a real problem, as they meet Southend and other strong teams'.[28]

There followed a difficult match with Luton Town, also at the Cottage, and the margin of Fulham's

> '3-2 win just about reflected the merits of the two teams. Starting brilliantly with a goal in the first ten minutes, the home side faded away in the second half and the persistence of the Luton forwards frequently put the Cottagers' defence in a tangle. It was a game of patches,

with Fulham after an early supremacy giving way under pressure. Luton improved as the match progressed'.

For his part Frank having scored the first goal (his eighth in just 5 games) seemed to be favouring a leg injury, and as a result he did not attempt too much given the heavy ball.[29] This was confirmed by 'The Baker's Man' who reasoned that this was why Frank 'appeared to slow up as the game progressed'.[30]

The Cottagers then travelled back to the West Country for a midweek return match on September 16 against Torquay United. It was reported in the local press that:

> 'More than usual interest was manifested in the Torquay – Fulham match at Plainmoor last night. It was a rousing game, and the attendance of 5,000 lustily gave the home side every encouragement. When the United met the Londoners about a couple of weeks ago they went down by 10-2'.

On this occasion the hosts exhibited more backbone and only went down 3-2 to a very late and highly disputed goal.

Torquay opened briskly and were a goal up after six minutes, but Fulham responded, through Frank and Hammond and led 2-1 at the break. Both teams strove hard in the second half and Torquay levelled. Then the home side appeared to have scored a third from a corner but the referee ruled, controversially, that a Fulham player headed clear off the line. All the resulting appeals were ignored and with time running out, Fulham:

> 'raced away and Finch scored, and the Torquay players

vainly surrounded the referee in an appeal for offside. As Fulham left the field considerable feeling was displayed, and a large crowd assembled round their dressing-room. One young fellow was escorted away by a policeman. Mr C. Deer, [chairman of the Torquay club] spoke to the crowd, which afterwards dispersed'.[31]

The Fulham club's next outing in the crowded early season schedule was at Ninian Park just 3 days later. So rather than travel back to London, the club stayed in Teignmouth for a couple of days of light training, team building, fishing and most probably a few rounds of golf.[32]

It was therefore a well rested Fulham side that rolled into Cardiff to maintain their winning ways and in doing so produced one of their finest performances of the young season.

'Playing delightful football the Cottager [sic] were 2 goals up in the first twenty minutes. With long accurate passes they swung the ball about among the forwards in great style, their combination being excellent. Hammond was again the inspiration of the front line, and had a great understanding with Newton. It was as a result of clever passes between these two that Hammond scored his first goal, and obtained the second shortly afterwards with a splendid drive'.

Cardiff improved somewhat in the second half, but conceded again when Frank nipped in and shot into an empty net, after the Cardiff 'keeper fumbled a cross from Proud.[33]

ARTHURIAN of the *Western Mail* considered that Cardiff

were defeated 'more thoroughly, perhaps, than the final score indicates.' He believed that:

> 'Too frequently is it urged that a side plays as well as its opponents will permit, but this was not the case at Ninian Park on Saturday, for there were so many occasions when the City players were in possession of the ball, only to throw their chances away ... There was no happy understanding between half-backs and forwards, and the weakness stood out in bolder relief because Fulham excelled. There was this difference, too, Fulham were dangerous whenever striking distance was reached, but from similar positions Cardiff were rarely a menace'.

It was noted too that Fulham's overall superiority was established early in the game. This was the result of the master strategist Hammond 'initiating and developing' their attacking movements. Significant too was the practice of Fulham's inside forwards dropping back to shadow their opposite numbers which severely reduced the potency of the Cardiff attack.[34]

This 3-0 victory meant that Fulham remained among the division leaders, being one of only two sides that had won six games; and thanks to the ten goals against Torquay the side had scored more than any other club in the division.[35]

Both Frank and Jim Hammond received a mention in J. Robertson's 'SPOTLIGHT ON THE STARS' after Robertson met up with McIntyre's immediate predecessor as manager, Ned Liddell. He reported that Liddell was:

'quite enthusiastic about the play of Frank Newton, Fulham's "livest" wire for many years. Newton had a goal at Cardiff yesterday and has only once failed to score since the season opened. Mr Liddell is naturally, also greatly interested in Jim Hammond, one of his "discoveries" who scored twice at Ninian Park'.[36]

A brief reality check followed when the club returned on September 26 to the Cottage and lost 3-1 to Northampton Town. Evidently Northampton's goalkeeper, Hammond, performed brilliantly and kept his namesake at bay, but not Frank who notched Fulham's second half consolation goal.[37] 'The Baker's Man' concurred, and thought that the Cobblers' goalkeeper, if asked,

> 'would probably declare that the second half was about the most hectic period he had ever experienced. Our lads knew where the goal was alright, and some of the pile drivers sent in by Newton & Co. were good enough to have won a dozen matches'.[38]

By the end of September Fulham had 12 points from 6 wins in the 8 games played, and had scored 29 goals. At the time, Southend United and Brentford led the Division with 13 points apiece, Fulham and Bournemouth & Boscombe came next with 12 points, followed by Watford on 11.[39]

The following weekend Fulham travelled to Reading's purpose-built Elm Park ground and once more failed to sparkle. The 'Biscuitmen' started slowly and unquestionably rode their luck in the first half. Overall, Fulham played the more attractive football whereas their hosts were often ragged. It was simply poor finishing and a failure to deal with set pieces that led to the Cottagers' downfall. Reading went ahead midway through the first half but shortly before the interval Frank equalised. Subsequently Reading played with 'terrific keenness' and scored no less than three times from free kicks. Newton added Fulham's second but it was not enough. Nonetheless, Frank probably derived some pleasure from adding two goals to his already impressive tally particularly against his friend and former Stockport colleague Joe Smith who had recently been appointed Reading's new manager.

Smith's opposite number, McIntyre, however, was less than happy, and with an important encounter with Southend United looming it was time for Fulham to make defensive adjustments.[40] Consequently, he dropped Ernie Beecham in goal in favour of Jake Iceton, and replaced William Hickie at left back with the weighty, but exceptionally quick Joe Birch who had been acquired from Bournemouth & Boscombe in the week of October 4.[41]

The Division leaders, Southend United, arrived at Craven Cottage on October 10 for an eagerly anticipated fixture but the result was inconclusive. A record crowd for the season, some 25,000, packed into the Stevenage Road ground and was treated to a thoroughly entertaining game which concluded with honours even, 1-1.

In the opinion of the reporter in the *West London Observer*, Fulham,

> 'were perhaps a little fortunate to share the points in a splendid exhibition of fast and clever football. Southend fully maintained their reputation as one of the finest

sides in the division, and amply demonstrated their supremacy as the unbeaten leaders of the League'.[42]

Fulham went ahead ten minutes into the second half through Barrett, but Southend were not 'dismayed' and equalised shortly afterwards. The visitors sustained the pressure, and Jones whistled a thunderous drive from 40 yards out which skimmed the crossbar with Iceton well beaten. Fulham clearly tired as the half progressed and by the end could do little more than keep the onrushing Southend forwards at bay. However, despite Southend's heroic efforts, no winning goal was forthcoming, and after ninety minutes Fulham were content to settle for the draw. The report mentioned also that 'Birch, the new full back, played a sound game, but Iceton was not an improvement on Beecham'.[43]

'The Baker's Man' offered an insight to the tactics employed which almost certainly reflected those of the management.

> 'We have heard a lot of late about various formations that are successful, but I have come to the conclusion that the only tactics of value must be carried out spontaneously in accordance with the run of the game. Preconceived ideas have a habit of going astray, and can be beaten when they become, as they are apt to do, stereotyped. The tactics employed by both the Cottagers and United emphasised this. Without any slavish adoption of the much boosted W formation they did the right thing in seeing that neither centre forward could do a great deal of damage. Each realized that in both teams there was a leader capable of winning the game'.[44]

The week following the Fulham first team slipped down to Margate for a bracing, seaside break, and on October 17, Clapton Orient tracked across London to face a 'fortified' Fulham side. The Orient started well and were quicker on the ball than their hosts. Nonetheless, both sides created opportunities but failed to capitalise. After the break the Orient held on for a few minutes until Fulham finally struck promotion form. Then the flood gates opened and the Clapton defence fell apart. The first goal came when Hammond crashed 'home a terrific shot' after which Fulham went into overdrive and the Orient's fate was sealed when Price scored from a set piece and Frank netted Fulham's third. The crowd was also afforded some further entertainment by Fulham's centre half, Gibbons, who 'with some Carnera-like methods' continually dispossessed the battling opposition forwards. But he could not prevent the Orient's consolation goal shortly before the close. However, this only occurred after the Cottagers had added two more. The first of which resulted from a penalty, awarded after 'Newton crashed in a pile-driver with the goalkeeper hapless, but Broadbent calmly caught the ball in an effort to save the situation.' Barrett scored from the spot and Hammond closed out the scoring when 'he found the net with an unstoppable drive'.[45]

A visit to Swindon Town was next up and this game demonstrated 'both the character in the side and how much luck is needed over a season to win a title'. At half-time Fulham trailed 2-0. Swindon's second was scored by Fulham's former striker Harry 'Abe' Morris who was reported to have looked suspiciously offside. After the break the Cottagers clawed their way back through Newton and Price but needed a 'dramatic last minute penalty save by Iceton to hold on to a point'.[46]

The view expressed in the *West London Observer* was that Fulham encountered a Swindon team that 'strongly belied' their position in the league table, and were fortunate to escape with the draw. Dominant in the first half, Swindon faltered in the second, and five minutes in Frank rose to head his side's first goal, his fourteenth of the young season, from Finch's well judged centre. Later Price equalised 'with a grand shot', before Iceton was called upon to perform his last minute heroics.[47]

A week later 'Fulham's Brilliant Victory' was celebrated in the local press after the Cottagers, playing at home, thrashed Norwich City. Fulham were judged to have 'delighted a gate of 15,000 with a brilliant victory by four clear goals.' Fulham clearly played well and Norwich were second best from the start. Hammond scored the Cottagers' first after 10 minutes 'almost walking the ball into the net ... The second came after 22 minutes ... Newton cleverly placing a carpet touch for Finch to shoot hard into the corner of the net.'

With half-time approaching, Fulham's inside left, Price, was admonished by the correspondent in the *West London Observer* for unsportsmanlike conduct.

> 'Play was held up when Smith, the Norwich left back, was injured in tackling Price. The defender fell heavily and it would be more commendable had the Fulham forward gone to his assistance [rather] than walking away in an attitude of indifference'.

Initially, after half time, Norwich pushed hard, but fell further behind when Frank,

> 'accepted a pretty header from Finch and found the net with a high left foot shot. Fulham were now playing fast and clever football and it was not long before they went still further ahead. Hammond ... swung across a perfect cross for Richards to head a beautiful goal'.

The win was conclusive, but before signing off our correspondent could not resist a further dig by adding that Taylor, the Norwich right winger, was 'applauded for a sporting action in leaving the ball and going to the assistance of Birch when the Fulham back was injured'.[48]

In November 1931 London's *Evening Standard* published Rowland Allan's timely article offering an insight to McIntyre's priorities in developing this successful Fulham side.

> 'They play their football with that precise accuracy with which the Guards form fours, although with considerably more variety. They keep the ball out of the air. Their centre-half back Gibbons is in touch with his forwards when the team is attacking and with his full backs when they are defending. The basis of their attacking scheme is the old and elementary one of working the opposing defence out of position. Hammond does most of the foundation work, not with quite the dazzling independent artistry of Alex Jones, rather with the more orthodox cunning of David Jack, and with a greater deadliness in shooting than either of them. Hammond makes Newton a better centre forward than he otherwise would be. Newton is as good as Lambert, of the Arsenal, used to be. I notice a striking similarity in the fearlessness and the untiring performance of these two

centre forwards. Price is one of those small, unobtrusive players who appear to arrive at the danger point on tip toes; the sort you do not notice on the way, but cannot miss when they have arrived and are executing a devastating piece of attacking business. The wing men close in towards goal in what they call the modern style. It appears to be called modern because a lot of people do not know that in great teams like Aston Villa, Preston North End, Newcastle United and others it was done 30 or so years ago. It is to be hoped an occasional failure will not tempt Fulham to abandon their obvious idea that a great football team is built up on attack: further more, their frequent success should not lead them to sacrifice directness and efficiency merely for spectacular effects'.[49]

Other football analysts were meanwhile wondering which club would be the most likely to beat Southend United to the Third Division South title. The *West London Observer* remained loyal to their base.

'There are two clubs in W. London which can go a long way to answer the question and they are Brentford and Fulham. It would be a haphazard guess for anybody to pick out any Third Division club as the one for promotion this season ... but a one point lead at the beginning of November as Southend enjoy over Brentford is a very narrow advantage. Both Brentford and Fulham are finding their feet now and it will be a disappointment to followers of football in West London if one, or both of these club [sic] do not finish above Southend'.[50]

In a similar vein it was reported that J.A. McIntyre

> 'and his men believe that the keenest competition will prove to be Northampton and Brentford. Mr McIntyre explained that these two combinations [were] more formidable than Southend because they are equipped with superior reserves'.[51]

At the end of October Fulham, with 18 points were third in the Division, 3 points behind Southend, 2 back of Brentford and level with Watford. All teams had played 13 games while Fulham still enjoyed a considerably better goal average.[52]

A trip to Brighton and Hove Albion followed, on November 7 and after twenty minutes the Cottagers were two goals ahead. The team began 'in fine style with a polished display of ball control'. Hammond's opening goal after 10 minutes was hotly disputed but not so Frank's, 20 minutes later, when he buried a perfect cross from Richards. 'The crowd saw a game which produced many fine movements, the Cottagers attacking with splendid precision.' Brighton were not however prepared to roll over and, despite missing a penalty, were on level terms at the interval. Thereafter the game was evenly contested until Fulham's third goal. This prompted Brighton to redouble their efforts, but it was to no avail, and the visitors returned to South West London eagerly anticipating their upcoming home fixture with Mansfield Town.[53]

Mansfield were not thought to be a particular threat and with the prospect of second place a real possibility fully 16,000 passed through the Stevenage Road turnstiles on November 14. At the start Mansfield's left winger, Death, sounded an early alarm when he 'crashed a shot only inches over the cross-bar.' Indeed, after 20 minutes the visitors were one up and judged to be full value for their lead. At the outset Mansfield controlled a 'lively ball' better than their hosts, but on the half hour Fulham hit back when Frank headed a Hammond cross towards goal and Finch was on hand to bury the rebound.

A hard fought second half followed, and after Frank had twice gone close, it was Barrett who finally stepped up to spare Fulham's blushes midway through the half. This narrow 2-1 victory moved Fulham into second spot in the Division ahead of Brentford who surprisingly lost 1-0 at home to Norwich City.[54]

The trip across to Vicarage Road on November 21 provided Fulham with an excellent opportunity to consolidate their league position since Watford were just 2 points behind them. Nonetheless, Fulham came out flat, produced a truly lacklustre performance and lost 3-1. The majority of the 14,000 plus crowd must have gone home well satisfied for not only had the 'Hornets' maintained their 100% home record but now were mounting a serious challenge for league honours. Both sides played attractive football at times but the hosts remained focused until the final whistle. On the other hand, Fulham played the more scientific game but were shot-shy. Instead of capitalising on scoring chances, the Cottagers 'paid the penalty of over-passing, the ball being sent from one forward to another in front of goal …' Frank scored the consolation goal, his 19th in the 16 games played to that point. Behind him was Jim Hammond with 14, so jointly they had accounted for 33 of the side's 48 goals.[55]

The first round of the FA Cup now interrupted the regular league schedule and Fulham would have been confident they would see off their visitors, Guildford Town, then members of the Southern League.[56] This they did without undue drama on November 28 before a fair sized crowd of 12,000. Both goals in the 2-0 win came courtesy of Hammond.[57]

The Cottagers' next league fixture involved a visit to Bournemouth's Dean Court on December 5, prior to taking on Yeovil and Petters United at the Cottage in the second round of the FA Cup. A disappointingly small crowd of approximately 5,000 turned out to witness Bournemouth's lacklustre display in which they offered little resistance. Fulham were soon 2 goals ahead, scored by Finch and Frank, and the convincing 3-0 victory was sealed when Frank netted his second shortly before the break. Overall it was intricate forward play that assured the 'Cottagers' success, the passing and centres sent over from the outside men often having the home backs flustered'.[58]

The Cup-tie against Yeovil and Petters United on December 12 would have been a Football Pools home banker, and other than the travelling fans among the 15,147 inside the Cottage, most, if not all, would have marked their pools entries accordingly. Indeed, many among the travelling support may also have done so, assuming the fixture was even on the coupon. The West Countrymen were not a negligible force and in fact subsequently went on to win the Western Division of the Southern League in 1931-32.[59]

On match day itself Fulham almost failed to turn up and a typical Cup tie tussle ensued.

> 'Fulham took the opposition too lightly at first and never recovered a grip on the game, and were lucky to live to replay. Yeovil and Petters played the Scottish short-passing game really cleverly, and on the run and quality of the play deserved to win by at least two goals'.[60]

The West London press was somewhat less harsh and emphasised that the Cottagers essentially played much of the game with ten men, with the injured Barrett banished to hobble on the left wing. As a result the forwards lacked cohesion and Hammond for once

> 'had a most unhappy afternoon, being entirely unable to find his centre-forward with the carpet passes which Newton seldom fails to accept. The home pivot scarcely had an opportunity throughout the game'.[61]

At the close honours were even, neither side having troubled the scorer.

The FA regulations specified that any replay was to be held during the following week. Thus, on Thursday, December 17 a record home crowd of 8,004 packed into the Huish Athletic Ground. But the home fans who were late, unfortunately for them, missed the best of the game, as the hosts went one up after 5 minutes. Fulham then steadied the ship and the teams turned around even thanks to an equaliser from Frank. During the interval McIntyre finally succeeded in lighting a fuse under his charges. The response was almost immediate and Fulham outscored their hosts 4 -1 over the final forty-five minutes. A relieved Fulham manager and team eventually came away with a conclusive 5-2 victory; Frank scored three of these. Fulham finally were through to the third round and their reward was another visit to Watford's Vicarage Road on January 9, 1932.[62]

After this match Fulham probably stayed in the West Country as they were scheduled to play Bristol Rovers at Eastville 2 days later on Saturday December 19, the third of four consecutive away league games. The 'ground was in the grip of winter, but it was early judged to be playable, and so it proved.' Inevitably the frigid conditions reduced the crowd to a disappointing 5,000, and at half time with fog rolling in from the Bristol Channel the referee denied the players a break. Instead they 'had refreshments taken out to them'.[63]

Jim Hammond excelled in this encounter, scoring early in each half as the visitors twice took the lead; adopting 'their characteristic long-passing game Fulham looked very promising, and seemed more at home on the frozen turf. In their first attack the Cottagers went ahead'.[64]

However, the final 2-2 scoreline represented a point dropped and one further downside was the injury Frank sustained. This resulted in his being *hors de combat* for the critical 'top of the table' clashes with Brentford on the mornings of both Christmas and Boxing Day.[65]

While turkeys were being basted in West London a crowd of 26,731, a record to that point in the season, descended on Griffin Park for the clash of the division's Titans. The resulting 0-0 draw would have disappointed the home support, but for Fulham it was a reasonable result and whetted appetites for the return game the following morning. A win would put Fulham a point behind Brentford.[66]

'Before a record gate for the season of approaching 25,000 Fulham defeated Brentford, the League leaders, by the odd goal in three, at Craven Cottage on Boxing Day and rose to within one point of their rivals. The game opened sensationally, Fulham at once assuming the attack, and the Brentford goal having two amazing escapes'.

An intense struggle was waged throughout the first half. 'The Brentford front line combined well and came near to taking the lead' from a goalmouth scramble and Hammond went close at the other end. Finch was prominent for the hosts and Fulham were fortunate when Gibbon nearly put 'through his own goal.' Then on the half hour Fulham were awarded a penalty after Perry was brought down. 'Hammond took the kick, but to the dismay of the home supporters he shot tamely on the wrong side of the post.' But redemption came five minutes later as Richards collected a Finch centre and scored with a shot that 'many thought the goalkeeper should have saved.'

The fierce action continued after the break but was 'spoiled by too much feeling, the referee having to say a few words to more than one player.' Finch, who had a 'magnificent game', was unlucky when he he hit the woodwork with a 'splendidly judged shot'. Then with five minutes left, 'amid intense excitement', the issue was settled when Perry buried a rebound from one of Finch's rasping drives. Brentford scored a consolation goal a couple of minutes before the end but on balance, unquestionably 'Fulham were superior and deserved their victory'.[67]

After playing 2 hard games in 2 days, Fulham faced another 'in form' side, Queen's Park Rangers [QPR], thankfully at

Craven Cottage. Nonetheless, QPR were enjoying a seven game winning streak and consequently had surged up the league table. So quite predictably, despite inclement weather, the fans streamed through the Stevenage Road turnstiles on the Monday afternoon of December 28. The majority of the 23,701 would have left disappointed.

> 'Fulham had a fine opportunity of getting on level terms with Brentford at the head of the division ... but they badly let down their supporters by being beaten 3-1. The Cottagers seemed to be feeling the effects of their holiday games, for they were far below the team that defeated Brentford two days ago. The Rangers ... played like a promotion side and thoroughly deserved the two points on the run of the game. Fulham were handicapped by playing against a driving rain in the first half, and they often carried on their short passing movements when a direct snap at goal would have been more desirable'.

It was the excellence of the visitors' defence that made the difference. Frank returned to the Fulham forward line, but as a unit they were well contained by the Rangers' mid-field. The hosts fell behind late in the first half and conceded a second after the interval; but with just seven minutes remaining Frank pulled one back. Fulham then strove desperately for an equaliser, but it was QPR that struck on the break, and the Fulham forwards in particular were left to rue their missed opportunities. For some there was perhaps a silver lining of sorts, for despite dropping two invaluable points:

> 'the Fulham FC directors have a little consolation in the fact that the attendance of over 23,000 was a record for a midweek match, and the takings amounted to £1,485. With the other fine gates for the Christmas matches, and the game with Southend earlier in the season, the Cottagers should this year be able to reduce their bank deficit'.[68]

The New Year opened with a game at Coventry City's Highfield Road, McIntyre's previous managerial stomping ground. Conditions underfoot were shocking and greatly influenced the outcome, a thrilling 5-5 draw. The *Coventry Evening Telegraph* reported:

> 'There were about 8,000 spectators when the game commenced, and a steady drizzle made conditions somewhat dismal. The ground was an absolute quagmire in places, making ball control extremely difficult'.

Despite the field conditions the game proved to be one of the most thrilling seen at Highfield Road for some considerable time. Fulham pressed from the start and early on enjoyed the 'lion's share of the play'. Frank scored twice and at half time Fulham led 2-1. The local view was that 'The Bantams' did not deserve to be behind at the interval as the side had played 'good, vigorous football throughout.' However, the unsuspecting spectators were on the brink of witnessing a truly extraordinary burst of activity:

> 'in a hectic ten minutes after the interval four goals were scored. The City equalised, took the lead, lost it, missed

> a penalty, and regained their advantage. Then Fulham equalised, and went ahead in somewhat lucky fashion, but Lake's equaliser for the City five minutes from the end was more than deserved'.[69]

Two hat-tricks by opposing forwards, Frank grabbed Fulham's, in the same game was rare indeed and perhaps ensured that City's missed penalty was passed over. It was described in one source as being awarded in the last minute. It was not, but its execution brilliantly reflected the problems encountered under foot. It was none other than 'Clogger' Watson who stepped up, but his 'shot got stuck in the mud, and Iceton only had to pick the ball up as it rolled gently towards him'.[70]

The *West London Observer* noted that in all the lead exchanged hands 8 times in what was one of the most exciting games of the season. Otherwise, the report added little and blandly concluded that 'the Fulham forwards, although a bit shaky at times, showed all their customary dash, and combination'.[71]

The third round of the FA Cup was played on January 9, 1932 and 15,978 packed into Vicarage Road. It was a hard fought, close encounter, played 'at a fast pace on a sticky ground, with the ball feeling like lead.' The result, a 1-1 draw, was felt to be a fair reflection after Watford responded to Fulham's goal which was scored by Frank late in the game. But of more immediate concern at the Cottage were the injuries sustained by Gibbon and Barrett, as the loss of the two was felt 'likely to prove a serious handicap in the race for promotion and Cup glory'.[72]

The replay took place on Thursday, January 14 and an excellent crowd in excess of 23,000, undoubtedly much to the directors' delight, packed into the riverside ground. However, this was Fulham's sixth game in just 3 weeks and both the crowded schedule and heavy grounds were exacting a toll on the players.

> 'If at any one stage Fulham looked uncertain during the 1931-32 season, it was at the turn of the year when they went five games without a win. Fortunately, two of these were in the Cup, when Watford won a Third Round replay at the Cottage 3-0 after a 1-1 draw at Vicarage Road. Losing in the Cup was less important than the fact that both 'Sonny' Gibbon and Bert Barrett were seriously injured. Gibbon so badly he did not play again in the first team that season'.[73]

Gillingham, still one of the lesser lights in the division, were next to arrive at the now somewhat shaky ramparts of Craven Cottage. Many among the home support may have marked it as another home 'banker' on the pools coupon.

Because of the injuries sustained at Watford, Fulham were compelled to make adjustments. John Dudley came in at right half for one of his rare appearances, and James Hindson, for his first team debut, at right back.

> 'Gillingham were by no means the superior side, but they succeeded because they adapted themselves to the conditions and realised from the outset that first-time methods were more likely to produce results than the ill-conceived tip-tap finesse of the Fulham forwards'.

With the wind behind them, Gillingham's long sweeping passes to their wingers proved productive and at the break they led 1-0. In the second half Fulham with the wind in their favour responded strongly but the visitors' goalkeeper was in terrific form. 'Hammond was badly off colour and Newton received hardly a single opportunity from the inside forward.' To the disappointment of the majority of the approximately 15,000 inside the ground, it was 'The Gills' that recorded the second goal and went on to shut out the high scoring Cottagers, the only side to do so throughout the 1931-32 season. Fulham's failure to beat a struggling side was blamed on the forwards who 'persisted in pattern weaving methods against a robust defence.' Also, somewhat harshly, the debutant Hindson was singled out as being 'in no way a success'.[74]

As John Robertson noted:

> 'Fulham must be an exasperating side to their followers. They lost at home yesterday to lowly Gillingham [who appoint a new manager tomorrow] and allowed Crystal Palace to range alongside Brentford in the leadership of the Southern section'.[75]

As matters stood on the evening of January 17, 1932 Fulham had won just one of their last six league games and both the manager and directors must have viewed their declining prospects with increasing alarm. Certainly the impact of diminishing gate receipts was very well understood.[76]

This run of poor results necessitated manager McIntyre to step up. The depth of the Cottagers' bench was being exposed as injuries mounted. McIntyre readily recognised the areas in which performances could be improved but there was insufficient time to make immediate changes before an in form Crystal Palace side was due at the Cottage.

At the best of times a Monday afternoon fixture in mid-January is not to be welcomed and particularly so for a side struggling to recapture their mojo when promotion prospects hung in the balance. Crystal Palace were enjoying a good run and were now second in the Division behind Brentford. No doubt Palace would have been anxious to get at the under performing Cottagers particularly as in their last 5 league games the team had only scored 8 goals, and 5 of these had been in the freewheeling 5-5 draw with Coventry City. It was critical now for Fulham to regain momentum. As expressed in the *West London Observer*, it was time for the club to return to 'the goal standard', as the attendance at the Palace game, just over 8,500, showed how quickly gate receipts declined when Fulham departed from it.[77]

A reading of McIntyre's 'riot act' very probably rang out in the home dressing room prior to the Palace match. The atmosphere would have been heavy, with heads bowed, as the players absorbed their manager's robust thoughts. But the details remained inside the dressing room as McIntyre would surely have demanded. He made one change in the side, bringing in Richards on the right wing, and returning Finch, in place of Penn, to the left wing.

Relief must have swept over not only McIntyre but also the faithful as Fulham broke loose in the first 15 minutes and scored three excellent goals. In so doing they:

'told their own story to the "Jeromoiads" [sic] who

prophesied that Fulham would crack-up like Southend. The "Cottagers" played as if they were determined to show that they have come out of the doldrums, and in triumphing by four clear goals over the Palace, played some of the best football since the opening of the season. Richards ... was the fastest player on the field, and repeatedly ran the Palace backs to a standstill. In contrast with Saturday's tactics, the home team indulged in long passing movements and, splendidly supported by the halves, the forwards moved in attack in one line'.

Hammond, Newton and Richards shared the three first half goals and Newton's second soon after the interval rounded out the scoring and sealed a very welcome result. Crystal Palace were judged to have been unlucky not to score, but the Fulham defence held firm and a critical 2 points were secured.[78]

McIntyre must have felt both relief and satisfaction that the decline was arrested so decisively. In effect it marked not only a prompt reversal of form, but proved the springboard that launched the Cottagers on a run of 8 wins and 4 draws over the following 13 games.

On a foggy Saturday, January 23, Fulham travelled up to Luton and came away with another resounding victory. In a brief report carried in the *Sunday Pictorial*, it was fine football, or what could be seen of it, that allowed Fulham to:

'beat the home side decisively by three goals to one. Little could be seen of the play for a great part of the game owing to the fog, which, at times, blotted out both goals from the stand. The London club's goals came in the first half through Newton, who achieved the hat trick. Had not Fulham lost Finch in the second half, through injuries, the score against Luton would have been much greater'.[79]

The local press provided further detail.

'Their victory was thoroughly deserved, and although they finished the game with only ten men ... they thoroughly mastered the home team. The feature of the match was the clever tactics employed by the Cottagers' forwards, and Newton, the leader, did the hat-trick. Fulham pressed from the start, and after the game had been in progress only three minutes Newton took up a long pass from Hammond, ran between the Luton backs and scored. The effect of the early lead was noticeable .... The Cottagers penned the home team into their own half, and five minutes later ... the ball was passed to Newton to get his second goal'.

Frank's third arose from a defensive error, 'and again the watchful Newton nipped in.' There was effectively no way back for Luton although they did score before Finch retired injured. As a result the hosts increased the ferocity of their attacks but Fulham's defence held and the Cottagers 'further strengthened their position as league runners up'.[80]

Cardiff City arrived at the Cottage the following Saturday, January 30, and again proved to be no match for the increasingly confident and much improved Fulham side. 'The Bluebirds' did well enough during the first half and at the interval only trailed by one goal. But after the break the wheels came off, three further goals were conceded, and well before the end Cardiff was a tired and beaten side.

Fulham 4 Cardiff 0, January 30, 1932.
Frank rises to score Fulham's second from a Jack Finch cross.

Frank was in robust form and marked Cardiff's card early in the first half by netting twice within four minutes. Unfortunately, both efforts were ruled 'offside'. But the friendly reporter from the *West London Observer*, probably an avid supporter, was having none of it and felt compelled to observe 'on the second occasion Newton was unquestionably on-side.' He continued by stating that Fulham fully deserved to take the lead when after 30 minutes Hammond, from 25 yards out, 'crashed in a left foot drive which sailed into the right hand corner of the nets.'

Five minutes into the second half Fulham scored a second after Finch neatly set up Frank. 'Almost immediately afterwards Newton should have scored again, but he drove high over the bar from only five yards.' But then, when put through by Price, he kept his head down and netted Fulham's third 'with a stinging shot'. It fell to Richards to perform the last rites and complete a decisive 4-0 triumph.[81]

Despite exiting the FA Cup, January was a good month for the Cottagers. The side had recovered its poise after a poor run which culminated in the miserable home loss to Gillingham. Since then Fulham had put together a 3 game winning streak, scored 11 goals and given up only 1. The club, now with 35 points from 26 games, was well in striking range of Brentford, and two points ahead of Exeter, followed by Reading and Crystal Palace. Fulham also had a significantly better goal differential of plus 31 versus Brentford's 21; the best of the other three was 14.[82] Of Fulham's 73 goals scored Hammond and Frank had accounted for 51; Hammond with 19 in 26 league games and Frank's quite remarkable figures of 32 in 24.[83]

A trip to Northampton Town's County Ground followed and was fraught with danger as Fulham had lost 3-1 to "The Cobblers" at home in September. In what was regarded overall as a hard fought game Fulham:

> 'put up a good display of spectacular football, but found Northampton a strong team on their own ground. It was from the only slip made by Hammond, the home goalkeeper, that the visitors won. Newton, with his usual characteristic of being in the right place at the right time, completely beat him in a swift raid. Fulham's defence

showed up unexpectedly well, and with the halves backing up the attack, the front line was polished and forceful'.

Proceedings followed a similar pattern after the interval. Fulham were at times hard pressed to defend their lead but the defence maintained their shape and successfully defied their hosts.[84] These were important points for the Cottagers as they enabled the side to move level with first placed Brentford.

The following encounter with Joe Smith's Reading side was an altogether more entertaining affair. Some 15,000 packed into Craven Cottage on February 13 and witnessed a see-saw battle in which the 'Biscuitmen' went ahead three times. Reading 'were making a well-timed run for the top. They had won six on the trot … scoring 25 goals in the process, and were the in-form side.' However, Reading had to settle for a 3-3 draw when, after Hammond had scored twice, they surrendered an own goal.[85] The point moved Fulham clear at the head of the Division, although Brentford had a game in hand.

Southend United, with whom Frank's brother William played in the 1920-21 season, were increasingly desperate to turn matters around after they had lost their way following a good start to their season. On the eve of the Cottagers' visit to their Kursaal Stadium, the once division leading 'Sandpipers' trailed the new league leaders by 9 points and were doing no better than treading water in 8th position.[86] But on this day Southend effectively ambushed Fulham 'with a fine exhibition of that speedy, confident football that for so many weeks kept them at the top of the division.' The hosts stuck effectively to their game plan and Wilson at centre half, the mainstay of the Southend defence, put the shackles on Frank to 'such effect that the centre was robbed of all opportunities of adding to his big bag of goals.' The teams ended the first half with a goal apiece but after the interval the home side improved, recapturing some of their excellent early season form and added three unanswered goals to record a decisive 4-1 victory. [87] Fulham remained in first spot, but the league was tightening and only 4 points now separated the top 8 clubs.

A week later, on February 27, 1932 the Cottagers travelled to Lea Bridge Stadium for a confrontation with the might of the Orient. At the time Clapton were languishing at the wrong end of the division table, but on this day they were considered the better side. For long periods the Orient dominated proceedings and the defence successfully checked Fulham's high scoring forward line. In fact it was felt that had Clapton 'contained such a sharp-shooting opportunist as Newton' the home side would have been well ahead by the interval. But they did not and therein was the difference, as it was Fulham's centre half Gibbons 'who sent a long pass up field, from which Newton shot the ball into the top of the net to score the only goal.' A defensive battle ensued for the remainder of the game but on the balance of play 'Fulham were distinctly lucky to take both points, for their display was not up to that expected of league leaders'.[88] Other correspondents supported the view that Fulham again rode their luck as the 'defences showed to splendid advantage, and the work of the Fulham men was a feature of the game.' Gibbons in particular received special mention as he 'never relaxed his efforts'.[89]

The report in *The People* agreed that luck and "Bonzo" were significant factors.

> 'The Cottagers' horseshoe must have been dancing somewhere yesterday! Fulham owe the valuable two points they won to their luck and to "Bonzo" Newton's deadly knack of grabbing his chances. He had two in a game played in a boisterous cross-wind against the Orient at Leigh Bridge. First he sent in such a fine shot that Blackwell stopped it only by a remarkable one-handed effort. From the other, Fulham's prolific centre-forward scored. This happened on the tick of the half hour, and the Orient had been pressing nearly all the time'.

Further comment was cited as emanating from the directors' box. 'A Fulham director, at the close, said "Our boys have not played so badly in any match this season."'[90]

Also of particular significance is the reference to "Bonzo" Newton as this is the first and only reference in a newspaper report that I have located. Consequently I believe it reasonable to conclude that it was a recently acquired appendage that originated in the Fulham dressing room. The correspondent included it here as he wished to inject an element of humour while displaying his 'inside knowledge'. The question is how did the nickname originate?

One plausible explanation can be traced from the roots of a travelling show which was 'disbanded after 126 years on the roads of Britain.' The show's closure was first announced in August 1931,[91] and its final public performance was to be held in Newcastle on November 31.[92] Mr Frank Bostock, the owner of 'Bostock's Circus', or 'Bostock and Wombwell's wild beast show', had negotiated the sale of his animals to the recently established Whipsnade Zoo, located in Dunstable, Bedfordshire.

The Zoo opened on May 23, 1931 and the 'collection of animals was boosted in 1932 by the purchase of a collection from a defunct travelling menagerie and some of the larger animals walked to the zoo from Dunstable station'.[93]

The journey South from Glasgow was described in some detail in the *Liverpool Echo* on Monday, January 18, 1932. The headline, spread across 5 columns, read: 'The Sea Lion's Merry Night On The Zoo Train'. The first two sub-headings continued: 'ONE GLORIOUS FEAST', and 'Bonzo Eats Two Stones Of Herrings'. The copy was provided by a *Liverpool Echo* 'reporter who travelled on the train'.

'BONZO'S NIGHT OF IT'

'Then at Lancaster we stopped at a deserted platform to wait for an express train which thundered by with a glitter of lights. The roar awakened the lions. Answering roars came from the shuttered coaches, and ears accustomed to listening for the danger sounds of the jungle strained tense and alert. "Bonzo," the eleven year old sea lion, was the merriest on the train. He decided to make a "night of it." First of all he sat up in his comfortable caravan- which was curtained off to shield him from possible draughts which might give him a cold – and looked wistfully at the two stones of herrings that had been put in to last him eighteen hours. "Bonzo" determined to have one glorious feast and risk the indigestion of the morrow. So he polished off the whole of the herrings, not forgetting to preface his meal by saying grace – a thing that few sea lions have been taught to do. Then in his deep bass voice he sang his famous song, which is something like a foghorn's rendering of "John Brown's Body" and was meant to be a sea lion's serenade to the dawn'.[94]

Frank enjoyed fish, and kippers were most certainly consumed regularly.[95] In addition his musical talents were widely recognised, but whether Frank included 'John Brown's Body' in his musical repertoire remains unknown.

By the end of February 1932 Fulham were top of the Third Division (South) with 40 points from 30 games, second were Brentford on 37 from 29, followed by Exeter City and Reading with 36 from 30. Crystal Palace also had 36 points but from 29 games and one point adrift of them were Norwich City and Brighton and Hove Albion also after 29 matches. The situation remained very tight, but Fulham still had a considerably better goal differential of plus 30, while the best of the other challengers was Norwich City with plus 18.[96]

On Saturday March 5 Swindon visited the Cottage. Prior to this match Frank had only missed the games over Christmas 1931 against Brentford. Otherwise, he was present throughout. However, in the Swindon game he was carried off. The report in the *Sunday Dispatch* would have raised concerns:

> 'I was sorry to learn that Frank Newton injured his spine at Fulham. It may be some time before he is again fit to play. This will be a big blow, for Newton, who is the League's highest scorer, has been depended upon to round off the artistry of Price and Hammond. It is to be hoped that Fulham's promotion prospects will not be ruined by the mishap'.[97]

The match report in the same newspaper provided the detail:

'Newton in scoring his thirty-fifth League goal of the season sustained concussion ... from a collision with an opposing full-back. There was a tense silence as the ambulance men carried the unconscious player off the field. The loudest cheer heard in London this winter – the whole of the grandstand rose at [sic] him – greeted his return 40 minutes later. Chairman John Dean says Newton showed indomitable pluck. Immediately he came round he refused to have his boots off, and insisted on returning to the field in spite of the protests of the doctor. He then went outside left. But it is improbable that he will play again for some time, as this injury usually affects the neck and is often stubborn and difficult to cure'.[98]

Concern among the fan base is reflected in two extant items of correspondence from West London. Both provide insights to Frank's character and hint at his being held in high regard in the community at large. The first, from a Mr Cope of Margravine Gardens, Baron's Court, dated March 7, was sent directly to Frank.

'Dear Sir,

I was very sorry indeed to see you met with an accident on Saturday. I really had thought the worst had happened by the way you fell and also when they had to send for a stretcher but was very much relieved and surprised to see you come on the field again. I admire your pluck but

think you should have rested, I trust no ill effect will come through you continuing to play I should like here to also say how I admire the many nice little things I have seen you do on the field such as shaking hands with a goal keeper and fetching the ball for the opposing side things so little seen in professional football today all best best wishes for your speedy recovery and may your team gain promotion.
Yours respectfully,'

Another letter appears to have been sent to the club and then handed on to Frank. This was sent from Thorney Hedge Road, Gunnersbury, London, W 4. Dated March 6, 1932, it reads:

'Dear Sir,
I was amazed at the pluck of Newton in returning to the field after his crash yesterday. Many a player would have skirted the desperate effort he had to make to score that goal, when it must have been obvious to him, in the fraction of a second in which he had to think, that a particularly nasty fall was inevitable. When Newton reappeared from the dressing room, trotting in that confident & determined manner of his, my spirits were cheered, & I was filled with admiration of a whole hearted player.
Yours faithfully,' [99]

The fact that so many column inches were devoted to Frank's injury possibly reflects the lacklustre nature of the game which was attended by some 18,000 fans. It was also poorly refereed, and the match 'deteriorated precipitately after Newton's mishap.'

In the first half referee Rous 'badly erred when a Swindon defender palpably handled in the area', but Fulham's 'confident' appeals were ignored. Later he did award Fulham a penalty for 'hands', but it was judged to be 'a doubtful decision'. However, it had no bearing on the result as Barratt fired his drive directly at the goalkeeper. Rous' afternoon did not improve as he waved away objections to Swindon's second goal ten minutes from time after he consulted his linesman. On this occasion 'the point should never have been allowed, the left winger clearly running the ball over the line before' he crossed for the centre forward to score. As it was the goal stood and Swindon escaped with a 2-2 draw.

The correspondent writing in the *West London Observer* was obviously less than impressed with this and other decisions. Frank's injury highlighted the dangers of paying too much heed to a hasty, post game medical diagnosis often influenced by the need to meet a Saturday evening copy deadline as was the case for the *Sunday Dispatch* reporter. By contrast, the match report in the *West London Observer* did not appear until the following Friday by which time it could be reported: 'Happily, Newton's injury did not prove so serious as was anticipated', and concluded that the most memorable features of the game were the scrappy 'football and a deplorable exhibition of weak refereeing'.[100]

Frank was not passed fit to play in the 2-2 draw at Norwich on March 12, but he did return a week later for the home fixture with Brighton and Hove Albion. Frank was closely marked by Brighton's centre half, Mooney, but his 'dash and enthusiasm' provided sufficient evidence that he had effectively recovered from injury. The Cottagers played well and 'were definitely superior' in winning 3-0. Brighton defended stoutly in the first half against a 'scientific and persistent attack', and there was no score at the interval. The hosts subsequently continued to press and built an insurmountable three goal lead through Finch, Hammond and Wrightson. In fact,

> 'Hammond, who crossed over to inside left to accommodate Wrightson, the recently acquired forward from Manchester City, took some little time to settle down, but after the breather the whole front line delighted a gate of 20,000 with a splendid exhibition of fast and clever football. Wrightson made a capital [home] debut, his clever positional play making perfect openings which were a constant source of danger to the Brighton defence'.[101]

McIntyre moved for Wrightson in early March as he wanted additional forward cover over the final 10 games of the season. He is thought to have been less than convinced with Wood on his 1st XI debut against Swindon. Wrightson was acquired from Manchester City for a large fee, £1,200, and McIntyre put him straight into the side at inside right. Hammond assumed the number 10 shirt and Price was dropped and not selected again for the balance of the season.[102]

After Brighton's defeat the Fulham faithful would have eagerly anticipated the upcoming Easter fixtures. Although the side was faced with 3 games in 4 days, expectations were high as the opposition clubs were mired in, or close to, the foot of the Division. Bottom of the table Thames were to host Fulham on Good Friday, and Mansfield Town did likewise the following day; the return game with Thames was scheduled for Easter Monday. Many of Fulham's fans must have anticipated a six point haul.[103]

The Cottagers travelled to Thames' cavernous West Ham Stadium, capacity 120,000, and must have struggled to locate the meagre crowd of 5,000 within. Somewhat surprisingly both clubs failed to find the net and the resulting 0-0 draw would have been a major disappointment to the Fulham fan base.[104]

On Easter Saturday the team went North to Mansfield to take on 'The Stags' at their Field Mill ground. Once more a slim crowd of only 7,000 turned up reflecting the harsh reality of their poor league position. In this game Fulham were fully extended to win the encounter 2-1, and in doing so did well to overcome 'the determined efforts of the home forwards'. Mansfield were judged to have produced a 'plucky' performance, but for the visitors it was two more invaluable points that maintained their position at the head of the Division.[105]

After a day's respite, Thames turned up at the Cottage and

> 'Fulham ran riot ... and by scoring eight goals ... brought their total to within four of a century. A splendid performance delighted a Bank Holiday gate officially returned at 20,000'.

The first goal came after 15 minutes through Finch, and although little was seen of the Thames attack the second did not come until

> 'Wrightson, playing with delightful cleverness and

coolness, eluded two opponents and slipped a beautiful pass to Richards. From the winger's centre, Newton raced on to crash a great left foot drive to the back of the net'.

Almost as soon as the second half commenced Hammond added a third. A key moment then arose when Thames were awarded a hotly disputed penalty. The Thames centre half Pritchard stepped up and smacked his shot against the cross-bar. With that the visitors' heads went down and the home support was then treated to fifteen minutes of the Cottagers' champagne football.

'Richards scored a fourth goal, and three minutes later Newton again beat the goalkeeper with a wonderful effort. By sheer persistency and pluck the centre beat three defenders and shot hard into the corner of the net. Fulham were now playing like a team inspired, and further goals came from Hammond, Richards and Hammond in the order named, the eighth goal being obtained right on time'.[106]

This eight goal feast enhanced the Cottagers' position at the head of the Division. At the beginning of April the club led Reading by 4 points, Southend United by 5, while Brentford was now seven points adrift. Unsurprisingly Fulham still enjoyed a considerably better goal differential, being plus 42. This was quite extraordinary as the best amongst the chasing pack was now plus 7. The season was approaching a climax and all had played 36 games other than Brentford.[107]

Therefore, with just 6 games remaining, 4 of which were

at the Cottage, Fulham were now truly in control of their destiny. First up was a fourth meeting with Watford who were unfortunate to find Fulham in sparkling form and enjoying an unbeaten run of seven matches prior to this 'Local Derby'. The attendance mirrored this success and over 24,000 fans poured through the Stevenage Road turnstiles.

> 'Fulham have not played better football this season than they did in outplaying Watford, the team that removed them from the Cup. From Newton, who brought his total for the campaign to 39, with two dazzling goals to Iceton, beneath the bar, scarcely anybody throughout the ninety minutes put a ball or a foot wrong ... [Watford] were up against a fine side at the apex of their form'.[108]

The correspondent in the *West London Observer* was equally as enthusiastic.

> 'Scoring five times against Watford, ... Fulham passed the century mark for the season and equalled the club record of 101 goals. The entire side were at the top of their form, and a splendid exhibition of fast and clever football showed that, barring accidents or injuries, Fulham are "all set" for the promotion stakes'.

Finch scored the first and Frank added two more to put the Cottagers 3-0 up by half time. Heavy rain during the interval changed conditions under foot but did not detract from the home side's performance. After Frank had hit a post, 'Hammond headed a beautiful goal – the 100th of the season.'

The crowd responded with a mighty roar of appreciation acknowledging the achievement. The fifth goal was the final act and came about when Frank 'sold a perfect dummy' and provided Hammond with a gilt edged opportunity which he promptly accepted.[109]

After this result John Robertson in the *Sunday Dispatch* speculated that Fulham 'should give London a fourth club in the Second Division' in the 1932-33 season. Fulham's chairman John Dean was also in fine form and got a little carried away when, after the game, he was reported to have indicated:

> 'that if increased gates justified the step, they will build a grand stand on the river side of the Craven Cottage ground and increase the holding capacity to 100,000'.[110]

However, of more immediate importance, with the prospect of promotion looming ever larger, was the necessity of protecting the nucleus of the team and deciding which players to maintain on the books over the Summer. In fact Fulham were the first club to release their list of re-signed players for the 1932-33 season.[111] Included were: Iceton, Birch, Tilford, Oliver, Gibbons, Barrett, Richards, Wrightson, Newton, Hammond, Finch, Price, Peters and Tompkins.[112]

The Cottagers eight game unbeaten streak ended at Selhurst Park on April 9 when Crystal Palace won 2-0. This defeat, however, had only a limited impact on Fulham's promotion prospects as the best that any of their challengers could do that day was draw. So it was back to the Cottage on April 16 to meet Bournemouth and Boscombe, a side that Fulham had convincingly turned over 3-0 in December. On this occasion the visitors once again offered little resistance and went down by a similar score, further fuelling Fulham's promotion drive. The hosts led 1-0 at half time courtesy of Wrightson's effort after half an hour. Fulham continued to press in the second half and Frank, having finally beaten the offside trap, exploited a glaring defensive error and scored the second. Shortly thereafter, when Finch was fouled inside the area, Frank was summoned and 'hit the ball with such force that it was in the net and out again in a flash'.[113]

Now, with just three games of the season remaining, Fulham travelled to Wood Lane, Shepherd's Bush where the QPR's directors, with a collective rush of blood, or at least far too optimistically, had taken out a lease on the 100,000 capacity White City Stadium. In the 'Official Souvenir' programme it was stated that the club had bid "au revoir" to their Loftus Road home. Fortunately 'adieu' was not mentioned, as the move proved to be a financial disaster and the club came close to being wound up. Money was lost every week as the crowds simply did not materialise. As the directors discovered the atmosphere, when such stadia are less than a quarter full, is appalling. Secondly, the QPR fans did not appreciate being separated from the pitch by a dog track which compared disastrously to the intimate surroundings at Loftus Road.[114]

The attendance for this 'local derby' was in excess of 21,500, and inevitably many Fulham fans would have been disappointed to witness the enforced delay to the Cottagers' promotion celebrations as the side went down 3-1.[115] It did mean, however, that should such celebrations prove appropriate they would take place at Craven Cottage after victory over

Bristol Rovers.

However, Bristol Rovers had absolutely no intention of facilitating Fulham's victory parade to the sunny uplands of Second Division football. Having lost two of their three previous matches, Fulham opened apprehensively.

> 'The occasion seemed too much for the excited Fulham players, who in the first half especially were quite unable to settle down. The play of the Rovers, on the other hand ... was far superior to Fulham's, and they well deserved the lead ... after 20 minutes'.[116]

From the start Bristol carried the game to their hosts and 'controlled a lively ball much better.' The Fulham defence was stretched and Bristol 'dominated the game for long periods'. Then misfortune struck when Pickering, Bristol's left back, was lost through injury. Prior to this Fulham 'seemed to be all at sea' against a well organized and fast moving side. Hammond was singled out as being less than effective, but he was not alone as the 'entire side seemed over anxious.'

McIntyre's words during the interval had a calming effect and encouraged Fulham to 'attack with much more confidence' to which the crowd naturally responded. Appropriately an approving roar enveloped the ground when after 8 minutes Finch put the Cottagers back on level terms. After which Finch veritably tore into the Bristol defence and the home side started to dominate. Finally, twenty minutes later, Barrett turned in a corner, and this was followed minutes later by a third when Hammond converted from a set piece to put Fulham 3-1 ahead. Bristol however were not finished and with barely eight minutes remaining a hiccup occurred when Pickering, now on the right wing, raised the tension when he surprised Iceton to slot Bristol's second. But the Cottagers were not to be denied and at the final whistle the side had earned the vital points and a very welcome return to the Second Division.

Fulham FC Division Three Champions, 1931-32.
Back row, l to r: Len Oliver, 'Sonny' Gibbon, Jake Iceton, Joe Birch, Frank Penn.
Front row, l to r: Bill Richards, Jim Hammond, Frank Newton, Johnny Price, Jack Finch, Syd Gibbons.

'With a new flag flying proudly at the masthead proclaiming the championship of the division, Craven Cottage on Saturday was one of the happiest football grounds in the country'.[117]

Reading were the runners up and Joe Smith would have marked both Fulham's progress and Frank's extraordinary goal scoring accomplishments. The club acknowledged the Cottagers' success in a congratulatory telegram.

'BRAVO FULHAM.

> Fulham, the Third Division [South] champions, received the following wire from Reading FC, their nearest rivals. "Heartiest congratulations on your well-earned promotion. We have had a good run together. May we have many more in the future. Cordial good wishes and good luck in every respect."'[118]

The pleasure, or otherwise, of playing the final game of the season at a rocking Craven Cottage was the lot of Exeter City. The afternoon was primarily one of celebration during which a football match took place.

> 'The directors' stand was be-flagged in honour of the occasion and a souvenir programme contained the photographs of the Fulham players who have won fame during this memorable season. Fully 16,000 spectators gave the players a rousing reception'.

The Fulham players managed to maintain their concentration and became more dominant as the game progressed. Hammond scored the first when he shot 'through a crowd of players' after which Fulham continued to press. However, just prior to the interval Exeter, very much against the run of play, surprisingly equalised. Exeter's right winger set up the goal, but in the opinion of many was 'palpably offside'. The referee remained impervious to Fulham's protestations and at the interval the scores were level.

Souvenir Program marking Fulham's promotion from Division III South to Division II. Printed for the home game v Exeter City, played on May 7, 1932

Frank sprang to life in the second half and scored his forty second and third goals. Appropriately, his second goal was a typically opportunistic effort. Yet the correspondent of the *West London Observer* could not resist having a further 'go' at the referee.

> 'Deplorably weak refereeing on the part of Mr A.G. Attwood, of Newport, threatened to spoil an interesting game, several extraordinary decisions against both sides rousing the ire of the crowd. It was regrettable that the concluding match of a splendid season should have been marred by most incompetent refereeing'.

At 'stumps' the Cottagers justifiably had won the game and the goals were most fittingly shared between Jim Hammond and Frank Newton. At the conclusion of the match there was an 'enthusiastic demonstration by the crowd, several players being carried shoulder high' off the pitch. Mr Morton T. Cadman representing the Football League Management Committee presented the Championship Shield to John Dean chairman of the Fulham board of directors, and medals to the individual players.[119]

Under McIntyre's guidance the club had enjoyed an exceptional season for not only had the manager built an excellent first team but he ensured the side had 'strength in depth'. As a result of which McIntyre had produced an admirable Reserve side which finished a respectable sixth in the London Combination League. In addition, the club defeated a strong Crystal Palace Reserve side, that included a large number of Palace first team players, to win the London Challenge Cup 2-1 at Selhurst Park.[120]

After delivering Fulham's first major honour in the club's 52 year history, their 21st season in the Football League, McIntyre's position was unassailable.[121] Hence there was no need to recognise or even acknowledge the existence of the Fulham FC Supporters' Club. Nonetheless, their membership was not prepared to be shunted into the shadows and decided to organise a 'celebratory' first annual dinner. This "Promotion Dinner" was held at Pritchard's Restaurant in Oxford Street and somewhat ironically in Pritchard's celebrated 'Dean Room', very probably so named for the occasion!

Inevitably there were a number of speeches and not a little point scoring. The first guest to rise was Councillor Nanson, of Brighton, Chairman of the Federation of Supporters Clubs. While he raised a glass to the promotion success, he went on to refer to

> 'the relationship existing between the FA and the Supporters Clubs, and expressed surprise that the Directorate of the Fulham Football Club had taken up such a singular attitude of opposition when they had nothing to lose and much to gain'.

The Chairman of the Fulham Supporters Club, Mr G. Bell, responded appropriately and in the course of his speech he touched on the relationship between the local supporters and the Fulham Football Club. He considered

> 'it was due to laziness on the part of the directorate to ascertain the nature and composition of the Supporters Club or, alternatively, an ill defined fear. They had pursued

in all their dealings, even when rudely and ignorantly slighted, a pacific attitude. Through their efforts, Fulham had a larger away following than ever before. Moreover, they had organised support, which was to the financial advantage of the club. Mr Bell, continuing, said the irony of the situation was that while the Football Club refused to have anything to do with them, they actually took advantage of a very cheap fare to Norwich (both players and officials) which the Supporters Club had secured'.

Before the acting Secretary toasted 'Our Guests and Visitors', Mr W. Reed read out a letter from Sir Frederick Wall, Secretary of the FA. In it Sir Frederick expressed his 'regret that another engagement prevented his attendance'. He also offered his congratulations to the Supporters Club on its success during its first year. Mr Reed noted that:

> 'This was in striking contrast to the unstamped postcard handed to an official curtly stating that he did not intend to be present. Another letter was from Mr G. Allison, the well-known B. B. C. commentator and director of the Arsenal, who was to speak at the dinner, but at the last minute had to go to Paris'.[122]

These late withdrawals and the manner of them clearly indicated that McIntyre's view of such clubs still held sway and would do so until he was forced out.

The great achievement of gaining promotion was formally recognised by the Fulham directors in August 1932 when they hosted a dinner at London's Holborn Restaurant. In total 38 of the club's directors, management and players attended. James McIntyre was seated to John Dean's right. In a report of his address Dean lauded manager McIntyre's achievements.

> 'The chairman said that in twelve months McIntyre had revolutionised affairs at the Cottage, produced order out of chaos and with judicious and inexpensive additions had provided the best and youngest team ever seen at Fulham. Never in the club's history had there been such harmony at the Cottage and he looked forward to a long association with the manager. McIntyre, for his part, received an honorarium of £450 and became a shareholder in the club'.[123]

To the players went the spoils; well, to most of them.

> 'At the end of the season, the board sought permission to pay a £25 promotion bonus to the eleven players mainly responsible for the success. In the end, watches and chains were presented to the eleven, and to Gibbon and Price. The League, however, refused to allow a similar presentation to Frank Penn, who had played in only nine matches. The watches which cost £375 [in total], were paid for by John Dean'.[124]

In all 26 players had turned out for the club over the season. Price and Gibbon had featured 31 and 22 times respectively. Hopefully Penn did not feel too badly at being excluded as he joined 11 of his colleagues, all of whom had played in 9 or fewer matches.[125]

Upon reflection, Frank would have had few regrets around the decisions taken earlier in the year. During the Summer of 1931 Frank and his wife travelled South from Romiley and on August 15 Frank made an immediate impression on all associated with Fulham FC when he scored a hat-trick in the first inter-squad game. His leadership of the line 'was a feature of the match', and he proceeded in short order to make the number 9 slot his own. He then set about terrorising defences throughout the Southern Section of the Third Division. In all he scored 43 league goals in 39 games, a club record that still stands. Although Aleksandar Mitrovic equalled it some 90 years later in the 2021-22 season, scoring 43 goals, it took him 5 more games in which to accomplish it.[126]

While Frank no doubt relished his outstanding individual record he would have been the first to acknowledge the contribution and support of his teammates. He was fortunate to play alongside talented seasoned professionals in what quickly became a well settled forward line. In particular, the ever present, 'Jim' Hammond proved a brilliant foil for Frank. Hammond enjoyed his most productive season of the ten he spent at Craven Cottage, 31 goals in 42 games. Many were the defences that succumbed to their talents and jointly they accounted for 74 of Fulham's 111 League goals.[127]

Frank commenced scoring almost from the moment he strode onto the hallowed turf of Craven Cottage. He followed his hat-trick in the inter-squad game with two goals in the home win over Coventry City on the season's opening day, and 4 days later with another hat-trick at Exeter. In the 7 games that followed he added a further 8 goals and thereafter in the next 8 league encounters he scored at the rate of a goal a game. After 17 matches he had hit the back of the net 21 times.

Due to injury Frank missed the 2 games with Brentford over Christmas 1931 but after Frank's 25th game (against Northampton Town on February 6, 1932) he had 33 goals to his credit. He didn't score over the next 2 games and then missed the Norwich fixture as a result of the injury sustained in the Swindon game. Then he finished the campaign strongly with a further 8 goals in the final 7 fixtures.

Of his 43 goals, 22 were scored at the Cottage, but his three hat-tricks were all recorded away from home. Frank scored consistently throughout the season, but only scored once over his last 6 away matches.[128]

In the Souvenir Programme, produced for the final game of the season with Exeter City, tributes were paid to all the players. Frank's citation was as follows:

> 'Frank Newton has proved to be just the centre forward we wanted. He has led the attack splendidly, showing an excellent understanding with both wings, while he ably maintained the reputation he gained with Stockport County, for whom he scored 150 [sic] goals in 3 seasons. His total prior to today was 41, and had he been able to play in all matches it is possible that the record which has been set up by Clarence Bourton, Coventry City (49) would have been improved upon'.[128]

His colleague, Jim Hammond, who played in 32 games at inside right, and over the final 10 matches of the season at inside left was also lauded.

'Jim Hammond with his 30 goals has also gone near to [a] record for an in side [sic] forward, and his part in the success of our attack has probably been the most valuable asset of all. That he has developed into one of the most brilliant players in his position in the country is the popular verdict of all critics, for not only has his individual skill and cleverness been a conspicuous factor, but Newton is indebted to him for some wonderful co-operative efforts'.[129]

Certainly Frank had prospered from playing along side a player of Hammond's calibre, and by the close of his first season with Fulham Frank had furthered his already considerable reputation as a robust, opportunistic goal scorer with a lethal shot. He was a popular member of a talented side. However, his success to date had been confined to Third Division football. It remained to be seen how he would cope with the demands of the Second Division.

1932 – 1933

An air of optimism swirled around Craven Cottage on the eve of the 1932-33 season. Hopes were high that the team which performed so well in winning promotion would adapt and respond positively to the increased demands of Second Division football. With this in mind McIntyre moved to add depth to the club's attacking options and revisited Southampton from where he now signed William Fraser, an inside forward, Albert Jepson, an outside right, and centre forward Arthur Haddleton. All had played occasionally between 1930 and 1932 for the Saints first team and collectively had scored 32 goals.[1]

A 'Special Correspondent' caught the pre-season mood prevailing at the Cottage in the 'Football Prospects' column of the *Daily Mirror.*

> 'ALL MERRY AND BRIGHT AT FULHAM
> Southampton Forwards Who Have Joined Promoted Club
>
> Fulham's twenty-seven professionals are remarkably fit and well, and Mr J.A. McIntyre, their secretary-manager, is optimistic of the team's chances in the Second Division. Three new forwards – all from Southampton – have been obtained and everything points to a good and successful season. Fulham's new players ... found the net sixteen times when they appeared for the Saints last season. Haddleton obtained nine of these goals in sixteen games, but, despite his promise, I cannot see him ousting Frank Newton from the leadership of the attack. In fact it is also hard to see how Hammond and Wrightson can be dropped from the inside berths'.[2]

The initial pre-season practice game was played at Craven Cottage on August 13 before a reported 10,000 spectators, and resulted in the first team forwards scoring 4 goals to the 'reserve' side's 3. Of the new Southampton signings, Haddleton and Fraser acquitted themselves well but Jepson at outside-right 'looked as if he was in need of a course of skipping which would quicken him up'.[3]

The second practice game failed to provide much further assistance around team selection. Other than for three players, the recognised first eleven played the reserves, and the latter monopolised the play through both halves. The versatile Peter Malloy,

> 'at centre half, was conspicuous throughout, playing a fine forceful game. Consequently, Newton, in the middle, had little rope, and when he headed through five minutes before the "breather", it was all against the run of the play. Hammond had great difficulty in keeping his feet, and there was much amusement when a wag in the crowd advised the popular Sussex batsman to send for his cricket boots. Of the old stagers, Frank Penn the ever green left winger, gave a most pleasing display ... Among the new men, Haddleton showed every promise of being a sound deputy for Newton'.

Frank scored twice and despite his poor touch Hammond scored the other. For the reserves Haddleton and Richards accounted for one apiece and Wood scored three.[4] The reserves won the game relatively easily 5-3.[5]

Fulham's league season opened on August 1 with a visit to Bradford City's Valley Parade, a ground Frank knew well from his Stockport days. Team selection was straight forward; the side remained unchanged from that selected in the last seven games of the 1931-32 season.[6] However, the day was not a success as Fulham went down 2-0, and Frank injured an ankle late in the first half. The Cottagers were reported to have made a promising overall impression against their 'doughty opponents but were 'handicapped' by Frank's injury and missed good scoring opportunities.[7]

A week later Swansea Town visited the Cottage and 17,000 fans were on hand to witness the home opener, a game that left most at Craven Cottage in high spirits. Frank was not past fit and his place was taken by Haddleton. On his Fulham debut he led the line well and scored 2 of the goals in what was a straight forward 3-1 victory. John Robertson in the *Sunday Dispatch* considered Haddleton had 'thoroughly justified his inclusion' and that Frank would 'find it no easy matter to get back into the team'.[8] J.J.S. in the *Daily Mail* was more cautious in stating that 'Haddleton … as leader of the home forwards, did not show the dash of Newton, but he certainly had a splendid idea of direction'.[9]

Just two days later, on Monday, September 5, Chesterfield visited the Cottage and Fulham 'started like a championship team' when Finch quickly put the hosts one up. Expectations rose among the 10,000 on hand that more were to come but the 'Spireites' regrouped and surprised Fulham by twice coming from behind.

> 'All the goals came in the first half. The second half was a mere battle of strength. Charges were more common than ball play ... Both sides were equally at fault, and the whole business was regrettable, for both could, if they had pleased, have played good football'.[10]

Frank remained out injured and missed the trip to play Notts County the following Saturday, September 10. The Cottagers started slowly and within 5 minutes were a goal down. The

County maintained the pressure 'and for nearly half an hour Notts played so well that defeat seemed very improbable.' Then a goalkeeping error, from which Haddleton capitalised, changed the balance of the match. Fulham stepped up 'and soon established a definite superiority'.[11] After The Magpies lost a man injured Haddleton added a second. With time running out, the County redoubled their efforts to take something from the game but Fulham resisted stoutly and departed with their first away win of the season.[12]

A good action shot of Haddleton, 'Fulham's Sharpshooter', was included in John Robertson's column in the following day's *Sunday Dispatch* of September 11.[13] Having scored 4 goals in 4 games 'the in form' Haddleton was selected for the home fixture with Port Vale; quite possibly in preference to a less than match fit Frank.

Nearly 22,000 packed into the riverside ground but most would have left disappointed at the result, a 1-1 draw. 'The Cottager' spelt it out in the *Sunday Dispatch*:

'CHANCES WASTED

Fulham Without Punch In Their Final Moves.

FULHAM'S football since the club's return to the Second Division has, on the whole, been good. It will not create confidence, however, if Fulham continue to drop points at home through ineptitude in their finishing movements. Since the opening match the Cottagers preferred Haddleton to Newton as leader of the attack, but the dash of the player who was successful as a goal scorer last season might have been an advantageous asset in this game'.[14]

The view in West London was considerably more pointed:

'FULHAM WANT NEWTON
FORWARDS NEED A LEADER.

The Fulham directors will have had much food for thought as a result of the game with Port Vale ... The forward line was completely out of gear for the want of a leader. The match ended in a draw, but the visiting goalkeeper ought to have had to pick the ball out of the net on more than one occasion. Haddleton's feeble display was responsible for many calls from the crowd of "We want Newton."'[15]

Charles H. Harvey in the *Daily Mail* offered a slightly more sympathetic view of Haddleton's performance if, as he stated, what he had been told was correct. 'Haddleton, however, showed a lack of confidence in his ability as a marksman, while too many shots were attempted from long range'.[16]

It would appear that Haddleton was unfortunate as the game with Port Vale on September 17 proved to be Haddleton's last in the Fulham first team. Clearly McIntyre had seen enough, and certainly by Christmas he no longer considered Haddleton adequate cover for Frank so that when Frank later missed 4 consecutive games over the Christmas-New Year period Haddleton was not selected.[17]

Following Port Vale's visit Fulham were placed mid table having won 2, drawn 2, and lost 1 with 6 points after 5 games. Bradford City were top with 11 points, followed by Stoke City and Plymouth Argyle with 9 each; all had played 6 games.[18]

Meanwhile, Frank now fit again had been selected to lead the line in Fulham's Reserve side against Brentford in a top-of-the-table Combination League battle on Monday, September 19. But on the day McIntyre held Frank back as he had decided to reinstate him in the first team at New Cross, on the upcoming Saturday, September 24. To that point in the season Millwall had not conceded a goal at the Den, but 'Newton hopes to celebrate his return … by spoiling this record'.[19] For Haddleton the decision proved terminal; his time at Fulham was effectively up. He subsequently was moved on to Swindon Town and debuted with them on September 16, 1933.[20]

Frank 're-appeared to lead the Cottagers' in front of a good sized 'Derby' crowd of some 28,000 at Millwall's Den.[21] Fulham played football 'of the highest order – accurate passing amongst the forwards, plenty of thrust, and well directed shooting'. And it was Frank who opened the scoring when he finished off an intricate move between Hammond and Richards.[22] In today's parlance, 'it was a game of two halves', as

> '[the] early exchanges were all in Fulham's favour and the Cottagers made an excellent impression with everything they did – apart from their shooting. Their clever approach work, forward combination, and accurate passing were a delight to watch'.

However, there was a tendency at times 'to overdo the pattern weaving'.

After the interval 'Fulham fell away badly' as Millwall 'exerted a stronger influence on the game'. The first Millwall goal was hotly disputed and when play resumed 'several players seemed to have difficulty in controlling their feelings.' Certainly there was little improvement after "Millwall's pertinacity' led to a second goal.[23] The game was summed up by 'The Spotter' in the *Daily Express* who shared the view that Fulham started strongly but were badly off the pace in the second half and 'could do little right; they never rallied; they beat themselves'.[24]

By the end of September the Cottagers were doing no better than holding their own in their new surroundings, being mid table with 6 points from 6 games. McIntyre needed to strengthen the side and it was to the defence that he first turned. At the time McIntyre viewed this as a priority, to which the *Daily Mail* made reference: 'Fulham are negotiating for the transfer of a first-class full-back, and hope to sign him on in time to play on Saturday against Southampton at Craven Cottage'[25] To this point in the season Birch and Tilford had filled the positions of right and left back respectively but there had been mention that Tilford, in particular against Port Vale, 'sometimes showed poor judgement;[26] and in the Millwall game, 'Neither Birch nor Tilford looked sound, against such forwards …'[27] In another game against Chesterfield, 'Abel worried the lives out of the Fulham defenders'.[28] Despite these shortcomings the anticipated signing did not immediately materialise, and the Birch – Tilford partnership continued uninterrupted until January, 1933. McIntyre held Tilford in high regard from his time at Coventry, and in February, 1932 had brought him to Fulham, paying Coventry a fee of £750.[29]

An article appeared in the *Daily Mail* at the end of September, attributed to 'Arbiter', Frank M. Carruthers entitled 'Footballers Old At 30.' Frank was soon to cross that threshold and may have been only too aware of the milestone. The main thrust of 'Arbiter's' remarks concerned the declining longevity of a career in professional football. He considered that the average career span of about twelve years for a professional footballer was shortening. He argued that the alteration of the offside rule in 1925 had quickened the pace of the game and that 'the life of the player would inevitably be shortened. I am afraid this fear has been realised. In a football sense a man now begins to grow old at 30.' He was 'convinced that in the raging tearing game of today' a player was required to have 'more speed than used to be essential and that without it he cannot hope to hold his own.' In 1931 Frank was at the peak of his goalscoring achievements and his opinion may have differed, but the underlying message was one of which he must have been well aware. Also he would have agreed wholeheartedly with 'Arbiter' when he wrote that a player,

> 'would be less at a disadvantage if he were afforded the protection to which the rules entitle him. Much of the slap-bang tackling which we see and which is tolerated by indulgent referees is unfair, and it is due to the excessive keenness with which the game is played. Back or half-back going into a tackle today may hope to secure the ball, but he makes his effort so thoroughly that if he should fail he succeeds in another way that is almost as effective. He stops the man. I am sorry to say that I have seen far too much of this double-purpose tackling this season'.[30]

Until the onset of the 1932-33 season Frank had remained

relatively free from injury throughout his soccer career. Given the robust, fast and physical manner in which he played and the often shocking conditions, some compared to 'no man's land', others frozen or waterlogged, it is surprising that he did not suffer more joint or ligament problems.

At this point of the season, post the Millwall encounter, it was time to regroup at the Cottage and the players would have been aware that McIntyre was casting an eye over the transfer market. The manager would have made it abundantly clear that he expected more and the upcoming game against his one time employers, Southampton, was a good time to start. He may also have felt piqued that the players he had signed from 'The Saints' during the closed season had disappointed. Haddleton may have been unlucky, but Fraser and Jepson had not impressed and neither had played in the first team.

Despite the team's perceived deficiencies McIntyre would have enjoyed the afternoon of October 1, as did the Cottagers.[31]

'Fulham's Great Display' was how the *West London Observer* headlined their extensive, glowing report of the match.

> 'Adverse weather conditions only served to accentuate the brilliance of Fulham's display against Southampton, at Craven Cottage on Saturday, when they won 4-2. The football of the Cottagers was splendid and with the exception of Price the entire side came through with flying colours. The inside-left was the one weak link and was often more of a hindrance than a help'.

The home side settled quickly and applied early pressure but after 15 minutes it was Southampton who scored. Fulham persisted and after 24 minutes 'Richards sent across a perfect corner', Frank rose to meet it and put it over the goalkeeper's head to equalise. Then barely 5 minutes later Frank capitalised on

> '[an] opening made by Hammond – easily the best player on the field. Newton took a cross pass with splendid judgement and from seven yards he headed well out of the goalkeeper's reach. It was a splendid goal'.

However by half time 'The Saints' were back on terms as the result of a Tilford blunder.

The Cottagers remained dominant in the early going after the interval until, following some narrow escapes around the Southampton goal, Hammond finally put Fulham ahead. Southampton protested vigorously, but Mr W.P. Harper, who controlled the last Cup Final, was having none of it and barely broke stride in awarding the goal. Fulham continued to play 'splendidly' and Richards 'who throughout had been a thorn in the visitor's defence', added a fourth. As Fulham tired on the increasingly treacherous surface Southampton rallied but their efforts fell short and were finally seen off 4-2.[32]

This was an important confidence boosting win that marked the beginning of an excellent seven game unbeaten run which put the club up to fourth in the Division by the end of the first week of November. Fulham were then a point ahead of Tottenham as well as Bury, but trailed Stoke, Bradford and Plymouth Argyle.[33]

Despite the criticism of Price's performance against 'The Saints' he of the 'dazzling feet' was selected the following week for the trip up to Bury. 'The Shakers' were unbeaten on their own ground, and before a dismally small crowd of

5,000, Fulham did well to take a hard earned point. The team started strongly, made 'a great impression', and after thirty-two minutes it was Price who scored. However, there followed a 'dramatic turn of the tide after half-time', prompted in part by the reduction of Fulham to ten men, as Bury pressed forward in 'hurricane style'. Although Fulham were later restored to eleven the Bury side maintained the pressure and with time running out a 'fierce drive was deflected off Barrett into his own net.' In summary it was a 'gruelling' game from which Fulham were, according to the account in the *West London Observer*, perhaps unlucky not to take both points.[34]

Lincoln City, winners of the 1931-32 Northern Division title, were one point ahead of Fulham when the side visited the Cottage on Saturday, October 15. 'Cottager' in the *Sunday Dispatch* succinctly concluded:

> 'Newton's deadly opportunism – he scored two fine goals – Hammond's masterly long passes – he has seldom played better – and the speed of the whole Fulham side on the ball beat Lincoln City'.[35]

Lincoln's game plan depended upon the successful operation of their offside trap. This approach did not go down well with the majority of the 25,000 spectators who recognised the ploy within the first five minutes when Hammond netted only to discover that the referee had blown up for 'offside'. However, after 16 minutes, with the Lincoln left back again appealing for 'offside', Richards centred and Price hit the net from 'just inside the penalty area.' Undaunted, Lincoln persisted with their game plan and a minute into the second half Richards, to the increasing frustration of the crowd, was again pulled up. However, shortly thereafter,

> 'the winger was compensated when Newton snapped up his centre and crashed the ball to the back of the net. Fulham maintained the pressure and the Lincoln custodian was injured in turning a terrific shot from Hammond round the post. From the corner Newton was just too high with a great header. Price and Finch were on the top of their form, and a great piece of work by the winger led to Newton obtaining the third goal with a rasping shop [sic] which left the goalkeeper helpless'.

Despite trailing by three goals Lincoln were not finished and in the final 15 minutes mounted an unlikely but determined fight back. It started with a hotly disputed penalty after which Fulham responded when Frank added his third. But no, he too was ruled 'offside'. Five minutes before the end Lincoln scored a 'palpably handled' second goal which was allowed to stand despite considerable disquiet on the home front. Ultimately it mattered little, and it was felt that 'Fulham were worthy winners of a hard-fought game'.[36]

It was some nineteen years since Fulham last visited Turf Moor. However, on October 22, 1932 'The Cottagers' succeeded in finding their way there once more. The harsh realities of the severe economic depression throughout Lancashire's milling communities continued to limit attendances and fewer than 6,000 turned out. Unfortunate, as Fulham produced some champagne football as 'The Baker' reported: 'For the greater part of the game Fulham played the best football seen at Burnley this season and were awarded by a lead of three goals'.[37] The Cottagers led 2-0 at the interval on goals by Frank and Gibbons. They continued to press subsequently and Frank added a third with 'an excellent screw shot over his head.' Alarmingly, and similar to the previous week against Lincoln, with a commanding lead and only 15 minutes remaining, Fulham again failed to circle the wagons and 'The Clarets' scored two quick goals. Worse still was that Burnley scored again 'just on time', leaving the visitors a long trip home in which to rue their carelessness.[38]

McIntyre would have been furious with his side's late defensive lapses in successive weeks. As a result his search for a quality full back moved up a gear and his watching brief became more focused. His concerns would have been reinforced as a result of the following week's game with Bradford Park Avenue at Craven Cottage. Fulham initially took the lead when Richards 'caught the goalkeeper napping with a dropping shot.' However, Telford in particular struggled to contain Geldard on Bradford's right wing who had a hand in both Bradford goals. He 'caused Fulham's defence any amount of anxiety by his cleverness and, after half an hour, from a corner-kick he caused Iceton to punch the ball through his own goal'.[39] Bradford's second resulted from Geldard running 'rings round Barrett and Tilford' and setting up Suggett for a tap in. Fulham came back into the game and drew level when Frank latched on to a fine pass from Finch and the teams went in at the break tied 2-2.

It was raining hard after the interval and Bradford's defence was put under immediate pressure. This was survived initially despite some anxious moments, but after 15 minutes the diminutive Price put the Cottagers ahead with a spectacular drive. Bradford responded and Iceton had 'few idle moments' in the Fulham net. Regardless, the decisive Fulham goal came when Price 'swung over a beautiful centre for Newton to cleverly head' the fourth. The final goal, scored by Finch, 'crowned a good afternoon's work' and would have sent most of the 20,000 plus spectators home well pleased.[40]

At the end of October 1932 McIntyre and many others would have been confident that his charges were adapting well to the demands of Second Division football. There was of course room for improvement when Fulham set off for the West Country to take on Plymouth Argyle, a side then enjoying a run of good results having lost only one of their previous ten matches and still undefeated on their Home Park ground. Plymouth were tough opposition and occupied third spot in the table on 17 points. Comparatively, Fulham were seventh with 14 points, 6 behind the leaders Stoke City.[41]

The club's trips to the South West often featured a stop over in Teignmouth. Today it would be described as a 'team building' exercise, but then more probably involved nothing more strenuous than a round or two of golf, sea fishing and some light training.

> 'The Cottagers, who spent the greater part of the week preceding the match at Teignmouth, amply justified the preparation which Manager McIntyre gave them for the occasion, and although the Argyle had more of the game than Fulham, the visitors took advantage of every scoring chance that presented itself and collected both points'.

Plymouth started with the wind behind them and subjected the Fulham defence to a thorough examination. Their efforts were rewarded shortly before the interval and the Cottagers turned around a goal down. As the second half progressed Fulham worked their way further into the game and from a set piece Frank levelled. Then, much to the delight of the 20,000 on hand, Plymouth regained the lead and

> 'continued to press, but could not get past Fulham's defence. Late in the game the Cottagers rallied magnificently. Hammond created an opening for Newton to get on terms again, while in the last minutes Finch finished off a final attack by scoring the winning goal'.

The credit for this excellent, hard fought victory was attributed to an improved defensive performance. 'It was the alertness of the forwards in seizing their opportunities, and the stoutness of the defence that carried Fulham to victory. The backs played one of the best games this year, while Iceton was brilliant'.[42]

The Cottagers had now gone six games without defeat and on November 12 an expectant crowd in excess of 20,000 wound their way to the Stevenage Road ground. The majority hoped to witness the steam-rolling of Oldham Athletic; but that was not to be. The game in fact was a tight encounter that was settled by Frank's early goal.

> 'During the first quarter of an hour Fulham's co-ordination, both fore and aft, was delightful. The Oldham defence was over-run. The movements of the Fulham forwards were fast and accurate and when Newton scored

> after six minutes, his goal suggested more to follow. Fulham, however, failed to live up to their promise. From a brilliant side they slumped to the ordinary, and Oldham not only held them, but were dangerous when they got going'.[43]

Having weathered the opening storm, Oldham improved and came close to scoring on numerous occasions. The visitor's centre half Gray 'for the most part held Newton in a grip of iron', and Frank's colleagues, despite some clever approach work, failed to impress. The Fulham defence again took the honours and it was primarily through their efforts that the 'Latics' left empty handed.

As a result Fulham vaulted into third spot in the league, 4 points behind Stoke City and 2 back of Bradford City, but now 1 point ahead of Tottenham, Bury and Plymouth. They also held a game in hand over the latter three.[44]

A visit to Manchester's Old Trafford stadium followed and 'Exile', reporting in the *Sunday Dispatch* on November 20, felt compelled to head his column 'GLORIOUS FAILURE'. He enthusiastically conveyed the events played out before 35,000 fans.

> 'The drama of the brilliant Fulham side fighting hard to keep intact a long sequence without defeat, and United's struggle to maintain a slender lead that they often looked like losing! Here was football with all its lure and thrills! Fulham's was a glorious failure! United will not meet a finer side this season. There was an amazing goal rush near the interval, and Manchester United had seen their early lead wiped out by a Fulham dash that

produced two goals. Then the Old Trafford side struck back with two. Four goals in six minutes! Such was the brilliance of the attacks. Gallimore shot on the run from 20 yards range for the first goal. Price began the quick scoring, getting an easy goal with the United's backs at fault. A minute later an inspired goal, described by Billy Meredith as the best he had seen for many years was got by Richards, who cleverly slipped the ball past the advancing goalkeeper. Fulham's lead was short lived, as Brown, the game's cleverest winger, equalised with a glorious shot. Before the interval Ridding put the United in front. Fulham deserved a point for the way they fought to wipe out United's lead, now increased in the second half by another goal from Galimore. The way those two clever schemers Price and Hammond swung the ball from wing to wing or down the middle to the ever-eager Newton always threatened to overwhelm the Manchester defence. From a corner-kick Newton headed through, and Jones deflected the ball on the way. Only some cleverly conceived off-side tactics by Mellor and Jones kept Fulham from equalising. In the closing minutes they were within an ace of scoring again when Finch's 10-yards drive was saved by Moody's wonderful anticipation'.[45]

The home supporters would have found the 4-3 victory highly entertaining. But from the Cottagers' standpoint it terminated a fine unbeaten run stretching back to the end of September during which Fulham had won five and drawn two.

As early as late November speculation was mounting

regarding which club might best be able to mount a sustained promotion drive. Stoke City, now leading the Second Division, visited the Cottage on November 26 and most in the large crowd of approximately 28,000 experienced something of a reality check as their heroes went down 3-1. Charles Buchan reported on the game and his assessment did not flatter the Cottagers. He headed his report, 'Stoke Rout Fulham', and was unsparing in his analysis.

> 'Fulham's hopes for promotion received a nasty jolt when they suffered their first home defeat of the season. Stoke City ... were their conquerors at Craven Cottage, and they well deserved their decisive victory. They were real promotion candidates, Fulham were not, and during the whole game Stoke held an undeniable superiority. The Potters were solid in every department, whereas Fulham had decided weaknesses both in the forward line and in defence. Only for a brief period in the second half, after Hammond and Wrightson changed positions did Fulham reveal form worthy of their high position in the League. Much of Fulham's troubles could be traced to the poor positional play of Birch and Telford. They played so squarely that one long pass ... beat both and allowed Mawson ... sufficient scope to engineer many dangerous movements'.

In Buchan's opinion Stoke exposed a fragile Fulham rearguard and immediate lessons should be learnt if Fulham were to progress. He emphasised that the Cottagers 'must concentrate without delay on finding a defensive plan of campaign and on improving their tackling'.[46]

The local press acknowledged the significance of Stoke's victory, noting that they played 'Like Champions' and amply demonstrated why they were at the head of the Second Division. Mention was made that Wrightson replaced the 'incomparable' Price, but he (Wrightson) 'was by no means to blame for the defeat.' The closest Fulham came occurred when Frank levelled early in the second half. But Stoke scored another almost immediately and never looked back. The report concluded emphatically that Fulham 'were soundly beaten, and a better side than Stoke City will not be seen at Craven Cottage this season'.[47]

McIntyre would certainly have been concerned with the back to back losses, in particular the decisive manner of Stoke's triumph. With two London 'Derby' games upcoming on December 3 and 10 against Charlton Athletic and Tottenham, positive results now were crucial if Fulham were to recover their poise. By the beginning of December Fulham had slipped to 8th, in the Division II standings with 18 points from 15 games, well behind the leaders Stoke City on 25 points from 16. Tottenham were second on 21 points while at the bottom of the table Charlton were lodged behind Chesterfield, West Ham and Burnley.[48] A victory at the Valley on December 3 was now mandatory if Fulham were to remain in touch with the leading pack.

The home side dominated proceedings initially and at the interval went in a goal to the good. By then Charlton should have established a winning margin, but fortunately Tootill, making his Fulham debut in goal following his recent transfer from Wolverhampton Wanderers, had only retrieved the ball from behind him once. Ultimately, the game turned on an extraordinary incident that arose just after the break.

> 'Three Fulham forwards in offside positions saw the ball sent down the field, and retired to allow Wright, in the Charlton goal to field the ball, as their positions put them out of play. Thinking that the referee had whistled, stopping the game for a free kick, the goalkeeper threw the ball down. Newton grasped the situation at once, and running up shot into an empty net. There was tremendous excitement at this "gift" goal and while the Charlton team vigorously protested to the referee they did not deter him from ruling that the goal was quite in order'.

Subsequently Fulham's performance improved and Hammond scored to put the Cottagers ahead 2-1. Their good fortune held for the balance of the match despite Charlton continuing to press and create enough chances 'to have scored a dozen goals.' The majority of the 25,000 inside the Valley had their expectations raised momentarily when Tilford conceded a penalty in the closing stages. Up stepped Pearce, but he failed to seize the moment as he shot wide and thus ensured Fulham's hard earned 2-1 victory.[49]

As John Robertson noted in the *Sunday Dispatch*:

> 'Fortune continues to frown on Charlton, who ought to have beaten Fulham, but there is no excuse for a player who does not play to the whistle or for one who misses a penalty-kick. The goalkeeper's error in throwing down the ball and allowing Newton to score at will can have had few parallels'.[50]

A more formidable challenge awaited Fulham at Craven Cottage on the following Saturday with the visit of the high flying Tottenham Hotspurs. However, on the day Spurs' luck, like Charlton's, was also out. In this instance they had to play most the match with ten men after Tottenham's inside left Greenfield broke his leg in a goalmouth scramble. This unfortunate accident arose just after Richards had put Fulham ahead in the fourteenth minute. Then just five minutes later Finch was fouled in the Tottenham penalty area. Frank strode up, hit a thunderbolt of a shot directly at Nicholls in the Tottenham goal. The goalkeeper managed to keep the ball out, much to the dismay of the home support, but was pole-axed and out cold for some three minutes. Despite missing such an excellent opportunity, Fulham continued to press the ten men and Frank made partial amends on the half hour.

The atmosphere inside the ground and throughout the first half was described in the national press:

> 'One! Two! Three! Four! Five! Six! Seven! The Swan[sea] song composed by the Tottenham supporters the previous Saturday filled the air when their champions took the field at Craven Cottage. Atmospherics were bad, however, on the Fulham wavelength, for after the echo had rebounded with One! Two! the theme song was blotted out. It was no musical comedy that was provided. It was drama all the way through. The Hotspurs, unconquered since Sept. 24, were two goals in arrears fifteen minutes after the curtain had been rung up and had lost the services of Greenfield, their inside-left for the remainder of the play.

Before the Spurs lost Greenfield, Fulham had shown a superiority in tactics and fully deserved the goal with which Richards opened the scoring, although it was a Tottenham blunder which led up to the opportunity being presented to the West London side.

The accident to Greenfield followed and while he was being carried off on a stretcher Fulham were awarded a penalty kick, Rowe fouling Finch. Newton took the kick. The shot struck Nicholls on the forehead and laid him out as effectively as an upper-cut to the chin by Jack Doyle. That missed penalty cost Fulham a point. Newton soon atoned for that failure when Hammond got Nicholls unbalanced with a shot that left the Fulham centre in a favourable position. A neat flick with his left foot the wrong side of Nicholls and the Fulham crowd were in ecstasies. Two goals up in fifteen minutes against such an all-conquering side as the Spurs was more than the most optimistic of them expected. The Spurs were not disorganised, but their sharpshooters were allowed little scope by a solid Fulham defence, which had Gibbons as the pivot. After the interval a different tale has to be told'.[51]

Although the Cottagers were ahead 2-0 at the break it was all change thereafter. Frank went close at the outset but Tottenham reduced the deficit after ten minutes and continued to press the Fulham defence.

'Spurs were playing like a team inspired, and the great contingent from Tottenham let forth a terrific roar when Hunt smashed a terrific shot into the roof of the net

> to level the scores. The Cottagers were outplayed, and the football of the Spurs was amazing. In the last quarter of an hour Fulham staged a partial recovery, but the forwards seldom looked like scoring. With two minutes to go, Hammond, who had faded out after a nasty kick in the face, drove in a typical shot but Nicholls brought off a marvellous save, flinging himself full length and grasping the ball on the line. It was a wonderful effort and the crowning feature of a glorious display'.[52]

'Cottager' in the *Sunday Dispatch* praised 'Tenacious Tottenham' for defying the handicap of being a man short for so long and he considered it to have been one of the 'keenest local duels' witnessed at the 'Cottage for many a day.' With respect to the Fulham players he singled out Gibbons as the best man on the field, Hammond for his effectiveness in attack and Newton, Barrett and Finch for the 'impressive fashion' in which they combined.[53]

It was clearly an afternoon of exhilarating football and one to which the wretched cliché 'a game of two halves' could reasonably be applied. Overall the draw was viewed as a just result.

Fulham had enjoyed a good run since losing their opening match to Bradford City at the end of August. In the following sixteen games the side had won 8, drawn 5 and lost 3. Frank had enjoyed an extraordinary run of success after returning against Millwall on September 24. Since then he had recorded 16 goals, and only failed to score in the draw at Bury. Over the same period the team had scored 29 goals and were fifth in the Division, 8 points behind Stoke, 4, 3, and 2 adrift of Bradford City, Spurs and Bury. Fulham had played 17 games, one fewer game than the others.

There then followed a run of indifferent results, 2 wins, a draw and 5 losses. By January 22, 1933, Fulham had slipped to tenth, 7 points behind the joint leaders Bradford City, Stoke and Bury.[54] In addition the club had exited the FA Cup at Chester losing 5-0 which was a truly shocking result.[55]

This downward spiral commenced at Blundell Park where Fulham obligingly provided Grimsby Town with their first home win in seven weeks. Fulham, playing into a strong wind, were caught short by 'The Mariners' aggressive start and after only two minutes were a goal behind. Surprisingly there was no further scoring in the game as the hosts held on grimly to their slim advantage. Fulham did improve in the second half and rallied strongly towards the close; in the Grimsby goal Tweedy served his side splendidly to keep his goal intact.[56]

Fulham then returned to Craven Cottage to prepare for three games in four days over the Christmas period. Regrettably, the Christmas spirit of 'good will to all men' was in short supply after Nottingham Forest's visit.

> 'No excuses can be offered for two valuable points being presented to Nottingham Forest ... Even if their football was not so pretty, the play of the visitors was much more effective. In the first half a ridiculous blunder by Oliver gave Nottingham the lead, and in the second half there was the extraordinary position of Fulham having two thirds of the play but with a score seldom looking likely. Newton was blotted out by Graham – a great centre-half, and Hammond was useless. A heroic display by Finch was the one redeeming feature of a poor exhibition'.

To make matters worse for the hosts shortly after play resumed in the second half Newton and two opponents were injured in a goalmouth scramble. As a result Frank was 'off the field for some minutes, and when he returned he was limping badly.' He continued to lead the line but he was less than effective and with ten minutes remaining, 'Newton, who had been hobbling about in the centre, retired to the left wing, and the re-arranged line struggled on to the hopeless end'.[57]

As a result Frank did not play in the next five games only returning to the side on January 21 against Notts County. In the interim Wrightson assumed the number 9 duties. Over this period Fulham beat and drew with West Ham on December 26 and 27, beat Bradford City on the last day of the month at home and lost away to both Chesterfield and Swansea on January 2 and 7. Matters failed to improve when on January 14 Fulham travelled north to play the high flying Chester side. The Third Division North leaders ran riot and unceremoniously dumped their visitors out of the FA Cup 5-0. This game proved to be the final first team appearances for both Wrightson and Tilford.[58]

The headline of the Swansea match report proclaimed: 'Fulham Need Newton Missing Link In Forward Line.' The view was that the sooner Frank returned 'the better for the Cottagers. There is a lot of leeway to be made up.' Consequently, there was considerable relief when he was finally pronounced fit to return against Notts County on January 21.

To this point in the season the County had not lost to a London side, and at Craven Cottage the team produced one of their best performances. The Cottagers got off to a flying start and were two goals up within eight minutes and 3-2 ahead at half time. The goals came through Hammond and Frank whose brace came from his 'head and foot – both efforts provided by Richards' centres.' Notts County took control after the break and scored two unanswered goals. While it was felt that Fulham had the more polished attack, particularly prior to the interval, the County looked the better balanced side and were well served by their defence, notably the backs who were judged better 'than the Fulham pair'.[59]

This 4-3 defeat meant Fulham had lost three games in a row during January, a disastrous run. While the team had scored five goals, ten had been conceded and the club was 10th in Division II.[60] McIntyre continued to make adjustments to the defensive alignment, bringing in Hindson at left back for the trip to Port Vale's Old Recreation Ground.[61] And most probably he was simultaneously warming up his Southampton connections, or at the very least intensifying his watching brief across the transfer market.

The Port Vale pitch, as a result of attempts to improve the surface, was covered in sand. Nonetheless, the 'frost bound pitch' was held responsible for a series of mistakes that resulted in two goals being scored in the first three minutes. The second, Fulham's equaliser, was scored by Frank. Subsequently, before a disappointing crowd of only 5,000, the combatants 'quickly settled down and despite the climatic conditions there was plenty of good constructive play.' The Cottagers continued to assert themselves, with their forwards 'splendidly supported by the halves', Finch scored the deciding goal ten minutes after the interval. This win, the first in 1933, represented two important points and maintained Fulham's mid-table position.[62]

A London 'Derby' followed against Millwall which generated

considerably more interest and attracted a crowd of over 15,000 to the Cottage. What transpired was the familiar 'old story of a glorious half hour and then the inexplicable fade out'. The feeling was that Fulham should have established a winning margin before half time, and most definitely should not have been 'struggling to avoid defeat' in the closing stages.

> 'Newton was in great form and after eighteen minutes he opened the score. Price brought the goalkeeper to his knees with a shot from close range and from the resultant scrimmage Newton shot into an unguarded net. Fulham had had the best of the play and the success was well deserved. Just before half-time Newton snapped up a through pass and crashed a terrific shot from fully thirty yards out. The goalkeeper made a flying leap and turned the ball round the post'.

And that was as close as Fulham came for the hosts then gave up a goal after a sustained spell of Millwall pressure, and matters did not improve when a 'painfully off colour Hammond' ballooned over from three yards. The tiring Fulham side attempted to rally but it was often 'only Iceton' in the Fulham goal, 'who stood between Millwall and the lead.' A draw was viewed to be a reasonable result but Hammond was singled out for his poor performance. 'Newton, handicapped through the weakness of Hammond, strove valiantly, and when the centre forward had the ball there was always hope'.[63]

A particularly significant trip to Southampton followed on February 11. The match resulted in a draw, this time 2-2. But,

'Fulham came very near to making football history on Saturday when they visited Southampton. The Cottagers have not won on this ground since the War, and after being two goals up in the second half, they survived a great revival on the part of the home team ... Fulham were seen to best advantage in the first half, when they played convincingly, and looked good value for both points. The forwards combined cleverly, their passing movements being executed with sound judgement'.

Fulham's first goal came through Richards when Finch, after 'a brilliant solo run', put him through on goal. Southampton stormed back but after some ten minutes of intense pressure around Fulham's goalmouth, during which time Southampton forced 'nearly twenty corners', Frank 'got away and put the Cottagers two up.' 'The Saints' captain Keeping then scored from the penalty spot and in the fading embers Southampton equalised and rescued a point.[64]

An unsatisfactory conclusion in some respects, but more importantly it took McIntyre back to Southampton, his old stomping ground, a club where he remained well connected and on which he now focused his sights. Critically, he would have been aware that the 'Saints' were experiencing a period of considerable financial pressure and therefore the club's directors could be susceptible to a generous approach for certain of their more prominent players. On February 17 the *Daily Herald* reported:

'After negotiations which had lasted all day Fulham last evening secured the transfer of two of Southampton's outstanding players, Keeping their captain and left back, and Arnold, who has done exceptionally well at outside-left. The news will be received with dismay by the Saints' supporters, for Arnold and Keeping had done much to keep the team in their present position, and the club's reserve strength is not of the best. Both players will be included in the game against Bury at Fulham tomorrow. Mr J. Dean, chairman of Fulham, admitted that the fee agreed on was the biggest ever paid by the club'.[65]

A prominent but unidentified member of the Saints' Supporters Club was contacted for his view which he could only describe as a tragedy for the Southampton football club. On the other hand, the directors would have welcomed the resulting infusion of £5,100 into the club's depleted coffers.[66]

It transpired that in one swoop McIntyre had resolved the most troublesome of his defensive problems and had significantly strengthened his attacking options, besides indirectly improving the depth of the reserves. Keeping was known to McIntyre as he was managing the club when Keeping signed professional forms in December, 1920. Since then he had made 300 appearances for Southampton, and had

'earned representative honours playing on the FA Tours of Canada in 1926 and South Africa and Rhodesia in 1929. He also played for England against The Rest, for the Professionals against the Amateurs and, in 1931, for the Football League against the Irish League at Blackpool'.

Arnold had joined Southampton in 1928, when he also

signed for Hampshire C.C.C., and had already played for England at Lords in 1931 against New Zealand.[67] These were significant signings and both names went directly onto the team sheet for the home fixture with Bury.[68] Frank was a late withdrawal from this game for which no reason has been established, and his place was taken by Perry.

A crowd of over 21,000 were inside Craven Cottage to see for themselves what impact the new signings might make against a good Bury side.

> 'Playing in their first match for FULHAM, Arnold and Keeping, formerly of Southampton had much to do with the saving of a point against BURY. The former headed a fine goal, while Keeping, who defended soundly placed a free -kick so well towards the end of the game that Perry had little difficulty in bringing the scores level. Fulham were distinctly lucky to avoid defeat. Bury held a two-goal lead for a long time – and deserved it. Their forwards swung the ball about to good effect, and backed up by efficient middle-line service, gave the Fulham defence a gruelling time. Perry was not a big success as Fulham's centre-forward, and the front line was far from impressive'.[69]

Similar views were expressed in the local press in which it was noted that Finch, now moved to the right wing, 'was not a success' while Perry 'strove valiantly in the middle but is not a Newton.' As noted the debutants did impress. Arnold, although poorly supported by Barrett, 'showed class and pace' and was expected to prove an excellent acquisition. Keeping in turn, although 'handicapped by the fact that he was in strange company ... played a magnificent game'.[70]

A difficult but fruitless trip followed on the Friday night of February 24 to Lincoln where a blizzard dumped a foot or more of snow on Lincoln's Sincil Bank ground. Local officials realised early that 'play would be doubtful, but a staff of men set to work to clear the touch lines.' Nonetheless, referee Adams of Nottingham called the game off after a noon pitch inspection. A no brainer given that 'in some parts of the ground the snow was 12 inches deep, and drifts had made the conditions particularly bad on the Sincil Bank side of the ground'.[71]

Fulham's next scheduled game was against Burnley on March 4 but this clashed with the sixth round of the FA Cup in which Burnley were drawn to play Manchester City at Turf Moore. The league fixture was rescheduled for the Wednesday following and Fulham potentially had a Saturday off. Commercial interests prevailed, however, and with Chelsea FC in a similar position (their scheduled opponents were Derby County) such a financial open goal was not to be missed. The arrangements for a 'friendly' between the S.W. London neighbours had probably been made shortly after the 5th round was played on February 18. The 'friendly' was held at Craven Cottage on March 4 and 'provided a splendid entertainment for over 20,000 spectators.'

A recovered Frank returned for this game which was a see-saw battle that raged from end to end and it was one in which Fulham never trailed. At the interval Fulham were a goal up, Arnold scoring 'with a rasping shot from close range'. They should have been further ahead since Chelsea were 'not in the picture.' But ten minutes later Chelsea were level and as 'so often has happened at Craven Cottage this season, Fulham went to pieces for a spell'. It was Arnold who then shook the hosts out of their lethargy when he broke 'away and sent over a perfect centre. Hammond drove in a shot which McIntosh could only push out. Newton was on the spot, and the ball was in the net.' However, within three minutes Chelsea had equalised once more. Arnold continued to be 'a rare thorn' in the side of the 'Pensioners' defence 'he was playing a great game', and once more had the ball in the back of the visitors' net only to be ruled offside. With time running out it was Hammond who restored Fulham's lead but yet again Chelsea equalised, this time directly from the kick-off. 'On the general run of play, Fulham were definitely superior', but overall the local correspondent considered the draw a fitting climax to a thrilling game. More important from Fulham's perspective was the mounting evidence that McIntyre's recent business with Southampton might well prove transformational.[72]

Burnley arrived at the Cottage, more in hope than expectation after losing their quarter final FA Cup match. Their start in this mid-week game before 10,000 Fulham supporters was calamitous as in the opening two minutes the Lancastrians shipped two goals. The first was scored almost before the visitors arrived on the pitch. 'Newton kicked off by passing to Hammond, and the ball travelled in a long pass to Finch. He centred, Newton headed, and without any opponent ever touching the ball, Wood put it straight into the net.' Two minutes later Arnold broke in, shot hard and a Burnley defender turned it into his own goal. But that was as good as it got, for after 'the best start of the season, the Cottagers faded away miserably and were lucky to win by 2-1.'

'For the remainder of the game, Fulham did nothing but spoil their opening efforts. By clever passing the Burnley forwards mastered the defence, and did everything but score. Arnold was the only forward to give the home supporters any hope. Keeping was the best player in the Fulham defence, where Oliver and Barrett spent a dismal afternoon ... providing passes for the opposition'.[73]

Both Arnold and Keeping had made a strong impression and had gone some way to reinvigorating the Fulham side. The trip to Bradford Park's Horton Park Avenue ground on March 11 reinforced this view as Fulham finally 'played like a promotion team', winning 4-1.

'Arnold, the new Southampton transfer, was the star of a team of Cottagers strong in every department. He scored a goal and made the openings for the other three. With Hammond and Newton at the top of their form, the front line at one period of the game carried all before it. Gibbons and Keeping were the best of a stiff defence'.

The first half was a fairly even affair and at the interval Fulham led 1-0. The goal was scored by Frank when he headed home an Arnold cross. Bradford equalised soon after the interval, but then Arnold commenced his demolition job.

'The rest of the game was definitely in Fulham's favour, with Arnold always threatening danger to the home defence. He brought the ball up into a promising position for Hammond to put Fulham ahead, and a few minutes later repeated the trick for Newton to get a third goal'.

Fittingly, it was Arnold who scored the fourth a few minutes from time.

The overly optimistic view was expressed somewhat prematurely that by scoring three second half goals Fulham's tendency to 'fade out' had been put to rest.[74]

With this win the Cottagers had now won 3 and drawn 3 of their last six games and had not lost a league match since encountering Notts County on January 21. As a result Fulham had climbed to 8th in the Division but remained seven points behind the leaders Tottenham and Stoke City.[75]

The week of March 13 was an active one. First, Arnold was selected to play for 'The Rest' in an England trial match at Portsmouth on March 22 and Hammond was selected as a travelling reserve.[76] Second, with the closure of the transfer season upcoming, Fulham signed George Rounce, a centre forward, from Queen's Park Rangers for a fee of £450.[77] Of more marginal significance was Arsenal's signing of Ray Bowden, Plymouth Argyle's exceptional goalscorer for a then record Arsenal fee of £5,000, mentioned here as Plymouth were due at the Cottage on Saturday, March 18.[78]

The England trial match, in which Hammond did not participate, was considered 'an unsatisfactory test of England's football strength'. The result, a 5-1 victory for the Rest, meant 'little knowledge could be gained from the trial'. 'Corinthian' in the *Daily Herald* attributed this to the Rest having a 'mad moment' which lasted four minutes, during which time they scored three goals. Sagar, in the England goal, was injured after 25 minutes and left the field with England 3-0 behind. Blenkinsop took over and yielded the fourth before Sagar returned in the second half. Finally, Crooks on England's right wing played 'half crippled for the greater part of the second half'.

For his part Arnold acquitted himself well, and 'used his great pace magnificently in the general upsetting of the England defence.' He was instrumental in setting up the opening goal when he finally received a pass 'that could be turned to account. He had to run at a tremendous pace, and then take a flying kick at the ball', which Sagar could only palm into the path of Hulme who scored.[79]

Plymouth Argyle, a point behind Fulham but now without Bowden, generated a good deal of interest among the 25,000 inside the Cottage on the afternoon of March 18. There was a very late line-up change in the Fulham side when Wood was switched to play at left half, a position unfamiliar to him, after Barrett pulled up injured just before the kick-off. The Reserve side was already *en route* to Southend for a London Combination game, and Wood was judged to be the best man immediately available to step into the breach. As a result Rounce made his first team debut at inside left, having just been transferred from QPR on March 14.[80]

The game started badly for the hosts who were a goal down after eight minutes while playing into a strong breeze. But Fulham soon levelled after Finch made a dazzling run and found Arnold in front of goal. Honours remained even although the right side of the Plymouth forward line exploited Wood's defensive weaknesses and came close to again edge in front. Just prior to the break Plymouth did net, but the effort was ruled offside.

After the interval it was the Cottagers turn to remonstrate

vociferously when the referee disallowed what appeared to be their second goal. Some twelve minutes later the Argyle players were at it once more 'in a body' when Frank appeared to have scored Fulham's second. On this occasion the referee consulted his linesman and then pointed to the middle. His decision took many by surprise and even the match reporter felt compelled to observe: '… Newton beating Harper from close range, but the goal should never have been allowed. The centre forward was at least three yards offside when he received the ball.' Just four minutes later the stuffing was completely knocked out of "The Pilgrims" when Frank scored his second.

Rounce was considered to have 'played a splendid game', and Wood, who clearly had an uncomfortable afternoon at left half, was absolved of blame for being 'quite unable to hold the Plymouth right wing' in check. In deputising for Barrett, Wood 'did the utmost a forward can be expected to do in a strange position'. Although Keeping was under constant pressure and Arnold lacked support, Wood 'struggled valiantly to fulfill [sic] what was so obviously an unfair task.' Nonetheless, it was reported that 'Fulham's defeat of Plymouth Argyle … would have been even more pronounced had it not been for a glaring weakness at left half'.[81]

Rounce retained his inside left position and travelled up to Greater Manchester for Fulham's fixture on March 25 against a rapidly improving Oldham Athletic side. At the beginning of March the "Latics" were bottom of the Second Division with 20 points from 29 games. However, the side had climbed to sixteenth with 28 points on the eve of their game against the Cottagers. The ensuing game was a hard fought affair during which the hosts displayed great determination and vigour.

Nonetheless, Fulham went a goal up through Arnold midway through the first half and the 'defence gave nothing away.' Oldham finally got themselves back on level terms but then Fulham's forwards came on and 'showed a cleverness in combination ... that was delightful to watch and much above the form shown by the home side.' It was Arnold who added the second and Hammond the *coup de grâce* shortly before the final whistle. Fulham were judged to have 'played as well as they ever have done', and the defence 'distinguished itself by the confident manner in which it dealt with the opposition'.[82] The *Daily Herald* in its brief review of games played in the Second Division enthused:

> 'Fulham's display was sufficiently good to suggest that they have a First Division team in the making. There is nothing wrong with their defence, and they were well served by their attack, despite the fact that Newton was by no means as thrustful [sic] as he can be'.[83]

At the beginning of April 1933 Fulham were fifth in the Second Division, seven points behind Stoke City but with a game in hand. Tottenham were second, one point back, also with a game in hand and a superior goal average. For the Cottagers, April promised to be a critical month with fixtures against both Stoke and "Spurs", besides a further six matches. Of the latter, the first was against Manchester United at the Cottage on April 1. United were four points behind Fulham at the time and very probably had someone from their organisation at Boundary Park on the previous Saturday.

Fulham were compelled to make an adjustment to the

forward line as Arnold was away on England duty at Hampden Park.[84] As a result, Finch reverted to his once familiar position at outside left and Richards was recalled to the right wing. The contribution of the rearranged line was noteworthy.

> 'Finch... on the wing was in great form, and his many sparkling duels with Mellor were features of the game. Hammond, too, was at his best, while Rounce contributed some clever dribbling and neat passing'.[85]

The local press coverage was considerably less inhibited. In an item headlined 'FULHAM'S FIFTH CONSECUTIVE WIN', the correspondent in the *West London Observer* let rip:

> 'Saturday was one of Fulham's great days. They scored their fifth successive win, defeating Manchester United by 3-1 and 30,000 people paid to see the Cottagers give another dazzling display. Fulham went ahead in spectacular style from the kick-off. Manchester made five positional changes for the match, and the home team's policy of getting into their stride in the first minute was highly successful. Fulham's forward line moved down the field from the kick-off together. Finch centred the ball and Newton gave them an early lead. For the first twenty minutes Fulham were the attacking side, and during that time Tootill only had two shots to deal with'.

United were not unduly perturbed by their host's fast start and subsequently came more into the game but they were considered fortunate to equalise three minutes before the interval. This set back did nothing to deter Fulham and after the break 'treated the crowd to another electrifying goal, scored within a minute of the restart. Finch followed up a pass, eluded the back and put the Cottagers ahead again.' Manchester then came on once more but the Cottagers defence soaked up the pressure and it was Hammond who ensured the win when he netted the third following 'a fine pass from Newton'. However, although there was no mention of Hammond being injured, he missed the team's next four matches and did not play again until April 17, Easter Monday, against Preston North End. This was a serious loss that upset the balance and cohesion of the forward line, but not, other than against Lincoln City, the results.[86]

After their run of five straight wins Fulham were fourth in the Division, still seven points adrift of Stoke and five behind Tottenham, but with a realistic although outside chance of promotion. Frank continued to make an outstanding contribution having scored 26 goals in only 21 league games. However, any buzz of excitement around Craven Cottage on that Monday morning was short lived. In fact, it was virtually extinguished by Wednesday evening after the rescheduled fixture at Lincoln. Although noted as a 0-8 score line in the *West London Observer*, the official result was 0-3. Nonetheless, it was dismal and 'unexpected'. The match itself was covered in just two paragraphs, which mentioned the forwards as being 'very subdued', and once more, after a promising opening, the side again 'fell away'.[87] The report in the *Daily Herald* provided more detail, and concluded:

> 'the principal factor in the impotence of Fulham's attack was the way in which Moulson completely blotted out

Newton. The big centre-half never left his rival, and in consequence, Newton had a most unhappy match'.

Significant too was the fact that Birch, at right full back, suffered a serious head injury 'and though he pluckily returned 10 minutes later heavily bandaged, he was never his real self afterwards.' He was injured in a collision which resulted in Lincoln's first goal. His injury in fact was so severe he did not return to the Fulham first team until September 1933.[88]

The immediate task now facing the Cottagers was to re-establish a foothold in the promotion race. In reality this was a monumental task for on Saturday, April 8 they were scheduled to play the Division leaders, Stoke City, on their Victoria ground. A formidable assignment against the side which had conceded fewer goals than any across all four divisions. To compound matters Hammond remained out through injury and now was joined by Birch whose place at left back was taken by Hindson.

'After the set-back at Lincoln, Fulham made a triumphant return to form ... when visiting Stoke City'. As was anticipated, the game was played at a 'terrible pace' and proved a monumental battle of the defences. Fulham were subjected to the full force of Stoke's awesome attacking power. The storm raged for fully twenty minutes 'almost without a brake [sic]. Stoke attacked with tremendous energy', with 'Matthews a young right winger, being the trickiest opponent.' Stanley contributed a number of 'capital centres', but the visitors' defence held despite there being 'many exciting escapes on the Fulham goal-line, [and] Tootill played superbly in the face of the determined onslaught.' Gibbons and Keeping were the backbone of the Fulham defence while Price twice beat the Stoke rearguard and had the ball in the net on each occasion. The first was judged to have been offside but the second stood and Fulham retained their 1-0 advantage at the interval.

Upon the resumption Stoke pressed forward once more but Fulham weathered the storm and inevitably Stoke's pace finally 'slowed perceptibly'. It then fell to Finch and Arnold to carry the attack but on 'too many occasions excellent approach work and accurate passes were wasted in front of goal. Newton was not happy in the re-arranged forward line, and he did not have a good match.'

A 1-0 victory at Stoke was a fine achievement, even if it was by the narrowest of margins.[89] Frank, despite his run of poor form, was a team player and would have been delighted with both the result and Fulham's decision to re-sign him along with sixteen others for the upcoming 1933-34 season.[90]

After the victory at Stoke the Cottagers were fourth in the Division, now four points behind Tottenham and five back of Stoke, still with 'an outside chance of promotion'.[91] 'Corinthian' outlined the situation:

> 'Fulham's progress will be watched anxiously during the next few days. As I have already mentioned, there is a chance of this club advancing three steps in successive seasons – which no other club as ever done – Southern to Second and Second to First. Leaving out Stoke and the Hotspur for the time being, let us look at what Fulham have got before them. To-morrow, they are at home to Preston, and on the following day they receive Charlton. It would not be an extravagant assumption to say that they will get four points in those two games. On Monday,

> Fulham go to Preston, and should they be good enough to obtain five points in three matches, they will be on the heels of the leaders. This is more likely, because Stoke have to go to two places, Charlton and Chesterfield, where they will find their opponents so greatly in need of points that there will be no quarter. Lowly though Charlton and Chesterfield are, the fact remains: Stoke could scarcely have two harder games on successive days. They receive Charlton on Monday, and it would not surprise me if Stoke got less than three points out of the three games'.

He continued by considering a number of permutations and concluded 'that the Hotspur have got a severe Easter before them'.[92]

Fulham's supporters certainly believed in the 'outside chance' and on Good Friday 28,000 packed into the Cottage ground to welcome Preston North End for an 11.15 a.m. kick-off. Preston opened strongly and subjected the Fulham defence to a thorough examination. In response Fulham gave as good as they got and opportunities were missed at both ends. The half finished scoreless. The Cottagers continued to press after the break and with fifteen minutes remaining Arnold finally capitalised. There was no further scoring and Fulham obtained the points; however, 'their display was far from convincing'.[93]

On the following day, April 15, before a crowd of some 20,000, Fulham started brightly against Charlton. Playing with a strong breeze they dominated from the outset. After Frank had missed an early chance Wood made amends and the Cottagers were one up within five minutes. Another followed after a quarter of an hour as Frank set up Wood three yards out for his second. Charlton offered sporadic resistance but remained two goals down at the interval. In the second half the visitors committed more men forward and came close on more than one occasion. But the Fulham victory was sealed following:

> 'an amazing piece of work by Arnold. The outside-left received the ball almost on the half-way line and beating both the wing half and the full back, he ran the ball right to the goalpost, where Newton was waiting for the easiest of easy chances'.

Charlton concluded the scoring shortly thereafter when they registered from the penalty spot.[94]

It was noted that many thought Charlton would fade quickly after conceding two early goals. They did not and actually mounted a 'fine struggle against the odds'. Of the Fulham forwards Wood received honourable mention as in addition to scoring two goals he

> 'played much excellent football. His understanding with Finch and Newton left little to be desired. When Wood got the first goal he displayed admirable judgement in running to a position where Newton could send the ball to him, and his shot was perfect'.[95]

After this match the *Daily Herald*'s 'Corinthian' had altered his view of Fulham's promotion prospects as both Stoke and Tottenham were now three points ahead of the Cottagers. He pointed out that even if Fulham could win at Preston there would still be the 'awkward affair next Saturday to face. Should the Hotspur win on that occasion and Stoke beat Lincoln in the Potteries, on the same day, Fulham's gallant struggle will be at an end'.[96]

The Fulham side would have travelled up to Preston on Easter Sunday as the match was scheduled to kick off at 10.45 on Monday morning. A crowd of 15,000 attended at Deepdale which was a reasonable turn out as the result was of little consequence to Preston in mid-table. For Fulham any realistic prospect of promotion was also dependent upon results elsewhere.

The local West London press considered that 'Fulham were always more dangerous' in attack and that 'Barratt and Gibbons, playing confidently, had the measure of the Preston forwards.' Finch scored the first Fulham goal shortly before half time and Rounce netted a 'brilliant' one in the second half. Although Preston revived after these set backs their only goal resulted from a penalty ten minutes before the end.[97] After Preston scored Fulham understandably played eight men behind the ball, determined to secure both points.

The correspondent in the *Daily Herald* considered he had witnessed a close encounter that might well have gone 'the other way round, for there was little between the teams.' He wrote that the Fulham defence was sound and in attack 'Newton did a great deal of running about after the ball without being able to get in any really good shots, and Arnold was about Fulham's most dangerous raider'.[98] Another report maintained that Fulham while taking two points away from Deepdale, 'were extremely lucky to do so'.[99]

Attention turned afterwards to the other results. From the Cottagers' standpoint they could have been better: Stoke beat Charlton as expected but Spurs dropped a point at Plymouth. So at the end of the day the Cottagers were three points behind Stoke, both having played 39 games, and Spurs in second were 2 points ahead of Fulham but with a game in hand. The goal differences were significant as Fulham were plus 15, compared to plus 44 and 34 for Tottenham and Stoke. The Cottagers' upcoming visit to White Hart Lane on April 22 loomed massive, for it was the first of the three remaining games, all of which had to be won.

In the week prior to the critical North London encounter Frank was once more interviewed by B.J. Evans of London's Evening *Star*. The article was published on the day of the match, April 22, 1933, under the headline 'Frank Newton, Fulham's Dashing Centre-Forward.'

'According to Frank Newton, Fulham's centre-forward, the Cottagers are very nearly in the First Division now. He spoke in no boastful vein when I chatted with him at Craven Cottage this week, but just expressed his honest convictions and those of his colleagues. "When I was in the Army", said Frank, "I boxed and played football for my company or my regiment; never for myself. In the Fulham club the *esprit de corps* is exactly the same. I have not scored as many goals myself this season; my record is 27 goals in 28 matches – two injuries kept me out of the team for several games – but it was not for want of trying. The fact is that we are now playing a different type of game, and play to our wings and inside men. As long as we get the goals, I am quite content. Pretty stuff does not win matches – only goals. That is the spirit at Fulham. Nobody is jealous at somebody else getting the goals. All we want is to score them. At the same time, I was sorry to be injured twice and thus miss Cup-ties for the first time since I have been a professional footballer. We expect to beat the Spurs today, even though they have not yet been defeated at home this season. They play real football, and so we have the chance to play them on their – and our – merits.

When I was interviewed last year in 'The Star,' I said we should gain promotion to the First Division this season. I still believe this, and so do the other ten in the team. If we lose one of our three remaining games, the other team will deserve their victory, for we are going out full of determination and fight. And, should we [stall] at the post this time, we shall go up next year. Our success this season will be sufficient encouragement to all of us. The team has been strengthened in every way by the coming of Keeping and Arnold. Since they were in the side we have lost only one game, at Lincoln, and have gained 23 points out of a possible 28. Keeping is the best full-back I can imagine. With one kick he will turn defence into attack, because he always finds his man with it. It was a great advantage to get the two new players from the same club, because Keeping knows just how to feed Arnold, who cuts in and scores. Talking of Johnny Arnold, we were all proud of his gaining his cap for soccer, and it would not surprise me if Jim Hammond followed suit soon. He was reserve in the last trial match, and should play for England next year. He would be a grand man to take away on tour with an England XI, because he is a born footballer and can fit in with any company. At least 50 per cent of my success with Fulham has been directly due to Hammond. A feature of life at Craven Cottage is the support the players get from the Governor [Mr McIntyre] and the chairman, Mr Dean. In return, we would do anything to make them happy, and I think we gave them a good Easter gift in six points from three matches. I have been with clubs, and have heard from many colleagues who have had the same experience – that of being shouted at and bullied by a manager at half time and at the end when a match was lost. That is so disheartening that it often starts a team on a losing sequence. With Mr McIntyre it is 'Do your best, boys,' before the game and a smile of sympathy and a 'Hard luck' if we lose, or the same smile of congratulation if we win. No wonder we are always trying our hardest on the field! Another Fulham asset is that the players are all good-living lads. We go to the pictures together, and are great pals off the field, while on it each man is playing only for his club. Though there are some great footballers in our team, there are no 'stars,' in this sense, that every man is just a member of the team'.

Frank wrapped up the interview by saying his ambition was to assist in getting the club into the First Division, and his wish was to remain with Fulham until his playing days were over.[100]

Unfortunately Frank missed the match because of a groin injury and the opportunity to perform before the largest crowd to witness a Fulham game that season. Some 46,750 souls were packed into White Hart Lane that Saturday anticipating a decisive struggle. However, decisive it was not, as both sides were terrified of making the crucial error that might result in defeat. 'Neither goalkeeper had a strenuous day, such was the excellence of the rival defences'.[101] But early in the game Tottenham were effectively reduced to ten men when Howe 'was injured so badly that he was little more than a passenger.'

The game was played with 'a vigour and speed that never relaxed.' But after the interval the game deteriorated and became 'scrappy', although the pace was maintained. Shortly before the end Fulham's Wood, deputising for Frank, appeared to have scored the winning goal, 'but the referee thought otherwise, and gave a free kick which mystified many of the crowd.' The feeling was that the referee blew up after the ball had crossed the goal line. The *West London Observer* reported that the match had been the Cottagers' 'hardest struggle to get a point' all season, and that the ten man Spurs side 'did well enough to merit a good deal of credit, as well as a point.' The concluding comment was that Fulham, having dropped a point 'must surely give up all promotion thoughts, until next season'.[102]

The report in the *Daily Herald* was more critical of the referee as their report appeared under the caption: 'ONE MORE 'LET-OFF' FOR TOTTENHAM', followed by the sub-caption: 'Fulham Robbed of Penalty Kicks'. It was felt that the visitors 'proved themselves to be a team superior to the Hotspur ... and yet it can be said with truth that the goal-less draw was a fitting result, because neither team deserved to win.' Other than the failure of the referee to award the penalties, the 'best feature of the match was the defensive play of Fulham.' In particular that of Keeping and Hindson 'who did some brilliant things in the way of tackling that little, but sturdy outside-left, Evans'.[103] After this 'tussle at Tottenham' McIntyre was reported to have said: 'Well, I am a trifle disappointed: but if we cannot go up, I am glad to see Hotspur promoted.' This was, as 'Corinthian' observed, 'distinctly the right spirit'.[104] For the more optimistic supporters, there still remained the remote possibility of promotion. Firstly, Frank was due to return from injury to face Grimsby, 'having made an exceptionally quick recovery…'[105] Secondly, prospects for a home win 'at the expense of Grimsby this afternoon' were considered 'bright'.[106] To gain promotion Fulham now had to win both their remaining games and Tottenham could do no better than draw one of their remaining three. A most unlikely outcome.

And so it proved, for Fulham entertained a less than spectacular Grimsby side on Saturday, April 29 and surprisingly went down 1-0. 'Fulham sealed their own fate, and put behind them their last prospects of First Division football next year.[season]' The post game atmosphere around the Cottage must have been dismal, more particularly so as Tottenham also went down to defeat. The Cottagers were judged to have been unlucky,

> 'because the best of their play was sufficiently good to merit them a point. Considering their lowly place in the table, the visitors showed up surprisingly well, but even the re-appearance of Newton at centre-forward failed to save the Cottagers. Grimsby's strength was in their half-back line; their display was one of the few at Craven Cottage which has bettered the home line'.

Frank's deteriorating goal scoring form was also underlined over the ninety minutes for not only did he narrowly miss two good opportunities but late in the game the Cottagers were awarded a penalty. There really was no need to underline the growing disappointment amongst the home support, but the crowd's dismay was 'clearly demonstrated' when Frank shot directly 'into the goalkeeper's hands'.[107] Certainly not the desired conclusion to a promotion drive but perhaps inevitable given this was only the club's second defeat in their last sixteen matches. It also must have provided McIntyre, Fulham's board of directors, and in particular Frank himself with some serious questions since he had scored only two goals in his last eight league appearances. Age and a declining strike rate would have been amongst Frank's most pressing concerns as the season ran down.

Inevitably the final game of the season at Nottingham's City ground was nothing if not anti climatic. This fact was underlined by the miserably small attendance of 4,000, undoubtedly the most ardent of home supporters. Much to their credit the Cottagers 'started with all their usual skill and dash, but faded out as the Forest improved.' The first half ended scoreless and was considered 'a true reflection on the even run of the play.' Forest improved after the break but both sides missed good opportunities and it was not until late in the game that the hosts took the honours. Fulham evidently should have registered 'at least two goals' but again failed to score for the third consecutive game.[108] A truly disappointing end to a season that just three games earlier held at least a remote prospect of First Division football.

Spirits around Craven Cottage would have been well

depressed after such a miserable finish to the season, despite the fact that no side had previously finished as high in the Second Division following promotion to it. Nonetheless, McIntyre remained ever watchful for opportunities to improve the side. Both he and Frank would have been well aware that performance levels seldom improved beyond the age of thirty, and Frank would turn 31 in November 1933.[109] It was perhaps with this in mind that he had paid QPR £450 for George Rounce in March 1933 and on June 1 he signed Samuel Abel, from relegated Chesterfield FC, for £500.[110] McIntyre also brought in a player by the name of Wraith from Scarborough FC who was reported to have scored 57 goals for his club in the 1932-33 season.[111]

At some point in May McIntyre and the board of directors had arranged for the club to tour Sweden in June 1933. This was a sound proposition given the dwindling prospects of promotion as it could provide an uplifting diversion that would rebuild team morale in preparation for the 1933-34 season. On the last day of May the *Daily Mirror* published a notice that Fulham FC planned to visit Sweden. The club 'who have seldom embarked on Continental tours in the past have concluded negotiations for a visit to Sweden next month. Mr Jimmy McIntyre, the manager, will be in charge of a party of 15 players'.[112]

The club played a total of four games between June 8 and 17, 1933. The limited British newspaper coverage relied mainly on statements from Reuters. The opening match was played against a combined Gothenburg side which the tourists won 3-1. The goals were scored by Finch, Price and Wood.[113] The second game was probably played two days later against I.K.

[Idrottsklubben] Brage located in Borlarge, a side that had finished second in the Northern section of the Swedish Second Division. Fulham recorded a second victory by a score of 3-0. Fulham led 2-0 at half time, through goals by Gibbons and Rounce, and the latter rounded out the scoring after the interval.[114]

It was then on to Stockholm on Wednesday, June 14 to take on A.I.K. [Allmanna Idrottsklubben] before some 6,000 spectators. The translated press headline read: 'Skilled Fulham outplay A.I.K., 6-1'.[115] The first half was reasonably competitive and the tourists only led 1-0 at the interval. In the second half the hosts were overwhelmed. In all Frank scored three goals, Finch two and Wood the other. Frank fired his first after 17 minutes. Fulham's third goal came on the hour when Frank buried a cross from Finch with a 'stone-hard, low, diving header', and he scored the fourth from another Finch cross. Overall the game was closer than the score line suggests. A.I.K. initially had some good chances and could have turned around 3-1 up.[116] However, the hosts were shot shy and when the opportunity did arise tended to shoot from distance. The steadfast Fulham defence and the failure of the A.I.K. half backs to control the mid-field evidently proved to be the difference.[117]

A fourth match was played on Friday, June 16 against I.K. Sleipner at their Indrottsparken ground in Norrkoping. Fulham's 3-2 defeat was the only loss of the tour, but provided a good tonic for the 4,907 supporters in the ground who were digesting the disappointment of their recent relegation from the Swedish First Division. Sleipner were judged to have produced their best game of the season and fully deserved to win what was a close, entertaining encounter. The only regret was the side had not produced form like it earlier in the season.

Sleipner won the toss and chose to play with the setting sun behind them. The home side started briskly and were a goal up after seven minutes. The advantage was short lived as Oliver headed past Persson in the Sleipner goal just four minutes later. Fulham scored a second from a goalmouth scramble after twenty five minutes. And then, shortly before half time, Sleipner got back on level terms. After the intermission, during which an award ceremony was held for local school sides, play flowed from end to end with numerous opportunities spurned.

> 'Eventually, the pace slowed, and both sides were preparing to share the honours, when 'a goal, with a capital G, arose "like a bolt from the blue." A Sleipner attack, that no one really believed in, developed when Wetterstrom set up Hjelm who put his foot through the ball and Sleipner's victory over Fulham was a fact'.

The headline in the local *Ostergotlands Dagbland* read: 'Sleipner in splendour, Fulham were subdued, 3-2 in a close match'. The reporter, 'Este', was generous in his account. He considered Fulham's play was characterised by the 'rarely seen ability to vary the pace of the game, good judgement in exploiting openings and "last but not least" a desirable speed on the ball.' Their mobility was also striking and encouraged the Sleipner side to raise their game which resulted in the first half being 'especially entertaining for those who had come to witness this English lesson in modern football.' The Fulham defence in particular received praise. Gibbons at centre half was likened to a 'majestic cliff', Barrett was singled out for his 'outstanding tackling talents' and Keeping was praised for his calm and steadying influence. Tootill in goal exhibited a safe pair of hands 'and also had a rare, beautiful kick, which should be a role model for our own goalkeepers.' Persson, 'was without a doubt the best player on the field' and made a massive contribution to his side's victory. In fact, without exaggeration, 'it can be safely stated that we have rarely seen' such a fine goalkeeping exhibition in Norrkoping. 'Este' concluded by thanking 'both teams for a truly entertaining and memorable match'.[118]

It is worth noting, in the light of later developments, that Frank possibly played in just one of the four games. This in itself would have been an indication of the management's concerns regarding a successor to lead the line.

The outstanding success of Fulham's 1932-33 season was something to celebrate. The side came very close to gaining promotion to the First Division in consecutive seasons; something which no other club had done. Inevitably there was much gnashing of teeth at having fallen short in the final stretch. But the side had truly exceeded all expectations as 'Corinthian' indicated prior to the heavy Easter schedule.

> 'Fulham's progress will be watched anxiously during the next few days. As I have already mentioned, there is a chance of the club advancing three steps in successive seasons – which no other club has ever done – Southern to Second and Second to First'.[119]

Much of the credit for the side's success inevitably must go to James Alfred McIntyre and his astute activity in the transfer market from the time of his appointment in April 1931.[120] His first inspirational move in the transfer market was the acquisition of Frank Newton, the free scoring centre forward from Stockport County. This move had finally solved the long running saga of the club's search for a centre-forward. Also in his first full season in charge he acquired Richards and later Telford from Coventry City. Over the summer of 1932 he revisited Southampton and signed three more players. And then, after Fulham had visited the Dell on February11, 1933, he made two brilliant acquisitions in Johnny Arnold and Mike Keeping. The total fee of £5,100 for them both which was a record for the club to that point quickly proved to be an exceptionally good investment that delighted the chairman, the club's directors and supporters. The impact the two made on the side was immediate and effectively placed Fulham firmly in the promotion shake up. By way of example, the goals against average per game fell, after their acquisition, from 1.78 to 1.07 over the last 14 games of the season. Similarly, the club's win-draw-loss record over the first 28 games read 11, 8 and 9, for a total of 30 points, or 54 per cent of those available. Comparatively, 20 points were amassed over the last 14 matches from 9 games won, 2 drawn and 3 lost, for a vastly improved 71 per cent.[121] These figures also underline how wretchedly disappointing were the final 3 games of the season during which the team failed to score.

Nonetheless, once the club reassembled after the Summer break; optimism reigned as the focus shifted to the season upcoming. A sense of continuity would have prevailed since the club had been quick to re-sign their players prior to the close of the 1932-33 season. 'Corinthian' reported at the time:

> 'I have the assurance of Mr Dean that there is not a player on their books who has any doubt as to his future so far as the coming summer is concerned. That is not only splendidly human, but wise from the club's point of view'.

Mr Dean commented:

> 'If one of our players is entitled to a benefit he gets it. We do not keep him waiting, and then apologise for not being able to give his money to him until months afterwards'.[122]

Finally, the words, once more from 'Corinthian', would have encouraged the Fulham fan base when he commented, after the draw at White Hart Lane:

> 'It can be said for Fulham that, had they risen to the First Division, they would have had small need to alter their team. In this match of Saturday last their team defence was far better than many I have seen in the First Division. Keeping was a human iceberg'.[123]

There must have been many around the Cottage who now relished the prospects of the 1933-34 season.

On the other hand, Frank might have entertained some concerns around the new season for a number of reasons. First, his form over his last seven league games in 1933 was below par in so much as he only scored one goal. Second, in November 1933 he would turn 31 and in the season just finished he had played in only 31 league matches. He possibly played in the reserves early in the season when Haddleton was preferred, but he would have been increasingly aware of the physical demands required of him to perform every week at the top of his game. Accordingly time lost through injury would have been an increasing concern. Third, on the Swedish tour, while he did slot 3 goals in the 6-1 romp against A.I.K. Stockholm, he did not score; however, he may well have played in only one game. Finally, McIntyre was naturally always ready to improve the team when the opportunity arose, and he had signed Rounce from QPR in March, 1933 and Abel from Chesterfield in June, 1933. Frank was well aware that he was the oldest of all the inside and centre forwards on Fulham's books.[124] As the 'senior pro.' Frank had good reason to feel vulnerable.

1933-34

At the end of his second season with Fulham, Frank had scored 70 goals in seventy games, both he and the club had enjoyed great success, and his popularity with the supporters was assured. However, he would certainly have logged that McIntyre had done a deal with Chesterfield that brought their highly regarded centre-forward Samuel Abel, born 1908, to Craven Cottage. Abel had 'scored 57 goals in 96 League games for his previous clubs',[1] prior to signing for Fulham on June 1, 1933.[2] Given Frank's extraordinary success over the previous two seasons Abel's acquisition could best be explained as an endeavour to add further cover to the club's number 9 slot. However, Frank's decline in form at the end of the previous season and the approach of his 31st birthday were both factors that would have been taken into account.

By the first week of August life was beginning to stir around Craven Cottage as the first trial game was scheduled for Saturday, August 12. As was customary the possible first team defence, the Whites, took on the Stripes who were composed of the probable attack and the Reserve defence. The game, played before approximately 7,000 spectators, was deprived of much 'of its value as a criterion of the coming season's form' as both Hammond and Arnold were still tied up with their County Cricket obligations and Abel was out injured with a swollen ankle.[3] Nevertheless, it did provide an opportunity for the management to look over their other new additions. These were: Wraith, from Scarborough, 'whose acquisition is likely to be a great asset', and three others who were considered outstanding prospects:

> 'Gore, an eighteen-year-old outside right from Morris Motors, who gave every indication of turning out a first class winger. Draper, a right-half secured from Arsenal, who put in a useful performance, while Styles, a new amateur, played well in goal'.

The Whites won the game 3-0 on goals from Wood, Wraith and an unidentified other. Frank and Rounce were considered to be the pick of the Stripes' front line.[4]

The second trial game was played on the following Saturday and provided a more acceptable result in so much as the probable first team won 6-3. Arnold was still absent since Hampshire C.C.C. refused to release him until the end of August, and Abel was still injured. However, Hammond had returned and 'was the brain behind many attacks'.[5] Both Frank and Price certainly appreciated his creative talents as they scored three and two goals. The opinion was that the prospective first team's 'front line could scarcely have been seen to greater advantage. They played a fast clean and exhilarating game with excellent combination that was reflected in the score'.[6]

The season opened with two home fixtures, the first against Port Vale on Saturday, August 26, and two days later the Cottagers entertained Blackpool. Fulham started well by winning both games. However, 'Cottager' was not convinced by the manner of the 3-0 victory over Port Vale. He considered that Fulham dominated the game in every respect, from start to finish, apart from the quality of their finishing which was dismal.

> 'In every other department they were exceptional —real First Division. Once they had settled down they looked so much better that the match was almost a farce. But—one goal amid all those chances in the second half! Their own supporters, even though Fulham were three goals up by then, began to get restive and started to remind Hammond that he wasn't playing cricket now'.

He singled out Price, that 'canny inside-forward', for his contribution in setting up Finch for the first goal; he also

> 'started the move which ended in Newton scoring the second and gave Newton the pass in the second half for the third. But after that—oh, Fulham. The chances they missed'.

He concluded that this failing would have to be sorted out if First Division football was to remain a realistic prospect.[7]

The local press report was brief but similar, as the scoreline was not considered to be a fair reflection of the home side's superiority. Included was the comment that Frank 'missed many chances' although he was trying hard. Nonetheless, he did score a couple of goals and that should have settled any immediate anxieties.[8]

Two days later on a sultry riverside evening there followed a tight struggle with Blackpool that ultimately the Cottagers edged 1-0. Despite the 'terrific heat', 15,000 attended and witnessed two contrasting styles of play. 'Fulham's fast footwork and clever inter-passing was in direct contrast to the visitors' more boisterous methods.' The outcome was made safe in the second half when, after a period of 'brilliant football', Price settled the matter.[9]

Despite certain shortcomings in attack, the club had started their new campaign reasonably well. And with Arnold's return from his cricketing duties the team should have been in confident mood on the trip up to Notts County's Meadow Lane the following Saturday. However, it was to prove an unfortunate day for not only did the Cottagers go down decisively, 4-1, but both Frank and Keeping were injured. Inevitably, it was 'Robin Hood' who reported on the game, and even he felt compelled to note: 'it is only fair to say that the Londoners had a slice of ill-luck … when Keeping injured his ribs …' After being off for five minutes he returned on the left wing, 'but appeared to be in pain.' The County took full advantage of the reorganised Fulham defence and were three up by half time. Fulham improved afterwards, but the hosts eased up after notching a fourth. Then to compound Fulham's problems Frank had to go off for repairs to a badly cut eye. It was not Fulham's day, and they

> 'were never wholly outplayed. Price and Newton being lively, but ... [even] allowing for Keeping's mishap, Notts were the better side, though Fulham were not disgraced'.[10]

The game received scant coverage in the *West London Observer* but their correspondent did note that Frank was up against

> 'Walker, a newly recruited Scottish International centre half, who was the mainstay of the County men. He persistently shadowed Newton, and an unshakeable defence did the rest'.

Keeping's injury was described as a pulled muscle, but because of the necessary positional changes, 'Fulham were too disorganised to do themselves justice.' It was acknowledged that the County fully deserved their victory.

> 'They settled into their stride right from the kick-off, and gave Fulham no time to settle down. Their movement showed a wonderful combination, and the forward line behaved like a machine. Playing with a speed that was gruelling to the Cottagers' defence, they secured a grip on the game which they only once relaxed'.[11]

Frank did not play in the next two fixtures, a visit to Blackpool on Monday, September 6, which resulted in a disappointing

4-3 defeat, and a 1-0 home triumph over Swansea five days later. There then followed a visit to the Den on September 16, with Fulham positioned seventh, only 2 points behind the league leaders Grimsby Town and Preston North End.

This London 'Derby' was eagerly anticipated and 35,000 crowded into Millwall's New Cross Stadium for the needle encounter. 'The match at the start promised to develop into a thrilling "Derby"', but with the respective defences dominating, it 'slowed down to an ordinary affair'.[12] The only goal of the game came midway through the second half when Frank nodded a Finch cross on to Hammond who headed past the Millwall keeper.[13] Otherwise, Frank did not enjoy his afternoon as Hancock, Millwall's centre half, similar to Walker at Meadow Lane, shadowed him closely throughout.

> 'Newton was never comfortable and rarely kept in touch with his wings, and furthermore he too often erred in his judgement even when the ball was sent to him with a perfect pass'.[14]

Despite the failings in attack the first away win of the new season would have been welcomed. Few realised, however, on the evening of Saturday, September 16, storm clouds were gathering.

CHAPTER VI

THE TRANSFER OF FRANK NEWTON TO READING FC, AND THE DEPARTURE OF JAMES MCINTYRE

The transfer of Frank Newton to Reading FC resulted from the combination of John Dean's long standing interest in acquiring Jack Lambert, and Herbert Chapman's activity in the transfer market on behalf of Arsenal.

Dean's interest was flagged up in the *Derbyshire Football Express* as early as November 1929.[1] On the other hand Chapman's concerns were flagged up when he signed Ernie Coleman a centre forward from Grimsby Town FC in March 1932 for £7,500.[2] Chapman opened the cheque book again in September 1933 when he paid Sheffield United £8,250 for Jimmy Dunne, another centre forward.[3] This move immediately raised interest elsewhere. 'CHATTERBOX' in his weekly column in *Reynold's Illustrated News* on October 15 stated: 'I can tell you of at least four clubs whose managers asked if they could have Lambert within 24 hours of the news that Dunne had signed for the Arsenal being broadcast.' The four clubs were Leicester City, Everton, Manchester City and Swindon Town. Despite the level of interest there was no bidding war as a week later 'CHATTERBOX' reported:

'Fulham got Jack Lambert cheaply, considering the competition ... The fee was under £3,000, I hear, and where will you find a man as good and experienced in the country to-day for that sum?'

He concluded with the telling observation: 'But the biggest fee is not necessarily the most profitable. Arsenal and Fulham are good friends. One good turn deserves another!'[4]

I suspect that the visit of the Arsenal Reserve side to the Den on September 9 is of particular importance as Fulham played there the following week September 16. It is my belief that the Arsenal players left a good amount of information behind regarding the impending changes in the Arsenal dressing room. The air at the Den would have been thick with gossip and rumour linking Lambert to Fulham and this would have been picked up by the Fulham players, Frank most especially. It is even possible that an agreement had already been reached between Arsenal and Fulham to trade Lambert.[5]

Jack Lambert who was transferred from Arsenal to Fulham in October 1933.

From Frank's standpoint uncertainty regarding his future was nothing new. He had already encountered it at Stockport. At Fulham he may already have felt his position too was exposed after the arrival of Abel from Chesterfield. By this time there certainly was already adequate cover for the number 9 jersey at Fulham; in addition to Abel, Wood and Rounce were already under contract. Fresh in Frank's mind as well would have been the limited playing time he had on the Swedish tour, an excellent opportunity to blood the potential replacements.

If he had concluded by September 17, after Fulham's visit to the Den, that Lambert was yet another potential addition to the squad he would have realised that his opportunities would be severely impacted.

In my opinion, I believe Frank clearly recognised McIntyre was looking to replace him; he was aware of course that he was not getting any younger and that the physical demands were increasing. Possibly as well he entertained no great appetite to re-establish himself at a new club where the expectations would be high.

In short, he would have been content to remain with Fulham but the suggestion that the club was to move for Lambert proved to be the catalyst that decided him to jump before he was pushed out of Fulham's League side. The interest of Joe Smith and their long standing friendship clinched the move to Reading FC and a return to Third Division football.

It was not just the addition of Lambert that would have influenced Frank. Others were also noticing the precariousness of his position. Witness the comment 'CHATTERBOX' made in his September 10 statement that Frank, after the injury he sustained against Notts County, 'is going to find it hard to get back. There are golden opinions at Craven Cottage of Abel, the sturdy lad from Chesterfield'.[6] Helpfully he closed by noting:

> 'If this should meet the eye of a good centre-forward, on whose head there is only a small fee - or preferably none at all – I can give the address to which he should apply immediately "Joe Smith, Manager, Reading Football Club."'[7]

And this is precisely what I believe he did. He would have advised Joe probably on September 17 that he was leaving Fulham and that he would inform McIntyre of his decision at the start of the week. For his part Joe would have gained permission from his chairman to proceed if a reasonable fee could be negotiated. Then on September 18 or 19, more probably on Tuesday 19th Frank met with McIntyre.

Given the personalities of Frank and McIntyre I think their meeting would have been tense. McIntyre was dogmatic, autocratic and voluble, and would have reacted badly to a challenge from one of his squad. Frank in turn could be impulsive, and had a firm belief in his own worth after his time in the Army and success on the football field. Importantly too he had a clear view of how he should be treated.

Whatever passed between the two the outcome was clear: Frank Newton was moving to Reading FC. The fee agreed would partially have reflected McIntyre's desire to be rid of Newton and needed to be a sum that Reading could reasonably meet. There remained the matter of how to best spin this sudden development in the Wednesday morning papers. It was decided to represent the reason behind the request for the transfer as the deterioration of Mrs Newton's health which would benefit greatly from Reading's better air quality; and of course, manager McIntyre would not stand in Florence Newton's way.

The transfer was widely reported in the National press. The *Daily Herald*'s account appeared on September 20, 1933.

> 'FRANK NEWTON, the Fulham centre-forward, who joined the London club in 1931, was yesterday transferred to Reading. Joe Smith, the present Reading manager, was attached to Stockport when Newton played for the Northern club. Newton's wife has been ill for some time, and the player has intimated that he thinks she would have a better chance of [a] complete recovery out of London. The club have consented to release the player, though they are not happy about it'.[8]

The *West London Observer* broke the news to it's readership under the headline: 'COTTAGERS' LOSS'.

> 'A bombshell was dropped in local football circles early in the week when it was announced that Frank Newton, ... had been transferred to Reading. Outside the personnel of the Cottagers' management, the news came as a tremendous surprise, for Newton has become one of the mainstays of the Cottagers forward line. The reason given for the transfer is that Newton's wife had become ill as a result of her being in London, and a change being imperative, the management placed no obstacle in the player's way when he asked for a transfer'.[9]

Florence Newton whose deteriorating health was cited as the reason for Frank's sudden departure from Fulham to Reading on September 19, 1933.

Coverage in the *Daily Mirror* reported 'READING IN BIG TRANSFER DEAL', and went on to state:

> 'Reading last night secured the transfer of Frank Newton, the Fulham centre forward – the man who led the Londoners to promotion in the season 1931-32. Newton thus becomes associated with an old colleague in Joe Smith the Reading manager, who was well known in his playing days as the Bolton Wanderers' inside left. When Smith left Bolton in the middle of the season 1927-28 he went to Stockport County, where he became associated with Newton, and the transfer can be attributed to the friendly connection which sprang up between the pair in those days. Mr J.A. McIntyre the Fulham manager,

said the transfer had been most unexpected and surprising, and that Reading paid a very substantial price for him. It will be recalled that last season Fulham, when approached, declined to entertain any offer for Newton. Mr Joe Smith said that Newton would play in Reading's team against Southend at Elm Park on Saturday'.[10]

'Chatterbox' provided the most informed view and reflected the depth of his connections within the game.

'Joe Smith the Reading manager, has done a great stroke of work for his club in getting Frank Newton, the Fulham centre-forward. He got him cheaply, too, and as Joe and Frank played together at Stockport they know each other pretty well. Fulham could have held out for much more than Reading paid, but Mr Smith had been asking for [the] first chance for weeks, knowing the way things were going – and Newton wanted to go to Reading. I believe the fee was under £1,000. Many clubs would have liked the chance to offer more. But no doubt Reading will reciprocate when the chance comes'.[11]

By including the phrase 'knowing the way things were going', "Chatterbox" suggests he was aware of Frank's concerns regarding his place in the Fulham side.

By September 23 Frank's transfer had been welcomed in the local Reading newspapers. *The Reading Standard* provided their readership with a good photograph of Frank and a glowing report. Here was the leader to take the club back to the sunny uplands of the Second Division.

'The followers of the Reading Football Club were delighted to learn on Tuesday that Mr Joe Smith had secured the signature of Frank Newton, the famous Fulham centre-forward, at what must have been a substantial fee. Newton, who is one of the best shots in the country, comes to Reading at a critical moment, and it is to be hoped that under his leadership the points which lead to a higher division will be secured. The absence of a good leader has cost Reading points that the club cannot afford to lose, and Newton's record proves that he has all the qualities essential in a player who is a real leader. Manager Smith must know all there is to be known about his new recruit, for while he was at [the] Stockport County Club Newton was there creating a record as a goalscorer. It was at his own request that Newton was transferred, and it was with regret that the Fulham officials agreed to release him. Mrs Newton had been ill and her husband expressed a desire to secure an engagement with a club outside the Metropolis. It was only after lengthy deliberation that Fulham agreed to let him go, and Joe Smith is to be warmly congratulated in stepping in and securing a player about whom many clubs have been making inquiries in recent months. Newton went to Fulham from Stockport County in 1931 and he led his new club to promotion in his first season with them. There can be no doubt that the transfer fee asked by Fulham was a stiff one, but if Newton lives up to his reputation he will prove to be a good bargain'.[12]

Meanwhile back at Fulham the news of Lambert's transfer

was not immediately released to the press, despite the fact that he played his last game for Arsenal on September 19, as Dean wanted to announce his brilliant acquisition at the Fulham Shareholder's Meeting on the evening of Tuesday, October 10.

Mr Dean 'and his fellow directors were in high spirits over the transfer of Lambert' and the chairman in his address to the shareholders revealed:

> 'Today our energetic manager has again embarked upon a speculation. He has beaten the book, because the number of clubs after this player was almost legion. With his usual persuasive powers, Mr McIntyre has got one of the cleverest managers in football to part with an excellent fellow whom I know will fill the breach'.[13]

The breach was presumably that left by Frank's departure. The question of filling it turned out to be a different matter as the 1933-34 campaign proved disastrous. Fulham won but only 15 games, scored only 48 goals and finished in 16th position.[14]

The press were not slow to pick up on this downward spiral. In the week of November 11, 1934 an article appeared in a 'SPORTING GOSSIP' column entitled 'F. NEWTON MISSED BY FULHAM, Decline of a Most Promising Side'. It read in part:

> 'AT the beginning of the season it was confidently predicted that Fulham would do well. They played attractive football last season in the Second Division, were not far off promotion, and had an enviable away record. This season they are far from fulfilling their promise.

FOUR GOALS IN SIX GAMES

Of their first eight matches they won five and drew one, which was a very satisfactory start. Then they transferred Frank Newton, the former Stockport County shooting star, and have not won since. Their last six games have yielded them only 2 points and they have themselves scored but four goals in that time.

LAMBERT'S FAILURES

LAMBERT secured from the Arsenal presumably at some cost, has netted only two goals for his new club, which must be rather a facer to the people who wrote into Manchester City abusing the officials for not signing the champions' former centre-forward.

READING FORM

NEWTON has scored eight goals for his new club, Reading, and partly as a result of this Manager Joe Smith sees his side third in the table, only two points behind the leaders, Norwich. They have yet to lose at home and must be reckoned one of the likeliest teams to go into the Second Division next season'.[15]

On February 10, 1934, Fulham beat Bury 2-1 at the Cottage, a week after the side had gone down 5-0 at Lincoln. Despite this twelfth win of the season the directors had seen enough. It was time for a change in leadership and 'Corinthian' in the *Daily*

Herald reported on February 13: 'FULHAM WITHOUT A MANAGER'. This development was held to be a big surprise; nothing '... more surprising has happened in this epidemic of managership vacancies'. John Dean stated, 'Mr McIntyre's engagement with Fulham FC is now ended.'

In addition 'Corinthian' mentioned that the Fulham directors had agreed to a grant of £250 to McIntyre for 'his wise control of the club'. He continued by noting that had Fulham succeeded in gaining promotion the previous season 'he was to have four times as much'. He concluded:

> 'Mr McIntyre was one of the highest-paid managers in the game, and did not believe in signing contracts with a club. He was also a great objector to receiving assistance from supporters' clubs. He was content to stand or fall by his own doings. Mr McIntyre said to me yesterday: "I would rather not discuss anything about the matter just now. Each side has said its say, and the parting has not been so bitter as some might think."'[16]

What McIntyre did not want to discuss was the real reason behind his dismissal which was his agreeing to Frank's transfer. For in so doing he incurred the board's deep displeasure for taking the 'unprecedented action in transferring, entirely on his own initiative, F. Newton to Reading for the impossible price of £650'.[17]

As a result McIntyre was gone and Joe Edelston was appointed on an interim basis,[24] prior to Jimmy Hogan taking over in the Summer of 1934.[18]

CHAPTER VII

THE READING FC MONTHS, 1933-1934

1933-1934

At the beginning of the 1933-34 season Reading Football Club exhibited two weaknesses. First, the club required a strong, forceful leader of the forwards and secondly a centre half; 'although if Hayhurst would feed his forwards more he should fill the pivot's place reasonably well'.[1] Joe Smith attempted to address the first problem when he was reported to have made a successful 'visit to the soccer bargain sales' where he obtained William Butler from Bolton Wanderers and Samuel Wright.[2] And reassuringly, Hayhurst at the end of September 1933 was considered by F.W.L. in his 'Reading and County Sports Chat' column to have 'the making of a first class pivot'.[3]

Reading's season started poorly and on September 17 having played six games the club was in sixteenth position in the Third Division South. The team had five points from two wins and a draw, had lost their away games and had scored only seven goals while conceding ten. The team had also been shut out on three occasions. Even this early in the season the club's prospects were looking poor and the word promotion had probably been struck from the Reading FC lexicon.

Tuesday, September 19 was an exceptional day for Joe Smith. He had been contacted by his former Stockport footballing colleague Frank Newton who advised him that he was leaving Fulham and would be available if Reading wanted to sign him. Given the very short timeline, Smith moved quickly and obtained the approval of the Reading chairman to sign Frank assuming a reasonable fee could be agreed and this may well have also been determined. What is certain is that by the evening of September 19 Frank was on the books of Reading FC.

With the transfer completed Frank made his debut for Reading, the 'Biscuitmen', on September 23 at Elm Park. The day broke dull and the 'almost continuous downpour' reduced the attendance to 9,442.[4] Those who braved the elements were well rewarded for they witnessed a team transformed as Southend were thumped 5-0, a resounding victory in which Frank scored twice.

The press rushed to proclaim Frank's important contribution. The *Sunday Dispatch*, under the headline 'Newton's The Man', announced that 'much of Reading's virility was due to their new centre forward … Reading appear to have found in Newton the leader they have required ever since Palethorp left the club'.[5] Similarly, The *Daily Mail* reported that under Newton's leadership Reading had produced their best form of the season, but added 'the margin of five clear goals exaggerated their superiority'.[6]

Not surprisingly the local Reading press reports were far less constrained. Frank was the focal point of the attention.

'Linesman' in the *Reading Standard* was most supportive.

> 'Reading's victory was really a personal triumph for Newton, the new centre-forward, for it was the leadership of the ex-Fulham player which made all the difference. Unselfish, always on the move and getting into the position in which he could make best use of the ball, quick as lightning in making up his mind what to do with the ball and in carrying out his intention. Newton showed himself the possessor of all the qualities essential in a football leader, and he made the other forwards play to him as no other Reading centre-forward has been able to do – at least for several seasons.
>
> A BRILLIANT FORWARD LINE
>
> Reading were doing nearly all the attacking and this time they crowned good approach work by scoring goals ... If I were a centre-half Newton is the type of player I should least of all like to mark, for he was as elusive as the proverbial eel and it was almost impossible to keep him under surveillance ... and more important still welded the Reading attack into a force more united and solid than it has been this season. His quick passes made his colleagues keep up and he distributed the ball with such speed and accuracy that the Southend defence knew not which way to turn'.[7]

W.E. writing in the *Berkshire Chronicle* was equally as enthusiastic. He considered that Newton

> 'appeared to be just the man Reading have wanted to complete a good side. His leadership inspired confidence, and the Reading players showed up in a better light than they have done hitherto this season'.[8]

Reading led by two goals at the interval, both of which 'were of the spectacular variety.' The first was scored by Fielding with whom Frank had played at Stockport County between 1928 and 1930. Frank netted the second when he buried the rebound after a Fielding shot was charged down. There was some question as to who should be credited with Reading's third goal, Frank or Hayhurst? According to the report in the *Berkshire Chronicle*, Frank scored from a corner taken by Butler. According to several players the ball crossed the line, but it was then kicked out and Hayhurst banged it into the net again just to make sure.[9] The account in the *Football Chronicle* was judged to have settled the matter:

> 'I did not see the match, so am unable to give a definite personal opinion as to who scored Reading's third goal. Our reporter stated that Hayhurst scored after a shot from Newton had been charged out, and the players rushed to congratulate the centre half. Later, we heard that Newton's shot had actually scored, so we have agreed that the goal should be credited to Newton, making him two in his first match for Reading'.[10]

The *Reading Mercury* noted that Hayhurst crashed the ball into the net 'after Newton, while on the ground, had sent it over the line'.[11] Finally, F.W.L. stated a month later on October

20 in his 'Reading and County Sports Chat' column, that the two goals Frank scored for Reading against Watford 'brings his total of goals scored for Reading to four.' In listing the other goal scorers he credits Hayhurst with one, and this he scored in Reading's opening game of the season against Exeter City.[12]

The fourth Reading goal resulted from Frank heading the ball to inside right McGough who unleashed a brilliant left foot drive. Shortly before the end Frank netted 'what many considered was the best goal of the match'. However, the referee blew for offside, which in the opinion of W.E. in the *Berkshire Chronicle* was 'a bad decision.' The fifth goal was scored from a penalty.

Clearly, Frank could hardly have made a better debut at his new club and the *Berkshire Chronicle* devoted a number of column inches to Joe Smith's recent acquisition:

> 'with a new leader who is fully conversant with his job, Reading were a different team. If they can capture in other games this season the same mood which swept them to victory we shall soon see them near the top of the league table ... Newton was a fine leader, contriving to be just in the right spot at the right moment. His passes to the wing men were perfect, and it was not surprising that under pressure the opposing backs frequently became rattled'.[13]

This level of unbridled optimism was evident also in F.W.L.'s 'Reading and County Sports Chat' column in the same publication:

> 'It is surprising what a difference one man can make to a

team. This fact was very much in evidence on Saturday, when Frank Newton made his debut for Reading ... In fact, it is no exaggeration to say that it was largely through Frank Newton that Reading were able to defeat Southend by five clear goals, for he played a prominent part in four of the goals, at least, and was distinctly unlucky to be given offside when he had placed the ball in the net during the closing minutes of the match. Apart from the work he did in connection with [the] goals ... Newton made a big difference to the forward line, his ball control and distribution considerably speeding up the attack.

It is a matter of great satisfaction to know that Reading have found the man they have been looking for, and there need be no further anxieties about the centre forward position. If Newton can steer clear of injuries Reading should soon be repaid for the money spent on his transfer, and it ought not to be long before the club occupies a position much nearer the top of the table'.[14]

The level of excitement engendered by Frank's arrival and impressive debut performance had the local press in rhapsodic mood. Certainly he was welcomed with open arms and he did not let the Reading paying public down. Frank would have appreciated the acclaim and this allowed him to put his upcoming 31st birthday to the back of his mind.

Prior to the club's game at Coventry on September 30 the Reading directors and players were entertained at the Sonning Golf Club, courtesy of Walter R. Rivers who was the proprietor of the *Reading Standard*. It was golf in the morning, followed by lunch and speeches, and a medal round in the afternoon. In welcoming his guests Mr Rivers mentioned his keen interest in the football club and certain of the games he had attended both at home and away. He also

> 'congratulated the club and Joe Smith, in particular, on getting a centre-forward of the calibre of Newton, and in wishing the new player a happy time in Reading he hoped would lead the club into the second league'.

He closed by calling for a toast to the health of the football club's chairman, Mr J. Royale, who responded appropriately.[15]

The match at Coventry City was played before a crowd of 15,481, and ended in a hard fought 0-0 draw.[16] It was felt that Reading did well to get a point as City dominated and the honours rested with the Reading defence.[17] In response to the sustained pressure applied by Coventry the Reading inside forwards adopted the 'W' formation. This adjustment did not meet with 'Linesman's' approval who, writing in the *Reading Standard*, considered a

> 'three-forward formation is not the method of attack which will bring the best out of Newton ... The Reading leader had not more than half a dozen real shots and it was not until the last ten minutes that he had a "really good chance"'.[18]

On the Saturday following, Reading hosted Brighton and Hove Albion. This game was 'thoroughly entertaining', more particularly perhaps because the home side won 2-0. During the first half the home defence 'was as sound as a rock against quick moving forwards', Frank once more received indifferent support as the inside forwards again played deep. The outcome was settled early in the second half when the right side of the attack, McGough at inside and Butler on the wing, scored a goal apiece.[19]

Frank's afternoon was summed up by the appropriately named 'Shortbread' in the *Sunday Dispatch*. 'Newton worked hard as a leader, but he lacked support from the other forwards'.[20] Once more the tendency to revert to the more defensive 'W' formation was commented upon disapprovingly by 'Linesman':

> 'by their too rigid adherence to the oft-discussed W formation in attack in the first half Reading might easily have lost ... but fortunately, two quick goals after the interval acted as a tonic to the inside men, keeping well up, they played a more worthy part than they had done hitherto. While one has to concede the point that a W formation can, in certain circumstances, be a desirable plan for forwards to adopt, yet this game proved more conclusively than any other in which Reading have played this season that it is futile if the attacking men are unable to put other tactics into practice as well'.[21]

Watford visited Elm Park the following Saturday, and to the delightof the majority of the 9,000 spectators crashed 6-1. The game got off to an unfortunate start when Slater in the Watford goal broke a finger in a collision with Frank. He gamely chose to carry on but after an hour he departed and did not return.

At the time Reading were leading 2-0 on goals from Oxberry and Frank. Woodward took over from Slater and although he pulled off 'many remarkable saves' he could not prevent the rout. All of the Reading forwards scored once and Frank twice.

This resounding victory also gave 'Linesman' a further opportunity to mention his '*bête noire*', the W formation, which he was delighted to report had evidently been abandoned.

> 'Though the game with Watford ... was too one-sided to be really interesting, there were aspects of Reading's football in the first half which were distinctly encouraging. Outstanding of them was the lively work of the forwards, who played as a line and who did not once revert to the W plan'.

In summary he concluded: 'even at full strength, Watford were no match for Reading, but with only ten men their task was a hopeless one'.[22]

The *Berkshire Chronicle* was also quick to condemn the W formation.

> 'Spectators at Elm Park ... saw what could be done by abandonment of the old "W" formation ... but even had the opposition been complete for the whole ninety minutes, it is doubtful they would have withstood the oncoming tide ... for the greater part of the game Reading kept a line of five forwards – hence their virility'.

On page 20 in the same edition, F.W.L. commented that:

'There were two features of the match worthy of note. One was the fact that all five forwards scored and the other was that the "W" was conspicuous by its absence. Both matters for congratulation. I need say no more, I think'.[23]

For his part Frank 'headed two lovely goals, whipped in a number of other fine shots, and led a fast and determined line with dash and intelligence'.[24]

There followed an away match against local rivals Aldershot. Reading disappointingly went down 3-0 on Aldershot's Recreation Ground before a record crowd.[27] 'Linesman' headlined his column, 'READING BEAT THEMSELVES' and was most indignant as he considered Reading:

'lost their heads and gave up playing constructive football when the referee disallowed what, to me, seemed a perfectly legitimate goal ... Reading deserve all sympathy, for no-one apart from the referee saw the offence which led to the cancellation of the goal, but one does not expect a team of professionals to give up the ghost as readily as did Reading'.

Furthermore, 'Linesman', in full cry was not to be mollified. He felt that the incident altered 'the whole aspect of the game', and he described the disallowed goal in considerable detail.

'Reading had been doing most of the attacking and eventually the ball went to Oxberry, being deflected to him off a home player. Newton, seeing that he was in the path to goal, dropped prone to the ground and Oxberry, shooting over his body, netted. I see it reported by an Aldershot pressman that a player handled before Oxberry got the ball, but this, I think, can be but a guess on the part of a man knowing as little as most of us about what happened. The only logical explanation was that the referee considered Newton offside and if this had been so – and I am convinced that it was not the case – his dropping to the ground rightly could have been construed as interfering with play. If the referee gave it that by falling as he did the Reading leader obstructed the goalkeeper is [sic] seems an unfair penalty on a man using his brains. I really doubt if the referee is quite sure himself why he disallowed the goal'.

'Linesman' also used the occasion to continue his crusade against the W formation.

'Newton had the galling experience of seeing most of the balls intended for him blocked by the opposing centre-half and I could not help thinking that Reading are not likely to get the best value out of their new leader unless the other forwards will play up to him in the manner he desires. Often enough he called to them to give him passes along the ground and to his inside men to keep up so that he could have someone to whom to give the ball. But he was wasting his breath, for invariably it happened that he had to plough his way through on his own, or try to get the ball to wings which were always well guarded by the Aldershot halves'.[28]

'Wanderer' in *The Reading FC Record*, the club programme, concurred in his column 'Club Gossip'. He wrote that the team visited Aldershot 'with high hopes of recording our first 'away' victory of the season, but were doomed to disappointment.' He attributed this to the referee disallowing Oxberry's goal, scored after 35 minutes, 'for an alleged infringement by Newton. This decision was a staggerer to the players and proved to be the turning point in the game.' He concluded by stating that the decision to strike 'off what appeared to everybody else (including the Aldershot players, who made no attempt to protest) a perfectly good goal, had a big bearing on the subsequent play.'

Mr White, the referee, had his performance further examined in the 'ODDS and ENDS' column on page 5 of the same programme. He was criticised for giving 'a childish exhibition of finger wagging in Johnston's face for some imaginary offence.' In addition 'two palpable penalties for handling by the Aldershot defence' were ignored. As a result of the standard of refereeing witnessed, Reading lodged an appeal with the League as it was customary for the same referee to be appointed for the return match. As a result ugly scenes sometimes developed as had been recently witnessed at Portsmouth and Everton. The hope was that prior to the return match at Elm Park 'our protest to the League on the Aldershot match will have the desired effect.'

The columnist exhibited a more generous spirit towards Willie Robb in the Aldershot goal. He 'was a great goalkeeper, and made many wonderful saves when all seemed lost; one from Fielding and another from Newton bordered on the miraculous.' It was felt also that he was 'a real sportsman too, for he had no doubt as to the legality of Oxberry's goal, and said so.' Indeed, should there be 'a better goalie in Scotland … I should like to see him play, but I very much doubt it'.[29]

The game report in the *Reading Mercury* agreed that from the time of the disallowed goal Reading 'started going backwards' and failed to show any improvement in the second half. The side's defensive play, 'before a crowd of over 10,000' continued to be littered with errors, and the forward play was disjointed as the inside forwards insisted on playing too deep.[30]

Clearly, it was felt that the Reading side failed to take a questionable decision in their stride and respond positively. On this occasion heads dropped and Aldershot went on to record a straight forward victory.

Despite attracting the smallest crowd to that point in the season, the match on October 28 at Elm Park against Luton Town was very different to the Aldershot encounter.[31] On this occasion the home support witnessed 'a thrilling struggle' which a revitalised Reading side won 4-1. The game, played in arctic conditions and steady rain, provided the Reading faithful with 'just the tonic they were needing after the display at Aldershot'.[32] Having survived the home side's initial onslaught Luton started to play the better football and took an early lead. However, Reading were not perturbed, and after fifteen minutes Frank equalised. It was a 'wonderful back-header' from Fielding's cross into the box. The scores were level at the interval which was deemed a fair reflection to that point.

Luton maintained their robust performance following the break but fell away when their left back, McKay, deflected a Frank 'special' into his own net. After the second goal and with the wind now behind them, Reading surged forward and Frank completed his hat-trick from close range; and Luton's apparently well justified appeals for offside were ignored. The scoring was rounded out in the gathering gloom by McGough from a set piece.[33]

'Linesman' commented in part:

> 'Though Reading were at all times as good as their opponents, there were times when they raised the ire of their supporters by using short passing, dry weather tactics, on a ground not suited to such a style of play. Then fortunately, they began to open the game and with five forwards playing up, they showed some good team work, laying the foundation for a well merited success. We saw more of Newton in this game than we did at Aldershot and he made good use of the ball, making many first class openings for his colleagues while not forgetting the path to goal himself'.[34]

'Shortbread' in the *Sunday Dispatch* added a dimension when he commented in a succinct report:

> 'If Luton had possessed a certain forward as deft at turning shadowy chances into goals as Newton, they would probably have enjoyed a decisive lead against Reading at half-time. But in the closing chapter, Reading's more open methods, greater speed and stamina wore their cleverer opponents down. Newton completed a handsome hat-trick with a hook and a drive'.[35]

Again the forwards played as a line and no evidence was forthcoming of the dreaded W formation. This would have been welcomed by many in attendance of whom 'Spectator' was one. He predicted doom for the team and justified his prediction in a letter to the Editor of the *Reading Mercury*, his letter was published on November 4, 1933. It read:

> 'Sir, - Reading's victory at home last Saturday has raised hopes of promotion to League II. I am afraid those hopes are doomed to failure. Let me visualise what will probably happen to [sic] Reading's next away match, at Northampton on Saturday. Reading will most likely play three forwards and five halves. Northampton will concentrate on Newton, and his play will be rendered innocuous unless the two inside forwards are well to the front to divert the attention of the home defenders, and to take advantage of a faulty goal clearance or a judicious pass by our brilliant centre forward. Time after time at Elm Park this season have veritable gift goals gone a-begging because of the inside men lying back and actually getting in the way of their own halves, who are fully competent to look after THEIR part of the game. There may be some virtue in the "W" formation, but Reading have never been able successfully to exploit it, as the results, and, incidentally, the gates, have conclusively proved. Yours, etc., 'SPECTATOR".[33]

The message around the 'W' formation was clear and certainly reflected the thinking of 'Linesman' of the *Reading Standard*, and possibly that of the newspaper's proprietor Mr W.R. Rivers. 'Spectator' clearly stated his assessment of Frank's on field performances which was probably endorsed by many others.

I have to point out how full and entertaining Frank's life was away from football. Right after the Luton game Frank was required to swap his football gear for evening wear and be backstage at the Reading Town Hall, with trombone, for 8.00 p.m. sharp. The Guild Concert Massed Band went to work promptly under the direction of the famous BBC conductor and composer, John Ansell. The evening's programme was a popular one and

> 'opened with a stirring symphonic march by Silvio Mancini, and later the bands played the "Mirella" Overture by Gounod. The most ambitious work was Sibelius' "Finlandia," proving very popular when scored for military band, and was admirably played. Another popular item was the patrol, "Wee MacGregor," with blending of tunes and Scottish "effects," and this had to be repeated. An amusing trombone duet, "The Troubadours," was a great attraction, partly because of its gay tune, and still more for the reason that Mr F. Newton, Reading's centre forward, was one of the soloists; and this also had to be repeated'.[34]

The large crowd loved it, and at the close of the evening His Worship the Mayor of Reading alluded to Frank's 'performances, on the field this afternoon and at the concert that evening, and then shook hands with him amidst applause'.[35]

For Frank this evening was not a one-off for while he was with Reading he played with 'The Salvation Army [Band] on Sundays', and also 'played professionally in the band at the County Theatre'.[36] And prior to his transfer to Reading he had played in the Mortlake Brass Band and he was pictured playing the cornet in the annual procession at Shepherd's Bush on Sunday, May 14, 1933.[37]

On November 4, 1933, Frank travelled to Northampton Town's County Ground in an effort to improve Reading's pathetic away record, one draw in five games and a solitary goal scored. Despite this dismal showing the club were placed fifth in the division, with fourteen points from twelve games and only two points behind Charlton, Norwich and Crystal Palace. Comparatively, Northampton were mired two places off the bottom of the table with nine points.[38]

Unfortunately for Northampton Town their visitors finally produced a masterful performance on foreign soil and registered their first away win, 4-2. Although 'The Cobblers' 'did most of the attacking in the first half, it was always Reading who looked like getting the goals'.[39] The columnist in the *Reading Mercury* noted: 'a gratifying feature was that the Reading forward line showed such a fine understanding, the passing and interposing keeping the Northampton defenders continually on the move'.[40] The visitors led 2-1 at the interval through Fielding and Butler. Reading increasingly dominated the midfield in the second half and only solid defensive work by the Northampton rearguard kept the score down. Frank ghosted through the first period but subsequently became more focused and created 'many dangerous attacks', one of which set up McGough for Reading's third goal. Frank recorded the fourth when he knocked in a rebound from a McGough shot that Cave in the Northampton goal failed to hold.[41]

The first away win of the season was of course well received locally, but the *Reading Mercury* provided the initial, yet mild criticism of Frank's performance. 'On the whole Newton was rather disappointing. He kept his line together well, but did not make the most of the chances that came his way'.[42]

After this first away success it was back to preparing for the visit of 'a highly infectious' Torquay United side, thirteen places below third placed Reading in the league standings. It had been a difficult week for the Devon side's management as their attempts to quell a viral infection ran into difficulties. By Thursday, November 9 it was apparent that Torquay would struggle to put out a side at Elm Park. This 'epidemic of illness' cited by the *Sunday Dispatch* was such that 'late on Friday' Torquay had to sign two players from Exeter City, just to 'make up the numbers' for Saturday, November 11.[43] The players were Jack Kennedy and Tom Walters who turned out the following day at inside right and left.

Under such circumstances a Reading victory was totally predictable and so it proved. The hosts started strongly, and the forwards in particular exhibited some delightful football. Frank was set up by McGough after just six minutes. It was a good goal as Frank

> 'had but a narrow opening through which to steer the ball. Though perhaps the greater praise should go to McGough for his splendid work. I think it can be truly said that Newton is the only man in the team who could have got the ball into the net from such a position'.

Reading then eased up and allowed Torquay to equalise but Fielding restored matters shortly before the interval from the penalty spot.

The second half got off to a quick start as the sides traded goals; Frank netted his second, off the woodwork, putting Reading up 3-2. Torquay, although under pressure, resisted gallantly until the last fifteen minutes when, run off their feet, they conceded two more, both scored by McGough. Despite the makeshift nature of the forward line Torquay performed as well as the club could have hoped.

'Linesman' considered that both teams at times played good, bad and very bad football. Yet,

> 'there can be no doubt that the better side won, and won by a margin which no more than fairly reflects the superiority of the football craftsmanship. It was a game which, though lacking in the finer points, was always interesting to the spectators, and as Reading got five goals there will be few complaints that their football did not attain the standard we know is possible'.[44]

Following this game on November 11 Reading did not play at Elm Park again until December 23 when the club opened their Christmas programme against Swindon Town. In the intervening period Reading had a potentially difficult series of matches, two of which were against promotion rivals QPR and one with Norwich City. The side also had to play two FA Cup matches before taking on Clapton Orient in a league game on December 16.

The first difficult league match was scheduled for November 18 with QPR. In not dropping a point at home all season QPR had transformed Loftus Road into a veritable fortress. Reading arrived fully briefed for their visit and what ensued was a monumental defensive battle. 'Linesman' was engrossed.

> 'Reading may win the League, and if one may be permitted to enter the realms of very premature conjecture, they may win the Cup, but I doubt they will ever accomplish a more meritorious performance than that on Saturday, when, in holding the Rangers to a draw, they were the first team to bring back a point from the Loftus Road ground. It was the fastest and most thrilling game in which Reading have taken part in a long time, and though there can be no denying that the home side were the better footballers, yet a draw was not an unfair result for the visitors had done sterling work in defence'.

Whittacker in the Reading net was singled out for special mention as he achieved the 'seemingly impossible' in keeping his goal intact.

> 'Comparing the defences the honours rest fairly evenly, but in attack Reading were definitely inferior to their opponents, and the reason for this was weakness at inside forward. Newton must have found it heartbreaking trying to put himself against the home backs and centre half, and he cannot be blamed for playing so inconspicuous a part in the work of the team'.

Again the inside forwards were criticised for playing too deep so that when Frank did get the ball 'he never knew where to find his inside men'.[45]

With the spoils shared both teams turned to preparing for their respective first round FA Cup matches. For Reading this entailed a visit to Vicarage Road, a match Reading was expected to win after the side's good display against QPR. Reading, unlike Watford, did not undertake any special preparations although routine training was interrupted by a day spent on the Sonning golf course.

On the other hand, Watford slipped quietly out of town on November 22 to spend a few days at Clacton. In previous years, after a stay at the Grand Hotel in Frinton-upon-Sea, the club normally won Cup games:

> 'when refreshed by a sojourn at this bracing resort ... The fact that the club are embarking on special training so early in the cup campaign speaks volumes for their determination to oust Reading at the first attempt'.

It was recognised that Watford's chances of getting to the second round would diminish 'alarmingly' if the 'Biscuitmen' could force a replay. A large crowd was anticipated and in order to reduce the pressure at the turnstiles no change was to be given on the spot. But for those without the exact money a 'change box' would be provided.[46]

In the event the game was anti-climatic and Watford benefited little from the charms of Clacton. 'Linesman' had expected a hard fought encounter, but 'the opposition provided by the home club was so weak that the match was as one sided as the League encounter … at Elm Park.' The game was 'disappointing as a spectacle', and generated little passion among the home support in the crowd of 15,397. Perhaps not too surprising as the first goal resulted from the best movement that 'Linesman' had witnessed that season.[47] In all some six Reading players participated in the move. Wright initiated the play at left half when he passed to Oxberry at inside left who then moved the ball rapidly out to Fielding on the left wing who in turn slipped it to Frank. Frank promptly swung the ball across to Butler on the right wing. He trapped it and found McGough, unmarked in front of goal, and Reading were one up. 'The movement had been so rapid that the home defence were completely at a loss'.[48]

A goal two minutes into the second half as good as settled matters. On this occasion Frank smacked a hard cross from Butler under the helpless McLaren in the Watford goal. Although he exhibited a good turn of speed in executing the move, Frank 'injured his foot and thereafter his usefulness was impaired to some extent.' Nonetheless, from this point on Watford was a beaten side and after McGough added a third goal Reading's forwards did very much as they wished. 'Linesman' considered Watford as poor a side as he had seen all season. Their finishing was appalling, and 'would have discredited a third class amateur team ... In every department they were inferior to Reading, and almost from the first minute their defeat was inevitable'.[49]

Prior to the above reports appearing in the local press, the draw for the second round of the FA Cup had been announced. For Reading the dreaded banana skin popped out of the hat, an away encounter against non-league Sutton-in-Ashford. But first the club had a difficult league game to negotiate at the 'Nest', home of the Division leaders Norwich City.

A crowd of almost 11,000 were reported to have watched the game and those inside at the start were delighted to witness the 'Canaries' go ahead in the first minute. But Reading regrouped and playing the better football levelled the score through

McGough after 25 minutes. In the second half Norwich proved the stronger side and were on their way to a comfortable victory after adding two more goals. But with minutes remaining Oxberry pulled one back and a furious battle then ensued. It was an exhilarating finish as Norwich played everyone behind the ball while Reading exerted frantic pressure. Notwithstanding, their efforts went unrewarded and Norwich finally triumphed 3-2. Frank had a subdued game as he was effectively marked out of it by Halliday, the Norwich centre half, whose 'successful policing of Newton was an important factor in the game. Halliday was seldom more than a yard or so from Newton and Newton's usefulness to the side was greatly diminished'.[50]

Reading's FA Cup match against Sutton-in-Ashfield was afforded extensive column inches in the local press. Few if any of the Reading faithful were aware that Sutton Town FC, founded in 1885, played in the Central Combination League which was comprised of teams based in Nottinghamshire and Derbyshire. In addition Sutton had also enjoyed considerable recent success in winning the Derbyshire Senior League, for the third successive time at the close of the 1932-33 season. Sutton played at their modest Avenue Ground with a reported but untested capacity of 10,000 and their solitary stand could hold 300 on a good day. It was later somewhat optimistically reported that 'up to 16,000 could be squeezed in if necessary', but it remains uncertain that such a necessity ever arose.[54]

Sutton's officials rejected an offer from Reading to switch the venue to Elm Park. They were hopeful that the club could again exploit home advantage as had happened in the first round when Rochdale were defeated 2-1. In the qualifying rounds the club had enjoyed success against Grantham, Ransome and Marles, Spalding United and Burton Town. 'Sutton are a professional team, though all the players are in other work, … most … engaged in mining. The players are paid for each match, and the wages bill is not very large – probably under £10 per week'.[55]

The London football journalists considered that Reading would win, but Joe Smith was naturally more cautious.[56] A man of few words and master of the cliché, he provided the local press with the following:

> 'We are not looking upon the game as an easy show for us. We realise that all cup-tie opponents cannot be taken lightly and we are out to do our best. The boys are fit and optimistic, but we realise what we are up against. I have received many reports from friends who know Sutton and I know they are going to give us as stiff a fight as possible. Their playing pitch is somewhat peculiar, I am told, and that gives them some advantage, but we hope to prove the victors'.[57]

There was little by way of special preparation as both teams adopted a relaxed approach. The Sutton squad had undertaken no special training whereas the Reading players once again passed the Wednesday prior to the game on the Sonning Golf Course. On the Friday the side travelled by train up to Nottingham.[58]

It was 'A Correspondent' in the *Reading Mercury* who urged that all should be mindful of the cry 'Remember … Walsall!'. This was a reference to the FA Cup match played the previous

January when 'Arsenal, the team of the generation, visited Walsall and lost and all the football world was staggered.' Such would not be the case if Reading capitulated to Sutton but the thought no doubt passed through the minds of some of the 100 or so travelling fans who, at a cost of 7/6 return, piled into the Great Western Railway's 9.55 a.m. 'football special' to Sutton Central.[59] By 4.00 p.m. there had been no such disaster, although an air of deep disappointment hung over the Avenue Ground's home dressing room. Sutton could have done so much better had not two glaring goalkeeping errors gifted Reading the game. To compound their sorrows Sutton had scored the best goal of the match, and could so easily have earned a replay.

The state of the Sutton pitch came in for much criticism in the Reading press.

> 'There was little doubt that on their own enclosure Sutton Town were as near a match for Reading as one could possibly get. But what an enclosure it was! ... There was hardly a level square yard; and within the eighteen yards area it was one series of bumps. To make matters worse, snow had fallen, and although this had thawed off the greater part of the pitch, the wings remained very hard, and it was difficult to keep one's feet in places ... It was a distinct handicap to Reading and almost as good as a goal to their opponents'.[60]

Throughout the game itself Sutton adopted spoiling tactics, tackled first time and endeavoured to never let the Reading players settle. Despite these tactics once the visiting forwards did get on the move Reading always looked the more likely to score. The first breakthrough came after 12 minutes when Oxberry sent over a cross that Peake in the Sutton goal caught. Then, instead of throwing the ball out, he attempted a drop-kick and in the process spilt the ball. As he did this,

> 'the ever alert Newton was on him, and ... forced the ball into the net. It was purely an opportunist's goal, and one which the goalkeeper might easily have prevented'.[61]

The next goal was scored 15 minutes into the second half when Sutton were enjoying their best spell of the game. Wright at centre forward seized upon a poor clearance "and gave Whittacker no chance with what was really the best shot of the match.' This sent most of the meagre crowd of 5,116 into a frenzy, and set up a desperate battle for the decisive goal. The struggle continued unabated for a further 20 minutes until Reading finally scored with some 10 minutes remaining. Peake once more was at fault. On this occasion he caught a harmless cross but as he went to clear he 'dropped the ball, and was unable to escape the attentions of Newton, so that Oxberry was able to dash up and place the ball into the net.' It was a hard fought, sportingly conducted game in which Frank's efforts were again held to be disappointing, although he was judged to have worked hard and always 'kept in the forefront of the attack'.[62]

To this point of the season Frank had scored 12 league and cup goals for Reading in the 12 games in which he had participated. However, his honeymoon period with the local press was over and his performances were now subjected to greater scrutiny, and more objective assessments which contained some mild criticism. The comments that had recently appeared included: 'disappointing' against Sutton; 'usefulness greatly diminished' at Norwich; 'inconspicuous' and 'rather disappointing' against QPR and Northampton Town respectively. Despite these slights he was averaging a goal a game and remained a valued and integral part of the Reading team.

With the flurry of Christmas fixtures fast approaching, and still with only one away win to their credit, it was high time for the club to sort out this miserable record. The opportunity arose at Clapton Orient's Lea Bridge Road ground on December 16. Prior to this fixture Reading were seventh in the Division with 19 points from 16 games, just two points behind second placed QPR, but 5 back of league leading Norwich City.[63]

The "Oriental Chatter" column in the Clapton Orient Football Club (1906) Ltd. Programme of December 16 welcomed Reading FC:

> 'our players today entertain old friends and rivals from Reading. As you are probably aware, Joe Smith manages the affairs of our visitors, and it is a credit to the old inside forward of Bolton Wanderers fame that on several occasions this season I have heard Reading referred to as one of the best footballing sides in the Southern Section. Their position in the League Table may not justify those complimentary remarks, but that they are not better placed is due to the fact that Reading's form away from home has fallen a long way below the standard of play

> produced at Elm Park. Reading, who have a lively young inside forward named McGough eager and willing to add to his bag of ten goals. Just as anxious is Newton, the centre forward, who did more than any other player to lift Fulham into the Second Division ... It is these two forwards ... that Reading look to for goals. Manager Joe Smith came from a football academy which in his day was second to none in the whole of the country. He knows good football, and insists on scientific methods as against the rough and tumble style which so many wrongly associate with Third Division football'.

Reading started hesitantly against the Orient and on a bone hard pitch were a goal down within five minutes. The team subsequently regrouped and throughout the first half played 'the most attractive football they have shown so far this season.' The first Reading goal was not long delayed and after twelve minutes Oxberry scored his one hundredth league goal to equalise. The ball was crossed from the left wing by Chandler and

> 'Newton charged a defender off to allow McGough to find Butler. The outside man drew the other back, short passed to McGough and from his return centre Oxberry netted, a well-merited finish to a smart movement in which each Reading forward played his part'.

Reading now dominated and went ahead when Frank 'cleverly went through the two backs and beat the goalkeeper when he ran out placing the ball in the net just inside the post.' Then, shortly before half time, Frank headed 'a brilliant goal' from Oxberry's centre. Reading continued in the ascendancy after the interval until Hayhurst had to be assisted off 'with blood pouring from his face' after colliding with an opponent.[64] Joe Smith later advised 'Linesman' that Hayhurst had broken his nose but as no doctor was immediately available Hayhurst insisted on playing on. Thus after the bleeding had subsided he reappeared on the left wing. However, while Reading were short handed Clapton scored their second goal which made for a closer score line than the Orient deserved.

> 'No man worked harder for Reading's triumph than Oxberry, who was the outstanding player on the field. It was the clever constructive work which put Reading on the road to victory. Altogether some beautiful passing movements were carried out by the forwards at a remarkable speed. Newton proved himself a thoroughly elusive leader and took a lot of watching'.

Finally, 'Linesman' signed off observing that 'the doctor had not turned up when I left the ground at the end of the game. Hayhurst's nose deserved a better reward than it received'.[65]

After the weekend's fixtures Reading had shot up to fourth in the league table with 21 points but still 5 points adrift of Norwich City, although they now held a game in hand. Ahead of them were QPR on 23 points from 17 games, and Coventry City with 22 from 18. Below Reading the table was desperately congested as five clubs had 20 points. A run of good results over the crowded Christmas schedule, three games in four days, was now critical. Swindon Town were up first on December 23 at Elm Park, a game which was followed by home and away fixtures with Bournemouth on Christmas Day and Boxing Day.

Reading got their programme off to a good start by beating Swindon 2-0. The game was a scrappy affair and was primarily noteworthy for the poor finishing of both sides. There was no scoring in the game until Reading took the lead 12 minutes into the second half and just three minutes later added a second. The opening goal was scored by McGough 'with as good a left foot drive as one could hope to see from an inside right.' Reading's left half Wright netted the second with a fierce shot from distance. Having established a two goal cushion Reading subsequently encountered little difficulty in controlling proceedings for the balance of the afternoon. Overall Reading was 'better served in defence than attack.' The forwards were unimpressive. Frank and Butler in particular were singled out as not being 'at their brightest and both did many things we do not expect of them'.[66] The vast majority of the 11,427 in attendance would have left Elm Park well satisfied.

It was an early start for the Reading club on Christmas Day as they were scheduled for a morning kick off at Bournemouth. The 8,133 spectators on hand were treated to a 'really exciting first half, in which both teams went all out, and ... the play was fast and even'.[67] Bournemouth, or Boscombe as it was often referred to in the press, scored after ten minutes and very nearly added a second but the Reading woodwork intervened with Whittacker 'hopelessly beaten'. Immediately thereafter the:

> 'Reading attack swept down the field and scored through Newton ... Fielding, who with Butler, had shared the honours in the Reading attack, swept down the left and

> ... sent across a perfect centre which went right across the goalmouth. Luckily Butler had followed the ball, and he sent in a shot which Gold got to but could not hold, and the ball dropped amongst a number of players,'

one of whom was a lurking Frank who promptly lobbed the ball into the back of the Boscombe net. Although the hosts pressed Reading over the balance of the half honours remained even at the break.

In the second half Reading stepped up a gear and dictated play but Gold in the Boscombe goal was in fine form and was not to be beaten.

> 'The outstanding feature of this half was the runs of Butler, who in the first five minutes got clean away but shot just wide. Then Oxberry hit the post and just [moments] later fired in a hot stinging shot. It was lucky for Boscombe that Gold was in [a] direct line, otherwise Reading must have scored'.

The Reading forwards were judged to have performed well; both Fielding and Butler were singled out as 'fine raiders' and were well supported by Oxberry and McGough. Frank was not mentioned as an active participant during the second half bombardment of the Boscombe goal as he was being very closely watched by Coxford, the Boscombe centre-half.

> 'Coxford was satisfied to act as a third full-back. It was perhaps lucky for Boscombe that he did so, as he often stood between the goalkeeper and Newton, whose dashes

down the centre were a source of danger to the home defence'.

After 90 minutes the score remained 1-1 and was generally considered a fair reflection of the morning's entertainment.[68]

The return fixture on Boxing Day before a home crowd of 17,323, the largest to that point in the season, proved to be too much for Boscombe and they were stuffed 4-0. The margin of victory was thought by some to be 'somewhat flattering' although 'Linesman' considered the primary difference between the sides was their finishing, 'the visitors being erratic in the extreme'.[69]

From the start Reading went on the attack and within 5 minutes Frank had Reading's first goal. McGough went over to the right wing to take a pass, Oxberry then came across and moved the ball on to Frank and in a trice he was through a narrow opening and the ball was in the net. 'It was a neatly worked movement, but I should not have been surprised had the referee given the Reading leader offside'.[70] The home side maintained the pressure and Fielding scored the second just 7 minutes later. Boscombe for their part matched Reading in the midfield, but their forwards demonstrated no 'shooting ability whatsoever' which meant the score remained 2-0 at the break.[71]

The second half was similar to the first. Reading started quickly and had the ball in the net following a collision between Frank and Gold, the latter being injured. After Gold had received treatment the referee 'bounced the ball where the goalkeeper had been injured, a decision at which no good sportsman will cavil.' Nonetheless, local press opinion was divided on this point as the reporter in the *Reading Mercury*, not surprisingly, considered the goal should have stood. Regardless, Frank was not to be denied and when Reading's right half put a long through ball to Frank he buried it beyond Gold's despairing clutches. The final goal in the 4-0 triumph was headed home by McGough from Fielding's cross.[72]

'Linesman' felt that:

> 'Bournemouth were better footballers than the score would suggest and in their passing amongst the forwards they were just as good as Reading. Indeed, in the first half I think their football was really better than that of the home players, but their finishing was hopeless. Their defence was not always sound, the halves and backs being too closely bunched at times and getting in each other's way, and Reading proved to be their masters'.

He also mentioned that Frank, despite being closely guarded, made several openings for his colleagues which they failed to exploit as they were reluctant to follow up. After the second half got underway he felt that:

> 'Reading were the only team in it, and though they ought to have got more than two goals ... one cannot grumble at a four-nil win particularly after a strenuous holiday programme in which five out of six points were secured'.[73]

After the Christmas period the promotion race had tightened, although Norwich City still led the pack with 30 points from 21 games and QPR were now just 2 points behind with a game in hand. There followed Coventry City, 27 points from

21 games and then Reading and Charlton Athletic with 26 points from 20 games.[74]

Following their successful holiday season Reading travelled to the West Country to take on Exeter City. Shortly before the kick off the pitch was bathed in sunlight but this changed immediately before the start as the heavens opened and the ground was subjected to a 'terrific downpour'. Despite the ground cutting up badly Reading opened brightly and subjected the Exeter defence to a thorough examination during which they should have gone ahead. 'Butler made the best attempts, but the biggest miss of all was by Newton. He struck a post when really there was plenty of room to put the ball inside.' In addition Exeter were reduced to ten men when their right half was injured, although even then Reading failed to unlock the Exeter defence and were soon severely punished.

In a hectic fifteen minute period the Reading defence fell apart and conceded three unanswered goals. The first of these appeared to be scored from an offside position. The injured Clarke, having returned to play on the right wing, materially assisted in two of them. Reading did succeed in clawing one back: 'Oxberry, Fielding and Butler all took part in the movement, and the latter's centre was headed into the net by Newton.' But that was as close as Reading came, and indeed the fourth Exeter goal resulted from yet further confusion in the Reading defence.

This was the side's worst defeat since the 5-1 thrashing that Gillingham administered at the beginning of September. Defensive blunders were held responsible, but the whole team came in for criticism. The defence was:

> 'frequently badly spread-eagled, mainly through the neglect of the [Exeter] right wing where Clarke played a strong game despite his injury ... The passing of all the half-backs, however, was bad, mainly due to their being unable to control the heavy ball ... The Reading forwards were never really lively. Butler was the most prominent and he indulged in many dribbles, but, like Fielding, the ball seemed too heavy for him to lift over into the centre. Oxberry played a nice midfield game, but was seldom dangerous, whilst Newton was generally overwhelmed by opponents ... Reading's best spell was the final half-hour of the first half, and had they forced home their advantage during this period they might have at least shared the points'.[75]

The long return journey would have afforded the players ample time to reflect upon their failings and provided the management with an opportunity to devise a strategy for dealing once more with Gillingham at Elm Park the following Saturday.

The result at Exeter and the prospect of the Gillingham fixture failed to excite local interest and resulted in the season's smallest home gate of 7,528.[76] Fortunately for Reading, although they started slowly, the club led 2-0 after twenty minutes through Oxberry and McGough. The second goal resulted from Frank's cross, and as soon as McGough

> 'touched the ball the Gillingham defenders stood still appealing for offside. The Reading man hesitated, but then shot, Stanbury recovering from his surprise

sufficiently to touch but not to stop the ball. With Newton too closely guarded, and he was not at his best, there was no one to weld the forwards into a united line ... They kept the ball too close and we saw none of those swinging passes which would have forced the Gillingham defenders to break up the close formation they adopted'.

It would appear that those who stayed away got it right, as 'Linesman' considered it one of the dullest games he had witnessed that season. Gillingham were fortunate to find Reading on their worst form and but for Whittacker the visitors would 'undoubtedly have accomplished the unexpected in taking a point.' While winning the game was important, the most significant event in the game, and ultimately in the club's season, arose in the final few minutes when Frank was carried off after he collided with Stanbury.[77]

Towards the end of the week of January 7 further information regarding Frank's injury was forthcoming. When he was carried off his left knee was causing him considerable distress. 'On Tuesday water had settled on the knee, and there seemed very little chance of Newton being fit for tomorrow's game.' (This was the third round FA Cup tie against Oldham Athletic, scheduled for Elm Park on January 13.)[78] This wretched news was confirmed by Joe Smith on Thursday, January 11, when he announced that Frank had damaged a knee ligament and would be unavailable.[79] This was a serious development and one that impacted on Reading's promotion chances. The correspondent in the *Reading Standard*, almost certainly 'Linesman', attempted to rally the home support.

> 'It is bad luck that Newton should have been injured just before the Cup-tie and at the time of writing it is practically certain that his knee will not stand the strain of a game. Even though one must realise that his absence will severely weaken Reading's attack I refuse to be despondent and, still feeling Reading can win, chide those long faced followers whose gloomy comments suggest that defeat is our inevitable lot'.[80]

Unfortunately it was the long faces that proved correct as Reading went down 2-1 in what was a 'keen struggle'. The largest crowd of the season, 20,057, packed into Elm Park, and most would have been deflated to see Reading surrender their 1-0 first half lead.

> 'Though Reading had almost as many scoring chances as their opponents there will be few unbiased sportsmen who will deny that the better team won, but if – and a very big if it is too – Newton had been playing, it is a different tale I should be telling now'.

Inevitably, 'the forwards sorely missed the inspiration of Newton's leadership.' Edward Harston was selected in Frank's absence.[81] It was recognised as a tough ask for him and 'Linesman' was sympathetic.

> 'I hesitate to make any adverse comment on Harston's play ... He did his best, even if that best fell a long way below the best that Newton could have given us, I still think he deserves commendation for trying so gallantly'.[82]

Now out of the Cup, it was time to concentrate upon Reading's promotion battle. It started with the rearranged midweek home fixture with Newport County. Harston's return to the first team was brief for Thomas Forster was now selected.[83] Reading won the game 4-0 before a meagre crowd of 4,608 but 'Linesman' was certainly not impressed.

> 'In one of the dreariest and dullest games seen at Elm Park this season Reading defeated Newport County by four clear goals ... their conquest was so easily obtained that they had no need to play good football to get the points. A strong wind ... made it difficult ... but not even the difficult conditions can adequately excuse the players for showing such deplorable form – form hardly worthy of local amateur teams'.[84]

Despite the team's shortcomings management would certainly have welcomed the points, although the question as to who should lead the line remained. The matter became more pressing on the Friday after the Newport match when Joe Smith announced that Frank would be out for some weeks. It also transpired that Ridley, Reading's right back, had broken his jaw in the Cup match and would be missing for a further two weeks.[85]

Towards the end of January the club issued an update regarding Frank's recovery and was reported in the Reading Standard by F.W.L:

> 'Newton ... is making excellent progress, and at the time of writing these notes, I was informed by Mr Joe Smith

that there is a likelihood of his turning out shortly. He has already started light training and has practically recovered from the effects of his injury'.

F.W.L. also added that he was

'glad to take the opportunity of denying the many rumours current in the town that Newton had been suspended by the club. In view of the service Newton has rendered to Reading, it is thoroughly unsporting to circulate such rumours, particularly at a time when he is on the injured list'.[86]

It is unclear as to precisely what these 'many rumours' related, probably just idle gossip, but the club certainly had not suspended him.

The former Aldershot player Frederick Gamble was the late selection to lead the line on January 20 at Crystal Palace in a match that finished 0-0.[87] 'Linesman' commented at some length on the 'vexed question' of finding a replacement for Frank and the inclusion of Gamble.

'There could not have been many who approved of this decision, but as events proved the selection of Gamble was more or less justified. While not pretending that he is the ideal man for the job it would be unfair to suggest that he did not do his job as well as one could expect him to do. With Newton in the team Reading would have won, but Gamble was a definite improvement on the two men, Harston and Foster, who had led the line in the previous matches. He did not make the best use of his chances, and he had more than one, but he was a tireless worker and was so persistently trying to go through with the ball that the Palace defence could not afford to neglect him'.[88]

Gamble had done enough to retain his place the following week and he played in the 2-2 home draw with Bristol Rovers. On February 3 he was selected again for the match at Southend's Grainger Road ground which also ended 2-2. At the time Reading retained fourth spot in the league but were beginning to lose contact with their promotion rivals, having taken just three points from their three previous games. Norwich still bossed the division with 38 points from 27 games, followed by Coventry City and QPR with 35 points from 27 and 26 games respectively. Reading trailed them with 33 from 26 games.[89] The upcoming game on February 10 at Elm Park against Coventry City loomed large. It was truly a 'four pointer'.

Gamble's contributions were judged to be inadequate so the search to fill the number 9 spot continued. As none was located prior to February10 Oxberry was selected to lead the line with Charles Barley at inside left.[90] Reading won what was a robust encounter by a penalty goal to nil. The result was a welcome relief to the club's officials but Oxberry was not judged to be an adequate replacement for Frank. 'Linesman' in his game report conveyed yet further bad news:

'It is not likely that Newton will be able to kick a ball for some weeks and now, in the running for promotion, Reading once again find themselves without a leader likely to bring the continued success which is necessary if the club are to get back into the Second League. Newton's injury has cost the club at least a thousand pounds in cup-tie receipts, and is likely to cost them promotion as well, for on the form shown by those who have deputised for him there is no player on the books good enough'.[91]

Reading next visited Brighton and Hove Albion. An unchanged side was fielded but could only manage a 1-1 draw. Once more Frank was mentioned in the game report. In this instance it was 'hardly fair to compare Oxberry to Newton… [and] once again the absence of the latter undoubtedly cost Reading the second point'.[92]

In the light of later events the management was clearly now in touch with a number of clubs as the search intensified. And after the 2-0 loss at Watford at the end of February it became almost desperate.

'Giving their worst display of the season Reading lost to Watford ... and, in doing so, put themselves out of the running for promotion. Norwich won their match with the Rangers [Queen's Park] and now have an eight points lead over Reading, so unless the unexpected happens the Berkshire club are not likely to see the Second League, at least for one more season'.[93]

Finally on March 1 the Reading management announced that a centre forward had been acquired. It was hoped that the relatively inexperienced Charlie Gregory aged 22 would prove up to the task. The fee paid for him was not disclosed. He had played a total of 21 times for Manchester City as a centre half since he joined them from Doncaster Rovers at the beginning of the 1931-32 season. He had scored just 2 goals for City both in December 1933.[94] The 'necessary formalities were rushed through' and he was selected to lead the line against Aldershot only two days later. Reading won the 'local derby' 3-2 and Gregory scored on his debut.[95] This was only the second win in the club's last seven league games; unfortunately it was followed by a 3-1 defeat at Luton and a disappointing home draw with Northampton Town.

It was time for some good news to cheer the increasingly despondent Reading club and its supporters. It finally arrived when Frank was declared fit to return for the game at Torquay on March 24.

> 'Congratulations to Frank Newton on at last returning to play. Injured on January 6th, he has been very anxious to get back and this week was reported quite fit again. If his knee does not give him further trouble he should be of considerable service to the club yet'.[96]

Torquay were languishing close to the bottom of the Division and fewer than 3,000 spectators were on hand to witness Frank's reappearance. The *Reading Standard* reported that those who stayed away from the game missed one of Torquay's more spirited performances. In fact 'Reading were lucky to bring one point away with them.' It was Frank who opened the scoring, fortuitously and somewhat against the run of play, with a hotly disputed effort.

> 'He appeared to be offside but played to the whistle while Torquay's backs stood still and the goalkeeper advanced. Newton slipped when about to shoot, but his left foot just helped the ball on and it struck the post and entered the net with Maggs looking on and making no attempt to save. The goal was hotly contested by Torquay'.

but to no avail. The home side subsequently stormed back and subjected the Reading goal to an almost continuous assault throughout the second half. 'Play was more robust than scientific' and Torquay gave 'the Reading defence a gruelling time'. Eventually the home side equalised and there followed a futile but 'veritable scramble' as both sides searched for a 'winner'.[97]

As a result Reading were now fifth in the division despite their run of indifferent form, equal with both Bristol Rovers and Luton Town, but trailing league leading Norwich City by an insurmountable eleven points. There were only nine games remaining and with no realistic chance of promotion the club had to adjust and strive for a second place finish. This commenced with a challenging Easter programme. Reading were scheduled to play at the Valley on Good Friday morning; the following day QPR were to visit Elm Park and on Easter Monday Reading hosted Charlton Athletic.

The club got off to a good start by securing a point at the Valley from a 0-0 draw. As the scoreline suggests it was a game dominated by the defences as neither side could capitalise on the few chances created. Charlton were the more threatening particularly in the second half but there were close calls at both ends. Whittaker saved magnificently from Wilkinson on the Charlton right wing and Boulter their inside left missed the proverbial 'sitter'. Frank almost scored when put through by McGough. He 'shot as the goalkeeper came out to meet him, the latter just managing to deflect the ball with his outstretched foot – a narrow escape.' Fielding went close and later Wright in the Charlton net 'brilliantly saved a curling ball from Newton'.[98]

Not unnaturally the performance of the Reading forwards came in for some criticism:

> 'the passing ... was not always good and in all departments there was a fatal inability to keep the ball on the floor ... Newton would have had to be at least two feet taller to reach most of the balls which came his way, while, in addition, he had to work by himself most of the time, having to run half way to the wing to take a pass. The inside men were invariably too far back, while on the right wing Butler had an off day'.[99]

To take a point off seventh placed Charlton in an away game was quite acceptable. It offered some encouragement to the Reading supporters who were presumably the majority of the 10,864 fans who attended the following day's game with second placed QPR. They were fortunate as what they saw was considered a wonderful display of football. It

> 'was one of the finest, if not the finest, exhibitions of football seen at the ground this season. Reading have not been in such dazzling form for months ... In every branch of the game Reading were the masters of their opponents'.

Nonetheless, the first half featured only one goal, netted by McGough from a Fielding cross.

Events then moved quickly after the break when the inside left Barley struck the crossbar, Fielding collected the rebound and crossed to Butler who in turn centred for Frank to score

> 'with a glorious header. For a while it was just shooting practice for Reading, and Newton put the issue beyond doubt when he got the third with a shot that came as the finishing touch to good work by Butler and McGough. This would have been enough'.

There was more to come however, as first McGough, and then Fielding, with a stunning '*coup de théâtre*', netted in the closing minutes. [100]

The masterful performance of the Reading forwards in what was a 5-0 demolition job of a good QPR side was summarised in the *Berkshire Chronicle*.

> 'Barley's foot artistry probably caused him to be more prominent than any of the other forwards ... Fielding and Butler ... were in aggressive mood, the latter showing some of his best form ... Newton and McGough were ever a source of anxiety to the Rangers' defence, mainly by reason of the fact that they kept well in the forefront of the attack. In fact, Reading's fine victory was largely due to the abandoning of the old "W" formation and keeping a straight line of forwards'.[101]

The return game at home with Charlton was deemed to

be a 'scrappy affair' and typical of a game between two sides each playing their third game within four days. For the first 70 minutes the quality of the football was both indifferent and uninteresting. Reading were unable to recapture the devastating form enjoyed just 24 hours earlier. 'Territorially they [Reading] always had the better of the game, but their passing was not good and their finishing hopeless. Charlton were even worse in this respect' and although each side had good openings in the first half, both missed empty nets. There was no score at the interval.

As the second half progressed no discernable improvement could be seen and it was looking very much as though the crowd of 14,422 had been held captive for another lacklustre 45 minutes. Then with 20 minutes remaining Barley unexpectedly created an opening; he passed to Frank who set up a scoring opportunity for McGough.

> 'This goal was the crowning of the best piece of football I saw in the whole game ... It was a case of "all's well that ends well" so far as Reading were concerned, but after Saturday their football was disappointing, and, indeed was not so good as that in the match at Charlton'.[102]

After earning 5 points from 6, Reading had sole possession of fourth place, two points behind Coventry City and 3 behind second placed QPR. Norwich had virtually clinched promotion as the side was now 7 points clear.

On Saturday April 7 Reading travelled to Newport and beat the County to record their first 'double' of the season. Locally, there was a belief that Newport would provide stiff opposition as they were coming off a 0-0 draw with Norwich. But Reading never really let their hosts into the game. 'In the first half Reading scored two goals, both through Newton, but they had chances enough to have got half a dozen more'.[103] The first goal was scored after 15 minutes when McGough slipped the ball out to Butler who centred and before 'Emery could effect a save, Newton was on him and had headed the ball into the net.' The second goal came after another good move between Butler and McGough and Frank was on hand again to deflect it beyond Emery.[104]

Newport enjoyed one purple patch but it was brief and they were never seriously in contention.

Linesman wrote:

> 'In many quarters I heard the opinion expressed that Reading were the best team who have visited Newport this season and that their football was the cleverest seen on the Welsh ground, but even if this be true Reading can play better football still. It was ... one of the best games Fielding has played for Reading, and with Barley giving his full measure of support the left wing were almost good enough to beat the Newport defence by themselves, but just to make sure there was Newton always waiting in the centre and worrying the backs to such a degree that they could never settle'.[105]

As expected, the home game against league leading Norwich City attracted one of the largest crowds of the season, 12,486. They were treated to a 'ding dong' battle. Norwich, with a strong wind in their backs enjoyed the balance of play throughout the first half but the Reading defence was in resolute mood and although the Norwich approach work was well executed their finishing was poor. Reading for their part adopted an exaggerated 'W' formation which meant that the forwards seldom got moving. This strategy served the home side well in so much as the game was tied at the interval.

With the change of ends Reading abandoned the 'W' formation, pushed the inside forwards up, and proceeded to dominate the second half. As the game progressed Wharton in the Norwich goal increasingly found himself at the centre of the action. Twice in quick succession he fisted away good efforts from Fielding and 'turned a splendid header from Newton around the post.' Halliday at centre half kept a tight grip on Frank who almost inevitably 'was always a source of trouble when near goal'. Honours remained even until Reading scored with less than 15 minutes remaining when Halliday turned a shot from Butler into his own net. Up until that point the visitors played as though they would settle for the draw. But now they had to press hard to salvage a point but found the Reading defence, which had been excellent throughout, unyielding and in no mood to be breached.[106]

There followed a re-arranged fixture with Bristol City at Elm Park on Wednesday afternoon April 18. It attracted the season's smallest home gate, a meagre 3,750. The sides responded in kind and 'Linesman' described the encounter as 'one of the least exciting it has been my lot to watch this season and the football was so scrappy as almost to baffle description.' Despite his bafflement, he made an effort mentioning he found the first half 'particularly dull,' and the standard of finishing on both sides so poor that a draw seemed inevitable. He held out hope for an improved home performance after the interval as he anticipated Reading with the strong wind in their backs would run Bristol off the Park. 'Linesman' was quickly disillusioned as the visitors took the lead after only 2 minutes when Hayhurst put through his own net. This shook the Reading side out of their lethargy and for the next

> 'fifteen minutes Reading did everything but score, but at last the equalising goal was claimed by Newton. It was a fitting climax to the best movement of the game, for all five forwards played their part and the ball went from one to the other so quickly that the Bristol defence had no chance to prevent ... '

Frank from beating the wonderfully named Scattergood in the Bristol goal.

In his summary 'Linesman' reverted again to criticising the inside forwards for playing too deep which resulted in Frank being isolated.

> 'I doubt if the Reading leader touched the ball more than half-a-dozen times in the first half, and only once did he look like scoring. This was when he headed in a high ball from Fielding and Scattergood made a save which can only be described in the of-used [sic] superlative, brilliant'.

Despite this disappointing draw 'Linesman' predicted that Reading would win the return game at Ashton Gate the following Saturday.[107] There is little to choose between the various reports in the local press but 'W. E.' in the *Berkshire Chronicle* surpassed the others by closing with the superbly, cryptic comment: 'Mr Pinckston, the referee, added to the spirit of the afternoon, by his habit of using his linesmen to save his own legs'.[108]

After this mid-week game all that effectively remained to be decided was which team would finish second. Reading was now third in the division, on goal average, tied with QPR on 50 points. Norwich continued to head the division with 57 points followed by Coventry City 6 adrift. All four clubs had played 39 games.

The leg weary Mr E. Pinckston was again in charge of proceedings at Ashton Gate 3 days later. On this occasion his performance was considered to be over zealous, 'and some of his decisions were not easy to understand.' Particular reference was made to the free kick and the retaking of same from which Bristol scored their only goal. Regardless, his decision did not change the outcome as Frank scored once in each half for a 2-1 Reading victory. Of interest to Reading fans would have been the introduction of J.S. Liddle and D.J. Samuel; the latter making his first team debut, at outside and inside right. It was reported that both performed admirably and thereafter retained their places for the balance of the season. 'As usual Newton was a great forager after scoring opportunities and Oxberry showed all his old craft on his return to the team'.[109] Or, as the *Berkshire Chronicle* reported: 'Newton did a lot of skilful work in the centre, and was in position when any scoring was to be done'.[110] Frank's two goals raised his season's tally to 24, recorded in

24 appearances. The two points earned moved Reading into second spot, on goal average, ahead of QPR with Coventry now a point behind.

Regrettably the Elm Park terraces were not crowded when Reading played their last home game of the 1933-34 season. Fewer than 6,000 turned up to witness a convincing 4-0 victory over Clapton Orient. Reading's football was deemed 'as delightful as any they had shown all season.' The hosts started slowly but once the team warmed to their task the result was never in doubt. The 'Biscuitmen' dominated the midfield and placed the Orient defence under mounting pressure. Reading opened their account when Liddle netted the first 'as cool as any seasoned veteran.' The second and third goals were scored shortly before the break. The first of these when Oxberry, Samuel and Liddle participated in some excellent approach work which Newton finished off "by flinging himself at a pass from the outside right and rolling into the net with the ball.' The third came shortly afterwards when Liddle headed home a Fielding centre.

Trailing 3-0 at the interval the Orient rallied early in the second half but were let down by their errant finishing. Reading regained their ascendancy as the half progressed and Frank scored the final goal of the game when he converted 'a centre from Fielding by hooking the ball over the goalkeeper …'[111] 'Linesman' thought the team acquitted themselves well and he particularly welcomed the movement and cohesion exhibited by the forwards.[112] As a result of this victory Reading completed their 1933-34 home season undefeated. Of their 21 home games the side had won 17 and drawn 4 and in doing so had scored 60 goals while conceding just 13.

Reading's final game of the season was scheduled for Swindon

Town's County Ground and the outcome would determine the league runners-up to Norwich City. Prior to the game Reading held a one point advantage over Coventry City and two over both QPR and Charlton Athletic. Following the game with Clapton Orient, 'Linesman' considered that '... Reading must surely be firm favourites for the honour'.[113]

Sadly the game at Swindon proved otherwise and was:

'an inglorious finish to what might so easily have been a promotion-winning season. Reading played poor football and Swindon, though they never attained great heights in football ability, thoroughly deserved to win, for Reading missed their chances. Coventry drew in their last game and by reason of the better goal average finish as runners-up to Norwich, a position I thought Reading would claim. While one can serve no useful purpose in making excuses for Reading's failure to get back, a review of the season leaves one with only one conclusion, namely, that but for the injury to Newton, Norwich would not have had such an easy passage to the Second Division and that it might have been Reading who gained promotion. This is no over-statement of the case and one cannot but sympathise with the ill-luck which dogged Reading's footsteps at a critical time in the season. Not only did the injury to Newton rob Reading of the promotion chances, but put them out of the cup earlier than they would have been and, financially, cost them something well over two thousand pounds, this being accounted for by the loss of an extra cup "gate" and the money paid for Gregory'.

'Linesman' concluded that at Swindon nobody in the Reading team played close to his potential in the 3-1 defeat and the team work left much to be desired. 'Newton had very little chance, for he was closely watched by a taller man'. He closed by observing that the Swindon manager Ted Vizard was

> 'a shrewd judge of a footballer ... and some of his "captures" have more than proved their worth. Armstrong, [Swindon's centre forward] by the way, is on the open transfer list, and I am told that a hundred pounds would secure his services'.[114]

The reference to Armstrong suggests that 'Linesman' perhaps retained concerns over the centre forward spot and the lack of adequate cover. In particular he would have been aware that Frank would be 32 in November 1934.

There is no question that 'Linesman' was absolutely correct in his assessment of Frank's value to the side and in his conclusion that Reading's season might well have ended differently had he remained fit throughout. Frank's injury resulted in him missing ten games between January 17 and March 23 which derailed any realistic chance Reading had of promotion. His impact on the side's performance and the lack of adequate cover for him are reflected in the points gained at certain stages of the season. Of course, there are always numerous variables that determine the outcome of one, or a series of games, but an indication of his impact on the club's fortunes is apparent from the following. In the first six games of the season, prior to Frank's arrival, Reading gained only 42% of the points on offer, 5 from 12. Frank then joined the club and played in the next sixteen league games from which the team took 23 of the 32 points available, or a whopping 72%; After which the side accumulated only 11 of the 20 points, or 55%. In the final ten games of the 1933-34 season the club collected 15 of the 20 points possible, a return of 75%.[115]

It is worth recalling that F.W.L. in his column 'Reading and County Sports Chat', pointed out in September, 1933 that:

> 'If Newton can steer clear of injuries Reading should soon be repaid for the money spent on his transfer, and it ought not to be long before the club occupies a position much nearer the top of the table'.

Regrettably injury struck, and the percentages above speak volumes.[116]

1934-1935

The Reading club's first trial game of the new season was played between the Stripes and the Whites on August 11, 1934 and the second a week later between 'Newton's Team and Lawson's Team'. Both games were reported on by 'Linesman'. In the first, the 'Stripes' overwhelmed the opposition winning 6-0, before some 3,000 once more eager spectators.

> 'If the goalscoring efforts of Newton and the forwards he led ... are examples of what we have to come, I think Mr Joe Smith's prediction that the club will be "bang in the running" at the end of the season, is founded on something more than the optimism common in all camps at

this time of the year. The form shown in these matches is practically valueless as a guide to the true capabilities of the men playing, but ... the new players included more than one really useful player'.[1]

The second game was a closer affair and was won 2-0 by Newton's Team the 'Stripes'. Although the 'Whites' enjoyed the better chances in the first half there was no scoring before the interval which was attributed to poor finishing. After the break 'Joe Smith made five changes in order that all the fit players should be given a run'; Clark was one of these and scored both goals for the 'Stripes'. 'Linesman's' conclusion, based on the 2 games, was bland and non-committal: 'Reading should have two teams which will more than hold their own in their respective competitions'.[2]

Reading kicked-off their season at Lea Bridge Road and the 'Oriental Chatter' column in the Clapton Orient Programme welcomed them noting:

> 'since Mr Joe Smith took over the managerial reins the Berkshire club, which provides the opposition today, has finished second, third and fourth in the Southern Section table. Joe Smith, whose powerful feet were once worth thousands to Bolton Wanderers, feels that but for a spell of bad luck, Reading would have pipped Norwich last season. The injury to Frank Newton was certainly a bitter blow to the club's promotion aspirations, but you will see the ex-Fulham centre-forward well in the thick of it today'.[3]

Clapton Orient were certainly 'fired up' for the opener and both the Reading side and 'Linesman' were caught completely unprepared for the performance of a transformed Orient team. As 'Linesman' described it, the hosts 'proved to be a mightily more difficult proposition' than he had anticipated and he remained uncertain as to what this should be attributed. But it was obvious the Orient 'are a far better team than they were last season.' Nevertheless, he considered there were mitigating circumstances that led to Reading's 2-1 defeat. First the Orient side far exceeded Reading's expectations by playing a style of football vastly superior to their performances of prior seasons; secondly, the 'Orient players had no mean advantage of being familiar with a playing surface which must be almost the worst I have seen at so early a stage in the season.'

From the outset Clapton moved at a fierce pace and subjected Reading's defence to a severe examination. The first goal resulted from this early onslaught but the Reading defence then held firm for the remainder of the half. The visitors came more into the game at the outset of the second but it was the Orient that went two up when the Orient's right winger unexpectedly beat Whittaker with a direct free kick. 'Linesman' viewed this as a just reward for attempting the unexpected and demonstrated a 'spirit of enterprise which characterised the Clapton football all the way through.' He felt too that 'it was their quickness to seize an opportunity which made them so formidable a force.'

Reading were not to be outdone and Frank displayed his ability to improvise when he set up Fielding for Reading's goal.

'When a ball came down the field the centre-forward, instead of bringing it into the centre, went out to the corner flag, drawing the defence and leaving the goal open. Fielding raced in to the middle and when the ball came in he had it in the net in a flash'.

In the final 20 minutes Reading improved and engineered a number of chances but failed to convert them.

Frank Newton on the alert for an opportunity against Clapton Orient at Lea Bridge, August 25, 1934.

'Linesman' reported that the Reading forwards lacked not only 'a unity of effort' but also exhibited little cohesion and 'for a long time found it difficult to get together, the inside men dropping back far too often.' Overall 'Reading played well and, though there were weaknesses, these will probably be eradicated as the season progresses.' He concluded by noting that the Orient, despite

> 'the heat never relaxed, but the Reading defenders proved themselves just as good stayers. It was a thrilling game in which Orient claimed the narrow victory which they deserved'.[4]

On the following Wednesday evening Reading took on Bristol City in their home opener. It was an uninspiring affair although Reading showed

> 'flashes of form good enough to put and keep the club at the top of the table, but for every two minutes of scientific football there were six or more of bustling play in which there was little of the cool concentration of effort necessary to develop into a consistent match-winning combination'.

Initially Reading with the wind in their backs and the setting sun behind them pressed hard on the City defence. The first goal scored after thirty five minutes resulted from a defensive lapse that allowed the ever opportunistic Frank to pounce and net his first of the season. 'It may have been a trifle lucky that the centre-forward should have been given this chance, but his shot was a glorious example of first-time effort' and the goal richly deserved. McGough scored the second just five minutes later to give Reading the comfort of a 2-0 cushion at the interval.

The home side held their form through the first fifteen

minutes of the second half but then fell back and allowed Bristol to come on to them. Nonetheless, the defence held firm and there was no further scoring. 'Linesman' was critical again of Reading's attacking play and maintained his view that the inside forwards played too deep. As a result 'Newton had at least three, and sometimes four or five, defenders waiting to pounce … as soon as the ball came within ten yards of him.' In what he considered was a 'fast but scrappy affair' he emphasised that it was essential, if promotion was eventually to be achieved, that the forwards must attack as a cohesive five man unit, for when they did the Bristol 'defence were well beaten'.[5]

Gillingham visited Elm Park just three days later and provided Reading with their second scalp of the new season. Despite the 3-0 scoreline,

> 'their display can have given satisfaction to but few of their followers. It was a scrappy game in which there was more wild kicking than accurate passing and both sides missed many scoring chances'.

Reading should have gone one up early on when Frank had the ball in the net but he was 'incorrectly' judged to have been offside. Gillingham then suffered a similar refereeing injustice and the game which 'was far from reaching the standard we must see from Reading in the coming weeks' remained scoreless at the interval. It was nonetheless 'more interesting than that at Elm Park' the previous Wednesday.

At the start of the second half Reading 'put more vim' into their game and were rewarded when Frank opened the team's account. He worked 'hard without getting any luck. Evading the two men who were guarding him closely Newton got the ball away and after the right wing pair had worked an opening for him he took a return pass and scored with a rising shot at which Holland made but a feeble attempt so quickly did the ball go into the net'.

Even with Reading's improvement little of note arose until some ten minutes from full time when the hosts 'put their supporters in a better frame of mind for their Saturday evening football discussions' by scoring twice. Frank netted his second from 'a mighty shot which sent the ball into the net and cannoning out again'. After which Liddle on the right wing completed the scoring and provided Reading with a more flattering scoreline than the balance of play justified.

'Linesman' was pretty damning in his assessment of the proceedings.

'There was much to displease and not much to please and neither side set a high standard of football technique. Reading's form in this match would not carry them very far up the league'.

He found the Reading forwards little better than their opposite numbers and there was room for 'considerable improvement.' But he grudgingly conceded that they 'knew the way to goal even if they did not beat the goalkeeper as often as they might have done'.[6]

To this point in the new season, when judged against their form at the end of the previous season, Reading had performed below their potential. This view was shared by the management who now made 3 changes for the return fixture at Bristol City's Ashton Gate ground on Wednesday September 5. Gregory was brought in at right full back while Oxberry and Liddle were replaced by Chandler and Butler. However, 'Linesman' considered that the latter failed to produce the 'noticeable strengthening of the attack as I had hoped … ' The management must also have been disappointed as the 'first half was as dreary as the other games in which Reading have played in the past few days, and there were only three shots likely to beat the alert goalkeepers', of which two were credited to Reading's forwards.

The only goal of the match was scored by the City when Gregory was off the field having an injured knee treated. Afterwards Reading attacked with more urgency while Bristol focused on getting players behind the ball and packing their defence. McGough 'was more like his old self and foraging here, there and everywhere', while Fielding on the left wing proved himself 'a speedy raider' and 'some of his centres deserved a better fate.' On the other hand Frank, who had failed to have a shot on goal throughout the first 45 minutes, was 'being closely watched by J. Pearce, the ex-Army centre-half who is on trial with the City, he had few passes put to him in such a manner that he could hope to turn them to good advantage.' There then followed an unwelcome, critical assessment that all competitive sports people must fear.

> 'I think a younger and faster leader might have got a goal, for on at least three occasions Newton was in a favourable position but was too slow to get in his shot before he was bundled off the ball by a defender'.

Although Frank would have been aware of his increasing struggle to maintain peak fitness, to read this in the local press must have been a watershed moment the reality of which was soon confirmed.

For Reading this 1-0 failure was tempered by the knowledge that the team 'showed a team spirit' that apparently had been absent in the previous games; if the side could consistently perform as they had in the latter stages against Bristol they would certainly improve on their poor away record of the previous season. 'It took them a long time to get into their stride, but when once they did they were a force to be reckoned with'.[7]

Frank's name did not appear on the Reading team sheet for the trip to Swindon; Lawson, who had enjoyed some success in the Reserve side, was preferred. 'Linesman' observed that Reading failed to take a point from Bristol because of 'weakness in the centre'.

> 'When it was announced that Lawson was to lead the line tongues were set a-waging with the most surprising football news of the season, and yet the change was not altogether unexpected to those who saw the game at Bristol. Comparisons are always odious, but in this instance it is particularly difficult to draw a contrast. If Newton had Lawson's youthful energy and his abundant physical fitness there would be no need for any change, and if the younger man could be given the old Fulham leader's craft and knowledge Reading could not wish for a better centre-forward. Lawson was indefatigable in his efforts to make good and he got to many a pass which Newton could not possibly have reached, but when he

got the ball he did not always know what to do with it'.[8]

Lawson's elevation meant that Frank turned out for the Reserve side at Elm Park, in a London Combination League match against Clapton Orient's Reserve side. It was a keenly contested affair that Reading won 4-3, the winner being scored with 'nearly the last kick of the match'. Frank led the line, scored the first goal, had another effort disallowed and proved a constant threat to the Orient's defence. Based on the run of play the result was considered to be fully justified.[9]

Lawson retained his spot for the game with Northampton Town and Frank once more played for the reserves. Reading's teams did well in both matches winning them 3-1. Lawson scored Reading's second goal and 'was a persistent centre-forward, although he missed several good scoring opportunities'.[10] The *Daily Herald* report was somewhat more blunt: 'Lawson missed two wide-open chances in the second half'.[11] Frank for his part led the line well and scored the third goal although it was hotly disputed by Baker in the Northampton net.[12]

After this Reading first XI victory the club was eighth in the Southern Section of the Third Division with seven points from their six matches. Millwall had won all of their six games and headed the table, followed by Charlton Athletic on ten points, one ahead of Coventry City.[13]

On the following Wednesday evening, September 19, Reading took on Bristol Rovers at their Eastville Stadium in a Southern Section Cup-tie. Lawson was again preferred over Frank and he was judged to have been 'unlucky with more than one scoring effort, Ellis, the home goalkeeper, displaying exceptional agility in reaching two low drives.' Bristol scored their winning goal against the run of play and Reading, despite dominating, failed to capitalise 'and towards the close lacked coolness. The steadying factor of Newton was badly missed in the centre', the result being Bristol Rovers scrambled home to victory.[14]

The following week Frank was reinstated in the first team for the game with Bournemouth at Elm Park. 'From the first minute Reading showed themselves to be the superior attacking combination' and Gold in the visitor's net exhibited 'such wonderful anticipation and was so quick on his feet that it seemed impossible to beat him'.[15] Bournemouth survived Reading's initial onslaught and it was very much against the run of play when the visitors scored first. Reading

> 'were not long in arrears, for Newton obtained a really fine goal. Perfect combination on the left wing was followed by an accurate centre from Fielding. Newton obtained and shot hard, and although Gold stopped this first attempt he was unable to save the terrific drive with which Newton followed up'.[16]

Frank appeals for a penalty after being felled in the Bournemouth area at Elm Park, September 22, 1934.

Just prior to 'the interval Gold injured his knee when no one was near him', and immediately after the break Reading scored 'as lucky a goal as they will ever get'.[17] Gold, who continued to play brilliantly despite his injury, fielded Chandler's long range, speculative shot, but 'the slippery ball … somehow … spun out of his grasp' and fell across the goal line. 'It was an unlucky moment for Gold, who had given one of the finest displays of keeping seen at Reading,' but it sealed Bournemouth's fate.[18] Reading went on to claim victory through McGough's two goals, the second of which resulted from Butler and Newton's neat combination. Overall it was felt that the Reading

> 'forwards played with more confidence than in any previous match this season, and, although there was room for improvement in their marksmanship, there was never any doubt about their superiority. The line also seemed to keep better together, doubtless due to the manner in which Newton kept the attack going, despite the fact that he was well watched … '

by Messer the popular former captain of Reading.[19]

This decisive win moved Reading up to fifth in the league with 9 points from seven games. At this early stage of the season the club trailed Millwall, on 12 points, Charlton with 11, and both Coventry and Swindon one further back. All clubs had played seven games.

Reading's upcoming fixture was a visit to Watford's Vicarage Road, a game from which the visitors probably anticipated at least one point. Watford's indifferent although rapidly improving form had yielded just 5 points from 7 games. The day, however, proved a decided disappointment for Reading.

'It was an unpleasant game, for the football never attained a high standard' and 'the Reading forwards had so many easy chances of scoring that they ought to have had at least three goals'.[20] Reading, playing into a strong wind, did well to withstand the opening Watford bombardment and towards the end of a scoreless half Reading's defence had allowed them to establish a foothold in the game. Reading in fact had the easier chances in the half; the first of which arose when Fielding had a fierce shot headed off the line and the second when it was reported that ...

> 'Newton also had the hardest of luck when, racing clear of the backs, he put the ball over McLaren's head as he came out to meet him. The goalkeeper made a great effort,'

pulling off a miraculous save, just tipping the ball wide of the post.[21]

But worse was to follow for not only did the wind shift 180 degrees during the interval but Reading persisted in squandering simple chances. Frank was singled out as the worst offender,

> 'and then came the first of the "sitters" missed by Reading. Butler went into the centre and put the ball back to the right where Newton was waiting for it with no opponent within three yards of him. It was a chance from which a schoolboy ought to have scored, but Newton muffed his shot to such an extent that the ball had hardly sufficient pace to carry it to the goalkeeper. It was a costly miss, for Watford were quick to take advantage of the good fortune. Straightaway they carried the

ball into the Reading area with dazzling passes … for Barnett to net from close in'.

There followed three excellent chances for Reading to equalise but all were missed. The guilty parties were judged to be Frank, Butler and Chandler. 'Linesman' concluded that: 'In attack Reading were woefully disappointing' and Newton, amongst others, 'was off his game.'

'Reading played scrappy football, but in the second half they did well enough to entitle them to one of the points– but for appalling finishing they would have taken it, while there was more than an outside chance they would have got both'.[22]

Frank in action at Vicarage Road against Watford FC in what proved to be his final appearance for Reading FC, September 23, 1934

On the other hand, the *Daily Herald* merely stated that 'Newton was completely eclipsed by Armstrong'.[23]

However, events did not end there for more was forthcoming from Vicarage Road. It transpired that over post match 'boardroom drinks' the discussion, much of which no doubt reflected the visitors' frustration, turned to the failings of the Reading attack. Reading director Mr William Lee held forth and expressed his views in a forthright manner. He described the game and Frank's performance as a '*disgracefully weak exhibition and Newton was the worst centre-forward ever seen in the Third Division*'.[24]

Problems arose when Lee's comments developed 'legs' after being leaked. Not very surprisingly given the relatively small arena of Reading's footballing fraternity Lee's view soon came to Frank's attention. As previously witnessed Frank had form when he encountered disloyalty from a manager or an employer. On this occasion I doubt that there was any confrontation with Joe Smith given their long standing friendship and the circumstances surrounding his move to Reading. Rather, I would speculate that Frank advised Joe that he was no longer prepared to play for Reading and requested a transfer. In addition, I am certain Frank had maintained his contacts at Fulham, now managed by Jimmy Hogan, and was well briefed as to the happenings in the Fulham dressing room and beyond.

Firstly, James McIntyre and Fulham had parted company. The reason given in the board minutes cited his transferring of Frank to Reading on his own initiative.[25] Clearly the board, specifically John Dean, would never have approved the move had the opportunity arisen and most certainly not for £650.

The report in the *Daily Mirror* stated that a Fulham director had advised that 'McIntyre had no contract with the club so that either side was in a position to terminate the engagement at short notice'.[26]

> The reason ... according to the board minutes, was because of his unprecedented action in transferring, entirely on his own initiative, F. Newton to Reading for the impossible price of £650. The Fulham board allowed McIntyre's successors much less discretion'.[27]

I would suggest that when Frank became aware of Lee's view he promptly contacted Craven Cottage to indicate that he would be available shortly and was content, should there be an interest, to return to the Cottage. The suggestion would not have fallen on tin ears for it was by now horribly apparent that the acquisition of Jack Lambert had been an expensive mistake. Indeed much earlier in the year, March 24, 1934, Frank must have allowed himself a wry smile when he heard that Reading's Reserve side had beaten their Fulham counterparts 5-2 in a London Combination match at Elm Park. None other than Jack Lambert played at inside right that day.[28]

The first public indication of a problem in the Reading ranks arose on the afternoon of October 3, 1934 when Frank did not turn out for a charity match at Elm Park between Reading and Swindon which had been organised in aid of the Gresford Colliery Distress Fund.[29] Frank's failure to participate in this game is a firm indication that Frank was on his way out of Reading and that a deal perhaps already existed with Fulham. In any event no risks were going to be taken that might jeopardise the move. News of Frank's transfer was soon abroad and was reported widely on October 6. The *Daily Herald* commented:

> 'Nothing so astonishing among these signings-on has occurred as the return of Newton to Fulham. This centre-forward went to Reading from Fulham and is now back again, and will take his place in the team to receive Hull. I was told that Newton was transferred [to Reading] without the consent of his directors. Newton will be playing his 200th league game today and his tally of goals is 186'.[30]

The *Football Chronicle* also commented on the same day:

> 'I find today that the transfer of Newton has been received with mixed feelings by Reading's supporters. I understand that the club has tried unsuccessfully to secure the return of Palethorpe, now with Preston North End, and that further efforts are being made to secure a centre forward'.[31]

Unsurprisingly, there was not a mention of Florence Newton's health previously identified as a primary consideration in Frank's move to Reading. At that time a change of air was considered 'imperative' and the management would place 'no obstacle in the player's way'.[32]

Meanwhile, the Reading weekly local press, because of their publication dates, had to play catch up. While Frank's transfer of course was reported there was more emphasis placed on the closing of ranks locally and an understandable desire to 'move on'. F.W.L. in his *Berkshire Chronicle*, 'Reading and County Sports Chat' column of October 12 wrote:

> 'Have only just recovered from the surprises of last week-end. The first, of course, was the news that Newton has returned to Fulham, and the second Reading's sweeping victory over Newport County on Saturday.
>
> . . .
>
> There was much local disappointment when Newton was allowed to join the Reading club from Fulham, for he materially helped Fulham in their promotion to the second division.
>
> At any rate it is a nine days wonder that will have probably slipped from the memory by the time these notes are read, although I question if the various rumours as to why he went back to Fulham will have ceased circulation by then'.

Unfortunately F.W.L. did not elaborate but a further bullet point made reference to Frank's performance in his first game back at the Cottage against Hull City.

> 'Newton played for Fulham against Hull City on Saturday but though his side won, he did not score any of the goals, although he is credited with playing a part in one of them at least. The opinion of the London Press was varied, some speaking in praise of his efforts and others criticising him. John Bell, in the "Morning Post," says that Newton is the most thrustful [sic] leader Fulham have

had for years, whilst James H. Freeman, in the "Daily Mail," says that he did not seem fast enough'.[33]

On the same day the *Reading Standard*, in a dismissive 'Late Sport' item buried on page 23, noted that:

> 'Many rumours are current in the town regarding the transfer of Newton to his old club, Fulham, but, as is usually the case, the stories have no foundation in fact. As manager Joe Smith put it, Reading were not satisfied with Newton's playing this season, and when a representative of the Fulham club remarked to a Reading director that his club would be glad to have Newton back again, negotiations were entered into and the transfer made in the ordinary way. Reading are now seeking a new leader and have several in mind, but at the time of going to press nothing definite had been settled upon'.[34]

On page 19 of the same edition 'Linesman' was delighted to report that the post-Newton era had got off to a rollicking start on October 6 with a 6-1 home win over a hapless Newport County side.

> 'Reading's dazzling win ... came as a pleasant restorative to those many supporters to whom the news of Newton's transfer to his old club, Fulham, must have come as a considerable shock ... Reading find themselves once again with a centre-forward problem, but Oxberry provided so happy a solution [he scored 3 of the 6] against Newport that perhaps the prospects are brighter than some of

the dismal johnnies would have me believe. Obviously a new man will be secured if one happens to be going at the right price, but the team will not be the poorer if Oxberry can continue to fill the gap so admirably'.[35]

In all probability Frank remained oblivious of the final word on the Watford game and his performance therein. This appeared in the *Reading Mercury & Oxford Gazette* also on October 6.

'Newton was seldom a source of trouble, he had several chances of testing the Watford goalkeeper, but he failed dismally. With Butler he missed the two simplist [sic] openings imaginable'.[36]

Of course there was a desire locally to move on as quickly as possible. In part, in my view, because Frank in effect had advised the club that he had raised the drawbridge on his Reading career. During the period of the two matches that Frank was relegated to the Reserve side it became apparent that the club had no adequate long or short term replacement. An intensive search swiftly followed and 'Linesman' offered more on Joe Smith's travels up North in his 'Sport Shorts' column on November 2, 1934.

'I have been inundated this week by the inquiries as to the truth of the rumour that Palethorpe is returning to the Reading Football Club. When I put it to Joe Smith he replied: I am afraid we shall not get Palethorpe. It is true that we have made inquiries but the fee asked for

> the player was far too high and was out of all proportion. We are keeping our eyes open and have been after four or five centre-forwards, but the clubs have been asking First Division prices for Third Division players. At the same time we are determined to get one in time for the cup ties'.[37]

Frank would have been well aware that during his time at Reading Fulham had failed to prosper. He certainly would have logged that at the close of the 1933-34 season the club finished in sixteenth position and that McIntyre had resigned, or was fired, on February 12 after the 2-1 home win over Bury.[38]

The main impediment to Frank's return had been removed and had been replaced by Joe Edelston on an interim basis. Jack Lambert had turned out in 26 league matches in 1933-34 and had scored only 4 times.[39] The pitch was certainly rolled for a replacement and when the occasion arose Joe Smith naturally would not stand in Frank's way.

CHAPTER VIII

THE RETURN TO FULHAM FC, 1934

Season 1934-1935

At the time of Frank's return to Craven Cottage Fulham were languishing in tenth place in Division II with eight points from eight games, fully seven points behind league leading Bolton Wanderers. The club's away form was particularly poor with only one point from four games; the most recent was a 2-0 defeat at Gigg Lane before some 6,000 Bury supporters on September 29. The *Daily Mail* reported that 'Fulham pursued the tip tap method, and as a result brought about their own downfall.' The reporter advised that: 'the Fulham players, now that the heavier pitches are coming along, must realise that they cannot pursue tactics more suited to faster pitches'.[1]

Frank's problems at Reading and his willingness to return to Craven Cottage would have been sudden but welcome news to both the club's board of directors and supporters. The views expressed in the press were more varied.

'Arbiter', Frank M. Carruthers, stated in the Saturday edition of the *Daily Mail* on October 6:

'Some of the Fulham officials, including Mr Dean, the chairman, did not approve the transfer of Newton to Reading, and I was not surprised when yesterday they arranged for the return of the centre forward. He is a go-ahead player, and it has been felt that a man of his type was required. He is to lead the attack against Hull City'.[2]

Others were somewhat more uncertain. 'Chatterbox' in his column 'Right on the Inside of Sport' stated:

'Eyebrows were raised when Fulham got their old player Newton back from Reading. Had Mr Jimmy Hogan [manager] been harried into a bad deal? Here is the answer many people want: Fulham's books show a nice profit on the two transactions. Take it from me, Jimmy Hogan won't waste a farthing on transfer fees – he thinks too highly of his own juniors'.[3]

Similarly, 'Corinthian' when comparing recent signings in his column on October 6, considered none 'so astonishing' as Frank's return to Fulham from Reading. He also divulges he too was aware that Frank was 'transferred without the consent of his directors'.[4]

Indeed, the Fulham directors welcomed his return. Their general feelings were reflected in a telegram sent to Frank on October 6, from Charles Bradlaugh Dean, the chairman's son. It read: 'DELIGHTED TO HEAR YOU HAVE RETURNED BEST WISHES AND GOOD LUCK C B DEAN'.[5]

As can be imagined Frank's return to the friendly confines of Craven Cottage 'delighted the 20,000 spectators who braved the rain to give their old favourite a rousing reception.' Frank led the line, Fulham attacked effectively from the opening and at the interval were two goals up. The second was an own goal conceded by Quantock who, under pressure from 'Newton, kicked into his own net.' Jack Lambert was playing on the right wing and was not a success; he 'later missed two "sitters"'. In the second half Fulham went on to score twice more and ran out 4-0 to the good. Frank 'showed that he had lost none of his thrust and shooting ability, and may prove to be the missing link in the forward line'.[6] The *Daily Mirror* noted that Fulham's forwards were 'strengthened by the inclusion of Newton', and that he 'put that thrust into the attack which enabled Hammond and Price to use the ball to the greatest advantage'[7].

The following week Fulham travelled to Nottingham to take on Forest at their City Ground. While both teams had ten points from nine games, Forest were unbeaten at home while Fulham had yet to win on the road. A keen battle was anticipated and the 14,000 who attended were not disappointed. By all accounts, it was 'a most exciting struggle' in which there 'was not a dull moment'.[8] Forest produced 'their best performance of the season' and any result other 'than a draw would have been an injustice to either side after a really sparkling display'.[9] Fulham started strongly and twice came close in the opening minutes. Subsequently the visitors 'opened the game out with long swinging passes' and put the Forest defence under severe pressure. Fulham also 'held the upper hand in midfield, but inaccuracy as marksmen was their failing.' As a result the hosts led 1-0 at the break. In the second half 'Fulham continued to force the pace' and eventually Price drilled a superb equaliser from fully 25 yards. Play moved at a breakneck speed from end to end and although both goals were at times under extreme pressure there was no further scoring. The conclusion being: 'It was a great game and a fair result'.[10]

Bradford City were the next team scheduled to enjoy the pleasures, or otherwise, of Craven Cottage. Although Fulham were six places above them in the league standings they were only separated on goal average. C.A. Hughes of the *Daily Herald* stated: 'Not having seen Fulham for some weeks I was much struck by the improvement in the side, even though the changes have not been drastic.' He thought that the forwards had developed a better understanding, that their close passing game was skilful and that long swinging passes were utilised only to exploit an unbalanced defence. He also added that Frank was 'not yet the ideal centre, but he has a big heart and will no doubt settle down to give the best in him, as in the old days with Fulham.' He concluded by observing that: 'On this display Fulham are the best of the London clubs in the Second Division'.[11]

The local press was equally as enthusiastic, 'Fulham again gave a splendid display at the Cottage'. Price scored directly from the kick off and within two minutes Newton had the ball in the net again but was judged to be offside. After Bradford had weathered the opening storm there was no further scoring in the half despite Fulham's creative football. The Cottagers continued to press after the interval and Arnold added a second while Finch should have netted a third. Bradford then were fortunate in pulling a goal back, which finally injected a degree of interest for the 21,000 in attendance. At that point the home side unaccountably 'slackened badly', and seemed almost intent to let Bradford back into the game. That was until Arnold

> 'sent across a perfect centre. Newton timed the ball with that precision that has always stamped him as an artist, and neatly headed through. The Cottagers were full value for the victory'.[12]

This result moved Fulham up to sixth place in the table with 13 points, ahead of both Sheffield United and Nottingham Forest on goal average.[13]

The Cottagers were still without an away win. Hopes must have been high that the visit to Meadow Lane against the cellar dwelling Notts County, with only 4 points, would improve this state of affairs. But Fulham were perhaps unlucky to encounter the County when they had just acquired Stabb, a centre forward, and Steele on the right wing, both from Torquay United, whose contributions 'resulted in a big improvement.' The 14,000 plus home supporters left well satisfied with manager 'Charles Jones' team-building enterprise'.[14] 'Friar Tuck' in *Reynolds's Illustrated News* reported in a similar vein, 'the County forwards seemed to have regained much of their lost confidence, and played together as their supporters have not seen them do since the season commenced.' He concluded: 'all things considered, a draw was a fair result.'

The *West London Observer* also registered surprise while reporting that 'the Cottagers did well to gain a point.' The forwards came in for their share of criticism, as they were 'workmanlike in building their attacks but as usual, their shooting was weak.' The County opened the scoring and Stabb had the ball in the net again a minute later but this effort was disallowed. Arnold's contribution to Fulham's attack was of its customary high standard but his efforts went unrewarded until Frank got on the end of one of his corners and 'in a twinkling' the scores were level. In the second half the pace of the game was 'appreciably faster', but there was no further scoring.[15] On balance it was felt that Fulham were worth no more than the hard earned point.

There then followed an exceptional home match on November 11 against Southampton in which Fulham figuratively failed to turn up until the 60th minute. At which point the visitors were three goals up, and many of the 18,000 in attendance were no doubt contemplating an early exit.[16]

> 'Southampton were the superior team in every department, but they paid dearly for the error of changing their tactics after securing a three-goal lead. They substituted defence for attack and were unable to withstand Fulham's desperate onslaughts'.[17]

Fulham were being badly bossed at home. That was until Gibbons cast caution aside and forsook his centre half role to join his forwards. With 24 minutes remaining he scored his first of three goals. After this T.H.J. Reynolds reported that 'Fulham became really roused and Southampton perturbed. With the home rearguard joining in the bombardment … the Southampton defenders were in extreme difficulties'.[18] 'Chelstan' in *Reynolds's Illustrated News* commented on the latter part of the second half:

'However, the biggest thrill for Fulham's supporters had yet to come, Gibbons ... decided to do things himself, and proceeded to head a goal from Arnold's centre. Five minutes later he was up in the goalmouth again, leading a rush. The ball was banged in. And, with four minutes to go, here was Gibbons, again in the goalmouth, the only cool man among an excited, struggling bunch, and once more he got foot to the ball and put it into the net'.[19]

A truly remarkable hat-trick for Syd Gibbons, a man who made 299 league appearances in Fulham's first team over 8 seasons. He played at centre half in all but 2 of those games and in total scored but 10 goals!

The report carried in the *West London Observer* considered it 'undoubtedly Fulham's worst display this season,' which 'was only redeemed by their late effort.' After Southampton's second goal,

'it seemed that Fulham's cup of sorrow was complete when McIlwaine calmly walked past Birch and Hindson and shot past the helpless Tootill. For most of the game Fulham's efforts at cohesion were almost puerile. They deserve credit, however, for their splendid fighting finish, but it was the do or die spirit and not academic football that saved the game'.

There was a final comment that in part explains why Southampton may have considered it prudent to play defensively in the latter part of the second half.

> 'There was an amazing scene during the match when three Southampton players were knocked out within the space of a few seconds. The field looked like a battle ground as first-aid men carried the injured players from the field, two of them bleeding from the head. They were able to resume after the interval, however, with their heads bandaged'.

Significantly there was no specific mention of a Fulham forward.[20] It was a truly lamentable performance, and a confidence sapping one for the upcoming away game against the Division II leaders Bolton Wanderers.

Since Frank had arrived back at Craven Cottage Fulham had gone 5 games undefeated. However, a trip to Burnden Park was of a different order to any match the Cottagers had played to that point of the season. Bolton had lost once at home, whereas Fulham had yet to register an away win. Many must have marked their 'pools' coupon accordingly.

And they would have been quiet correct, for 'Fulham had one consolation about their heavy defeat at Bolton. It was inflicted by a team showing real promotion form.' Fulham did well at the outset and their approach work was smooth although good scoring opportunities were few. As the half progressed the side held out under increasing pressure until just moments before the interval when Hindson turned a cross into his own net. Matters developed differently in the second half when the home side hit their stride, and

> 'the London team's rearguard proved quite incapable of holding them, for they combined speed with their

> cleverness, whereas Fulham, though making many adroit moves, were slow-footed, and often did their work twice over'.

The assessment of Fulham's performance in the *Daily Herald* was accurate but harsh.

> 'Fulham flattered to deceive. They could not maintain their early form against such a side as Bolton proved themselves to be and finished up badly beaten with hardly a man doing justice to his reputation'.[21]

'Trotter' in *Reynolds's Illustrated News* concurred that the 20,000 spectators were treated to an 'exhibition of real football' in which 'the Wanderers and Fulham started off in brilliant style with fast, clever play.' Both sides demonstrated that they had 'fast-moving, clever forwards. Fulham's half-backs played splendidly in counteracting a long series of fine Bolton moves.' But matters deteriorated when 'bad feeling crept into the game … and free kicks were frequent.' Fulham tested their hosts but Bolton's sustained pressure eventually paid off when Hindson turned the ball into his own net. Play in the second half 'restarted as it had left off, the Wanderers going hammer and tongs', and when Bolton scored a second from a shot deflected by Birch, heads went down. The visitors were 'thoroughly leg weary' and incapable of containing 'the clever, sprightly Wanderers. It became merely a question of how many goals Bolton would get.' On the day 'Bolton played like a super-team' and in winning 3-0, 'simply ran Fulham off their feet'.[22]

The local press was equally constrained and coverage was brief. The only Fulham forwards mentioned were Arnold and Finch and that was because they 'both made one or two desperate efforts on the wings', but all to no avail. 'The Cottagers seldom got an opportunity of carrying the ball into the home territory after the resumption', and that was all that really needed to be said. No doubt most among their readership did not dwell on the result.[23]

Prospects appeared brighter for the week following when Oldham Athletic were due to visit the Cottage. Fulham were now ninth in the league standings while Oldham were three off the bottom. The Athletic had yet to secure an away win and had conceded 34 goals in 14 matches, more than any side in the division. On the day 'Chelstam' reported that Oldham were a much better side than their lowly league position indicated. He considered that the side's luck was completely out as their defence 'made the Fulham attacking scheme look poor'. That was until Frank scored in the second half from what appeared to be an offside position. However, the goal stood and finally injected

> 'some life into the Fulham forwards, and shortly afterwards Arnold went through the Oldham defence twice and scored both times. The first of these two, incidently, was deflected by Burke – more bad luck for Oldham'.

Overall the defences dominated proceedings and the aforementioned Burke at centre half 'marked Newton so well that the Fulham leader hardly saw the ball.' Once again none of the Fulham forwards received a positive mention other than

Arnold and it would seem probable that the majority of the 15,000 spectators enjoyed the result rather more than the spectacle.[24]

The account in the *Daily Herald* was similar and considered the forwards of both sides contributed little. The game ought to have finished goalless and it most probably would have done 'if the referee had not decided that Newton was on-side when he put the ball into the net at the end of 60 minutes dull and featureless play.' The view was that the Burke deflection 'finished Oldham.' But there was no praise for the Fulham forward line, nor indeed certain of the half backs.

> 'For some inexplicable reason the Fulham attack fell right away to the form of last season. Everything went wrong. The ball was passed nicely to the opposition by Price and Clark, while Newton allowed Burke to tower over him in the middle of the field, and hardly get more than a fleeting glance at the ball'.[25]

The *West London Observer* was quick to laud Arnold's contribution. He was 'irresistible', and once his colleagues provided decent support he scored two 'splendid goals.' Otherwise, there was little positive to recount. 'Fulham's attack was for the most part of the game unimpressive. There was no sparkle about their play'. It was acknowledged that there was some improvement in Fulham's performance after Frank's disputed goal but without Arnold's contribution it would have been an unedifying spectacle.[26]

Clearly, the side was not performing well and the upcoming game at Turf Moor would have been approached with some trepidation. Nonetheless, the team went off to Cleveleys on the following Tuesday 'for a week's special preparation', and readers were assured that this was to be no relaxed week of golf and ping-pong as 'the training apparatus goes North from Craven Cottage, and the boys will do exactly the same work as they do at home'.[27] But all their hard work made little difference as 'Fulham did not live up to their reputation of being football stylists.' It was felt that many of the 11,000 in the ground 'were somewhat disappointed, particularly in view of the fact that so much had been heard of the continental methods introduced by the Londoners' Burnley-born manager Jimmy Hogan.' The visitors failed completely to even suggest 'that they were a team of outstanding ability.' Yet again the finishing was poor and much effort and time was wasted in 'futile pattern-weaving.' So much so that Burnley dominated in every department and in many ways it was a 'stroll in the park'. Burnley were two up at the interval and Fulham never really threatened in the second half. Of the forwards only Hammond and Arnold were commended, but the former 'nullified good approach play by erratic finishing.' The tall Burnley pivot, Wallace, returned to the side and put in a 'strong defensive' shift, in effect nullifying any contribution that Frank might have made. To round it out things were no better on the right side where 'Finch and Lambert had a lean time'.[28]

The *West London Observer* also failed to find much positive to report, other than another fine display from Arnold. The view was that Fulham had again failed to meet expectations and were 'soundly beaten.' Tootill was in fine form in the Fulham goal, and 'had the forwards shown the same form as the goalkeeper, the result would have been vastly different.' Fulham did improve shortly 'before the interval, but both Hammond and Newton failed miserably in finishing.' After the interval Arnold scored to make it 2-1. But although this put 'new life into the attack' the success was short lived. The contest was effectively over before Burnley scored their third.[29]

Despite the poor run of results, one win in the club's last five matches, Fulham remained eighth in the division with 17 points from 16 matches. The side still remained without a win away from home and had performed very poorly in their last two away fixtures. In addition, four of Fulham's last six league games had been against sides which were in the top seven places in the division. They were therefore fortunate that the upcoming match was with Swansea Town, a club nine places below the Cottagers and similarly still in search of an away win. Given the context, the crowd of 17,000 might well have been less than optimistic that they would witness a resounding victory over the Welsh invaders.[30]

A.J. Webb reported on Fulham's 4-1 victory in the *Daily Herald*, but he was quick to reiterate Fulham's apparent problems.

> 'Fulham have yet to become a perfectly balanced football machine. There were obvious weaknesses both in attack and defence in this game, and, so far as the forwards were concerned, blemishes were made manifest by the brilliance of Arnold on the left wing. Finch, on the opposite wing, was not nearly so effective, and Newton, despite his two goals, fell away badly in the second half. Newton played his usual robust game up to the interval, and was

always well up the field, but afterwards he lost speed and was all too frequently robbed when in possession'.

Swansea also scored in the first half but thereafter never threatened to get back on terms against a dominant Fulham defence in which Gibbons was formidable. As Webb pointed out, Gibbons would have shared the honours with Arnold as the 'star turn' but for his contribution to a moment of sheer pantomime.

> 'The ball was placed on the spot for Gibbons to take the [penalty] kick, but the centre-half decided it was not sitting up properly, and he proceeded to give the ball a turn. This did not suit Referee Gibbs, who promptly turned it back again only for Gibbons again to handle the ball as the referee went away. Then a Swansea player joined in the fun, and so it went on, this childish quibbling, until Gibbons finally strolled up, kicked the ground behind the ball and watched his great effort trickle tamely outside. Ridiculous from start to finish'.[31]

Webb also commented upon the 'distinct scientific flavour' of the Cottagers' performance which was something that their new manager, Jimmy Hogan, had attempted to inject into their game. Hogan believed strongly that 'close intricate passing and dribbling' would ensure a team's success. His training methods and tactics were considered 'unconventional' by many; the Fulham players did not take to them and the board remained dubious.[32] Perhaps it was this revolutionary, more scientific approach, as opposed to one of improvisation, that led Webb to note that 'strangely enough, it was very often the most unorthodox move that baffled the Swansea defence.'

In the second half Swansea were second best and were 'easily outplayed' by the Cottagers. 'Generally speaking, it was a good, hard game, with Fulham always in the role of dictators'.[33]

'Chelstam' in his report agreed absolutely that Arnold was the 'stand out' player throughout the match. He also pointed out that Swansea suffered the misfortune of effectively losing their right-back in the first half; after the interval he was moved to outside right where he played 'in considerable pain'. Except for Arnold's contribution, 'Chelstam' considered it was a 'somewhat drab match. Newton could make no headway against Hanford, and the Fulham right wing [Finch] was again weak.' He also concurred with Hogan's view regarding 'the stifling effect of Herbert Chapman's third-back' innovation and considered Hanford had 'fallen into the modern centre-half fashion of playing behind his backs, which seems a shocking waste of talent.' Nonetheless, Hanford did effectively reduce Frank's contribution to the proceedings.[34]

The account in the *West London Observer* offered little more, but did note that with an open goal beckoning Frank 'nearly hit the corner flag' prior to scoring his first goal in the 27th minute. Hammond was also singled out for being 'decidedly off colour and about one in six of his passes found the man.' Otherwise, Arnold's genius was lauded; he had 'never played a finer game and if the rest of the forwards had accepted all the chances he gave them the score would have been doubled'.[35]

Fulham's next fixture was an international friendly against FK Austria, Wien, or as referred to in the English press FC

Austria, played at the Cottage on December 3. This was the second game in the touring Austrian team's five game visit to England. Their manager, Herr Robert Lang, explained that the tour was not 'being undertaken for any financial gain, but because we are happy to have the chance of learning football art right on the spot'.[36] FC Austria had already won their opening game against Liverpool at Anfield 2-0 on November 28.[37]

On December 4, 'Corinthian' reported on the match with Fulham which finished 1-1. He declared that not a single 'spectator could have left the ground at Craven Cottage without being convinced that our visitors were the better side.' He singled out in particular Havlicek, 'a great goalkeeper', Sesta as having 'few superiors as a back, if any, and Molzer … an outside-right fit to be in any British international team.'

For Frank it was the game that would haunt him for the rest of his life. His world changed forever. It provided the defining moment of his football career.

> 'Fulham, unfortunately suffered the penalty of playing a friendly game. Newton ... went through for a shot and fell to the ground, but there was not the slightest suggestion of a foul having been committed. Newton lay on the ground and waved to his trainer for assistance, not allowing anyone to touch his right leg. To those who have seen football accidents it was obvious that something serious had happened, and that a stretcher was necessary. Newton has a fractured fibula, just below the knee, but not a single player or official of the Fulham club would state that the incident was otherwise than an accident. It is a blow to Fulham to lose so effective a centre-forward,

but the club know that it was merely one of the incidents of the game'.[38]

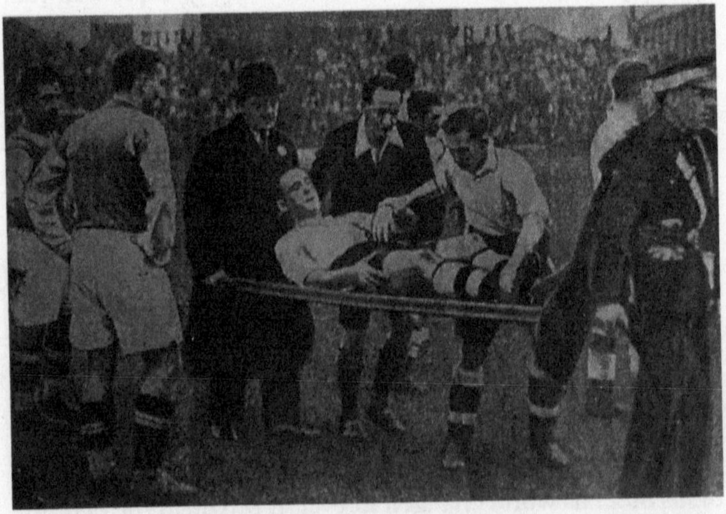

Frank Newton being stretchered off, under the watchful eye of team captain Len Oliver, after breaking his leg playing against FC Austria at Craven Cottage, December 3, 1934.

The *West London Observer* reported that as a result of Frank breaking his leg the game 'ended almost in tragedy for the home side.' And that it 'was just about the worst mishap that could have befallen the Cottagers with the heavy list of Christmas fixtures before them'.[39]

The Programme for the game ran to 12 pages and provided thumb nail sketches of the respective players. Interestingly on page 11 in a small boxed announcement it stated 'TO-NIGHT SEE THE FILM OF To-day's Match ON THE SCREEN' at the Palace Putney. It is assumed that this related to the Pathe News coverage, of which some 45 seconds are still extant on YouTube.[40]

Naturally there were many who were much distressed by the awful news and a number may well have put pen to paper. Unfortunately we are aware of the content of only two of the letters addressed to Frank. The first was brief and was sent by W.A.J. Parris, Hon. Secretary of the Reading FC Supporters Club on December 4. In it he expressed regret at learning of the accident and also hoped 'that it will not be long ere you are about again and that the accident will not interfere with your playing career.'

The second, dated December 10, 1934 is more interesting and was sent to Frank by Alf Stones, then residing in Sheffield. Prior to identifying himself, Stones states that he wanted to

> 'sympathise with you in your misfortune of a broken leg. I knew you had been injured against the Austrians, but not until I saw you in the 'People' reading a letter from Hugh Gallacher did I know it was a broken leg'.

Stones then identifies himself as the Captain and inside left of the Yorks and Lancasters side that beat the East Indian Railway side 1-0 in the final of the 1927 Durand Cup in Simla, India. Stones clearly had enjoyed his time in India, as Frank had done. In what was almost a lament, he wrote:

> 'How I look back on those days and wish they could all come back again (don't you?). Since I came home in 1929 I have always looked for your team's results and how many goals you got Stockport, Reading and Fulham, and I read an article about your career in Thomson's Weekly. Oh! Yes I've been interested in you although I only played

against you once. If you remember the day after the Durand Final you had a bad cold and you met some of our team in a cafe in Simla and we talked the game over. Well Frank if this letter of mine helps you forget a bit of your trouble I shall be satisfied'.

Stones mentions that 'his team Sheffield Wednesday' defeated the Austrians 3-0, and that while they played good football 'they play at the halt if you get me and that gets them no further forward.' He explained that he now worked on the trams, and after a day running about town he did not 'feel much like playing', after which he signed off wishing Frank the best Christmas 'circumstances will allow'.[41]

What Stones was referring to when he states 'saw you in *The People*' I believe was a photograph taken in Putney Hospital and published in the *Daily Mirror* on December 5, 1934. The caption reads: 'Still Cheery. – Frank Newton, the Fulham centre forward, who broke his leg in the match against FC Austria, in hospital at Putney yesterday.' It is also included in Frank's Scrapbook, but there is no reference to the item he was holding. If Stones is correct in identifying the *Mirror*'s sister paper *The People,* I assume that the letter Frank is holding is identified therein as being from Hughie Gallacher. Hughie Gallacher was the diminutive, 5ft. 5 ins, centre forward who played for Newcastle United before joining Chelsea in 1930. Frank played against him in the 'friendly' between Chelsea and Fulham on March 4, 1933, an encounter in which both scored.[42]

Inevitably, there followed much speculation as to when Frank might be fit or able to play again. Jimmy Hogan, initially feared that a long absence was inevitable, but he remained hopeful that Frank might 'reappear before the season closes'.[43] This optimistic view was countered on the same day when the *Daily Mirror* reported that Frank was out for the balance of the season because not only had he fractured his fibula, but 'he has also sustained torn muscles and ligaments near the knee'.[44] Despite this, at the beginning of January1935 Jimmy Hogan again took an optimistic view when he stated that Frank had left hospital and was 'getting on splendidly'.[45] And towards the end of the month a further positive view claimed that Frank hoped 'to begin light training in a few weeks'; however, he was still undergoing treatment.[46]

After January the press diverted it's attention once more to matters on the pitch. That was until an appalling announcement appeared in the *Daily News* on April 22, 1935 captioned 'Newton's Career Ended'. It was succinctly reported that complications had arisen 'and this Fulham centre-forward will not play football again'.[47]

The item in the *West London Observer* was also headed 'NEWTON'S CAREER ENDED'. Their readership was informed:

> 'The injury has failed to respond to treatment in the manner it was hoped, and it is understood that Newton will always be handicapped as a result of his unfortunate accident to such an extent as will make football an impossibility. Newton was the most prolific goalscoring centre-forward that Fulham have had for many years, and held the club's record'.[48]

Frank, despite having played before and entertained literally hundreds of thousands of fans since he started playing competitive football at the age of 17, was compelled to give up the Saturday afternoon grease paint in 1934. For almost all professional footballers retirement was followed by a period of adjustment. It was a radical change that some inevitably handled better than others. For Frank, similar to many whose careers ended between the two World Wars, it was difficult to adjust to a society mired in a deep depression. In Frank's case he had also to endure the additional frustrations of a physical handicap which would have haunted a once so active a sportsman.

Frank's career after football is not well documented. By 1940 the family had moved to Coventry where their home was destroyed in the November blitz of that year.[49] Thankfully there were no reports of injury. Frank and the family then settled in the Manchester area where he was reportedly employed as a brass moulder in the business of Charles Dean, son of the Fulham chairman. Here Frank was reported as being 'a glutton for work'.[50]

There are also records from 1943 showing Frank was Band Sergeant and Deputy Conductor of the 49th County of Lancaster Home Guard Band; not surprising in view of his lifelong interest in music. [51]

Marcus Heap, Stockport County's historian, described Frank's career after football:

> 'After his career was finished Frank Newton remained in London. As a star centre forward of his day he was friends with other notable London footballers such as

> Cliff Bustin and Alex James and was the godfather to the Welsh international Wally Barnes. Despite this he decided not to look for a job inside football. Fulham Football Club ensured that he [Frank] had a job as a brass moulder in a factory owned by the son of the [Fulham] Chairman. This led to an engineering career which he was to follow throughout the rest of his life. At the same time he undertook some scouting for Fulham which he later continued on a freelance basis - his most 'famous find' was the outstanding 'Busby Babe' full back Roger Byrne who Newton recommended to Manchester United'.[52]

Subsequently Keith Newton understands his father was later employed in a managerial capacity at the New Pear Mill in Bredbury, Stockport which at the time was owned by Stockport Limiteds.[53]

Finally Frank retired to the Tameside area, six miles from Romiley, where Keith recalls his father as being at his happiest amongst his family although he seldom spoke of his achievements on the football field. I understand that he started to write his autobiography but he never got much beyond the introduction.

In his final years his leg continued to cause him increasing discomfort and eventually he underwent a further operation at the age of 74. Sadly complications arose and he died shortly afterwards from a blood clot on November 9, 1977 just three days shy of his seventy-fifth birthday.[54] He was survived by his wife, Florence and his three children. To date no obituary has been located.

EPILOGUE

The question remains, 'How do Frank Newton's achievements in the Football League compare to those of his peers'? An impossible thing to do but it is reasonable to have a stab at it. A measure that I think permits an approximation is the ratio of goals scored and appearances.

An interesting article appeared in the August 25, 1934 edition of the *Football Chronicle* under the heading 'Scorers of Goals'.[1] The content primarily consisted of a list of players who had scored one hundred goals, the number of appearances each had made in the Football League and the clubs they were with at the outset of the 1934-35 season. At the head of this list was 'Dixie' Dean, Everton, who had scored 308 times in 320 appearances, a ratio of 0.96 goals per game, and in ninety-second spot was D.M. Robbie, Bury, who had achieved the 100 goal mark but in 404 outings. Frank, then with Reading, appears at number 27, with totals of 180 and 193, a remarkable ratio of 0.93. Others high on this list included Jimmy Clarkson, Plymouth Argyle, 0.95; Tommy Bamford, Wrexham, 0.87; Jack Bowers, Derby County, 0.87; C.F.T. Bourton, Coventry City, 0.86, George Camsell, Middlesbrough, 0.83; David Halliday, Clapton Orient, 0.83 and Edward Harper, Blackburn Rovers, 0.82.

The article stated:

> 'Nothing in League football exerts a greater appeal to the average man in the street than to know who get the

goals, yet hitherto the game's countless thousands of followers have been given surprisingly little in the way of detail concerning the leading scorers. For that reason the unique list below will be found to teem with interest in every line, for it tells at a glance the complete summarised record to the start of this season of every player who appeared in first-class company last campaign and has reached a century of Football League goals. In every instance the player's career has been traced right back to its start, and his complete goals and games in the Football League given, and a hundred and one points of particular interest arise from a study of the list, which also will be the means of settling many arguments. Where a player has retired from active service since the end of last season ... the club for which he last appeared is given, while the new ones of those who have moved from one League club to another during the summer months are stated'.[2]

It must be recognised that the figures above reflect the situation at the start of the 1934-35 season. So although Dean has a ratio of .96; by the time he retired it had fallen to .87. Similarly, C. Bourton's ratio had declined from .86 to .63 when he hung up his boots in 1939.

Interestingly Wikipedia maintains a listing of 'footballers in England by number of league goals'.[3] Although it is noted that the 'list is of footballers who have scored at least 100 domestic league goals in English league football', only those who had scored 200 or more goals are actually included. However, ratios between appearances and goals scored, seasons of participation, and the goals scored for their various clubs are given. Again the list is organised on a goals scored basis. Heading the table is Arthur Rowley with 434 in 619 appearances, a ratio of 0.70, while the last included is Bob Taylor with 200 goals in 577 appearances, a ratio of 0.35. Note Rowley is top of the list because of the number of goals he scored. His ratio indicates that it took him more games to acquire them.

Significantly, it is clear that players' goal scoring ratios in the inter war years were considerably better than those recorded after World War II. In fact only Brian Clough, Wally Ardron and A. Rowley compare. Clough's ratio of 0.92 is exceptional and reflect his unfortunate, early retirement through injury. Ardron's figures were compiled primarily in the post war years as were Rowley's. I believe that comparisons between the two eras only serve to underline the increasing emphasis placed upon a club's defensive abilities in later years.[4]

Finally, it has long been manifestly obvious that a player's longevity in the game is accompanied by a reduction in most, if not all aspects of that individual's performance. Accordingly this is reflected in the scoring ratios of all those listed above who played between the World Wars, with the exception of Tom Keetley who retired in 1933, and those whose playing careers were terminated abruptly through injury. Frank Newton was one such, but in his final few games in the 1934-35 season with Reading and Fulham his ratio fell from 0.93 to 0.91, perhaps an indication of what would have awaited him. Similarly, at the end of their careers Jimmy Cookson finished with a ratio of 0.88; 'Dixie' Dean 0.87; Ted Harper 0.80; Jack Bowers, George Camsell and Dave Halliday 0.78, and finally Clarence Bourton on 0.69.

The above is not intended to form a basis of comparison between Frank Newton and the likes of Dean, but in my view it does establish Frank's rightful place amongst the most celebrated of players active between the two World Wars.

ABBREVIATIONS

AJ, Aberdeen Journal
AN, Athletic News
BC, Berkshire Chronicles
BCT, Brecon County Times
BE, Burnley Express
BN, Burnley News
BNAP, Blyth News & Ashington Post
CDE, Cheshire Daily Echo
CEN, Cumberland Evening News
CET, Coventry Evening Telegraph
CMG, Civil & Military Gazette
CO, Cheshire Observor
DE, Daily Express
DFE, Derbyshire Football Express
DH, Daily Herald
DM, Daily Mirror
DMA, Daily Mail
DN, Daily News
DNY, Dagens Nyheter
DTCH, Derbyshire Times & Chesterfield Herald
ES, Evening Sentinal
EPG, Exeter & Plymouth Gazette
FC, Football Chronicle
FG, Football Gazette
FNP, Fank Newton Papers
HDM, Hull Daily Mail
ID, Idrottsbladet
LDP, Lancashire Daily Post
LE, Liverpool Echo
LEP, Lancashire Evening Post
LIE, Lincolnshire Echo
LM, Leeds Mercury
MEN, Manchester Evening News
NC, News Chronicles
NJ, Nottingham Journal
NL, Nelson Leader
OD, Ostergotlands Dagbland.
RIN, Reynolds's Illustrated News
RM, Reading Mercury
RMOG, Reading Mercury & Oxford Gazette
RN, Reynold's News

RS, Reading Standard

SA, Stockport Advertiser

SD, Sunday Dispatch. Note the British Newspaper Archive list this title under Weekly Dispatch (London).

SDI, Sheffield Daily Telegraph

SE, Stockport Express

SM, Sunday Mirror

SP, Sunday Pictorial

SS, Staffordshire Sentinel

SVD, Svenska Dagbladet

SWBA, South Wales Borders Archive, Brecon

TCJ, The Cottagers Journal

TE, The Englishman

TP, The People

TS, The Sportsman

TSI, The Statesman [India]

TSL, The Star (London)

WLO, West London Observer

WMSWN, Western Mail & South Wales News

YPLI, Yorkshire Post & Leeds Intelligencia

FOOTNOTES

INTRODUCTION

1. TP, 25/6/1923, p. 23.
2. fulhamweb.co.uk Fulham FC - Frank Newton.
3. St. Chad's Anglican Church, Romiley, BMD records.
4. https://ukcensusonline.com
5. St. Chad's Anglican Church.
6. https://ukcensusonline.com
7. ancestry.co.uk – Sarah Newton.
8. CDE, 28/9/1929, n. p.
9. CDE, 3/11/1928, p. 2.
10. CDE, 5/12/1927, p. 2.
11. CDE, 12/1/1928, n. p.
12. CDE, 31/3/1928, n. p., & SE, 5/4/1928, p. 4.
13. CDE, 3/12/1928, n. p.
14. FNP, Scrapbook, Press clipping, entitled 'WHAT FRANK NEWTON, STOCKPORT COUNTY, HAD TO SAY.' n. p. Interview held shortly after Stockport's win v Southport on 23/3/1929.
15. BE, 26/2/1913, p. 6.
16. BE, 16/4/1913, p. 6.
17. https://hydeunited.co.uk/ewen/fields/timeline
18. TS, 20/1/1917, p. 4.
19. TS, 27/1/1917, p. 4, 10/2/1917, p. 4 & 17/2/1914, p. 4.
20. MEN, 4/4/1917, p. 2.
21. MEN, 9/4/1917, p. 3.
22. TS, 10/4/1917, p. 4.
23. TS, 14/4/1917, p. 4.
24. MEN, 5/5/1917, p. 4.
25. TS, 29/9/1917, p.4, & 8/10/1917, P. 1.
26. MEN, 6/10/1917, p. 3.
27. MEN, 29/9/1917, p. 3.
28. MEN, 13/10/1917, p. 3.
29. BN, 20/3/1918, p. 3.
30. Harry's previous playing experience appears to have been with Manchester City, but only in Lancashire Section Subsidiary Competition games, or charity matches.
31. BE, 20/3/1918, p. 3.
32. LEP, 16/3/1918, p. 3.
33. BN, 27/3/1918, p. 3.
34. Wikipedia, Manchester City, 1918-19 season. However, there may be a problem with this entry as it is repeated in the 2 subsequent seasons.

35. BN, 3/4/1918, p. 3.
36. BE, 3/4/1918, p. 3.
37. The R.A.M.C. had a large facility in Blackpool, The Lancashire Military Convalescent Hospital, between 1916 and 1919. The Hospital ran a football side that competed in the Auxiliary Section of the Lancashire Combination Section.
38. BE, 30/3/1918, p. 3.
39. BE, 27/3/1918, p. 3.
40. BE, 3/4/1918, p. 3.
41. BE, 28/3/1917, p.4.
42. BN, 3/4/1918, p. 3.
43. BN, 28/8/1918, p. 3.
44. Ibid, & 4/9/1918, P. 3.
45. BN, 11/9/1918, p. 3.
46. BN, 16/10/1918, p. 3.
47. BN, 20/11/1918, p. 3.
48. BN, 5/3/1919, p. 3.
49. BE, 30/4/1919, p. 4..
50. BE, 15/1/1919, p. 4.
51. Jeff Kent, Port Vale Personalities, p. 213, & FG, 18/10/1919, p. 4.
52. CO, 10/9/1921, p. 2.
53. BE, 5/3/1919, p. 4.
54. CO, 5/1/1924, p. 4.
55. BE, 26/2/1913, p. 6.
56. LEP, 16/11/1916, p. 4.
57. BE, 24/1/1917, p. 3.
58. BE, 28/3/1917, p. 4
59. BE, 31/3/1917, p. 8.
60. Wikipedia, Manchester City, 1918-19 season.
61. DM, 7/8/1920, p. 11.
62. info@shrimperpublshing.co.uk Email, D. Goody to the author, 30/10/2009.
63. LEP, 26/8/1921, p. 4, & 2/9/1921, p. 4. Both these editions are titled: 'Lancashire Daily Post, Extra Special edition'. The British Newspaper Archives lists the Lancashire Daily Post under the title Lancashire Evening Post.
64. LEP, 1/4/1921, p. 3.
65. CDE, 4/4/1931, p. 2.
66. BE, 13/4/1918, p. 3, 17/4/1918, p. 2, 20/4/1918, p. 3 & 24/4/1918, p. 2.
67. BE, 20/11/1918, p. 2.
68. BE, 5/3/1919, p. 4.
69. CO, 10/9/1921, p. 2.
70. LEP, 24/3/1924, p. 7.
71. LEP, 14/4/1924, p. 7.
72. LEP, 30/3/1918, p. 3.
73. Telcon between Keith Newton and the author, 11/2/2022.

74. Elder Mill, Romiley. Wikiwand.com

75, Chadkirk Printworks, Marple. marplelocalhistorysociety.org.uk

76. Email, Hilary Atkinson, Chair Marple Local History Society to the author, 16/09/2021.

77. Ancestry UK, George Newton.

FRANK NEWTON JOINS THE MILITARY

1. BC, 12/10/1934, p. 20.
2. The Fischer Education Act, 1918.
3. SWBA, Ledger No. 2, Army Registration No. 3903015 – 4078, & 'STATEMENT BY A SOLDIER CONCERNING HIS OWN CASE', Army Form B 179a. Barcode (000482047), Frank Newton Service Number 3003429, W.O. 419. The National Archives, Kew, London.
4. FNP, Scrapbook, 'WHAT FRANK NEWTON, STOCKPORT COUNTY, HAD TO SAY'.
5. Barcode (ADT 0004820470).
6. FNP, Scrapbook, Press clipping, "B.J. EVANS Interview", conducted 26/9/1931, TSL, n. d.
7. Barcode (ADT 000482047).
8. Ibid.
9. DE, 15/5/1933, p. 5, & RM, 21/10/1933, p. 6.
10. Alan Sedunary, Heaven on Earth: The Official History of Reading F. C., 1871- 2003, p. 62, and The Little Book of Reading F. C., p. 62.
11. FNP, Scrapbook, Photograph, Lancaster Home Guard Band, 1943. Inscription verso.
12. Sniggary Barracks, THE GREAT WAR (1914-1918) FORUM. A photograph of what appears to be Hut 3, clearly has a sign 'BAND' nailed to the door. www.greatwarforumj.org/topic/94697. And J. Russell, 'Liverpool Ramblers AFC, 1882, The Complete History, 2013.
13. Barcode (ADT 000482047).
14. BCT, 21/8/1919, p. 2.
15. BCT, 1/5/1919, p. 8.
16. BCT, 21/8/1919, p. 5.

17. BCT, 28/8/1919, p 8 & 11/9/1919, p. 8.
18. BCT, 25/9/1919, p. 2.
19. BCT, 25/9/1919, p. 8.
20. BCT, 6/11/1919, p. 7.
21. BCT, 27/11/1919, p. 5.
22. BCT, 11/12/1919, p. 8.
23. BCT, 25/12/1919, P. 5.
24. BCT, 25/12/1919, p. 2
25. BCT, Ibid.
26. BCT, 18/12/1919, p. 8.
27. BCT, 1/1/1920, p. 3.
28. BCT, 26/2/1920, p. 6.
29. BCT, 15/1/1920, p. 6.
30. BCT, 22/1/1920, p. 3.
31. BCT, 29/1/1920, p. 2.
32. BCT, 7/2/1920, p.3, & 12/2/1920, p. 3.
33. BCT, 19/2/1920, p. 7.
34. BCT, 26/2/1920, p. 6.
35. Ibid.
36. BCT, 11/3/1920, p.3.
37. BCT, 1/4/1920, p. 7.
38. BCT, 8/4/1920, p. 5.
39. BCT, 29/4/1920, p. 5.
40. BCT, 6/5/1920, p. 5.
41. BCT, 26/8/1920, p. 3.
42. BCT, 30/9/1920, p. 6.
43. BCT, 23/9/1920, p. 2. Frank is incorrectly listed as E. Newton.
44. BCT, 30/9/1920, P. 6.
45. BCT, 14/10/1920, p. 3.
46. BCT, 21/10/1920, p. 3.
47. BCT, 28/10/1920, p. 7.
48. BCT, 11/11/1920, p. 6.
49. BCT, 4/11/1920, p. 7.
50. BCT, 2/12/1920, p. 8.
51. BCT, 11/11/1920, p. 6.
52. BCT, 14/10/1920, p. 6.
53. BCT, 25/11/1920, p. 5.
54. BCT, 13/1/1921, p. 3.
55. BCT, 6/1/1921, p. 8 & 13/1/1921, p. 3.
56. BCT, 4/11/1920, p. 7.
57. BCT, 13/1/1921, p. 3.
58. BCT, 20/1/1921, p. 7.
59. BCT, 3/2/1921, p. 8.
60. BCT, 3/3/1921, p. 5.
61. BCT, 20/1/1921, p. 7.
62. C.T. Atkinson, <u>The South Wales Borders, 24th Foot, 1687-1937</u>, p. 458.
63. RM, 23/9/1933, p. 17.
64. BCT, 20/10/1921, p. 7.
65. BCT, 26/5/ 1921, p. 8.
66. BCT, 1/9/1921, p. 8.
67. BCT, 13/10/1921, p. 7.
68. BCT, 25/8/1921, p. 6.
69. BCT, 6/10/1921, p. 5 & 13/10/1921, p. 7.
70. BCT, 20/10/1921, p. 7.

71. BCT, 27/10/1921, p. 5.
72. BCT, 3/11/1921, p. 5.
73. BCT, 3/11/1921, p. 8.
74. BCT, 10/11/1921, p. 7.
75. BCT, 27/10/1921, p. 5.
76. BCT, 17/11/1921, p. 7. The report states the game was between Brecon Depot and Builth Town.
77. BCT, 24/11/1921, p. 8.
78. Barcode (000482047)
79. BCT, 24/11/1921, p. 7.
80. BCT, 24/11/1921, p. 3.
81. BCT, 27/10/1921, p. 5.This Welsh Amateur Cup game v. Rhayader came about because "Hereford St. Martins when after drawing with Brecon at Hereford … were unable to replay a mid-week match at Brecon."
82. BCT, 8/12/1921, p. 7.
83. BCT, 15/12/1921, p. 5.
84. BCT, 22/12/1921, p. 2.
85. BCT, 29/12/1921, p. 8.
86. Ibid.
87. BCT, 12/1/1922, p. 6.
88. BCT, 9/2/1922, p. 5.
89. BCT, 16/3/1922, p. 7.
90. BCT, 12/10/1922, p. 6.
91. BCT, 19/10/1921, p. 6.
92. BCT, 26/10/1922, p. 7.
93. FNP, Scrapbook, Press clipping, ' Football. Welsh Amateur Cup. (First Round) Brecon v Builth Wells', n. d.
94. Email, S. Mogridge, Archivist, Royal Artillery Museum to the author, 27/1/2021.

INDIA, 1922 – 1927

1. SWBA, Digest of Service, 1919-1939, n. p.
2. Barcode (ADT 000482047), Frank Newton, Servicr Number 3903429, W.O. 419. The National Archives. Kew, London.
3. Ibid.
4. Ibid.
5. TSI, 9/5/1923, n. p.
6. TSI, 11/5/1923, n. p.
7. TSI, 13/5/1923, n. p.
8. SWBA, Ledger Z, 57, n. p.. Newspaper clipping ex TSI or TE, n.d.
9. TSI, 30/5/1923, n. p.
10. SWBA, Ledger Z, 57, n. p., contains an incomplete, unidentified newspaper clipping, n.d.

11. SWBA, Ledger Z, 57, n. p., contains newspaper clipping ex TSI, n. d.
12. SWBA, Ledger Z, 57, n. p., [1923], n. p., n. d.
13. CMG, 10/6/1923, p. 6.
14. SWBA, Ledger Z, 57, n. p., [1923], n. p., n. d.
15. SWBA, Ledger Z, 57, n. p., [1923], newspaer clipping ex TE, 26/6/1923, n. p.
16. Ibid.
17. SWBA, Ledger Z, 58, n. p., Sports Diary, n. p.
18. Ibid.
19. CMG, 10/7/1923, p. 6.
20. TE, 1/7/1923, p. 21.
21. CMG, 14/7/1923, p. 6.
22. CMG, 18/7/1923, p. 8.
23. CMG, 21/7/1923, P. 6.
24. CMG, 28/7/1923, p. 8.
25. SWBA, Ledger Z, 58, n. p.
26. Ibid.
27. Ibid.
28. Ibid. Note in newspaper clipping ex TSI, n. d., n. p., Simpson is credited with both goals.
29. Ibid.
30. Ibid, newspaper clipping ex TSI, n. d., n. p.
31. Ibid.
32. Ibid.
33. The final standings are calculated from the results recorded over the last 3 games of the season, based on the Division I table, after 13 games played, included in SWBA, Ledger Z, 58, n. p..
34. SWBA, Ledger Z, 58, Sports Diary, clipping from TS, n. d., n. p.
35. Ibid.
36. Ibid.
37. Ibid.
38. Ibid.
39. Ibid.
40. Ibid.
41. Ibid.
42. TE, 26/5/1927, p. 21.
43. FNP, Scrapbook, n. p., n. d.
44. TE, 16/6/1927, p. 21.
45. TE, 16/6/1927, p. 20.
46. CMG, 28/6/1927, p. 11.
47. CMG, 5/7/1927, p. 16.
48. TE, 7/7/1927, p. 21.
49. www.espncricinfo.com
50. CMG, 19/9/1927, p. 10.
51. CMG, 26/9/1927, p. 8.
52. CMG, 30/9/1927, p. 11.
53. CMG, 3/10/1927, p. 14.
54. FNP, Scrapbook, unidentified newspaper clipping, n. p., n. d.

55. FNP, Scrapbook. Interview conducted by B.J. Evans of TSL, on 26/9/1931, the day Fulham played Northampton Town at Craven Cottage. Headline: 'Frank Newton, Fulham's Scoring Centre-Forward'. n. p., n. d.
56. SWBA, Ledger Z, 57, n. p., n. d.
57. SWBA, Ledger Z, 58, n. p., n. d.
58. Ibid.
59. Ibid.
60. Ibid.
61. Ibid.
62. Ibid.
63. SWBA, Ledger Z, 57, n.p., n.d. Three of these games, and probably all four were reported in TE and/or TSI.
64. SWBA, Ledger Z, 58, n. p., n. d.
65. Ibid.
66. Ibid.
67. Ibid.
68. Ibid.
69. Barcode (ADT00048)
70. SWBA, Ledger Z, 57, n. p., n. d.
71. CMG, 14/10/1923, p. 6.
72. SWBA, Ledger Z, 57/58, n. p., n d.
73. Ibid.
74. Ibid.
75. Ibid.
76. C.T. Atkinson, The South Wales Borderers, p. 456.
77. SWBA, Ledger Z, 57/58, n. p., n. d.
78. Ibid.
79. Ibid.
80. Ibid.
81. Ibid.
82. Ibid.
83. Ibid.
84. Ibid.
85. SWBA, Digest of Service, 2nd Battalion SWB, 1919-1937, n. p.
86. C.T. Atkinson, The South Wales Borderers, p. 458.
87. SWBA, Digest of Service, 2nd Battalion SWB, 1919-1937, n. p.
88. FNP, Scrapbook. Interview conducted by B.J. Evans of TSL, on 26/9/1931. The appropriately named Johnny Basham was a Welsh boxer who became British and European champion at both welter and middleweight. His professional career extended between 1909 and 1929.

STOCKPORT COUNTY FC, DECEMBER, 1927 – MAY, 1931

1927-1928 Season

1, Peter Freeman, Stockport County Encyclopedia and History Update, 1994-2000, p. 94.

2. FNP, Scrapbook, Press clipping, 'Frank Newton, Fulham's Scoring Centre Forward'. B.J. Evans interview, conducted on 26/9/1931, printed in The Star, n. d., n. p..

3. Norman Rodgers (footballer), Wikiwand.com

4. FNP, Scrapbook, Press clipping,'WHAT FRANK NEWTON, STOCKPORT COUNTY, HAS TO SAY.'

5. CDE, 3/12/1927, p. 2.

6. CDE, 5/12/1927, p. 2.

7. FNP, Op. Cit.

8. CDE, 12/1/1928, p. 2.

9. Ibid.

10. BNAP, 2/4/1928, p. 5.

11. CDE, 31/3/1928, n. p., & SE, 5/4/1928, p. 4.

12. DFE, 10/3/1928, p. 15.

13. DFE, 28/4/1928, p. 15. The maximum retainer is given as £8 per week.

1928-1929 Season

1. DFE, 10/11/1928, p. 19.

2. Ibid.

3. DFE, 17/11/1928, p. 15.

4. CDE, 3/11/1928, p. 2.

5. CDE, 1/12/1928, p. 2.

6. SA, 1/12/1928, p. 2.

7. FG, 8/12/1928. p. 1.

8. Ibid.

9. FG, 1/12/1928, p. 3.

10. SE, 6/12/1928, p. 4.

11. CDE, 3/12/1928, n. p.

12. FNP, Scrapbook, Press clipping, "Busy Bee", byline. From CDE between 28/11 and 5/12/1928, n. p.

13. CDE, 10/12/1928, n. p.

14. SE, 13/12/1928, p. 4.

15. FNP, Scrapbook, Press clipping, 'Great Goal Marked My Worst Game!'.

16. SA, 21/12/1928, n. p.

17. CDE, 22/12/1928, n. p.

18. SE, 20/12/1928, p. 4.

19. CDE, 22/12/1928, n.p. 1930-31: R.W. Matthews was transferred New Brighton and did not play for the County

afr September 11, 1930.

20. CDE, 27/12/1928, n. p.
21. SA, 28/12/1928, p. 18
22. SA, 18/1/1929, p. 18.
23. SA, 25/1/1929, p. 18.
24. Ibid.
25. NL, 25/1/1929, p. 6.
26. SA, 25/1/1929, p. 18.
27. SA, 1/3/1929, p. 18.
28. SA, 8/2/1929, p. 18. It was also mentioned that: "During the match the pressure the crowd caused the barriers to give way in two places, and precipitated large numbers of spectators on the playing pitch. Constable Joseph Hodgson, who was on duty had his ankle injured by the collapsing railings and was conveyed to the Infirmary and after treatment sent home. Two spectators, Joseph Poole, 8, Clifton Street, Alderley Edge, and William Sutcliffe, of 43, King Street West, Stockport, were taken ill whilst the game was in progress, and were attended to by the St. John Ambulance Brigade and were taken to the Infirmary. In neither case was the condition serious and later in the evening they were discharged."
29. DFE, 16/2/1929, p. 19.
30. SA, 1/3/1929, p. 18.
31. Ibid. and CEN, 31/2/1929, n. p.,'CARLISLE COMMENT ON COUNTY'S VICTORY'.
32. SE, 28/2/1929, p. 4.
33. DFN, 2/3/1929, n. p.
34. AN, 25/2/1929, p. 8.
35. DFE, 16/3/1929, n. p.
36. SA, 1/3/1929, p. 18.
37. The International was played between Wales and Ireland on 2/2/1929. Wales won 2-1 before a crowd of some 12,000.
38. SE, 7/3/1929, p. 4.
39. SA, 8/3/1929, p. 18.
40. LE, 4/3/1929, p. 10.
41. SA, 8/3/1929, p. 18.
42. Ibid.
43. SA, 15/3/1929, p. 18.
44. CDE, 16/3/1929, p. 2.
45. SA, 22/3/1929, p. 18.
46. Ibid.
47. SE, 21/3/1929, p. 4.
48. SS, 16/3/1929, p. 10.
49. Peter Freeman, op. cit., p. 95.
50. CDE, 23/3/1929, n. p.
51. SA, 22/3/1929, p. 18.
52. SE, 28/3/1929, p. 4.

53. FNP, Scrapbook, Press clipping, 'WHAT FRANK NEWTON, STOCKPORT COUNTY, HAS TO SAY'. Interview conducted c. the week of 24/3/1929.
54. DFE, 30/3/1929, p. 15.
55. SE, 28/3/1929, p. 4.
56. SE, 4/4/1929, p. 4.
57. Ibid.
58. SA, 5/4/1929, p. 6.
59. SE, 4/4/1929, p. 4.
60. Ibid.
61. Ibid.
62. SA, 5/4/1929, p. 6.
63. AN, 1/4/1929, p. 8.
64. SE, 16/5/1929, p. 4.
65. SA, 5/4/1929, p. 6.
66. SA, 12/4/1929, p. 18.
67. FG, 13/4/1929, p. 3.
68. SA, 19/4/1929, p. 18.
69. SA, 29/4/1929, p. 18.
70. BNAP, 22/4/1929, p. 5.
71. SDI, 29/4/1929, p. 10.
72. SA, 10/5/1929, p. 18.
73. CDE, 4/5/1929, n. p.. Joe Smith went on to be player-manager at Darwen FC, 1921-31; manager of Reading FC, 1931-35 & of Blackpool FC, 1935-58.
74. Ibid.
75. SE, 16/5/1929, p. 4.
76. FNP, Scrapbook, Press clipping, 'Frank Newton, Fulham's Scoring Centre-Forward'. B.J. EVANS Interviews--. Believed to be from The Star with whom Evans was employed. 26/9/1931.

1929-1930 Season

1. SA, 23/8/1929, p. 13.
2. Ibid.
3. SA, 30/8/1929, n. p.
4. Ibid.
5. SA, 6/9/1929, p. 16.
6. LEP, 10/9/1929, p. 9.
7. SA, 6/9/1929, p. 16.
8. LEP, 10/9/1929, p. 9.
9. CDE, 5/10/1929, n. p.
10. CDE, 14/9/1929, n. p.
11. SA, 20/9/1929, p. 16.
12. AN, 16/9/1929, p. 12.
13. SE, 26/9/1929, p. 4.
14. CDE, 28/9/1929, n. p.
15. SA, 4/10/1929, p. 16.
16. LEP, 30/9/1929, p. 16.
17. CDE, 4/10/1929, n. p.
18. CDE, 5/10/1929, n. p.
19. SE, 10/10/1929, p. 4. James

P. Scullion, see D. Turner & A. White, FULHAM: A Complete Record, p. 189. Also, DFE, 12/10/1929, p. 11.

20. SE, 17/10/1929, p. 4.
21. SA, 25/10/1929, p. 18.
22. Ibid.
23. CDE, 2/11/1929, p. 2.
24. CDE, 26/10/1929, n. p.
25. Ibid.
26. CDE, 2/11/1929, p. 2.
27. SE, 14/11/1929, p. 4.
28. CDE, 16/11/1929, p. 4.
29. AN, 18/11/1929, p. 17.
30. FG, 23/11/1929, p. 1.
31. SE, 28/11/1929, p. 4.
32. DFE, 30/11/1929, p. 13.
33. SA, 29/11/1929, p. 16.
34. SE, 5/12/1929, p. 4.
35. DFE, 14/12/1929, p. 13.
36. DH, 3/12/1929, p. 13.
37. SE, 19/12/1929, p. 4.
38. CDE, 7/12/1929, p. 2.
39. SA, 27/12/1929, p. 16.
40. DH, 27/12/1929, p. 8.
41. SA, 27/12/1929, p. 12.
42. Ibid.
43. Ibid.
44. Ibid.
45. ES, 27/12/1929, p. 3.
46. ES, 28/12/1929, p. 8.
47. SA, 3/1/1930, p. 16.
48. Ibid.
49. Ibid.
50. Ibid.
51. Ibid.
52. Ibid.
53. SA, 10/1/1930, p. 19.
54. SA, 13/2/1931, p. 16.
55. CDE, 18/1/1930, p. 2.
56. www.netweather.tv Washout November – December 1929 – Historic Weather – Netweather.
57. DH, 30/12/1929, p. 9.
58. SA, 17/1/1930, p. 20.
59. Ibid.
60. DM, 18/1/1930, p. 19.
61. SA, 24/1/1930, p. 19.
62. Ibid.
63. SA, 31/1/1930, p. 19.
64. CDE, 3/2/1930, p. 2.
65. Ibid.
66. Ibid.
67. CDE, 15/2/1930, p. 2.
68. CDE, 3/2/1930, p. 2.
69. CDE, 15/2/1930, p. 2.
70. CDE, 22/2/1930, p. 2
71. Ibid.
72. CDE, 22/2/1930, n. p.

73. SA, 28/2/1930, p. 20.
74. CDE, 1/3/1930, n. p.
75. SA, 7/3/1930, p. 20.
76. LM, 3/3/1930, p. 9.
77. SA, 7/3/1930, p. 20.
78. Ibid.
79. CDE, 8/3/1930, n. p.
80. SA, 21/3/1930, p. 17.
81. AN, 17/8/1930, p. 9.
82. DFE, 22/3/1930, p. 11.
83. SA, 21/3/1930, p. 17.
84. LDP, 20/3/1930, p. 5.
85. LM, 21/3/1930, p. 11.
86. FG, 22/3/1930, p. 4.
87. SA, 28/3/1930, p. 20.
88. SA, 4/4/1930, p. 16.
89. DFE, 5/4/1930, p. 11.
90. SA, 11/4/1930, p. 17.
91. SA, 18/4/1930, p. 15.
92. SA, 25/4/1930, p. 15.
93. LE, 19/4/1930, p. 4.
94. CDE, 19/4/1930, n. p.
95. SDT, 20/4/1930, p. 7.
96. SA, 25/4/1930, p. 17.
97. SA, 2/5/1930, p. 20.
98. SA, 9/5/1930, p. 20.
99. Ibid.
100. CDE, 3/5/1930, n. p.
101. SA, 9/5/1930, p. 20.
102. DFE, 7/5/1930, p. 9.
103. SA, 22/8/1930, p. 7.
104. SA, 13/2/1931, p. 16.

1930-1931 Season

1. CDE, 9/8/1930, n. p.
2. SA, 22/8/1930, n. 7.
3. SA, 29/8/1930, p. 16.
4. Ibid.
5. SE, 4/9/1930, p. 4.
6. Ibid.
7. Ibid.
8. SA, 12/9/1930, p. 16.
9. AN, 8/9/1930, p. 13.
10. SDT, 8/9/1930, p. 7.
11. SA, 19/9/1930, p. 15.
12. SDT, 12/9/1930, p. 7.
13. LEP, 22/9/1930, p. 9.
14. SE, 18/9/1930, p. 4.
15. SA, 12/9/1930, p. 16.
16. SE, 18/9/1930, p. 4.
17. SA, 19/9/1930, p. 15.
18. SE, 18/9/1930, p. 4.
19. SA, 19/9/1930, p. 15. R.W. Matthews was transferred to New Brighton and didn't play for Stockport County after September 15, 1930.
20. LE, 22/9/1930, p. 10.
21. SE, 2/10/1930, n. p.
22. SE, 9/10/1930, n. p.

23. AN, 6/10/1930, p. 8.
24. SE, 16/10/1930, n. p.
25. SE, 23/10/1930, n. p.
26. YPLI, 20/10/1930, p. 15.
27. SE, 23/10/1930, n. p.
28. SE, 30/10/1930, n. p.
29, SE, 6/11/1930, n. p.
30. SDT, 3/11/1930, p. 10.
31. AN, 3/11/1930, p. 15.
32. SE, 27/11/1930, n. p.
33. Ibid.
34. SE, 4/12/1930, p. 4.
35. SE, 11/12/1930, n. p.
36. DH, 8/12/1930, p. 14.
37. SE, 18/12/1930, n. p.
38. SA, 19/12/1930, n. p.
39. SDT, 18/12/1930, p. 10.
40. SA, 19/12/1930, n. p.
41. SE, 25/12/1930, n. p.
42. SE, 1/1/1931, p. 4.
43. FG, 27/12/1930, p. 3.
44. SE, 1/1/1931, p. 4.
45. Ibid.
46. SE, 4/12/1931, p. 4, and 18/12/1931, n. p.
47. SE, 1/1/1931, p. 4.
48. AN, 28/12/1930, p. 9.
49. YPLI, 29/12/1930, p. 13.
50. SE, 8/1/1931, p. 4.
51. YPLI, 2/1/1931, p. 13.
52. SE, 8/1/1931, p. 4.
53. Ibid.
54. AN, 12/1/1931, p. 15.
55. SE, 22/1/1931, n. p.
56. SE, 29/1/1931, n. p.
57. SA, 6/2/1931, n. p.
58. Ibid.
59. SE, 12/2/1931, p. 4.
60. SA, 13/2/1931, p. 16.
61. Ibid.
62. CDE, 16/2/1931, p. 2.
63. SE, 19/2/1931, p. 4.
64. CDE, 21/2/1931, p. 2.
65. Ibid.
66. Ibid.
67. SA, 27/2/1931, p. 17. Horsfall had progressed through the County's ranks. He played in the club's youngsters trial game on 26/8/1930, SA, 29/8/1930, p. 16, and shortly afterwards in the County's Central League side, SE, 4/9/1930, p. 4, and 11/12/1930, n. p.
68. Ibid.
69. CDE, 23/2/1931, p. 2.
70. CDE, 28/2/1931, p. 2.
71. CDE, 2/3/1931, p. 2.
72. CDE, 7/3/1931, p. 2.
73. SE, 12/3/1931, n. p.
74. Ibid.

75. Ibid.
76. AN, 16/3/1931, n. p.
77. SE, 26/3/1931, n. p.
78. SE, 2/4/1931, n. p.
79. Ibid.
80. LEP, 30/3/1931, p. 9.
81. SE, 9/4/1931, p. 4.
82. Ibid.
83. LM, 4/4/1931, p. 9.
84. SE, 9/4/1931, p. 4.
85.CDE, 6/4/1931, p. 2.
86. SE, 9/4/1931, p. 4.
87. Ibid.
88. Ibid.
89. Ibid.
90. SA, 17/4/1931, p. 17.
91. SE, 23/4/1931, p. 4.
92. SA, 17/4/1931, P. 17.
93. SE, 23/4/1931, p. 4.
94. Ibid.
95. SE,30/4/1931, n. p.
96. Ibid.
97. CDE, 2/5/1931, p. 2, and County's Reserve team goal scorers CDE, 9/2/1931, p. 2.
98. CDE, 2/5/1931, p. 2.
99. SE, 7/5/1931, p. 4.
100. Ibid.
101. Ibid.
102. CDE, 9/5/1931, p. 2.
103. Simon Burton, The Guardian, 16/11/2014, n. p.
104. DM, 13/5/1931, p. 5.
105. Alex White, 'The Men Who Made Fulham Football Club', p. 360. And Peter Freeman, pps. 94 & 95.
106. AN, 25/5/1931, p. 5.
107. AN, 8/6/1931, p. 6.
108. AN, 15/6/1931, p. 7.

FULHAM FC, MAY, 1931- SEPTEMBER, 1933

1931-1932 Season

1. DFE, 30/11/1929, p. 10.
2. DFE, 20/12/1930, n. p.
3. Dennis Turner & Alex White, p. 196.
4. DM, 10/10/1930, p. 22.
5. DE, 10/10/1930, p. 17.
6. Ibid.
7. DM, 10/10/1930, p. 22.
8. Dennis Turner & Alex White, p. 281.
9. Dennis Turner, 'Fulham Football Club, The Official 125 Year Illustrated History, 1879-2004', p. 48.

10. DM, 18/6/1931, p. 22.
11. Dennis Turner & Alex White, pps. 133, 130, 169, 80, 198.
12. DM, 19/5/1931, p. 5.
13. 'The Cottagers Journal', "The Baker's Man", 'Tales of the Cottagers', Souvenir Programme, Fulham v Exeter City, May 7, 1932, p. 6.
14. RIN, 6/9/1931, p. 22.
15. WLO, 23/10/1931, p. 3.
16. "The Programmes – 1932-33 – 10 Footballs". 10Footballs. com
17. FNP, Scrapbook, Press clipping, 'Fulham's Chief Problem Has Been Solved'. n. p., n. d.
18. DN, 18/8/1931, p. 13.
19. FNP, Scrapbook, Press clipping, 'Frank Newton, Fulham's Scoring Centre-Forward'. B.J. Evans interview conducted on 26/9/1931, published in The Star, n. d., n. p.
20. The Cottagers Journal, Tales of the Cottagers, 27/8/1931, p. 6.
21. WLO, 21/8/1931, p. 2.
22. SD, 30/8/1931, p. 18.
23. WLO, 4/9/1931. p. 2.
24, Ibid.
25. EPG, 3/9/1931, p. 6.
26. Dennis Turner, Ed., 'Cottage Chronicles, An Anecdotal History of Fulham Football Club, 1879-1993', p. 95; and WLO, 11/9/1931, p. 2; also The Cottagers Journal, Tales of the Cottagers, 7/9/1931, n.p.
27. The Cottagers Journal, Tales of the Cottagers, 7/9/1931, n.p. The figure of 150 goals is incorrect but subsequently appeared in the press on numerous occasions.
28. WLO, 11/9/1931, p. 2.
29. WLO, 18/9/1931, p. 2.
30. The Cottagers Journal, 26/9/1931, n. p.
31. EPG, 17/9/1931, p. 7.
32. Dennis Turner, Ed., p. 95.
33. WLO, 25/9/1931, p. 2.
34. WMSWN, 21/9/1931, p. 4.
35. Ibid.
36. SD, 20/9/1931, p. 19.
37. WLO, 2/10/1931, p. 2.
38. The Cottagers Journal, 10/10/1931, n. p.
39. www.11v11.com
40. WLO, 9/10/1931, p, 2, & Dennis Turner & Alex White, p. 283.
41. Dennis Turner & Alex White, pps. 80 & 283.
42. WLO, 16/10/1931, p. 2.

43. Ibid.
44. The Cottagers Journal, 17/10/1931, n. p.
45. WLO, 23/10/1931, p. 2.
46. Dennis Turner, Ed., p. 96.
47. WLO, 30/10/1931, p. 2.
48. WLO, 6/11/1931, p. 2.
49. Dennis Turner, Ed., p. 100.
50. WLO, 6/11/1931, p. 2.
51. SD, 1/11/1931, p. 21.
52. www.11v11.com
53. SM, 8/11/1931, p. 31; and WLO. 13/11/1931, p. 2.
54. WLO, 20/11/1931, p. 2.
55. Dennis Turner, Ed., pps. 96 & 54; and WLO, 27/11/1931, n.p.
56. Paul Marsh, 'The Association of Football Statisticians, NON LEAGUE ANNUAL, Anual No. 1', p. 59, n, d.
57. Dennis Turner & Alex White, p. 282.
58. Ibid.; and WLO, 11/12/1931, p.2.
59. Paul Marsh, p. 53.
60. SD, 13/12/1931, p. 16.
61. WLO, 18/12/1931, p. 3.
62. Ibid.
63. TP, 20/12/1931, p. 19.
64. WLO, 25/12/1931, p. 2.
65. Dennis Turner, Ed., p. 97.
66. Ibid,
67. WLO, 1/1/1932, p. 2.
68. Ibid.
69. CET, 2/1/1932, p. 1.
70. Dennis Turner, Ed., p. 97.
71. WLO, 8/1/1932, p. 2.
72. WLO, 15/1/1932, p. 2.
73. Dennis Turner, Ed., p. 97.
74. WLO, 22/1/1932, p. 2; Dennis Turner & Alex White, pps. 108 & 283, note this was Hindson's debut in the Fulham first XI.
75. SD, 17/1/1932, p. 18.
76. When home attendance figures for the seasons 1931-32 and 1932-33 are compared, gate receipts increased by approximately 28%. These figures provide an indication of the margins that could be anticipated. Attendance figures taken from Dennis Turner & Alex White, op cit., pps. 282 & 284.
77. WLO, 22/1/1932, p. 2.
78. Ibid.
79. SP, 24/1/1932, p. 27.
80. WLO, 29/1/1932, p. 2.
81. WLO, 5/2/1932, p. 2.
82. www.11v11.com
83. Dennis Turner & Alex White, pps. 282 & 283.

84. WLO, 12/2/1932, p. 2.
85. Dennis Turner, Ed., p. 98.
86. www.11v11.com
87. WLO. 26/2/1932, p. 2.
88. WLO, 4/3/1932, p. 2.
89. SD, 28/2/1932, p. 19.
90. TP, 28/2/1932, p. 20.
91. LE. 21/8/1931, p. 12. The reference states that the show will close at Christmas time in Glasgow.
92. LE, 28/11/1931, p. 12.
93. Whipsnade Zoo – wikipedia.org
94. LE, 18/1/1932, p. 9.
95. Confirmed in a telcon of 11/2/2022, between Keith Newton and the author.
96. www.11v11.com
97. SD, 6/3/1932, p. 22.
98. SD, 6/3/1932, p. 23. There was some confusion as to how long Frank was off the field. SD notes 40 minutes, but the WLO, 11/3/1932, p. 2, states 10. If the injury arose after 13 minutes of play in the second half, 10 minutes would appear to be correct.
99. FNP, Scrapbook, letters dated 7/3/1932 and 6/3/1932.The name of the Gunnersbury correspondent cannot be deciphered.
100. WLO, 11/3/1932, p. 2.
101. WLO, 25/3/1932, p. 2.
102. Dennis Turner & Alex White, pps. 198 & 283.
103. Dennis Turner & Alex White, p. 282; and www11v11.com
104. Thames AFC - wikipedia.org
105. WLO, 1/4/1932, p. 2. The 3 games played over Easter were all reported in this edition.
106. Ibid.
107. www.11v11.com
108. SD, 3/4/1932, p. 21.
109. WLO, 8/4/1932, p. 2.
110. SD, 3/4/1932, p. 20. Dean's thinking may well have been coloured by the move of Queens Park Rangers to the White City Stadium for the 1931-32 season. The directors took out a long term lease, soon much regretted, on the 100,000 capacity venue, where 80,000 could be accommodated under cover.
111. WLO, 8/4/1932, p. 2.
112. SD, 17/4/1932, p. 27.
113. WLO, 22/4/1932, p. 2.
114. 'The Move to White City Stadium, 1931-32', qprreport.proboards.com
115. Dennis Turner & Alex

White, p. 282.

116. SD, 1/5/1932, p. 25.

117. WLO, 6/5/1932, p. 2.

118. SD, 1/5/1932, p. 25.

119. WLO, 13/5/1932, p. 3.

120. Ibid.

121. Dennis Turner, 'A History of Fulham Football Club, 1879-1979', p. 58.

122. WLO, 13/5/1932, p. 2.

123. Dennis Turner, p. 58.

124. Ibid.

125. Dennis Turner & Alex White, p. 283.

126. Wikipedia, List of Fulham FC, Records and Statistics, Goalscorers.

127. Ibid. pps 282-283.

128. The Cottagers Journal, 7/5/1932, p.6.

129. Ibid, p. 7.

1932-33 Season

1. www.11v11.com
2. DM, 10/8/1932, p. 18.
3. DH, 15/8/1932, p. 14.
4. WLO, 26/8/1932, p. 2.
5. DH, 22/8/1932, p. 14.
6. Dennis Turner & Alex White, pps. 283 & 285.
7. WLO, 2/9/1932, p. 2.
8. SD, 4/9/1932, p. 18.
9. DM, 5/9/1932, p. 14.
10. DM, 6/9/1932, p. 15.
11. DM, 12/9/1932, p. 14.
12. Dennis Turner & Alex White, p. 284.
13. SD, 11/9/1932, p. 20.
14. SD, 18/9/1932, p. 18.
15. WLO, 23/9/1932, p. 2.
16. DM, 19/9/1932, p. 16.
17. Dennis Turner & Alex White, pps. 284 & 285.
18. SD, 18/9/1922, p. 18.
19. DE, 24/9/1932, p. 2.
20. Dennis Turner & Alex White, p. 167.
21. WLO, 30/9/1932, p. 2.
22. DM, 26/9/1932, p. 17.
23. WLO, 30/9/1932, p. 2.
24. DE, 26/9/1932, p. 17.
25. DM, 29/9/1932, p. 15.
26. DM, 19/9/1932, p. 16.
27. DE, 26/9/1932, p. 17.
28. DM, 6/9/1932, p. 15.
29. Dennis Turner & Alex White, pps. 62, 80 & 194.
30. DM, 28/9/1932, p 15.
31. Dennis Turner & Alex White, lists no entry under Jepson or Fraser. Albert Edward

Jepson, an outside right, was transferred to Brighton & Hove Albion in May 1933. DH, 23/5/1933, p. 14. Fraser went to Northampton Town during the closed season in 1933. DH, 27/6/1933, p. 15.

32. WLO, 7/10/1932, p. 2.
33. www.11v11.com
34. WLO, 14/10/1932, p. 2.
35. SD, 16/10/1932, p. 22.
36. WLO, 21/10/1932, p. 2.
37. SD, 23/10/1932, p. 24.
38. WLO, 21/10/1932, p. 2.
39. SD, 30/10/1932, p. 20.
40. WLO, 4/11/1932, p. 2.
41. www.11v11.com
42. WLO, 11/11/1932, p. 2.
43. SD, 13/11/1932, p. 22.
44. www.11v11.com
45. SD, 20/11/1932, p. 22.
46. NC, 28/11/1932, n. p.
47. WLO, 2/12/1932, p. 2.
48. www.11v11.com
49. WLO, 9/12/1932, p. 2.
50. SD, 4/12/1932, p. 20.
51. FNP, Scrapbook, Press clipping, 'TEN SPURS HOLD FULHAM', unattributed, n.p., n.d..
52. WLO, 16/12/1932, p. 2.
53. SD, 11/12/1932, p. 22.
54. www.11v11.com
55. Dennis Turner & Alex White, p. 284.
56. WLO, 23/12/1932, p. 2.
57. WLO, 30/ 12/ 1932, p. 2.
58. Dennis Turner & Alex White, pps. 284 & 285.
59. NJ, 23/1/1933, p. 9.
60. www.11v11.com
61. Dennis Turner & Alex White, p. 285.
62. WLO, 3/2/1933, p. 2.
63. WLO, 10/2/1933, p. 2.
64. WLO, 17/2/1933, p. 2.
65. DH, 17/2/1933, p. 14.
66. Dennis Turner & Alex White, p. 75. Also, DH, 28/8/1939, p. 8; 'Corinthian' states in part in an article entitled "TRAFFIC in FOOTBALLERS", "… there are many clubs who have to rely on the coaching and the eventual selling of players in order to keep their bank managers quiet. Southampton almost broke their supporters' hearts when they allowed two international players, Keeping and Arnold, to go to Fulham; the officials were quite frank about it, but much explanation was necessary to

convince the good supporters of that town that it was a question of straightening out a banking account or doing without football.

From Fulham's point of view the thousands of pounds spent was a sound business stroke. With the aid of those two men the club was nearly promoted to the First League, and the interest thus created in Fulham's matches brought hundreds of pounds extra through the turnstiles."

67. Dennis Turner & Alex White, pps. 75 & 111.
68. DH, 18/2/1933. p. 14.
69. DH, 20/2/1933, p. 15.
70. WLO, 24/2/1933, p. 2.
71. LIE, 25/2/1933, p. 6.
72. WLO, 10/3/1933, p. 2.
73. Ibid.
74. WLO, 17/3/1933, p.2.
75. www.11v11.com
76. DH, 16/3/1933, p. 18.
77. DH, 15/3/1933, p. 14, & Dennis Turner & Alex White, p. 188.
78. Ibid. Also, see Western Daily Press, 15/3/1933, p. 4; and PlymouthLive, Sport, "The Plymouth Striker sold to Arsenal for £5,000". G. Sparks, 6/1/2018, updated 22/1/2018.
79. DH, 23/3/1933, p. 18.
80. DH, 15/3/1933, p. 15.
81. WLO, 24/3/1933, p. 2.
82. WLO, 31/3/1933, p. 2.
83. DH, 27/3/1933, p. 14.
84. DH, 3/4/1933, p. 18. This proved to be Arnold's only appearance for England. The game was played before 132,000 spectators and was won 2-1 by Scotland.
85. Ibid.
86. WLO, 7/4/1933, p. 2.
87. Ibid.
88. DH, 6/4/1933, p. 14.
89. WLO, 14/4/1933, p. 2.
90. DH, 13/4/1933, p. 18.
91. WLO, 14/4/1933, p. 2.
92. DH, 13/4/1933, p. 18.
93. WLO, 21/4/1933, p. 2.
94. Ibid.
95. DH, 17/4/1933, p. 13.
96. Ibid.
97. WLO, 20/4/1933, p. 2.
98. DH, 18/4/1933, p. 14.
99. FNP, Scrapbook, Press clipping, 'EIGHT DEFENDERS', unidentified, n. d.
100. FNP, Scrapbook, Press clipping, TSL, 22/4/1933, p. 18.

101. FNP, Scrapbook, Press clipping, 'THE GRIM ROAD TO PROMOTION', unidentified, by Renard, probably 23 or 24/4/1933, n. p.

102. WLO, 28/4/1933, p. 2.

103. DH, 24/4/1933, p. 18.

104. Ibid.

105. DH, 28/4/1933, p. 18.

106. DH, 29/4/1933, p. 18.

107. WLO, 5/5/1933, p. 2.

108. WLO, 12/5/1933, p. 2.

109. DM, 21/9/1933, p. 15, and 28/9/1933, p. 15. Both articles carry the by-line 'ARBITER', (Frank M. Carruthers), and are respectively entitled: 'WHY CENTRE FORWARDS FAIL), and 'FOOTBALLERS OLD AT THIRTY'.

110. DTCH, 3/6/1933, p. 9, RIN, 20/8/1933, p. 22 & Dennis Turner & Alex White, p, 152.

111. DM, 31/5/1933, p. 30.

112. Ibid. Neither Arnold, nor Hammond were included as both were under contract to Hampshire C.C. and Sussex C.C. respectively. Dennis Turner & Alex White, pps. 75 & 105. Arnold opened the batting for Hampshire against Sussex, at Horsham, on June 10,1933. Hammond did not play in that game, but was selected to play for Sussex against Cambridge University, at Hove, on June 17, 1933. TP, 11/6/1933, p. 24, and 18/6/1933, p. 20.

113. TP, 11/6/1933, p. 22.

114. DM, 12/6/1933, p. 27.

115. DNY, Dagens Nyheter, 15/6/1933, n. p.

116. Email, Svante Printz, to the author, 24/5/2021.

117. ID, 16/6/1933, n. p.. "Varfor aro engelsmannen snabbare an svenskarna?"

118. Email, Benka Karlsson to the author, 17/5/2021, with attachments of articles from OD, 17/6/1933, n. p., and SVD, 17/6/1933, n. p.

119. DH, 13/4/1933, p. 18.

120. DH, 2/4/1931, p. 14.

121. Dennis Turner & Alex White, pps. 111, 284 & 285.

122. DH, 12/4/1933, p. 18.

123. DH, 24/4/1933, p. 18.

124. Dennis Turner & Alex White, Abel, p. 152; Hammond, p. 105; Perry, p. 130; Rounce, p. 188; Wrightson, p. 198. Wikipedia, Haddleton and Wood.

1933-1934 Season

1. Dennis Turner & Alex White, p. 152.
2. RIN, 20/8/1933, p. 22.
3. DH, 14/8/1933, p. 15.
4. WLO, 18/8/1933, p. 2.
5. DH, 9/8/1933. p. 15, & WLO, 25/8/1933, p. 2.
6. WLO, 25/8/1933, p. 2.
7. RIN, 27/8/1933, p. 24.
8. WLO, 1/9/1933, p. 2.
9. Ibid.
10. RIN, 3/9/1933, p. 24.
11. WLO, 8/9/1933. p. 2.
12. DH, 18/9/1933, p. 14.
13. WLO, 22/9/1933, p. 2.
14. RIN, 17/9/1933, p. 24.

TRANSFER OF FRANK NEWTON TO READING FC AND THE DEPARTURE OF JAMES McINTYRE

1. DFE, 30/11/1929, p. 10.
2. Ernie Coleman, Arsenal.com
3. Jimmy Dunne, Arsenal.com
4. RIN, 15/10/1933, p. 23.
5. DH, 14/9/1933, p. 18, & 15/9/1933, p. 18.
6. RIN, 10/9/1933, p. 23.
7. Ibid.
8. DH, 20/9/1933, p. 14.
9. WLO, 22/9/1933, p. 2.
10. DM, 20/9/1933, p. 23.
11. RIN, 24/9/1933, p. 23.
12. RS, 22/9/1933, p. 15.
13. WLO, 13/10/1933, p. 3.
14. Dennis Turner & Alex White, p. 287.
15. FNP, Scrapbook, Press clipping, unattributed, 'F. NEWTON MISSED BY FULHAM', week of 11/11/1933, n. p.
16. DH, 13/2/1934, p. 14.
17. Dennis Turner & Alex White, p. 62.
18. Ibid.

READING FC, SEPTEMBER, 1933 – OCTOBER, 1934

1. SD, 20/8/1933, p. 16.
2. SD, 27/8/1933, p. 18.
3. BC, 29/9/1933, p. 20.
4. Alan Sedunary, 'Heaven on Earth: The Official History of Reading FC, 1871- 2003', p. 216. Sedunary credits Frank's second goal to Hayhurst.
5. SD, 24/9/1933, p. 21.
6. DMA, 25/9/1933, p. 17.
7. RS, 29/9/1933, p. 15.
8. BC, 29/9/1933, n. p.
9. Ibid.
10. FC, 30/9/1933, p. 4.
11. RM, 30/9/1933, p. 17.
12. BC, 20/10/1933, p. 20.
13. Ibid.
14. BC, 29/9/1933, p. 20.
15. RS, 29/9/1933, p. 6.
16. Alan Sedunary, p. 216.
17. RM, 7/10/1933, p. 15.
18. RS, 6/10/1933, n. p.
19. RM, 14/10/1933, P. 15 & RS, 13/10/1933, p. 19.
20. SD, 8/10/1933, p. 19.
21. RS, 13/10/1933, n. p.
22. RS, 20/10/1933, p. 15.
23. BC, 20/10/1933, p. 20.
24. SD, 15/10/1933, p. 25.

25. RM, 21/10/1933, p. 16.

25. Alan Sedunary, p. 216.

26. RS, 27/10/1933, p. 15.

26. FNP, Scrapbook, Reading FC Record, programme, Reading FC v Luton Town, 28/10/1933, pps. 4 & 5.

27. RM, 28/10/1933, p. 17.
28. Alan Sedunary, p. 216.
29. RS, 3/11/1933, p. 19.
30. RM, 4/11/1933, p. 17.
31. RS, 3/11/1933, p. 19.
32. SD, 29/10/1933, p. 21.
33. RM, 4/11/1933, p. 7.
34. RM, 4/11/1933, p. 3.
35. Alan Sedunary, p. 62.
36. DE, 15/5/1933, p. 2.
37. DH, 30/10/1933, p. 18.
38. RS, 10/11/1933, n. p.
39. RM, 11/11/1933, p.17.
40. RS, 10/11/1933, n. p.
41. Ibid.
42. SD, 12/11/1933, p. 21.
43. RS, 17/11/1933, n. p.
44. RS, 24/11/1933, N. P.
45. Ibid.
46. RS, 1/12/1933. p. 19.
47. RM, 2/12/1933, p. 21.
48. RS, 1/12/1933, p. 19.

49. RS, 8/12/1933, p. 19.
50. Ibid, and 'Sutton Town Football Club', Nottinghamshire Archives, www.inspirepicturearchive.org.uk
51. RM, 2/12/1933, p. 21. Note, states 'It may be possible to get 10,000 people in the ground.'
52. RS, 1/12/1933, p. 19.
53. RS, 8/12/1933, p 19.
54. Ibid.
55. Ibid, and RS, 1/12/1933, p. 19, RM, 2/12/1933, p. 21, & 9/12/1933, p. 21.
56. RM, 21/12/1933, p. 17.
57. Ibid.
58. Ibid.
59. DH, 11/12/1933, p. 18.
60. Clapton Orient Football Club (1906) Ltd., Programme, 16/1/1933, p. 3, "Oriental Chatter", & RS, 22/12/1933, p. 13.
61. Ibid, & RM, 23/12/1933, p. 5.
62. RS, 29/12/1933, p. 13.
63. Ibid.
64. RM, 30/12/1933, p. 13.
65. RS, 29/12/1933, p. 13.
66. RM, 30/12/1933, p. 13.
67. RS, 29/12/1933, p. 12.
68. Ibid.
69. RS, 29/12/1933, p. 13.
70. Ibid.
71. Ibid.
72. Standing based on DH, 8/1/1934, p. 14, discounting the results of January 7, 1934.
73. RS, 5/1/1934, p. 13.
74. Alan Sedunary, p. 216.
75. RS, 12/1/1934, p. 15.
76. BC, 12/1/1934, p. 16.
77. RS, 12/1/1934, p. 15.
78. Ibid.
79. www.readingformerplayers.co.uk
80. RS, 19/1/1934, p. 15.
81. www.readingformerplayers.co.uk
82. RS, 19/1/1934, p. 15.
83. Ibid.
84. BC, 26/1/1934, p. 20.
85. www.readingformerplayers.co.uk
86. RS, 21/1/1934, p. 13.
87. DH, 5/2/1934, p. 13.
88. www.vintagefootballers.com
89. RS, 16/2/1934, p. 15.
90. RS, 23/2/1934, p. 15.
91. RS, 3/3/1934, p. 19.

92. www.statcity.co.uk
93. RN, 30/9/1934, p. 22.
94. FC, 31/3/34, p. 4.
95. RS, 29/3/1934, p. 13.
96. BC, 6/4/1934, p. 16.
97. RS, 6/4/1934, p. 15.
98, Ibid.
99. BC, 6/4/1934, p. 16.
100. RS, 6/4/1934, p. 15.
101. RS, 13/4/1934, p. 15.
102. BC, 13/4/1934, p. 20.
103. RS, 20/4/1934, p. 15.
104. RS, 20/4/1934, p. 17, & BC, 20/4/1934, p. 20.
105. RS, 20/4/1934, p. 17.
106. BC, 20/4/1934, p. 21.
107. RS, 27/4/1934, p. 15.
108. BC, 27/4/1934, p. 20.
109. BC, 4/5/1934, p. 20.
110. RS, 4/5/1934, p. 19.
111. Ibid.
112. RS, 11/4/1934, p. 19.
113. FC, 5/5/1934, p. 4. Calculations based upon results listed in item headed: "READING FOOTBALL CLUB GOSSIP."
114. BC, 27/9/1933, P. 20.

Reading F. C., Season 1934-1935

1. RS, 17/8/1934, p. 16.
2. RS, 24/8/1934, p. 14. William Butler is identified incorrectly in the press report as Joe.
3. Clapton Orient Football Club (1906) Ltd., Official Programme, 25/8/1934, p. 3, "Oriental Chatter".
4. RS, 31/8/1934, p. 15.
5. Ibid.
6. RS, 7/9/1934, p. 15.
7. Ibid.
8. RS, 14/9/1934, p. 13.
9. Ibid.
10. RS, 21/9/1934, p. 15.
11. DH, 17/9/1934, p. 17.
12. RS, 21/9/1934, p. 15
13. Ibid.
14. Ibid.
15. RS, 28/9/1934, p. 19.
16. BC, 28/9/1934, p. 20.
17. RS, 28/9/1934, p. 19.
18. Ibid
19. BC, 28/9/1934, p. 20.
20. RS, 5/10/1934, p. 15.

21. BC, 5/10/1934, p. 20.
22. RS, 5/10/1934, p. 15.
23. DH, 1/19/1934, p. 19.
24. Alan Sedunary, p. 62.
25. Dennis Turner & Alex White, p. 62.
26. DM,26/10/1934, p. 14.
27. Dennis Turner & Alex White, p. 62.
28. RS, 29/3/1934, p. 13.
29. DH, 3/10/1934, p. 18.
30. DH, 6/10/1934, p. 18.
31. FC, 6/10/1934, n. p.
32. WLO, 22/9/1934, p 2.
33. BC, 12/10/1934, p. 20.
34. RS, 12/10/1934, p. 23.
35. RS, 12/10/1934, p. 19.
36. RMOG, 6/10/1934, p. 21.
37. RS, 2/11/1934, p. 15.
38. Dennis Turner & Alex White, p. 286.
39. Dennis Turner & Alex White, p. 287.

FRANK RETURNS TO FULHAM F. C., OCTOBER, 1934

1. DM, 1/10/1934, p. 19.
2. DM, 6/10/1934, p. 14.
3. RIN, 14/10/1934, p. 23.
4. DH, 6/10/1934, p. 18.
5. FNP, Scrapbook, Telegram to Frank Newton from C. B. Dean, 6/10/1934, n. p
6. WLO, 12/10/1934, p. 2.
7. DM, 8/10/1934, p. 30.
8. DM, 15/10/1934, p. 31.
9. DH, 15/10/1934, p. 19.
10. RIN, 14/10/1934, p. 24.
11. DH, 22/10/1934, p. 19.
12. WLO, 26/10/1934, p. 2.
13. DH, 22/10/1934, p. 18.
14. DH, 29/10/1934, p. 19.
15. WLO, 2/11/1934, p. 2.
16. DH, 5/11/1934, p. 18.
17. WLO, 9/11/1934, p. 2.
18. DH, 5/11/1934, p. 19.
19. RIN, 4/11/1934, p. 24.
20. WLO, 9/11/1934, p. 2.
21. DH, 12/11/1934, p. 19.
22. RIN, 11/11/1934, p. 24.
23. WLO, 16/11/1934, p. 2.
24. RIN, 18/11/1934, p. 24.
25. DH, 19/11/1934, p. 19.
26. WLO, 23/11/1934, p. 2.
27. RIN, 4/11/1934, p. 23.
28. DH, 26/11/1934, pps. 18 & 19.
29. WLO, 30/11/1934, p. 2.

30. Dennis Turner & Alex White, p. 288.
31. DH, 3/12/1934, p. 19.
32. Dennis Turner & Alex White, pps. 62 & 63.
33. DH, 3/12/1934, p. 19.
34. RIN, 2/12/1934, p. 22.
35. WLO, 7/12/1934, p. 2.
36. AJ, 27/11/1934, p. 4.
37. DH, 29/11/1934, p. 18.
38. DH, 4/12/1934, p. 18.
39. WLO, 7/12/1934, p. 2.
40. 'The Cottagers Journal' Official Programme of The Fulham Football Club, 3/12/1934. The extant footage can be found on YouTube, Fulham v Austria 1934. 'News In A Nutshell', British Pathé News. Frank is the 8th Fulham player jogging out to the pitch from the Cottage.
41. FNP, Scrapbook, Letter, A. Stones to Frank Newton, 10/12/1934, n. p.
42. WLO, 10/3/1933, p. 2.
43. DN, 12/12/1934, p. 15.
44. DM, 12/12/1934, p. 31.
45. DE, 1/1/1935, n. p.
46. DE, 24/1/1935, p. 16.
47. DN, 22/4/1935, p. 12, a similar account appeared in DE, 12/4/1935, p. 13.
48. WLO, 26/4/1935, p. 2.
49. Keith Newton in conversation with the author, 19/4/2022.
50. FNP, Scrapbook, unattributed press clipping, n.d., n.p.
51. Marcus Heap, *The Hatter Historian*, November, 1997
52. Pear New Mill – Wikipedia en.m.wikipedia.org
53. Marcus Heap, Op Cit.

EPILOGUE

1. FC, 25/8/1934, p. 8.
2. Ibid.
3. Wikipedia, 'List of footballers in England by number of league goals' / List of players. As of May 10 2023.
4. Ibid.